ROMANOV
AUTUMN

ROMANOV AUTUMN

The Last Century of Imperial Russia

CHARLOTTE ZEEPVAT

SUTTON PUBLISHING

This book was first published in 2000 by
Sutton Publishing Limited · Phoenix Mill
Thrupp · Stroud · Gloucestershire · GL5 2BU

This edition first published in 2006

British Library Cataloguing in Publication Data
A catalogue record for this book is available from the British
Library.

ISBN 0 7509 4418 8

Typeset in 10/12.5 pt Goudy.
Typesetting and origination by
Sutton Publishing Limited.
Printed and bound in Great Britain by
J.H. Haynes & Co. Ltd, Sparkford.

Contents

List of Plates

Preface and Acknowledgements

The Romanov dynasty ruled Russia for a little over three hundred years and its name and story exerts a lasting fascination. In recent years attention has focused almost exclusively on the dynasty's dramatic end and this book seeks to widen the picture, drawing material from the last century of imperial rule. It was a compelling time and a time of contrasts, when the Tsars reached the peak of their wealth, their prestige and their power, yet also faced the growth of forces which would destroy them. Each of the last four Tsars, Nicholas I, Alexander II, Alexander III and Nicholas II, tried to steer his own course between reform and control. All four were hard-working men who cared desperately for their country; they made mistakes, but many of the questions that daunted them remain unanswered to this day – this in itself should make us doubt the harsh judgements often passed on them. Their public lives were conducted against a glittering backdrop, unrivalled in the West: too often we forget that behind the glamour the Romanovs were just ordinary people experiencing the joys, confusions and problems of ordinary human life.

In its last flowering the dynasty produced many sympathetic and gifted characters – and some who were far less admirable. It built and embellished the palaces that stand today as a powerful reminder of all that has gone – yet for at least two generations the last century of imperial rule has been a hidden period in Russia. I first visited St Petersburg in 1993 as guest speaker on a tour of the last Tsar's palaces which I had helped to research and plan. Our Russian guides then knew little of the dynasty in its final century and they were surprised by our interest. They listened eagerly, borrowed notes, and by the next summer they knew the stories quite as well as we did.

But they were also beginning to see a tidal wave of books on the last four Tsars being published in their own language. Some were translations of books long familiar in the West, but others drew from their own rich archival sources that were just coming to light. With each year that passes, the interest grows and the knowledge and understanding deepens.

Romanov Autumn draws on five years' experience of working on tours of St Petersburg and, in the interim, of researching the palaces and the people who owned them. I have always been fascinated by Russia and the Romanovs, but the changes of recent years have injected a note of excitement into the story, and this book draws heavily on Russian sources. The individual chapters started life as articles written for *Royalty Digest* magazine over a seven-year period. For the book I have substantially revised some, completely rewritten others, added new chapters and woven all together into a loosely chronological structure that tells the central story through the experiences of individual members of the dynasty, of the palaces that housed them and the people who worked for them. The perspective shifts and changes, threads of the story cross and re-cross but the central theme remains: a royal family in its years of growth, its years of prosperity, its crises and its disintegration. The final chapters tell the stories of those who escaped, and of those who did not.

I wish to thank Her Majesty The Queen for permission to quote from documents in the Royal Archives at Windsor. The staff of the Royal Archives are always patient, well-informed and helpful, and I am grateful to them for their contribution to individual chapters. Paul Minet, the Editor of *Royalty Digest*, published the articles in their original form and has given the book his wholehearted support. I am also grateful to Holts' Tours for trusting me to tell these stories to successive coachloads of their customers.

In the course of seven years, numerous friends and friends of friends have helped me with material, ideas and advice on the subject of imperial Russia, and I hope they will enjoy the result. My thanks are due to David Horbury, Frances Dimond, Father Terence

Maclean Wilson, Elena and Sergei Yablochkin, Svetlana Gorokhova, Anastasia Kornienko, Vladimir Trifonov, Bob and Charmian Godfrey, Arthur Addington, John Wimbles, Nancy Tryon, Marion Wynn, Sue Woolmans, and Gil Martin – and my apologies to anyone whose name should appear on this list. I would also like to thank my mother, who tries hard to put up with my Russian ramblings, my editors Jaqueline Mitchell, Kate Platt and Clare Bishop, and Sheila Watson, my agent.

On Names, Dates and Titles

All the main characters in this book were Russian, by birth or marriage, and their names would have been written first in Russian, second in French – which was widely used in Court and society until the late nineteenth century – then in English, German, Danish and so on, to suit the place where they happened to be or the person they were communicating with. The versions given here are as close as possible to the original Russian, with the sole exception of the Tsars, whose names seem too well known in their English versions to change.

Then, as now, Russians used two names: a Christian name and a patronymic – the name of their father with '-ovich' or '-evich' at the end, meaning 'son of' and '-ovna' or '-evna' meaning 'daughter of'. So, for example, Dmitri Konstantinovich, 'Dmitri, son of Konstantin'. Foreign princesses who married into the family took on a Russian Christian name if their own did not translate. Some used their own father's name as a patronymic, others adopted a name with particular significance for the Romanov family. Unlike our middle names, patronymics are used regularly in Russian, and for anyone writing on this subject they offer an invaluable way of distinguishing between two people with the same Christian name.

The calendar in use in Russia until February 1918 was the old-style, Julian Calendar. In the nineteenth century this was twelve days behind the Gregorian Calendar used in the West: by the twentieth century the difference had risen to thirteen days. Wherever possible in this book, events described that took place in Russia are given two dates: first, the old-style, Russian date; second, its Western equivalent (e.g. 24 July/5 August 1824). References to events outside Russia have only the new-style date.

The titles of the imperial family pose many problems for a non-Russian writer, though in their original forms they were blissfully simple. From the sixteenth century onwards, the man who ruled Russia was the *Tsar*. His wife was the *Tsaritsa*. Each of their sons had the title *Tsarevich* (son of the Tsar), and each of their daughters *Tsarevna* (daughter of the Tsar).

Peter the Great introduced the first complication by changing his own title to *Imperator* (Emperor), on 22 October/2 November 1721. His wife became an *Imperatritsa*. From this time onwards, the official title of the Russian sovereign was *Imperator* or *Imperatritsa*, though the earlier title survived in the imperial anthem, in place names and expressions (like Tsarskoe Selo, 'the Tsar's Village'), and in the long memory of the Russian people. As the nineteenth century drew to an end and interest in Russian culture and history grew the old forms were heard more often, but they were not used on formal occasions.

The titles of Peter's family were also altered. His surviving daughters, Anna Petrovna and Elisaveta Petrovna, became *Tsesarevna*, instead of *Tsarevna*, but this title would never be used again. *Tsarevna* came to be used in later years for the wife of the heir to the throne. Peter's grandchildren bore the titles that would apply to every legitimate child born to a Russian sovereign, or to a sovereign's son, until the Revolution: *Velikii Kniaz* (Grand Prince), and *Velikaya Kniazhna* (Grand Princess). A woman who married into the family became a *Velikaya Kniaginia* (also Grand Princess, with the variation indicating a married woman – like the difference between 'Miss' and 'Mrs' in English).

There were a few later changes. The future Alexander I had an additional title. He was *Tsesarevich i Velikii Kniaz*, 'Tsesarevich' signifying that he was heir to the throne. This title was not automatic, but was afterwards given to the Heir at birth, or at the moment when his position was recognized, and it was said that once given it could never be removed. In 1886 Alexander III tried to control the size (and cost) of the family by demoting the children of his cousins, great-grandchildren of an *Imperator* in the male line, to *Kniaz* (Prince) or *Kniazhna* (Princess).

So, during the last century of imperial Russia, the imperial family consisted of an *Imperator* and an *Imperatritsa*, the *Tsesarevich i Velikii Kniaz*, his wife if he had one, known as the *Tsarevna*, and a varying number of *Velikii Kniaz, Velikaya Kniaginia, Velikaya Kniazhna, Kniaz,* and so on. The fun begins when their titles have to be expressed in other languages.

Germans used a straight translation: *Imperator* became *Kaiser*, the Heir was the *Großfürst Thronfolger*, his brothers and sisters *Großfürst* or *Großfürstin*, and their cousins *Fürst* or *Fürstin*. (The German title *Fürst* is translated as *Prince*.) But in French, *Velikii Kniaz* became *Grand-Duc* and *Velikaya Kniaginia* (or *Kniazhna*) *Grand-Duchesse*, while, for some reason, *Kniaz* on its own, the lesser title, was translated as *Prince*. English followed suit with *Grand Duke, Grand Duchess, Prince* and *Princess* – an odd and uncomfortable translation, because in England a prince outranks a duke. The distinction between a Tsar's son and a German Grand Duke (*Großherzog*), which is clearly made in both Russian and German, does not appear in French or English. We add to the confusion by a bungled attempt to use Russian titles: *Tsarina*, often seen in English and French, never existed in Russian, and the Heir's title should not be *Tsarevich* but *Tsesarevich* (which survives in English only as the name of a horse race).

So which version of the titles do we use? There are no right answers, and anyone who reads about the imperial family will get used to seeing and using several versions of their titles and names. Flexibility is the key. The accepted usage in English has always been *Emperor* (or *Tsar*, or even *Czar*), *Empress* (or *Tsarina*, with either spelling), *Tsarevich* (or occasionally *Cesarevitch*), *Grand Duke, Grand Duchess, Prince* and *Princess*. Some early writers tried to remedy the original error by using *Duke* instead of *Prince*, but this has died out. In this book I have returned as closely as possible to the Russian, using *Tsar* and *Tsaritsa, Tsesarevich, Grand Prince, Prince,* and so on, except in direct quotations from sources using other versions or other spellings.

Many readers will find this usage strange and some may be irritated by it, but I appeal for their patience: its very unfamiliarity makes an important point. For the greater part of this century there has been a deep gulf between Russia and the West, and most of our knowledge of the last three Tsars has come from the memoirs of those who escaped the Revolution, or from non-Russian sources. The exiles had experience of the imperial Court, but they were also affected by later events. They blamed or praised, demonized or sainted, handing down a twisted tapestry of fact, supposition and gossip, with no documentary evidence to check their view. The Soviets were selective, releasing only those documents that could be used to support their own version of events. Properly researched biographies of the later generations of Romanovs, from Russian archival sources, were an impossibility until recent years. Now, documents newly released from Russia are broadening the picture, and in time deeper and more considered studies may emerge, and may change even the most cherished and familiar of ideas. For anyone interested in this subject, this is an exciting and unpredictable time.

1

The Other Nicholas and Alexandra

TSAR NICHOLAS I AND HIS WIFE TSARITSA ALEXANDRA
FEODOROVNA

*'When one looks back it is frightening to think how time passes.'. . . Russia was
at the height of its power when Nicholas I wrote these words to his sister,
remembering a day more than thirty years before, when he had ridden away to
war beside his brother, Tsar Alexander I.[1] He was just seventeen then, with no
idea of succeeding to the throne and no responsibilities. He was happy and,
though he did not know it, he was about to meet the girl he would marry. In
Berlin the King of Prussia's daughter Charlotte welcomed the Russian visitors.
She was fifteen; tall, pretty and rather naïve. Nicholas was handsome; they were
both fresh from the schoolroom and each found the other irresistible, though their
families insisted on a year's delay before they could even become engaged. The
defeat of Napoleon and the re-ordering of Europe was far more pressing than the
hopes of two romantic teenagers – though the thought that their marriage would
reinforce the political alliance between their two countries would not have escaped
either family. Three years were to pass before Charlotte was received into the
Orthodox Church with the name 'Alexandra Feodorovna', which she would use
for the rest of her life and, on her nineteenth birthday, she and Nicholas were
married in the chapel of the Winter Palace. It was 1817, a hundred years before
the Revolution and the collapse of the dynasty.*

Nicholas was born to be a soldier, and it was the only life he
wanted. Too young to have felt the tensions that led to the
murder of his father, Tsar Paul, he was the product of a
secure childhood in an unusually united family. When he was born
in the Catherine Palace at Tsarskoe Selo in the summer of 1796,
his brothers Alexander and Konstantin were almost grown up. He
was closest to his sister Anna, just a year his senior, and to his

1

younger brother Mikhail; later the three would call themselves the 'Triopathy' and wear special rings engraved with their motto 'Firmness and Hope'. They gave a similar ring to their mother, the Dowager Tsaritsa Maria Feodorovna, making her a member of their circle.

Maria Feodorovna was a strong woman, and it was her firm will that brought unity to her large family, overriding the differences in their ages and upbringing. She had been forced to give up her elder sons to Catherine the Great, her mother-in-law, and this deepened her determination to bring up the younger children in her own way. Nicholas was taught to speak four languages and he studied the classics, economics, law and political science. He played the flute and his paintings could have been the work of a professional artist, but no amount of persuasion would make him as charming and polished in company as his mother wished him to be. Both Nicholas and Mikhail found the parade ground more fun than the dance floor. 'Your brothers act like complete invalids', she complained to Anna, 'and never dance a step',[2] and she 'went for' the brothers 'because at parties they retired into corners and looked bored'.[3]

Alexandra remembered this with amusement in a memoir of her first years with Nicholas. In private, she said, he was a different person, and 'he and I were only really happy and pleased when we were alone in our rooms with me sitting on his knees while he was being loving and tender'.[3] It delighted the Dowager Tsaritsa to see them: 'Nicky is a dear husband. It is impossible to be more careful, more attentive than he is of his wife' . . . 'his wife is delightful and lives for him, anticipating his every wish, all his thoughts; doing everything she can to please him'.[4] Within weeks of the wedding Alexandra was pregnant. She fainted during Mass and, after carrying her to her room, Nicholas rushed up to a young page-in-waiting and announced that he was going to be a father. The baby, a boy, was born with pleasing symbolism in the Kremlin, the historic heart of Russia, 'in Holy Week, on the most beautiful of spring days, while the bells were still ringing in the great feast of the Resurrection. . . . Niki kissed me and burst into tears, and we thanked God together.'[5]

In fact, there was nothing accidental about the setting of baby Alexander Nikolaievich's birth. It had been engineered by the Dowager Tsaritsa to stress the national importance of the young family. Everyone knew that one day the throne would pass to Nicholas and the birth of a son confirmed his importance; he and Alexandra were the only ones who refused to face the inevitable. Alexander I's marriage was an empty shell and his two daughters had died in infancy. Konstantin was divorced. In 1820 he contracted a morganatic marriage, telling his mother that he wanted nothing to stand between Nicholas and the throne. Still, Nicholas would not discuss the succession. Alexander tried to raise the subject one evening after a family dinner, but Nicholas and Alexandra became so distressed that he abandoned the attempt. When Konstantin formally renounced his right to the throne in 1822, Alexander kept the document secret.

The couple's very happiness was a problem. All they wanted was to be together and to enjoy their children. The second baby was a girl, Maria; Nicholas soon overcame his disappointment, and his letters filled with adoring descriptions of the children. His mother agreed. 'I went to hug my dear grandchildren who are quite delightful,' the Dowager Tsaritsa wrote in 1820, seven months after Maria's birth. 'The little girl is getting much prettier and will be as pretty as her mother . . . [she] already cherishes her father who gives her a lot of attention and who is much amused by her. He truly loves her. As for the little boy, he's an angel and the best child possible.'[6]

A few months after this was written, Alexandra produced a stillborn daughter. It was her third pregnancy in as many years and the loss of the baby brought on a deep depression. Nicholas was all attention and kindness, nursing his wife with his own hands, though his mother noticed that he was 'distracted at the abstinence he must observe'.[7] The doctors advised a holiday and he took Alexandra back to Berlin; it suited them both so well that they returned to Germany the following year, and again in 1824, though by that time they had three children to leave with the Dowager Tsaritsa, and painful memories of another lost baby. Did they dream of leaving

Russia for good? Alexander I feared that this was a real possibility and in the spring of 1825 he summoned them home, saying that he needed their company. He presented Alexandra with land of her own at Peterhof, the imperial estate that had pleased her most at the start of her life in Russia. A few weeks after the gift was made she had another daughter, Alexandra.

There are a number of stories which suggest that Nicholas did not always observe the abstinence his mother admired, and one of the most persuasive dates from this time. It is said that at a Court ball in 1824 Nicholas met a Swedish girl, Marianne Rutenskiöld, that they had an affair which resulted in pregnancy, and that, for form's sake, a husband was found for Marianne. She had a daughter, Josephine, born near Smolensk on 12/24 May 1825, but her marriage failed, and Nicholas, who had by this time become Tsar, appointed her matron of one of the imperial cadet corps. He allowed her to live at the Farm at Alexandria Peterhof, and her daughter was brought up alongside his own children, even calling him 'Papa', and the Tsaritsa 'Mama'. In 1848, with the Tsar's permission, Josephine married a French artist, Joseph Fricero, and went to live with him in Nice, but she remained close to the imperial family and several of her children had Romanov godparents.

Stories like this tend to be believed automatically, and if this one is true it suggests a much more cynical view of Nicholas's marriage. Josephine certainly existed, and she was close to the imperial family. Her sons, Alexandre, Nicolas, and Michel, had suitably Romanov-sounding names. But there is a problem. The date of her birth suggests that she was conceived in mid-August 1824. On 24 July/5 August of that year Nicholas and Alexandra left Russia for Germany and did not return until Alexander I sent for them in March 1825. According to these dates Nicholas could hardly have been Josephine's father, and the whole idea of his infidelity gently falls apart. Simple friendship could explain the link between the Tsar's family and Josephine and her mother, and no one reading Nicholas's letters to and about Alexandra could doubt that he loved her and would continue to do so until his death. If his eye ever strayed, it meant nothing to him.

When Alexander I called his younger brother home in 1825 he was rapidly losing interest in life. The Tsar was tired, and on doctors' advice he took his sick wife on a journey south that autumn, appointing Nicholas as his regent. No one was prepared for the news of Alexander's death in distant Taganrog; it came as a body blow to the whole family. Nicholas led the imperial guard in swearing allegiance to Konstantin, refusing to accept his brother's renunciation of the throne because no one had ever told him about it, or shown him the documents. From his home in Warsaw, Konstantin swore allegiance to Nicholas and the stalemate lasted almost three weeks, with each brother declaring loyalty to the other and Mikhail riding backwards and forwards between them. It would have been funny, if it had not been so dangerous. When Nicholas learned of a conspiracy in the army he bowed to the inevitable and accepted the throne. This happened at midnight on 13/25 December.

The air in the city was tense. Groups of soldiers were out on the streets, shouting for Konstantin. Their leaders were mainly young men from noble families, army officers who had seen how their peers lived elsewhere in Europe and had returned to Russia bent on liberal reform. Some were republican, some not; they had no coherent leadership and Konstantin had no interest in them, but for a few hours the danger was intense. In the snow-covered courtyard of the Winter Palace, by the light of torches, Nicholas committed his little son Alexander to the protection of the loyal Finnish Guards. As morning came the rebels gathered on the Senate Square. Whole regiments were refusing to take the oath of loyalty to their new Tsar: when the Governor of St Petersburg tried to explain that Konstantin had renounced the throne, he was shot and killed. Before midday, Nicholas rode out onto the Square and loyal troops joined him. He spoke to the rebels and offered an amnesty but made no headway, and as darkness fell his generals urged him to fire on the crowd. He gave in and the Decembrist Rising was crushed by force.

No one could doubt Nicholas's bravery that day, but many have questioned his humanity. Ordinary soldiers who joined the revolt were pardoned but five of their leaders were sentenced to death, and almost three hundred exiled to Siberia. The new Tsar took a firm grip on the empire, imposing severe restrictions on individual movement and thought. He needed to take control quickly and to restore order, but the personal burden was crushing. Nicholas's devotion to duty was absolute, and his mother watched with concern as he sank under the weight of new tasks. 'He says that his reign has brought only trouble,' she wrote, 'he is overwhelmed with business, work. He never goes to bed before 2.00 or 3.00 in the morning. He does not even have time to have dinner in peace. . . . He is thinner, paler, in a way that is frightening.'[8]

All of this took a heavy toll on the family. Alexandra spent the day of her husband's accession in prayer with her children. She was terrified: as a child she had seen her family driven from Berlin by Napoleon's army, now her husband was facing armed men in the streets of his capital. The anxious hours of waiting left her with a nervous twitch of the head which visitors to the Court still noticed twenty years later; her health never fully recovered. The little Tsesarevich was affected too. His tutors saw a new timidity and a tendency to give up when things became difficult: he dreaded the day when the throne would fall to him.

The family needed privacy and were happiest at Alexandria Peterhof, the estate Alexandra had been given by her brother-in-law. This was their own place, 'our favourite little corner of earth'.[9] By 1832 they had seven children, and Nicholas delighted in them all. The Tsesarevich was handsome and lively. When he rode with the troops at his father's Coronation the Tsar nearly burst with pride. Nicholas adored his son, although it did concern him that the boy was inclined to dream and showed no enthusiasm for the army. Maria was small for her age while Olga had reached her mother's height by the time she was twelve. Young Alexandra was 'a little moppet' and when Konstantin, the second son, was born, his father cried for joy. He said Konstantin was 'small and ugly, but very unusual'. Next came two more sons, Nikolai and Mikhail; their father called them 'very agreeable . . . the apples of my eye'.[10]

The imperial couple were exceptionally good parents and no pageantry was allowed to complicate their children's lives. The young Romanovs were kept well away from Court and brought up simply; even the servants were instructed not to use their titles but to address them by their name and patronymic, Russian fashion. Evenings were always spent with their parents, or at least with their mother, playing games, acting and making music. Once, the French Ambassador asked if he might meet the Tsesarevich; he expected an audience in the Winter Palace and was amazed to be taken to the park at Tsarskoe Selo to watch the little boy at play with his sisters. The Tsar explained that he feared the effect it might have on his son if important men were presented to him in a formal setting.

Nicholas was preparing the Tsesarevich for a changing future, and even though his own rule was repressive he understood the calls for reform. He recognized that serfdom was unjust, yet knew that it was a fundamental part of the empire's organization which could not be removed easily. Count Kisselev, the Minister of the Imperial Domains, was asked to investigate measures that could be taken and the reign saw some cautious changes, but for complete abolition Nicholas found no support at all. He believed in the autocracy, seeing himself as the only defender that ordinary people had. He attended to even the smallest matters personally and travelled widely within the empire listening to individual concerns. He was harsh, but could also be kind; on one occasion he left his carriage to walk behind a lonely funeral cortège because there were no other mourners. Meanwhile life at his Court was a constant round of masked balls, dinners, and entertainments of all kinds. 'I like people to have fun,' he told his sister Anna, 'for it keeps them busy and eliminates the time to say silly things.'

Once order was established Nicholas worked to strengthen and extend the borders of the empire. He fought the Turks and imposed his will on the peoples of the Caucasus; in 1830 Poland rebelled and he suppressed the rising with ruthless efficiency, though he greeted the news that Europe was calling him 'the new Attila' somewhat ruefully. 'This poor Attila can only think of staying quietly at home, happy in being with his five-month pregnant wife and his children; his tastes are all domestic; in short, he is the least hostile and the most peace-loving person on earth; – what a strange fate!'[11] It would have amazed the Tsar's contemporaries to know that this was how he saw himself. As Europe was shaken by a series of armed risings, Nicholas's Russia became a fortress built to withstand Western influences, from which the Tsar could emerge to defend the traditional order.

Liberal historians have heaped some of their best insults on Nicholas I. He has been called cruel, brutal, tyrannical and despotic, and is rarely given credit for any positive achievements. But he was more Russian than any Tsar had been for over a century, and he responded to a new mood within the country, where people were striving to understand what being Russian meant. This was more positive than simply closing the border. From the start of his reign, Nicholas initiated a programme of public building and gave generous patronage to those artists who were trying to evolve a new style from the best elements of the old. He provided financial help for Feodor Solntsev, who travelled the empire collecting examples of traditional design, and he authorized the publication of Solntsev's findings. In the 1830s there was an ambitious plan to restore the Kremlin and add new buildings to harmonize with the ancient cathedrals and palaces. Little remained of the interiors of the Terem Palace, for example. Ever exacting, Nicholas rejected fourteen decorative schemes before he found one that was appropriate.

All of this work was undertaken with conscious seriousness: the Tsar saw the Kremlin as a national heritage to be preserved for the people. As Peter the Great had forced Russia to face west, so Nicholas was trying to turn it back to itself. He redesigned the appearance of his Court, issuing a decree in 1834 which introduced a formal dress for Court ladies based on traditional Russian costume. The decree defined the cut, colour and fabric, and the precise nature of the ornamentation to be used by ladies of differing status. Government officers were expected to wear uniform at all times. With all these measures the Tsar was creating an impressive and uniquely Russian backdrop for the public life of the country.

In private too, Nicholas I was an ambitious builder. He created houses, pavilions and chapels at Alexandria Peterhof, and his family's apartments in the Winter Palace were redecorated early in his reign. In 1837 much of the Winter Palace was destroyed by fire.

Nicholas co-ordinated the successful rescue of many treasures in person as the fire raged. When it was over, he made speedy restoration a priority; he was a generous patron, but he expected his deadlines to be kept. He liked to discover new artists and it was not unusual for a painter working quietly in one of the imperial parks to find himself invited home for tea with the Tsar. In 1844 Nicholas commissioned a massive rebuilding programme at Gatchina but, because he had grown up at the palace and the old rooms held many memories, he had paintings made before the work began to keep a visual record of the past. In all things he was immensely sentimental about the family, giving orders that rooms with a particular significance should be preserved untouched. Under his direction parts of the greater palaces became family museums.

The imperial family were avid readers. State censorship was tight, yet the reign saw an avalanche of books that are now regarded as classics; Pushkin, Dostoevsky, Turgenev, Lermontov and Gogol all flourished during Nicholas's reign. They were critical of the régime; official censors certainly interfered with their work, but they did not stop them writing. Nicholas himself attended the first performance of Gogol's play *The Government Inspector* at the Alexandrinsky Theatre. It seems a paradox but Nicholas I was at once fiercely repressive and yet tolerant. He lived by the motto on the 'Triopathy' ring that he had worn since he was young, 'Firmness and Hope': the autocratic firmness, which he never relaxed, and the hope for progress and reform in the future.

In 1842 Nicholas and Alexandra celebrated their silver wedding with a medieval tournament at Tsarskoe Selo in which the whole family participated. The idea of chivalry appealed to the romantic in Nicholas, who was a great fan of Sir Walter Scott. Scott's novels were regularly read out loud within the family circle. They had met in 1816, when, as a young man, the future Tsar was sent to Britain to study constitutionalism in action: once his own eldest son was grown up Nicholas allowed himself the freedom to travel again, leaving the Tsesarevich Alexander as his regent. He visited England and accompanied Alexandra on her visits to European spas; in 1845 and 1846 they spent time in Italy.

By this time the imperial couple had become grandparents. Their eldest daughter, Maria, was married to Duke Maximilian of Leuchtenberg, the Tsesarevich had married Marie, Princess of Hesse-Darmstadt, and both couples had children. It delighted Nicholas and Alexandra to watch the growth of a new generation, but there was sadness for them too; their first grandchild, Alexandra of Leuchtenberg, died when she was three and the Tsesarevich lost his eldest child, Alexandra Alexandrovna, just before her seventh birthday. In January 1844 Nicholas and Alexandra's youngest daughter, Alexandra Nikolaievna, married Friedrich Wilhelm of Hesse-Cassel. Like her mother she became pregnant within weeks, but she fell ill in the summer while staying at Tsarskoe Selo and gave birth prematurely. According to some sources she had scarlet fever, to others, measles. Whatever the truth, both she and her baby were dead before the day's end. Her parents were shattered. 'Our grief is lifelong,' Nicholas wrote, 'it is an open wound we shall carry to the grave.'[12] Within the family, the name Alexandra came to be seen as unlucky.

Nicholas and Alexandra's devotion to one another never waned. By the late 1840s Alexandra's health was declining and the couple's life became quieter. Lady Bloomfield, whose husband was the British representative in St Petersburg, was able to observe them together on several occasions and noted that Nicholas's behaviour towards his wife 'was touching and charming . . . it was so attentive and affectionate, and at the same time so respectful'. With age and experience the Tsar had gained the polished manners that his mother despaired of in his youth, and Lady Bloomfield was impressed by his charm, his gentleness, and his continuing good looks. She found the Tsaritsa 'very thin, but not so ill as I expected, and her face bore the traces of great refinement and beauty. Her eyes, which were blue, were set deep in her head, and the expression was more intelligent than pleasing. Her voice was soft, but she spoke rapidly and with decision.'[13] She was touched by Alexandra's kindness and surprised and pleased to be received in the private rooms of the imperial family without ceremony or formality.

But outside the domestic haven the late 1840s saw increasing unrest in Europe. Russia was not touched by the revolutions of 1848, though Nicholas tightened his grip on the country and sent an army to help the young Emperor Franz Joseph in Hungary. Nicholas's Russia had become a force to be reckoned with, but the reckoning was not far off. For generations Russia's rulers had eyed the Balkan countries, then under Turkish rule. Nicholas hoped to establish himself as protector of the Sultan's Orthodox subjects, and in 1853 his armies occupied the provinces of Moldavia and Wallachia. It was an expansion the West would not allow. The resulting war in the Crimea exposed every chink in the Tsar's armour and his empire, which had appeared so strong, did not have the resources or the organization to compete with a Western alliance. Depressed by his army's weakness in the Crimea, Nicholas's health suffered and he died in the Winter Palace on 6/18 February 1855. Officially death came as a result of influenza, but some said that an argument with the Tsesarevich over the conduct of the war had produced a fit of rage, causing a massive stroke. Suicide has also been suggested and others argue that Nicholas simply died of a broken heart. One of the most feared rulers in Europe, his own priority had never been power. As he told his sister, 'the only true happiness is an agreeable home life. The rest is only illusory.'[14]

Alexandra survived her husband for five years. She retired to the Alexander Palace at Tsarskoe Selo, and continued to give dinner parties for as long as her health would allow. The family and their doings were a constant source of interest to her and she warned her son against the dangers of reform. Of one thing she had no doubt: looking back on the day of her wedding she wrote 'with utmost confidence I placed my life in the keeping of my Nicholas and he has never betrayed that trust'.[15]

2

'Our Favourite Little Corner of Earth'

ALEXANDRIA PETERHOF

The estate that Alexander I presented to Alexandra when she was unhappy and homesick for Berlin was a generous gift: 115 hectares of wooded parkland on the shore of the Gulf of Finland, lying to the east of the great park at Peterhof. Peter the Great had once given this land to Prince Alexander Menshikov who had a stone palace, 'Moncourage', built on the site. In the eighteenth century Peter's niece, Tsaritsa Anna Ioannovna, bought back the land for hunting. In 1825, rechristened 'Alexandria' in honour of its new owner, the park became a summer playground, beloved of every generation of Nicholas and Alexandra's descendants while the dynasty lasted.

Alexander could not have chosen a better site, or a better present. His sister-in-law was thrilled with Peterhof when she was first taken there as a bride in the summer of 1817: 'when I discovered the sea, the old trees close to the shore, and all the fountains in the garden, I gave continuous little squeals of pleasure,' she remembered, 'I was really enchanted.'[1] But she found the Great Palace with its ornate interiors overwhelming, its yards of gold leaf tiring to the eye. To please her, her husband commissioned the English architect Adam Menelaus to build a house in the fashionable Gothic style, quite unlike the other Russian palaces. The 'Cottage' was built on rising ground with trees on three sides and a magnificent view of the sea, in sight of the naval base at Kronstadt.

From its completion in 1829 the Cottage was a family home, just large enough for Nicholas and Alexandra, their children, and two servants. It had its own garden and around this the park was carefully landscaped, with a number of smaller buildings, summerhouses and follies, some practical and designed to accommodate more servants and others added for appearance. Menelaus built a little Gothic house, the 'Farm', near the Cottage, which was used to provide extra schoolrooms for the imperial children, and the family had a private chapel dedicated to St Alexander Nevsky. This was also in Gothic style, like a chunk broken from one of the great European cathedrals and set down in the park.

The poet Zhukovsky, who taught Alexandra to speak Russian when she first arrived in the country, created a distinctive emblem for Alexandria Peterhof: a shield, bearing a wreath of roses encircling a sword. This was meant to represent Nicholas and Alexandra and the love that had remained constant from their first meeting. The device was used to decorate the outer walls of the Cottage and it appeared on furniture and smaller items commissioned for the house. Flags bearing the sword in the wreath of roses flew from the roof and from other buildings in the park, and later generations wove a romantic legend around the emblem. They said that it commemorated the imperial couple's first meeting in Berlin at the end of the Napoleonic Wars, when a tournament was held and Nicholas took part on behalf of his brother, the Tsar. The story told how the King's daughter threw him a wreath of white roses and he caught it on his sword. Tournaments were fashionable at that time so it may have happened, but, true or not, the tournament came to be part of the mythology of Alexandria Peterhof.

The park was the imperial couple's sanctuary, where they could shut themselves away from the public life they had never wanted and spend time with their children. But inevitably the outside world began to intrude. The Cottage became too small to hold a Tsar, with all his official duties. In 1842 an enlarged dining room and a terrace were added, though Nicholas regretted this terribly and clung to the idea that the house was still a simple family home. In the summer of 1846 the Bloomfields were invited to dinner and were touched by the intimacy of it all: 'nothing could have been less formal or pleasanter than the dinner', Lady Bloomfield remembered; 'their

Majesties both talked a great deal, and during dinner the Czarewitch's two eldest children, and their two cousins, the Grand Duchess Marie's, came into the room and played about. It was charming to see the Emperor and Empress's manner with their children and grandchildren; it was so very kind and affectionate, and the little ones were as merry and playful as possible. . . . When dinner was over, and we had adjourned to the drawing-room, the Empress said she must show me her private apartments herself. She took me into her sitting-room, bed-room, and dressing-room, and then into the garden.'[2]

The rooms of the Cottage were small – for a palace – and colourful, cluttered with little ornaments and family portraits. In the attic Nicholas had a study with a splendid view of the sea and he spent many hours there watching naval manoeuvres. In 1833 he had a wooden tower topped by an optical telegraph built on the shore, which enabled him to direct his ships and to communicate with the base at Kronstadt. This was visible from the Cottage, but the Tsar preferred to sit in the tower itself: in time rooms were added to enable Alexandra and the family to join him and take tea. The optical telegraph became another of the park's pavilions. In the summer of 1854 the shadow of the Crimean War reached Peterhof; 'for several days the entire enemy fleet was clearly visible from the balcony of the Cottage', the Tsesarevich told his aunt.[3]

As the Tsar's four sons grew up they were given their own dachas at Alexandria; the Farm was enlarged to provide a summer residence for the Tsesarevich Alexander, who married in 1841, while Konstantin had a datcha known as the 'Admiral's house' (from earliest childhood Konstantin had been destined for the Navy). Nikolai and Mikhail moved into the 'Cavalry houses'. After marriage, the three younger brothers would acquire whole estates of their own at Peterhof and would commission emblems based on the badge of Alexandria. These represented their regimental duties: for Konstantin, an anchor encircled by roses; for Nikolai, the crossed axes of the pioneer regiment; and for Mikhail, the field gun of the artillery. These devices were flown at Strelna, Znamenka and Mikhailovskoe respectively but the senior line of the family remained faithful to their sword.

Alexandra Feodorovna began to say, rather mournfully, that the Cottage had become too big for her and her husband once their children had grown up and moved away.

After Nicholas I's death, the Alexandria Park continued to be Alexandra's property and did not pass to the new Tsaritsa, her daughter-in-law Maria Alexandrovna. Alexandra went on using the Cottage but the focus of importance at Alexandria shifted to the Farm, which had become the summer residence of the Tsar. Maria Alexandrovna inherited the estate when her mother-in-law died, but the Cottage was left to its memories until her eldest son, the Tsesarevich Nikolai, was old enough to need a house of his own. Sadly his tenure was all too brief: after his death in 1865 the building passed to his brother.

The Farm was similar in style to the Cottage, but much larger. Along two of its sides were verandas supported by metal columns, which were camouflaged and painted to look like birch trees. Most of the upper rooms had balconies on the garden side with striped awnings to keep out the sun, and the exterior walls were painted a pale yellow with the emblem of Alexandria Peterhof on each of the highest gables. Paintings of the late 1850s show a children's wooden playhouse in the garden, shaped like a traditional peasant cottage.

Inside, the Farm was very light and airy, modern, and designed for comfort. In its large entrance hall the yellow walls were hung with engravings and there was a wide bay window, draped with net curtains. A simple curved staircase with an iron balustrade led to the upper floor and there were plain wooden chairs around the walls. Maria Alexandrovna collected glass ornaments and displayed some of her favourite pieces in her sitting room at the Farm. This was a very feminine room, its walls decorated with pale lilac and green flowered paper, colours that were echoed in a delicate tracery design painted on the ceiling and above the bay window. Ivy covered screens separated this window, with its table and chairs, from the rest of the room where the Tsaritsa had her day bed. Her husband's study, where some of the most important reforms of the new reign were discussed and planned, was dominated by the strong blue of the curtains, rugs and upholstery. A large portrait of

Nicholas I standing outside the Cottage faced his son's desk and looked down on his every move.

By the 1870s there were children spending their summers in the Cottage again, and a new generation was learning to love Alexandria Peterhof. Alexander II's eldest surviving son, Alexander Alexandrovich, his Danish-born wife Maria Feodorovna and their family brought new life to the house. Their children were attracted by the balconies and staircases, and by all the odd small corners that were so unlike anything they had encountered in the grander palaces. Most days the elder boys, Nicholas and Georgi, would be sent to see their grandfather at the Farm, and would play in his study while he worked. Young Nicholas treasured the memory of a day when he attended Vespers with the Tsar in the Gothic Chapel. A violent thunderstorm came on, the sky darkened, and the chapel itself seemed to shake. 'Gusts of wind from the open doors made the tapers burning before the ikonostasis to flicker fitfully. There was a long clap of thunder, louder than the rest, and all of a sudden I saw a fiery ball fly right over the Emperor's head through the open window. It whirled across the floor, went right round a chandelier, and in a flash was out of the door into the park. My heart stood still. I glanced up at Grandfather. His face was calm and unperturbed. Quietly he made the sign of the cross, not moving a step from where he stood as the fiery ball went past him. . . . After the ball had gone . . . I looked up at Grandfather again. A slight smile was on his face, and he gave me a nod. My terror had passed . . . and I set myself the task of always following Grandfather's example of calm.'[4] It was a lesson in courage and faith from one future victim of terrorism to another.

Tsaritsa Maria Alexandrovna died in 1880 and Alexandria Peterhof passed to Maria Feodorovna, who was destined to be the park's last imperial owner. With her husband, who became Alexander III, she continued to use the Cottage as her summer home and it was the Farm's turn to slide back into the shadows, to be used in summer by one or other of the new Tsar's brothers, by guests, or as a setting for imperial receptions.

Shortly after his accession, Alexander III noticed that his grandfather's optical telegraph was in a bad state. The original tower was only a wooden building and it had suffered from exposure to the sea winds. With the introduction of the electric telegraph it had fallen into disuse, but Alexander decided that it had historical importance and ordered the architect Anthony Tomishko to produce a reconstruction in stone. 'It will do for my children', he is supposed to have said, but the first people to use the new tower were his cousin Olga Konstantinovna, her husband King George I of Greece and their children. This gave the building its first name; the Tsar's nickname for the King's elder daughter Alexandra was 'Baboon' and he christened the tower 'Villa Baboon' in her honour.

The same years brought another visitor to the villa who would come to have an immense impact on the Romanov story. In June 1884 the Tsar's younger brother Sergei was married to Princess Elisabeth of Hesse-Darmstadt and among the guests who relaxed at Alexandria before and after the celebrations was the bride's twelve-year-old sister Alix. The Tsesarevich Nicholas, then sixteen, described the long summer days in his diary, with their family dinners, outings, and games in the garden: 'We all romped around a lot on the net . . . went out with Ernie and Alix in the break, with Papa driving . . . we fooled around a lot on the swings. Papa turned on the hose then we ran through the jet and got very wet.'[5] Nicholas was starting to take a close interest in young Alix and they scratched their names together on a window pane in the newly built villa. This must have seemed like a childish romance that would soon be forgotten: in fact, it sealed the future for them both.

Once Nicholas was old enough to need a house of his own he began to use rooms in the tower, sharing the villa with his brother Georgi, and after his accession in 1894 and marriage to Alix, he commissioned Tomishko to enlarge the building to provide a summer home for the family they hoped to have. It took a long time. In the early summer of 1897 Alix gave birth to her second daughter Tatiana at the Farm, where she and Nicholas were staying while they waited for their new house to be completed. Grand Prince Georgi wrote from the Caucasus to ask about the building's progress. 'When will the house by the sea at last be finished? I am intrigued to know what it will look like and how it will be joined to the old one. I keep thinking of how we used to live there together and how cosy it was; it's already 7 years how terrifying the way time flies.'[6] In fact, a new two-storey house was joined to the original villa by a raised and enclosed gallery above an archway large enough for a carriage or car to drive through. Kitchens and service rooms were added, but the building was still dominated by the tower flying the flag of Alexandria Peterhof. A small road led along the coast to the Maritime Gate, at the western boundary of the park, which joined the gardens of the Nikolaievich estate at Znamenka.

The focus of life at Alexandria Peterhof had shifted once again and, although the Tsar's mother still owned the park and used the Cottage in summer, the most important building in the dynasty's final years of power was Tomishko's 'New Palace'. Within its walls a second Nicholas and Alexandra came to love Alexandria, and their three youngest children, Maria, Anastasia, and the Tsesarevich Alexei, were born in the house on the seashore, where once the first Nicholas had directed his fleet.

The New Palace was bright and comfortable, a home rather than a palace, and the family's favourite room was Nicholas II's study on the second floor of the old building. Its walls were panelled with walnut to match the Tsar's desk; the chairs, upholstered in dark green morocco leather, had been specially ordered from England, and despite the darkness of the wood the room was always full of light. One window, facing west towards Kronstadt, had a balcony with a table that was continually piled with newspapers, magazines and books. The desk was set at right angles to the other window, which faced north across the gulf. In this study Nicholas II received his ministers and gave special audiences: there was a waiting room next door and offices and servants' rooms on the floor below. The dining room, beside the waiting room, was designed to look and feel like a room on board ship.

From the second floor of the old villa, the covered gallery led to the new building that held the rooms of the Tsaritsa and her lady-in-waiting, and the bedrooms, playrooms, and classrooms of the imperial children. The Tsaritsa's drawing room had white-painted woodwork, a floral design on the walls, and soft furnishings in a pink rose-patterned cretonne. Art Nouveau wallpapers decorated her daughters' rooms, while the prevailing colour for Alexei was blue: all was bright, modern, and designed for simplicity and comfort. Generations had passed but Alexandria Peterhof was still a sanctuary where an imperial couple could shut themselves away from the pressures of public life and enjoy being alone with their children.

After the Revolution, however, the gates of Alexandria were thrown open, and the public gained access to this once safe and very private world. In 1925 it cost fifteen kopecks to look around the Cottage and fifteen to go into the Farm, but entrance to the New Palace was a full twenty-five kopecks. Guide books stressed that there was nothing of artistic merit in the building except one portrait of Alexander III by Serov, but ordinary people were still attracted to the palace because of its association with the last Tsar and his family. Their personal possessions could still be seen, and the Tsesarevich's toys littered the nursery.

The guide books voiced official disapproval of the imperial family, but a generation of museum curators came to love the palaces for their beauty, and for the silent story they told. When news of the German invasion of 1941 fell like a thunderbolt from the summer sky, these curators were faced with a desperate race to save as much as they could from the advancing armies. The Great Palace was their priority, but four-fifths of the inventoried items from the Cottage and other pieces from the Farm and the New Palace were packed into crates and taken on a hazardous journey into Siberia, with collections from the other palaces outside the city. The packing continued until the very last minute, when the fighting could be heard quite clearly from the park. For almost three years the curators guarded their treasures and waited, until the end of January 1944 when they heard that Peterhof was free. When the news was confirmed they opened one of the precious crates and drank a toast to the liberation from the crystal glasses made for the Cottage, decorated with the sword in the wreath of roses.

The scene they faced on their return was heartbreaking. Unable to conquer Leningrad the Germans had set out to destroy the old imperial palaces, and they had almost succeeded. The Great Palace was a burned-out shell and the park had been mined. The Cottage was looted and battered, and the Farm had been used by the Germans as their local headquarters. The New Palace, right on the coast, had been too good a target for naval shelling: its destruction was completed by the Soviets in the 1960s.

Today the Cottage is open to the public once more after extraordinarily skilful restoration work, which was completed in 1978. Most tourists are taken to the Great Palace and miss the Cottage, which is hidden in the trees and reached by an unmade track. They miss a treasure. The building looks almost as it did in paintings of the 1840s, although the trees are thicker and taller than they were, which might have delighted the original owner: Alexandra Feodorovna loved solitude. Visitors are taken first into a small exhibition in the room that used to be her bedroom. The Soviets would not allow bedrooms to be restored as bedrooms; today the guides mention this as one of the oddities of the 'bad old days'. The exhibition includes some of the finely detailed nineteenth-century watercolours of the interiors by Eduard Petrovich Hau which provided invaluable guidance for the restorers.

The restored rooms of the Cottage are colourful and cluttered, reminiscent in some ways of Frogmore and Osborne in England, also of Hohenschwangau in Bavaria, though the house has a charm of its own and its painted staircase is breathtaking. Most of the decoration is in the original Gothic style, but one of the upper rooms has an Art Nouveau feel, recalling the years when Maria Feodorovna spent her summers at Alexandria. The Cottage is more personal and homely than the grander palaces, with portraits of Nicholas I and his family, and everywhere, on walls, balconies and chairbacks, and on the crystal glasses once used to toast the liberation, is Zhukovsky's emblem of the sword in the wreath of roses.

Beyond the Cottage and its garden, the Alexandria Park is at last emerging from its long sleep. The Gothic Chapel, where a very young Nicholas II learnt from his grandfather's example not to show fear, has been fully restored and work has begun on the Farm. The building is still shuttered and neglected, but the trees that grew up around it, enclosing it like Sleeping Beauty's castle, have gone, and, remarkably after so long, reminders of the past are everywhere. An old mosaic pavement; decorative wrought-iron work, rusting now, and hanging at odd angles; a few fragments of the original yellow plaster clinging to the walls; and, unshaken on the highest gable, one defiant shield still bearing the old emblem.

In time the Farm will be restored. The New Palace is beyond saving, though its ruins can be found, lost in the trees and bushes by the shore. Parts of the building are recognizable: the base of the tower, the archway that once joined the new and old wings, and odd openings that must once have been doorways and windows, lost in a meaningless tumble of brick. In old photographs the building looks striped. The broken fragments of the walls have alternate layers of ordinary red bricks and glazed yellow ones – the lost palace must once have been very colourful and bright, particularly in the full light of summer. Photographs of the last Tsar's children playing by the sea show that the shoreline used to be marked by a line of large boulders and they are there still, though reed beds have grown between them and the water.

This should be a sad place, but it is not. At Tsarskoe Selo it is easy to remember the tragic end of the dynasty. On a summer day at Alexandria Peterhof the silence and spaciousness still recall the generations who enjoyed the park and the times when they were happy. Nicholas I's family is remembered in tangible form at the Cottage. When the Farm is restored, Alexander II's time will live again, and even Nicholas II's family is not forgotten. In August 1994, to mark what would have been his ninetieth birthday, a bronze statue of Alexei, the last Tsesarevich, was erected beside the Cottage, on a spot where there was once a memorial to Nicholas I, his great-great-grandfather. In a setting that brings together the beginning and end of the story of Alexandria Peterhof, the little boy is shown leaning against a tree stump, looking down towards the hidden ruins of the New Palace where he was born.

3

A Useless Sacrifice?

GRAND PRINCESS ELENA PAVLOVNA

One day in the early years of the last century a young woman sat by a window in the Winter Palace. Through her tears she watched the grey, swirling waters of the Neva and wished for nothing more than oblivion. Grand Princess Elena Pavlovna was seventeen years old, bound in marriage to a man who showed no signs of affection or even of interest towards her, and the years stretched away before her, hopeless and empty. The Tsar came into the room but she turned her face away. Alexander I had no need to ask what was wrong; he sat beside Elena and began quietly to tell her something of his own life, of his troubles, hopes and fears. 'We do not belong to ourselves,' he said, 'we are tools in the hands of God, destined to fulfill his will; we are the means He has chosen. Our happiness consists in following His call; only thus can we do good.'[1] It was a hard comfort to offer, but Elena was touched by his kindness, and years later she would remember the incident as a turning point in her life. In fact, things would get a lot worse for her before she saw any improvement.

To marry into the Romanov family Elena had given up everything, even her name. Two years before the meeting she was Princess Charlotte of Württemberg, living with her father and sister in Paris. The two Princesses lived in modest circumstances, making their own clothes and studying at an institute. There they met a Miss Walter, a relative of the celebrated palaeontologist and anatomist Georges Cuvier. With their father, Prince Paul, Charlotte and her sister Pauline spent many evenings at the Cuvier house studying under the great man and drinking in the learned conversations around his table. It was for this intellectual existence that Paul had turned his back on his Stuttgart home in 1815, settling in Paris with his small daughters because he found life in the French capital more to his liking.

At home in Württemberg he had left a wife and two sons, and a very bitter legacy. The Württemberg family did not approve of his decision to settle in Paris. They ordered him to return home so his daughters could be brought up in a manner more suited to their rank, but he defied them. The Romanovs were convinced that his daughter's early life was unhappy. The only details we have come from the stories she told in later years to the women in her household, and there was no hint of unhappiness there. Perhaps she remembered what she wanted to remember. She told them about her life in Paris and her studies with Cuvier, she spoke of her father with fondness, but never mentioned her mother or Stuttgart. Princess Elizabeth Kurakin, whose own mother was one of Elena's ladies-in-waiting, believed that the Grand Princess had lost her mother in early childhood; in fact, Elena was over forty when her mother died. The arrangement of her disastrous but very grand marriage was probably the Württemberg family's way of reasserting its authority.

Elena first met her husband in the summer of 1822, but the engagement was settled months before the meeting. He was Grand Prince Mikhail Pavlovich, Alexander I's youngest brother, and his only interest was the army. To ordinary men in the ranks he was a harsh disciplinarian, even brutal, but people who really knew him valued his cheerfulness and generosity and his family adored him. Before the meeting Mikhail had shown little interest in marriage and his mother's constant concern was the lack of suitable princesses. She never seems to have thought of Charlotte, which was odd, as she too was a Princess of Württemberg and Paul was her nephew, born in St Petersburg and named after her husband Tsar Paul.

Once the engagement was confirmed, though, encouraging reports began to reach Russia. Charlotte was exceptional, they said, very mature for her fifteen years and, if not exactly pretty, she had a sweet and expressive face. She made the journey north in August 1823 and Mikhail rode to meet her at the border. He was impressed by her poise and apparent confidence and amazed to hear her greet his officers in Russian. At a reception held in her honour she charmed the two hundred guests by speaking to them individually. She told the historian Nikolai Karamzin that she had read his latest volume in the original language, and when generals were introduced her conversation turned to battles and strategy. Cuvier's teaching had produced a manner and a depth of intelligence that people did not expect in a girl of sixteen. A princess entering her new husband's home was supposed to be sweet, childlike and naïve, soft enough to be moulded into the ways of his family and country. This Princess already had a strong character of her own.

As the weeks passed praise for young Charlotte's unusual qualities mounted. She handled Court ceremonies well, she danced beautifully, her manner was suitably reserved. It was a front: in private her periods were delayed and she suffered painful stomach cramps; her first experience of the long masses of the Orthodox Church left her pale, sweating, and about to faint, but she held her ground. The danger signs were there; Maria Feodorovna noticed that her son was not attentive or loving, but she reassured herself time and again with the thought that nobody could be unhappy with her Mikhail. Only one person saw the situation clearly. Grand Prince Konstantin Pavlovich knew his brother all too well, and his summary of the problem was chilling. 'The married state', he wrote, 'is an accessory which he might have been able to do without.'[2]

Before Charlotte travelled to Russia Konstantin had tried to persuade Mikhail to call off the engagement. He had spoken to his mother and sister too, but no one would listen. The affair gained its own momentum. Charlotte was received into the Orthodox Church on 5/17 December 1823 and took the name Elena Pavlovna; her own name would never be used again. Her engagement was celebrated officially the next day and she wore a blue velvet gown with a long train, heavily embroidered with silver roses and leaves, and an emerald diadem. She looked magnificent. On 8/20 February 1824 she and Mikhail were married in a temporary chapel set up in the Tsar's reception room; Alexander had a bad leg, but the family would not think of holding the wedding without him.

Within a fortnight the marriage was in trouble. Mikhail claimed to be happy, but had no conception of what marriage involved. 'In spite of the fact that he could love his wife,' Konstantin told their sister Anna, 'he maintains a unique coldness and unawareness towards her. Whether it is the newness of the situation, shyness or another reason, I was not able to make it out.'[3] Konstantin liked Elena. He saw that beneath the intelligence and witty conversation she was very sensitive, and he tried without success to change his brother's attitude. In April Grand Prince Nicholas wrote that Mikhail was 'working hard now to get children for them, but it appears that this is still unsuccessful'.[4] More optimistic than his brother, Nicholas never saw the storm beneath the surface.

Elena produced her first child, Maria, in St Petersburg the following March. Within months she was pregnant again. The Dowager Tsaritsa, still inclined to hope for the best, praised her self control: 'she organises her time so well. All morning she spends studying in spite of nausea and vomiting.'[5] The deaths of Alexander I and his wife that winter robbed Elena of two of her most understanding friends in the imperial family. With the spring she was uprooted to Moscow for the birth of her baby, another little girl who was named Elizaveta for the dead Tsaritsa. Loyal crowds thronged the Kremlin and a Te Deum was sung, but isolated somewhere away from the celebrations Elena suffered weeks of milk fever and post-natal cramp. Mikhail was said to be in very good humour, and overwhelmed with work.

By the beginning of the next year Elena was pregnant again, and again she was suffering. Her first child was showing signs of consumption and seemed unlikely to live. Her third, Ekaterina, was born in St Petersburg in the summer of 1827, and this time Elena did not recover from the effects of the birth. Physically and emotionally she had no reserve of strength left. Her behaviour came under increasing criticism and the storm finally broke. She decided that the marriage was over. Then her own family closed its doors against her. Her mother, her uncle, the King of Württemberg, her grandmother, even her father in Paris refused to help. Marriage, however awful, was still marriage. The imperial family would allow only a temporary separation. While Mikhail went with the army to fight in one of Russia's interminable Turkish wars Elena travelled south to take the waters at Ems, leaving the children with the Dowager Tsaritsa.

She broke her journey at Konstantin's palace in Warsaw, and he was shocked by the state of her, and angry that his warnings had had so little effect. He told his sister 'one must agree that this young and charming woman was very gratuitously and very uselessly sacrificed. Her position is frightful . . . and what is worse, no one wants to put themselves in her place to understand it. My wife and I did our very best to bring up her morale which was at a completely low ebb.' Anna agreed: 'I too feel that she is a very noble person – completely sacrificed – who, in my opinion, only indulges in the small defects for which she is blamed because she has been provoked or soured by an uninterrupted succession of difficulties about which she is still both too young and too lively to become resigned.'[6] Both hoped that now Elena had made her stand Mikhail would have more respect for her, and would begin to value their life together. It seemed to be her only chance.

Elena stayed away from Russia for at least a year. The Dowager Tsaritsa died, and in her will left a strong clue to the way forward for her daughter-in-law, passing to her the administration of two charitable institutions. There was some concern about Mikhail's handling of his fortune, so his mother placed the family's finances on a sound footing by leaving a capital sum in trust which he could not touch. The couple had exchanged letters during their separation, and had reached a sort of truce: Elena returned to Russia, and at the start of 1830 she had a miscarriage. There would be two more children, Alexandra and Anna, but both died in infancy. In the spring of 1835 Mikhail and Elena took their daughters to a spa in Bohemia, but it was unusual for them to be together; while Mikhail spent longer periods travelling in Europe, Elena was beginning to make a life for herself in St Petersburg – a life that did not involve him.

At the Mikhail Palace in the city, and in her husband's summer palaces, the Grand Princess was creating a salon like those she had known in Paris in her youth, drawing to herself some of Russia's most creative and interesting people. She was one of the highest ranking ladies in the country, and it was a continual irritant to society that access to her circle did not depend on rank or money. She invited the clever, the artistic and the musical, and the rigid censorship imposed by her brother-in-law seemed to stop at her door. Gogol, Pushkin and Turgenev all enjoyed Elena's patronage, knowing that they could express any ideas in her house in safety and be sure of an audience.

As her confidence grew, Elena's sympathy went out to those who needed help. She became a good friend to the Tsar's sons and introduced them to a wider range of ideas and cultural influences than they could meet at home. When Princess Marie of Hesse-Darmstadt, Tsesarevich Alexander's fiancée, came to Russia as a shy and unhappy fifteen-year-old Elena was quick to befriend her, knowing just what it meant to be a stranger at Court. Alexander's brother Konstantin Nikolaievich was her particular favourite though, and when the time came for him to marry she introduced him to a young cousin on her mother's side, Alexandra of Saxe-Altenburg, who became Grand Princess Konstantin.

But the years that brought increasing personal confidence for Elena also brought tragedy. At the start of 1844 her daughter Elisaveta married her sister Pauline's stepson, Duke Adolf of Nassau. Elisaveta died a year later after giving birth to a baby who also did not survive. The next year brought news that Elena's elder daughter was also dying. Grand Princess Maria Mikhailovna had never been strong. She was in Vienna when the end came and her father appears to have been with her: it was he who sent news back to the family, and in their letters to one another it is his grief for both his daughters which is pitied. Elena is not even mentioned. This may simply reflect the old closed circle of the 'Triopathy' or it may show deeper divisions in the Mikhail family. In the summer of 1849 Grand Prince Mikhail was attending army manoeuvres in Warsaw when he suffered a stroke. He died there a few months later and again Anna and Nicholas wrote of their own sorrow and pain without ever mentioning Elena.

Whatever her feelings on her husband's death, as a widow Elena enjoyed greater independence. She broke from the custom of celebrating Easter at Court, preferring to be in her own palace with her daughter Ekaterina; in future she would relate to the imperial family on her own terms. Ekaterina married Duke Georg of Mecklenburg Strelitz in 1851, but he liked Russia and was happy for his wife to spend the greater part of each year with her mother. They surrounded themselves with interesting people. In 1848 the musician Anton Rubinstein came to St Petersburg and settled at the Mikhail Palace. With his help Elena founded what would one day become the St Petersburg Conservatoire. Five years later she invited Princess Kurakin to be her lady-in-waiting. The Princess had spent fourteen years outside Russia and had lived through the 1848 revolution in Paris, and she brought new ideas to the household.

Female education was an absorbing interest of Elena's, and she quizzed the Kurakin children on their studies in Paris. She sent her daughter's former governess Mlle Troubat back to France to observe education there and report on developments. Elena dreamed of improving the standards of education for all Russian women, a dream that was shared by the young Tsarevna Maria. Society watched the friendship between the Grand Princess and the rising generation of Romanovs with unease: she was far too keen on reform, and her ambitions went a long way beyond the classroom.

Under Elena's protection Russian intellectuals were free to voice their growing discontent with a system of landholding that made one man the property of another. Samarin's controversial paper on the abolition of serfdom was read and discussed in the drawing room of the Mikhail Palace, and Elena was so moved that she asked the Tsar for permission to free the serfs on the Poltava estates that she had inherited from her husband. Nicholas I refused. Even so, Elena began to run the estates on humanitarian lines which horrified the provincial governor, who complained that all discipline would be lost.

Concerns such as these paled in the face of real crisis. When the Crimean War began Elena did not join the general criticism of the Tsar and she set aside her love of France. She organized a privately funded aid society for the wounded, and founded an order of nursing sisters, all in the face of fierce opposition from the military hierarchy.

The Tsar trusted her and gave her what she wanted, agreeing to her request for an army commission for Pirogov, a leading surgeon. Elena's nursing sisters became the forerunner of the Red Cross in Russia, and her interest in medical and scientific work grew.

Once Nicholas I was dead, the new reign gave her a chance to effect real political change. She finally freed the serfs on her Poltava estates, and her salons were given over to the cause of abolition. She had known Alexander II since he was a small boy and encouraged him now in his plans for reform, supported by his brother Konstantin, by her friend Count Paul Kisselev, a lifelong advocate of abolition, and by the new Tsaritsa. They made a formidable team. On his own Alexander might have been swayed towards hard-line policies, but when his conservative ministers seemed to be gaining ground, Elena introduced Kisselev's nephew Nikolai Milutin to Maria Alexandrovna, and so manoeuvred him onto the committee that was working on the liberation. With Milutin and Konstantin at his side, Alexander pushed the reform through. The abolition of serfdom, which became law on 19 February/3 March 1861, was Alexander II's great achievement but he might never have managed it without his brother, his wife, and his aunt. The opposition was fierce. Elena was so unwavering in her friendship for Milutin that those who were eager to stop the emancipation tried to destroy her by hinting that there was more to the relationship than politics. She ignored them all.

The world that Elena had created after her awful experience of marriage was a world of women. Her life centred on her daughter and her ladies; she took close interest in their lives and ideas, and was always kind to their children. At her right hand was her lady-in-waiting, Baroness Editha von Rahden, who shared her concerns, kept her informed and dealt with her correspondence. The Baroness was charming, enthusiastic, clever, and very kind. She had time for everyone, though society did snigger at her over-zealous regard for etiquette; her curtseys were said to be twice as deep as anyone else's. Into this charmed circle men came only by invitation. Elena kept a slight distance around herself that discouraged informality. In his diary Kisselev described her as 'a woman of great intelligence and a heart of gold. Her friendship, not easily given, is like a rock. . . . She never chatters: she talks. Everybody who has met her marvels at the extent of her knowledge.'[7]

The salon at the Mikhail Palace was the place to be, and acceptance there still could not be bought, which was not popular. Thursday evenings were given over to meetings for artists and scientists; on other days there would be parlour games or parties, and always there was music. Sometimes Elena commissioned translations of books; Alexander II did not miss one of Baroness Rahden's readings from the memoirs of Baroness Oberkirchen, who accompanied his grandparents to Versailles in the time of Marie Antoinette. Konstantin Nikolaievich was a regular visitor too: there were those in society who had never forgiven him or Elena for their work in the cause of emancipation, and they still sought to undermine the Grand Prince by hinting at a conspiracy against the throne. In good times these rumours could be ignored, but they left a vague shadow that was never quite dispelled.

In the spring of 1862 Elena found a new use for the Mikhail Palace. Revolutionaries had set large areas of the city on fire, leaving thousands of people dead, injured and homeless. The Princess turned half of the palace into a canteen, and others followed her lead. It was typical of her to take a practical approach to national catastrophies, and also to very private ones. When one of her daughter's ladies, the younger Princess Kurakin, was grief-stricken after the death of a brother, Elena put her in charge of a home for old ladies which she had just founded. Then she worked alongside the young Princess, helping her to sort out day-to-day problems, and to learn more about herself in the process. Her help was given equally freely to those she did not know: without publicity or fuss she paid private pensions to numerous artists and musicians who came to her notice, enabling them to continue their work.

As time passed Elena spent longer periods travelling in Europe, and in 1863 she discovered a new interest. On a visit to her sister Pauline she met nineteen-year-old Princess Elisabeth of Wied, Pauline's step-granddaughter. Here was a girl who would benefit from contact with a wider world: Elisabeth was well read and artistic, intensely emotional and utterly wedded to home. Elena asked if the young Princess might accompany her on her travels, and the Wieds were delighted. That autumn Elena left with her for Lake Geneva, settling at the Hotel Beaurivage at Ouchy, and Elisabeth was overwhelmed by her kindness, and fascinated by the interesting people who gathered around her. 'I love my aunt more every day,' she wrote to her mother, 'I am happy to be near her, and when she is in the room I only think of her!'[8]

Together they travelled on to St Petersburg for the winter. The imperial family was welcoming and Elena made sure that her protégée made the best use of her time. 'Her day is filled up with music, reading, the study of Russian, and the time she spends with me,' she told the Princess of Wied, 'I have also entreated her always to have a good book in reading. To heighten her interest and get her to work herself, I advised her to write out parts and make comments upon it for you. Be it here or in another centre of the great world, we must remember that we deteriorate, if we do not try to get away from the frivolity that surrounds us by serious thinking and reading.'[9] Elisabeth studied the piano with Anton Rubinstein and Clara Schumann. On Monday evenings she and Elena visited the opera, on Tuesday there were Shakespeare readings, and dinner parties completed the week. The palace echoed with fine music. Then Elisabeth fell ill and Elena nursed her, helped by Grand Princess Ekaterina and Baroness Rahden. The Prince of Wied died during his daughter's illness, but she stayed in Russia until the next summer, when Elena took her home.

For the next three years Elisabeth accompanied her great-aunt whenever she travelled in Europe; whether the Grand Princess was playing bowls with General Moltke at Ragaz, hosting intellectual gatherings at Carlsbad or visiting the Great Exhibition in Paris, Elisabeth was continually by her side, and always conscious of how much she owed her. It was in Ragaz in 1866 that the young Princess first heard discussion of Prince Karl of Hohenzollern Sigmaringen, who would one day be King of Romania – and her own husband.

Elena's last years were occupied with her daughter and her three Mecklenburg grandchildren, and with her many interests. Her nursing order was flourishing and she had already endowed a small hospital, but this was not enough. She dreamed of founding a larger medical institution and made plans accordingly: these were not realized until after her death in 1873 but in time the Institute of Grand Princess Elena Pavlovna would train some of Russia's finest doctors and would keep her name alive until the Revolution. She had come a long way from the unhappy seventeen-year-old who longed for death. There were some who said that she thought too much of her own importance but they were few. She *was* important, thanks largely to her own efforts, and the agonies of the past had faded to stories by the fireside, told to encourage her younger ladies when their own lives seemed hopeless and empty.

Tsaritsa Maria Feodorovna

Vassili Zhukovsky

4

A Flight of Doves

THE EARLY YEARS OF ALEXANDER II

In the mid-nineteenth century the idea of a throne passing peacefully from father to son was a novelty in Russia, where for two hundred years the succession had been haphazard and often violent. Alexander I became Tsar in the wake of his father's murder and many suspected that he had been involved; the stain of this never really left him. His younger brother was forced to push his way to a throne he did not want by ruthless suppression of the Decembrist Rising. So when Nicholas I died in his bed, leaving a son who was capable, experienced, and ready to take over, even the dynasty's enemies were prepared to hope for a brighter future. But hopes like this had surrounded the new Tsar all his life.

Remembered omens, favourable or unfavourable, follow princes like a shadow. When the child who would become Alexander II, Russia's Tsar Liberator, was born in the Kremlin in April 1818, all the bells of Moscow were ringing to celebrate the Easter festival. A flight of white doves was said to have circled the rooftops of the Chudov Monastery, where, by tradition, imperial babies were christened. Often repeated, this story would come to symbolize an unbearable burden of hope and expectation. Describing the birth in later years, his mother remembered 'something grave and melancholy in the thought that this little creature would one day be an emperor'.[1]

There are fond glimpses of Alexander Nikolaievich's early childhood in the letters of his grandmother Maria Feodorovna. 'The little boy . . . is changing daily. He's a most delightful child. . . . He climbs trees, gets himself out of trouble, I think, balances on beams, jumps about. . . . Sasha is as agile as a little monkey.'[2] Protected by an unusually close and loving family, Alexander had no sense of his own importance. Grand Prince Nicholas was strict but he knew how to unbend and play with his children, and often took a supporting role in their games. When Alexander was six, the gentle Captain Karl Merder was appointed to replace his nurses and governesses, but the peaceful pattern of his life went on undisturbed.

The pattern was shattered in 1825, when Nicholas ascended the throne in confusion and violence. When the Decembrists fired the first shots on Senate Square the shedding of Russian blood by Russians seemed an appalling novelty; in time it would become all too familiar. Little Alexander would not have understood much of what was happening. In a few tense days he was taken from his home, entrusted to the care of the Finnish Guards in the torchlit courtyard of the Winter Palace, and left to stand beside his anguished mother as she prayed for her husband's safety. It was a terrifying introduction to the world of political power. From the start Alexander was trained to bring about the reforms Russia so badly needed, but he dreaded the forces misplaced reform could unleash. The shadow of those December days never really left him. But no prince could have had a better training: in 1826 Nicholas I offered the poet Zhukovsky the position of tutor, in partnership with Merder.

On the face of it, Zhukovsky was an unlikely choice. The illegitimate son of a landowner from the provinces, his mother was a teenage captive, taken to Russia after one of the empire's wars with Turkey. His father provided a good education designed to fit him for the civil service, but the young Zhukovsky found the work uninspiring. He drifted, until his poetry drew the attention of the Dowager Tsaritsa Maria Feodorovna. In her household Zhukovsky flourished, and when her son Nicholas married his princess from Berlin, the poet was chosen as her Russian teacher. It was Alexandra who urged her husband to entrust the Tsesarevich to Zhukovsky's teaching. The poet had proved himself immune to the temptations of Court life. Honest and idealistic, he spoke his mind without fear and never took advantage of the favour shown to him. He would die a relatively poor man.

Before his appointment had even started, he issued a vehement protest about the eight-year-old Tsesarevich's introduction to military life. The boy had been allowed to ride with the troops in his father's coronation parade: the crowds loved it and Nicholas could hardly contain his pride, but Merder noticed that Alexander was too excited afterwards to concentrate on lessons. 'Madam, forgive me,' Zhukovsky wrote to the Tsaritsa, 'an over-developed passion for the art of war – even if indulged in on the parade ground, would cripple the soul and the mind. . . . He would end by seeing his people as an immense regiment and his country as a barracks.'[3] At first the Tsar was angry, but faced with Zhukovsky's threat of resignation he gave way and listened to the poet's ideas.

Zhukovsky set out a nine-year curriculum for the Tsesarevich. Alexander was to have two companions to share his life in a structured school environment that no ceremonial would ever disturb. They would sleep, eat, work and play together: competition was frowned on, and the boys were encouraged to discuss their reading with one another, and to keep journals. At the heart of their studies were history, languages, and a profound sense of the nearness of God. As they progressed, the boys would be introduced to sciences, law and philosophy. Good behaviour was rewarded by a chance to put money in the poor box – a recipe for chaos in most classrooms. Military drill was just part of the programme, with fencing, gymnastics and riding; on Sundays handicrafts and outings took the place of lessons.

At his best, Alexander was a courteous and honest child, obviously bright, and naturally generous. Any sign of suffering or unhappiness moved him. But he was just a boy, prone to mischief and laziness, and his tutors noticed a worrying tendency to turn the smallest setback into a crisis. He cried too easily, often for no reason. Patiently, over time, Zhukovsky discovered Alexander's dread of his own inheritance, born in the violence of the Decembrist Rising. He was eleven when his mother gave birth to a second son. 'I am so glad,' he is supposed to have said, 'now Papa will be able to choose him as the Heir.'[4]

Kind though Zhukovsky was, his high-mindedness must have

added to his pupil's forebodings. He gave the boy an essay setting out his vision of the perfect ruler, and Alexander treasured it for the rest of his life. 'Respect the law,' Zhukovsky wrote, 'the law which is neglected by the Tsar will not be observed by the people. . . . Respect public opinion – for it often enlightens the monarch . . . public opinion will always be on the side of the just sovereign. . . . Rule by order, not by might. . . . Love thy people; unless the Tsar loves his people, the people cannot love their Tsar.'[5] The tutor also left a note on Alexander's school desk: 'You will one day walk into History. That is inevitable by sheer accident of birth. History will pass its judgement on you before the entire world and for all time.'[6] It was a daunting prospect for an eleven-year-old boy.

That same year, 1829, Alexander went on army manoeuvres for the first time. His father noticed a lack of enthusiasm, and friction increased between the Tsar and the tutors. Nicholas was adamant that more emphasis must be placed on military sciences. He was appalled when Zhukovsky chose as Alexander's history tutor Professor Arseniev, who had lost his University post for attacking corruption in the judicial system. Zhukovsky argued that Alexander must understand the real state of the country. A favourite religious teacher was dismissed for sympathizing with dissenters. As tensions between school and Court multiplied, Alexander began to play up in class and to fight with his companions. In 1832 Merder suffered a slight heart attack. Blamed for this by Arseniev, Alexander broke down and promised to behave.

He was on the threshold of an important change. In 1834, on his sixteenth birthday, he became the first Romanov prince to swear the Oath of Allegiance – in time, this would be an important rite-of-passage for all the men of the imperial family. The words and the setting were overwhelming: in the chapel of the Winter Palace before a congregation of courtiers, government representatives, foreign guests and clergy, the boy promised to obey his father 'in all things, without sparing my body, to the last drop of my blood'. 'Everybody was deeply moved',[7] Pushkin recalled. Many were moved to tears. Alexander came into his fortune that day and by his own choice gave generous sums of money to the Governors-General of St Petersburg and Moscow to be used for the poor. He was not told until much later that Merder, who had gone to Italy to convalesce, had suffered a second heart attack a few days before the ceremony, and had died with his pupil's name on his lips.

The Tsesarevich returned to the schoolroom determined to succeed. He felt guilt as well as grief for Merder, and only found relief in hard work. Three years remained of Zhukovsky's nine-year plan, and in the final examination the nineteen-year-old showed a remarkable breadth of knowledge, and depth of understanding. But he had also spent those three years being introduced to society. Everyone wanted to meet him, and for a boy accustomed to camp beds and functional classrooms there must have been huge temptations in this new life. Vague rumours of love were as inevitable as they were harmless and Alexander displayed a real horror of flattery; soon all agreed that their Tsesarevich could not have been more promising.

His formal training over, Alexander was sent on a seven-month tour of Russia, following a punishing schedule devised by his father. Accompanied by Zhukovsky and General Kavelin, Merder's replacement, the Heir travelled across the country at breakneck speed. 'Even when in bed at night,' Zhukovsky complained to the Tsaritsa, 'we feel as though we were still galloping.'[8] Towns en route arranged civic receptions, church services, banquets and balls, and local dignitaries queued to meet their future ruler. Peasants walked for miles just to catch a glimpse of Alexander's carriage. His party was shown around schools, hospitals, factories, charitable institutions and churches; Alexander looked and listened with interest, but he knew that there was more to see.

He began to demand unplanned halts in the dirtiest and most neglected villages where he would leave his carriage and walk, entering peasant huts as a guest. If this disrupted the official programme, he didn't care. To the peasants it must have seemed like a visitation from outer space, but if they were too overawed to speak, Alexander could see how they lived. His itinerary included a visit to Siberia, where imperial visits were unknown, but it was his own idea to explore convict settlements and talk to prisoners in chain gangs. In Tobolsk he made a special detour to meet the exiled Decembrists whose rebellion was a lingering nightmare to him. The conditions of their exile shocked Alexander so much that he wrote an impassioned appeal to his father. The Tsar heard and made changes.

It would be easy to be cynical about these stories. Alexander came from the most privileged level of society and when his tour was over he would go home. But his feelings were genuine and lasting: he insisted on seeing the true state of Russia, and it is no wonder that so many hopes came to rest on his shoulders. The challenge would come when the desire to do good had to be translated into hard political action. Then the certainties of Zhukovsky's teaching, that public opinion would favour the just ruler, and that the ruler who loved his people would always be loved by them, would lose the power they had once possessed.

For the moment, though, everything Alexander did was touched with gold. Russia loved him, and his next undertaking would be a tour of Europe, which his parents were keen to push forward as quickly as possible because the rumours of love had become a reality. At the start of 1838 Alexander developed an overwhelming crush on a Polish lady-in-waiting, Olga Kalinovskaya, and though he knew there could be no marriage he tormented himself with thoughts of what might have been. He would always fall in love too easily and too well: his father understood and was eager to push him out into the world, to keep him busy and to find him a suitable wife. The Tsar planned an exhausting schedule for his son which Alexander followed willingly, but it was not long before the pace began to tell. At Copenhagen in the early summer of 1838 he caught a cold that developed rapidly into bronchitis; for days he was confined to bed. At last his party reached Ems, but they were delayed there for three months by the severe racking cough and fever that the Tsesarevich was not able to throw off. For the rest of his life he would suffer from asthma.

With some reluctance, Nicholas I allowed his son to convalesce in Italy, but by the end of January 1839 the party was on the move again, touring the German Courts. It was no secret that Alexander was looking for a wife. His parents hoped for Princess Alexandrine of Baden but the eighteen-year-old princess made no impression on Alexander. From her father's Court at Karlsruhe he went on to Heidelberg but exhaustion was setting in, and on 12 March General Kavelin suggested an unplanned stop in Darmstadt. He intended a quiet night, but the Grand Duke of Hesse had other ideas, inviting the Tsesarevich and his suite to the theatre and then on to dinner. Most felt too tired to go but Alexander could hardly refuse. 'Not till next morning', Zhukovsky told his parents, 'did I learn of what happened that evening. To call him happy would be hardly enough. . . . The aim of all our travels is at last achieved.'[9]

Alexander had been stopped in his tracks, literally, by the Grand Duke's daughter. At fourteen Marie of Hesse-Darmstadt was still a child, but she was tall for her age and intelligent. She was lonely too, missing the mother who had brought her up away from Court, only to die of tuberculosis when Marie was eleven. For a short while during her early childhood her parents had been estranged, and it was whispered by gossips across the Courts of Europe that the Grand Duke was not her real father. Not everyone in Darmstadt was kind to Marie, and Alexander was too soft-hearted to resist this combination of youth, beauty and unhappiness. His party stayed in Darmstadt for a few days, and when the time came to leave he wore a locket containing a strand of Marie's hair.

On the evening of 19 March Alexander arrived in The Hague. He was to spend a month with his aunt Anna, Princess of Orange, and her family, to celebrate Easter and his twenty-first birthday. 'Sasha was charming in his Cossack uniform which suits him marvellously,' Anna wrote to her brother that night, 'the little moustache has prospered, and as for his appearance I can tell you that I find him a very handsome boy.' Days in The Hague were spent quietly, visiting and writing letters, and in the evenings Alexander would sit over tea with his aunt. He must have told her about Marie; she hints at this in another letter to the Tsar: 'I am certain that the differences of places and objects have not distracted him from the principal goal which was to occupy him.' She was delighted with her nephew. 'He has a great deal of tact, grace and dignity,' she wrote, 'with a naturalness which charms.'[10]

On 20 April Alexander left The Hague for England, and another successful visit. Queen Victoria was a year younger than he was and still unmarried, and she found his naturalness quite as charming as his aunt had done. He stayed a month, and was welcomed everywhere with enthusiasm. On 29 May he returned to The Hague, then, with his parents' permission, made his way to Darmstadt where the preliminary negotiations for marriage had already begun.

There is a well-established story that Nicholas I opposed the engagement and held out against it for a full year, forcing his son to fight for what he wanted. Almedingen describes how the furious Tsar demanded Alexander's return to Russia after the first Darmstadt visit, and writes that Alexander went back to face his father's anger before continuing his tour. Familiar though this scenario is, it is not supported by the evidence. Alexander's party arrived in Darmstadt on 12 March and stayed for a few days, reaching The Hague on the 19th. With no transport faster than the horse, they could not possibly have managed to fit a visit to St Petersburg in as well, even if the Tsar had ordered it, and besides, there is no sign that Nicholas did object: he wanted to see his son safely married. In April the Austrian Ambassador to St Petersburg reported the Tsar's acceptance of the Hesse alliance to his home government. In May Nicholas wrote to his brother-in-law in Holland, mentioning the Oranges' eldest son and adding, 'So mine too has found his lady-love; let us see what will happen; thus far the pretty English girls have not yet prejudiced Darmstadt.'[11] For one reason, and one reason alone, Alexander would have to wait to obtain his desire; Marie was not yet fifteen.

After a brief visit to the Hesse family Alexander returned to Russia, where his father began to introduce him to the business of state, and as the year turned he prepared to go back to Darmstadt. There could be no definite decision until he had seen the Princess again, his father said; he and the Tsaritsa would not try to influence their son, 'but it would delight us a great deal if the decision was affirmative'.[12] The engagement was announced in April. Nicholas I and Alexandra were in Europe themselves that spring, and they congratulated Alexander and Marie at Frankfurt in June. In August, a few weeks after Marie turned sixteen, the whole party set out for Russia. On 28 April 1841, the eve of Alexander's twenty-third birthday, he and Marie were married in the chapel of the Winter Palace.

Marriage brought Alexander more personal happiness than he had known since the distant days before his father's accession. He and Marie, now Maria Alexandrovna, were young, interested in literature, music and poetry, and their Court became the focal point for a circle of like-minded friends. Most of their evenings were spent dancing, listening to music, reading aloud and exchanging ideas. Their first child, Alexandra, was born at Tsarskoe Selo in the summer of 1842, and a son, Nikolai, followed a year later; with his birth the succession was assured and his grandparents were delighted. Then came Alexander, Vladimir, Alexei, Maria. . . . Alexander was a devoted father. His study in Tsarskoe Selo was hung with portraits of his wife and children, and his desk was heavy with miniatures of them. The children played beside him while he worked. Little Alexandra died of tubercular meningitis eight weeks before her seventh birthday and he treasured her blue silk dress for the rest of his life. She was a favourite with her father. Many years later, when his younger daughter Maria was about to marry, Alexander told Lady Augusta Stanley about the child he had lost, who 'was so devoted to Him She used to entreat to be allowed to sit in his room even when He was busy, and would remain there hours, quite silent, if only she might see her Papa.'[13]

But Alexander and Maria Alexandrovna shared more than just their children. Alexander was closely involved in the work of his father's government and sought his wife's opinion on everything. He took state papers home and they read and discussed them together. He respected her judgement, as he respected his aunt Elena, Maria's closest friend within the imperial family. Together the young couple read the newly published works of Turgenev and Gogol, which flew in the face of official censorship. Together they studied the latest reports on the state of the country, which were too controversial to show to the Tsar. Zhukovsky was still in the wings, urging Alexander on: 'Your heart does sincerely desire the highest good, and one day you will have great power under your hand . . . but you

<u>must</u> know what to do . . . the acceptance of any measure – once you know it to be good – must at once be followed by action.'[14]

In 1842 Alexander chaired a committee that his father had called to change the conditions of serfdom. Its aims were limited, but that did not prevent a storm of protest; there were powerful vested interests in Russia intent on preserving the system. The committee's actions were strangled by bureaucracy. Unrest increased. In some areas hopes had been raised by the talk of reform, and peasants became violent when those hopes were dashed, or fled from the land. Elsewhere there was violence because peasants were afraid of change. It was chaotic and disheartening, and the Emperor's only answer was to tighten the screw of repression. This set the pattern for the 1840s. With rigid censorship and draconian punishments, Nicholas I tried to shield Russia from the demands for change which were spreading across Europe, but nothing could silence the anger in the country. Alexander, at the heart of his father's government, attracted none of the blame for these policies. The touch of gold clung to him still.

Nicholas's reign was moving towards its painful end. After 1852, the Tsesarevich watched his father rush headlong into conflict with the European powers. Nobody wanted the Crimean War. Never a soldier at heart, Alexander hated the very idea of war and realized what the result of this particular war must be, but he could not oppose his father. He was virtually regent, with all power except the crucial power to decide overall policy, and Maria shared his anxiety as he poured over the Gospels and Zhukovsky's letters looking for encouragement, and watched events unfold. No amount of courage on the Russian side could make up for bad organization and bad leadership. By the start of 1855 Alexander could bear it no longer and dismissed the Commander-in-Chief, replacing him with a man of his own choosing. Two days later the news broke that Tsar Nicholas I was dead, and Alexander had become Tsar of Russia. He was thirty-six years old, and his country was on the point of collapse.

At this low ebb, hope focused on him as never before. Within the first few months of the reign he had relaxed censorship and lifted the ban on overseas travel, and he went on to abolish capital punishment and flogging. The Decembrists were freed at last. Even the régime's fiercest enemies looked to Alexander for a miracle. From England the exiled socialist Alexander Herzen, publisher of the journal *Kolokol* (*The Bell*), made an extraordinary promise. He would abandon opposition, 'if only I have alive within me the hope that You will do something for Russia. Sire, grant liberty to the Russian word. . . . Give us freedom of speech. . . . Give the land to the peasants.'[15] It was an extraordinary moment. Anything and everything seemed possible, and the doves were flying all over Russia.

5

Our Joy Since Birth

TSESAREVICH NIKOLAI ALEXANDROVICH

The emancipation of the serfs was Alexander II's great achievement, and he enacted an impressive number of other reforms in education, in the law, in government and the armed forces; he did his best to satisfy the great outpouring of hope that greeted his accession. But his reign saw a sinister new development. Terrorist groups, intent on pushing forward their own programme for the country, made the Tsar their target, and attempts on his life multiplied. The dreams began to die, and the hopes to fail. Alexander wavered between reform and repression. Even his marriage, which had begun so well and contributed so much to the positive achievements of his reign, also began to fail, its happiness to slip away. It happened gradually, but one of the steps along the road, though no one would have seen it at the time, was the death of the imperial couple's eldest son, the Tsesarevich Nikolai.

'I f I find a single sight as beautiful as this in any other country, I will know that my travels have been worthwhile.'[1] Nikolai Alexandrovich, the eldest son of Alexander II and heir to the throne of Russia, was standing on the balcony of the Cottage at Peterhof in the early summer of 1864, looking out on the woods, the sea, and the distant gleam of sunlight on the rooftops of Kronstadt. The next day he would leave on a prolonged visit overseas to complete his education and find a bride. He was twenty.

By all accounts the Tsesarevich was an exceptional young man; 'our joy since birth', the poet Tiutchev called him.[2] Tall and slim, he had inherited the bearing and temperament of his father with the looks and the intelligence of his mother, the Tsaritsa Maria Alexandrovna. He was born in St Petersburg on 8/20 September 1843, and the event was welcomed and celebrated as much as the birth of any first son in direct line to a throne: 'it is a wonderful happiness for us and for the Empire,' his grandfather wrote, 'may God preserve this dear child for us.'[3] Nikolai became heir to the throne at the age of eleven, as the Crimean War drew to a close, and he and his younger brother Alexander took their own small revenge on the enemy by creating 'Mopsopolis', a fantasy world set out in skilful pen-and-ink drawings, representing the English as pug dogs.

Nikolai was five years old when his elder sister Alexandra died, and his closest companions in childhood were his brothers and their Leuchtenberg cousins. They were happy, normal children. Anna Tiutcheva, a lady-in-waiting to the Tsaritsa, described a squabble between Nikolai and his brothers a few weeks after their father's accession. The boys were discussing their father, and

little Grand Prince Nikolai said, with an air of importance, 'Papa is so busy nowadays that he is making himself ill with exhaustion. When Grandfather was alive, Papa helped him, but nobody helps Papa; uncle Konstantin is too busy with his department, and uncles Nix and Misha are too young, and I'm still too small to help him.' At that, his brother Alexander leapt in with a will, 'That's not really the point, that you're too small, you're just too stupid.' 'It's not true, I'm not stupid,' the Heir objected crossly, 'I'm just too small.' 'No, no, you're just too stupid.' The Heir to the throne had reached the end of his patience with these disrespectful allegations; he grabbed a cushion and threw it at his brother's back. Grand Prince Alexei decided this was an appropriate moment to take sides, and in his turn he began to shout at the top of his voice, 'You're stupid and just stupid.' A fight started, and it fell to the nurses to go in and restore peace. The Heir moved away, deeply offended by his brothers' lack of confidence in his ability to help with the administration. . . .'[4]

Nikolai was educated for the throne, whatever his brothers may have thought, and he followed a rigorous, intense programme of studies designed for himself alone. Both parents adored him, but while his father could be rather severe, his mother devoted herself singlemindedly to him, almost forgetting her other children. He developed rapidly, showing a quick mind and an interest in serious questions which impressed and, at times, even worried those responsible for his education. His governor, Count Stroganov, remarked that the Tsesarevich's maturity of thought and expression seemed almost unhealthy in one so young. One of his tutors took a more hopeful view: 'if I succeeded in forming a student equal to Nikolai Alexandrovich once in ten years,' wrote Professor Soloviev, 'I would think I had fulfilled my calling as a teacher.'[5]

Such perfection . . . but there is a rather different picture of the Tsesarevich in the memoirs of one of his contemporaries. Once a week Nikolai attended algebra classes at the Corps des Pages on the insistence of his mother, who thought that it would do him good to study with other boys. Among those boys was Prince Peter Kropotkin, and he recalled that the Tsesarevich spent most of his time in class drawing – extremely well – and making amusing remarks to his friends. Nikolai was good-natured and gentle, he said, but took a flippant attitude to everything. All efforts to educate him were wasted and he failed his final examination in August 1861. It could be a different boy, but Kropotkin's account has to be read with caution. When his memoirs were written he was living in exile, having earned imprisonment in Russia and in France by his revolutionary activities. He had no reason to love the imperial family but his description does capture something of the humanity of the Tsesarevich. The drawings and humour ring true of the creator of 'Mopsopolis', and Nikolai may have found in the classroom a welcome break from the palace, where he was the only pupil of a high-powered and demanding team of tutors. He was, after all, just a boy, albeit a very gifted one.

Like his father before him, Nikolai was sent from the schoolroom on a tour of the Russian empire which lasted for three years. His mind was already turning to the future. In 1860 he had acquired or been given a photograph of Princess Dagmar of Denmark. She was only twelve then, he was seventeen, but the idea of marriage may have been put to him: certainly he began to see Dagmar in that light. His collection of photos grew, and in August 1863, while visiting Russia's southern cities, he assured his mother that no other girl could attract him now. His letter gives an appealing glimpse into the mind of a young man fully aware that he had been impulsive in the past, and desperate to be taken seriously. He did not know if he would ever meet Dagmar, he said; 'I leave it all to God, for it is a holy matter, a sacrament. . . . I treasure these feelings so much that it would be painful if you were to tell me they are an illusion that could change a thousand times, and so on. For how could they have lasted for three years? And why are they increasing and not decreasing?'[6] In June 1864 he left Russia, accompanied by Count Stroganov and a large suite.

Denmark was at war with Prussia that summer and the borders were closed, so the party's immediate destination was Bad Kissingen, where the Tsaritsa was taking the waters among a glittering company. The Emperor and Empress of Austria were there and the Grand Duke of Mecklenburg-Schwerin, and Nikolai stayed long enough to make a friend of the eighteen-year-old King Ludwig II of Bavaria. Then he went to Weimar on the invitation of his father's cousin, Duke Carl Alexander. Nikolai was amazed to find the atmosphere in the small German capital entirely Russian; in 1804 his great-aunt Maria Pavlovna had gone to Saxe-Weimar as a bride, and her influence was everywhere. He thoroughly enjoyed the visit. Soon there were rumours of an engagement with the Duke's fifteen-year-old daughter Marie, who was even taken to meet the Tsaritsa at Schwalbach, but Nikolai had other ideas. He left Weimar for Holland where he whiled away the weeks at Scheveningen, bathing in the sea. Another of his father's cousins, Queen Sophie of the Netherlands, and the Queen Dowager Anna Pavlovna, his great-aunt, were pleased to see him, but as soon as he could Nikolai hurried to Denmark for the long-anticipated meeting. In Copenhagen he was greeted by the Crown Prince and the King's brother, and the next morning royal carriages arrived to take them on the three-hour journey to Fredensborg: the King and all his family were waiting for them on the front steps.

Dagmar did not disappoint him. Queen Louise of Denmark's daughters were noted for their simplicity and the Princess greeted her prospective fiancé wearing a light summer dress under a black pinafore, with her hair drawn into a neat bun at the nape of the neck. According to Feodor Oom, the secretary of the Tsesarevich's Chancellery, who had been shown her photograph by Nikolai more times than he could remember, 'she shone with the freshness of her sixteen years'.[7] But the atmosphere at first was tense and uncomfortable. Falling in love with a photograph was a great deal easier than meeting a living girl – in full view of her relatives. For days no one knew what to say, and the King's embarrassment was worse than any. Nikolai liked the King Christian, responding to his openness and honesty, but was less sure about his prospective mother-in-law: in a long letter to his mother on 24 August/5 September he praised the King but refused to comment on the Queen, saying that he was too happy to be critical.[8] There was good reason for this happiness, for Nikolai was at last finding his courage and making real progress. He delighted in the palace's rural setting and found relief in lively games with Dagmar's little brother and sister. With the support of his aide-de-camp, Colonel Richter, he made the first tentative enquiry, through Crown Prince Frederik: would a hypothetical proposal be well received in the country generally, and might Dagmar return his feelings? The answer, hypothetically of course, was yes.

Time passed quickly, and the renowned jollity of the Danish family soon swept away any remaining shyness. There were outings to places of interest, informal teas and dinners where the conversation flowed freely, races, games, riotous laughter – a great release for the Danes, who had so recently endured the misery of war. Nikolai was enchanted with Dagmar, but assured his mother that he had been careful not to mention the subject of marriage, particularly to her, and had simply asked her parents if he might return.[9] Knowing that her son treasured such high expectations of the meeting, the Tsaritsa had advised him not to let his feelings run away with him. He was obliged first to see his parents, and to ask their permission to make a formal proposal.

Nikolai left Denmark and travelled south to join his parents at Heiligenberg, his uncle's house to the south of Darmstadt. He spent the first evening alone with his mother while the rest of the family went to the theatre. The Tsar and Tsaritsa were glad to approve his plans and he was keen to return to Denmark to propose, but first he was expected in Prussia for a full day of military manoeuvres with his father. On the way they stopped at Stuttgart to visit another aunt, Queen Olga of Württemberg, and Nikolai celebrated his twenty-first birthday in Germany. He cannot have been eager to salute the army that had just forced the Danes into a humiliating surrender, and he might have wondered if his presence there would cause offence in Denmark. Worse still, the night before the manoeuvres he suffered violent pains in his back, but still forced himself to take part. Eleven hours on horseback left him exhausted and this was the first sign that something was wrong; unfortunately it was a sign no one heeded.

As soon as he could, Nikolai hurried to Denmark and joined the royal family at Bernstorff. He spoke at once to the King, who explained the purpose of the visit quietly to his daughter, then brought the couple together. Walking in the park, a little way behind the King and Queen and one of their sons, both Nikolai and Dagmar felt shy and apprehensive. 'I wanted the earth to swallow me up,' he told his mother. But he forced the words to come, and they found a ready welcome: Dagmar accepted his proposal and they kissed and held hands. 'I could hardly speak,' he wrote, 'and although it was a cold autumn day, I was as hot as if I were in an oven.'[10] The engagement was announced officially that evening, 28 September, and in the days that followed gifts were exchanged and visits made. Also, the young couple were able to speak privately for the first time. Nikolai showed Dagmar the photographs of her that he had been collecting for five years. She surprised him with the revelation that she had thought of him long before their meeting, and had promised herself that she would marry no one else. It is always assumed that marriages at this level were political arrangements, but if this was really true of Nikolai and Dagmar, it was not the way they themselves perceived it. Nikolai assured his mother that no one had discussed the marriage with Dagmar in the past. It was important to him, this discovery that for her too the attraction had grown silently and in private. But he went further.

He had observed, he said, that many people in Denmark did see a political dimension to the alliance and he was careful not to encourage them.[11] For him at least, the engagement was a purely personal matter.

On 12 October Nikolai left to rejoin his family in Darmstadt. He was supremely happy, enthusing to his mother about his fiancée's artlessness, her loveliness and the kindness in her eyes, and earnestly praying for their future together. It delighted him that Dagmar would take his mother's name, Maria, on her conversion.[12] One object of his travels was now achieved, but a long programme of cultural visits still lay ahead before he could return to Russia with his bride.

Travelling in short stages through Germany and Austria, the Tsesarevich and his suite arrived in Venice on 30 October. They spent two weeks visiting museums, churches and theatres before moving on to Milan, where Crown Prince Umberto, the heir to the Italian throne, was waiting to meet them. Nikolai wanted to learn about the political system in Italy, but his questions to Umberto met with a disappointing response. Umberto said that Nikolai, as heir to an absolute monarch, might be obliged to know all about the law and the constitution; but for himself, he preferred to leave all that to the politicians. The Italians were impressed with the Tsesarevich's grasp of affairs, however; compared to their own princes he was extremely well informed, and his questions were penetrating and deep. In fact, he was receiving daily bulletins of news and information from the Chancellery in St Petersburg, which he read with close interest; this tour was meant to impress Europe with the man who would one day rule Russia. He met King Vittorio Emanuele II at a gala dinner in Turin, given in his honour, and on 11 November he and his party left for Genoa. Their first sight of the city in autumn sunlight, with the blue expanse of the Mediterranean beyond, was a nostalgic reminder of the Black Sea coast, and home. A Russian naval squadron was anchored off Genoa and the Admiral greeted Nikolai at the station. The Tsesarevich was so pleased to see men in Russian uniforms again that he invited all the squadron's officers to dine at his hotel.

Nikolai was longing for home, and decided to break from his official programme to visit his mother. The Tsaritsa's tuberculosis was bad that autumn and he had last seen her being carried on a stretcher to the station at Darmstadt, en route for Nice. Now she was staying at the Villa Bermond, a villa in name, but really a vast estate set on the side of a hill, famous for its orchards of fruit trees and fields of Parma violets. There were five houses in the park and the Tsaritsa and her suite filled three of them. Nikolai sailed from Genoa on the Russian corvette *Vitiaz*, travelling incognito as the 'Comte du Nord' – the travelling name his great-grandfather Paul had used over half a century before. Arriving in Nice, he settled at the Villa Diesbach and spent a few days with his mother before the *Vitiaz* returned him to Italy, disembarking this time at Livorno. Most of the suite were waiting in Florence, where a full programme of activities had been planned, but as the train drew into the station Nikolai was seized by agonizing back pain and his companions almost had to carry him to his reserved apartments in the Italia Hotel.

The next day he forced himself to his feet, determined to see the treasures of the Pitti Palace, but the effort was too much, and on returning he had to take to his bed. He remained there for the next six weeks. There was a swelling on his back; an abscess, the doctors said, and while he underwent a series of painful treatments his suite did all they could to distract him. His fifteen-year-old cousin Sergei of Leuchtenberg, who was living in Florence, came in every day to keep him company and to describe the wonders that he would never be able to see. On New Year's Day the Tsesarevich and his party left for Livorno, where the *Vitiaz* was waiting to take them by sea to join the Tsaritsa in Nice. Rooms had been prepared on the first floor of the Villa Diesbach; Nikolai's uncle, Grand Duke Ludwig III of Hesse, was occupying the ground floor, so the suite took up residence in a neighbouring hotel.

The pain had eased, but Nikolai dreaded a return to the suffering of the past months. He was very weak and unable to straighten his back, and he had to be carried up and down stairs. French doctors prescribed massage and steam treatment and he took daily rides, stopping outside the Villa Bermond so that his mother could come out to meet his carriage. People who saw them remarked on the affectionate relationship between mother and son; at every meeting Nikolai would take his mother's hand and kiss each finger in turn, and both of them struggled to hide the anxieties they must have been feeling. Throughout his short life Nikolai had been taught to master his emotions; walking one day in the Valley of Flowers, with a stick and a friend's arm for support, he said that he hardly dared to speak about Dagmar because he loved her so much, and if he thought of her, he would lose control.

Since the engagement the young couple had exchanged regular letters. While Nikolai struggled against his illness, Dagmar was learning the language and customs that must soon be her own. Her confession that winter that the Orthodox Church now seemed closer to the truth to her than the church of her childhood brought him particular delight: his letters bear witness to a profound faith, which he longed to share. The couple exchanged visions of the children they would have and of their life together in the Anichkov Palace, the traditional residence of the heir to the throne where apartments were already being prepared. In his weakened state, Nikolai clung to these dreams.[13]

As the weeks passed, he began to experience frequent headaches and sickness. The doctors said that he had nothing more serious than rheumatism, with perhaps a touch of malaria, and the Tsaritsa wanted to be reassured, but there were angry scenes between the doctors and Count Stroganov and the tension grew. Two French specialists, Nélaton and Rayer, had been called in at the end of January and they confirmed the diagnosis of rheumatism, much to the relief of those already treating Nikolai. On the other hand Professor Burci, who had treated him in Florence, was sending anxious messages through the Russian Consul warning that the spinal abscess that he had detected could only be aggravated by the present treatment, and was probably affecting the bone marrow already. His warnings fell on deaf ears. So confident was official opinion that at the end of February an emissary was sent to Copenhagen to make arrangements for Dagmar to meet the Tsaritsa, and even for the wedding.

In March Nikolai became weaker, and showed acute sensitivity to sound. He complained that the lapping of the waves on the beach made it impossible to sleep, so he was moved to the Villa Bermond. On 11 March the *Journal de Nice* published an optimistic bulletin about his progress. Two days later he attended a fête for the Chasseurs of the Imperial Guard, to review the troops and distribute prizes, but he was unable to leave his carriage and had to struggle to hide the pain. Another month passed, and far away in Denmark Dagmar began to worry about the tailing-off of his letters. On 7 April, after more than a fortnight's silence, she sent a desperate appeal to her 'dear Nixa', reminding him that with the approach of spring their next meeting was drawing near; her mind was filled with thoughts of him and she longed for news. She teased him with the joking, but perhaps real, anxiety that he had met someone else, and the letter took two days to write.[14] But the news, when it came, could not have been worse. On Easter Saturday Nikolai's condition suddenly deteriorated; he became feverish and could not see clearly. A telegram was sent to the Tsar who left St Petersburg that night with his own doctor.

During the same night Nikolai had a slight seizure that left his right side paralysed for some hours, and chaos reigned in the Villa Bermond. Silent crowds gathered outside. The Tsaritsa would not leave her son's bedside, and her ladies became so overwrought that Count Stroganov lost his temper, and told them that anyone who could not control herself had better leave. On Easter Monday, 18 April, the Tsesarevich was dressed and placed in an armchair to receive communion. News of his illness had drawn specialists from all over Europe, and one Professor Rehrberg from Vienna produced the first accurate diagnosis: cerebro-spinal meningitis. It was too late. Within days Nikolai was slipping into periods of delirium, when he could recognize no one. Until this moment the only adult relatives with the Tsaritsa were her brother Alexander and his wife Julie, Princess of Battenberg, but now, from all over Europe, the family began to gather. On Thursday Grand Prince Alexander arrived. Nikolai was pleased to see the brother whose gifts were apparent to no one but himself; compared to the Tsesarevich,

Alexander had always looked awkward and rather stupid, and people were inclined to dismiss him. Dagmar reached Nice on Friday with her mother, and at 2.30 p.m. the Tsar himself came to the Villa Bermond. The Tsaritsa woke her son to tell him that his father had come; he kissed her hand, taking each finger in turn, and asked what she would do without him. It was the first time he had mentioned death, and his father knelt by the bed in tears.

Nikolai was sleeping more now, though the slightest sound would wake him. On Saturday he saw Dagmar come into the room and whispered to his mother, 'isn't she beautiful?'[15] Dagmar spent a long time beside him that day, arranging his pillows and stroking his hand, talking softly all the while; for some time Alexander also stayed by the bed, holding his other hand. Later the legend grew that Nikolai had joined their hands and told them to marry after his death, but there is no suggestion of this in the early eyewitness accounts. The end came on the evening of Sunday 24 April. Outside, in the sunshine of early spring, French infantry and cavalry and Russian sailors mounted silent guard on the Villa Bermond, while the family, their suites and the doctors filled the Tsesarevich's room, and the clergy chanted prayers for the dying. Nikolai was beyond speech now, but a single tear was seen on his cheek.

Two days later the body was moved in a torchlight procession to the Orthodox Church in the Rue de Longchamps. Nikolai was to be taken home on board the *Alexander Nevsky*, with the ships *Oleg*, *Vitiaz*, and *Almaz* as his escort, and solemn ceremonies marked each stage of the procession until the coffin was safely on board. Only Count Stroganov remembered a morning some three months earlier when Nikolai, watching the squadron sail past his window, had fallen into a sort of trance. Coming to himself, he had said, 'I thought I was on board the *Alexander Nevsky*, and she was taking me on a long voyage. . . .'[16]

The voyage would be long, and hard. The *Alexander Nevsky* was almost lost in violent westerly gales off the coast of Portugal. The squadron put in to rest at Lisbon, then sailed on to Plymouth where the English ships *Liverpool* and *Royal Adelaide* fired a twenty-one gun salute, and Russian priests from London came on board to conduct a service. There was thick fog off the Danish coast and the ship almost ran aground on rocks in the Skaggerrak before reaching calm water, and a sad meeting with the Danish royal family. On 21 May/2 June the *Alexander Nevsky* finally arrived at Kronstadt, which Nikolai had admired from his balcony a year before. Now, with great solemnity, his coffin was carried onto the deck of the yacht *Alexandria* for its last journey up the Neva to the Cathedral of St Peter and St Paul. On Tuesday 25 May/6 June the Tsesarevich Nikolai, who was born to rule Russia as Nicholas II, was laid to rest. 'This was not just a man who has left us,' wrote his tutor, the historian Stassioulevitch, 'this was youth, beauty, a first love, scarcely awakened. . . . This was a young man who personified all the hopes which a million brave men place in the future. This was nobility, goodness, friendliness, the spirit of justice and fair-play. This was the symbol of all that is dear and sacred to us on this earth.'[17]

The tragedy changed the future for the whole dynasty, but its immediate effects bore particularly on two of the young people present at the Villa Bermond, Dagmar and Grand Prince Alexander. Dagmar did not attend Nikolai's funeral. She and her brother had a private meeting with the Tsar and Tsaritsa at Heiligenberg, where the Russians rested on their way home, but the Crown Prince was the only member of the Danish royal family to go on to St Petersburg. Still only seventeen, Dagmar was emotionally and physically drained by the experiences of the past few months, and her parents were keen to protect her from further suffering.

But there was also an unspoken agenda, which could be wrecked if it were raised at the wrong moment; both they and the Tsar and Tsaritsa wanted to see an engagement between Dagmar and Alexander, who must now step into Nikolai's shoes. The Tsaritsa's suggestion that this should happen immediately was too insistent, too likely to fail. Nikolai had been dead barely a month when Queen Louise wisely urged caution. She advised that Alexander be left alone to consider his position and reach his conclusions without undue pressure. On her own side, she saw that Dagmar would only be repelled and hurt by talk of another marriage. Her mind was still on Nikolai, and she needed time.[18] A few weeks later the Queen refused an invitation to take Dagmar to St Petersburg. A pilgrimage to the grave would be far too painful, she said, and the speculation such a visit would arouse could only be damaging. She could see how the situation would be read, and wanted to protect her daughter from envy and malicious gossip.[19]

But the Tsaritsa had good reason for her almost indecent haste, for, in the wake of Nikolai's death, she and her husband had a very reluctant and unhappy Tsesarevich on their hands. Alexander was shattered by the loss of Nikolai. Less than two years apart in age, the brothers were unusually close. Even in Denmark, celebrating his engagement, Nikolai's thoughts had turned to Alexander. 'I miss Sacha very much,' he told their mother, 'I would love to have him here.'[20] For Alexander this affection was tinged with respect, and something close to dependence. A few months after Nikolai's death, he confided to his diary the lasting grief and loneliness he felt 'without my friend whom I loved more than anyone else in this world'. He remembered how he had shared everything with his elder brother and hidden nothing, and he knew the feeling was mutual: though he still had Vladimir, Alexei, Sergei and Pavel, he was certain that not one of them could play the role Nikolai had played in his life.[21]

Tall, heavily built and clumsy, Alexander had always lacked his brother's winning manners and ease in company. He was less gifted intellectually, less attractive: people found him boorish, and he did nothing to dissuade them – though his diary reveals an unexpected depth of sensitivity and a ready gift for self-expression. But he was haunted by a sense of his own inadequacy, and soon after his elevation to Tsesarevich a cousin found him crying bitterly at the change in his fortunes. Alexander wanted only to be the younger brother: to make matters worse, he was also in love.

It was normal for a Grand Prince – for any prince – to develop an attachment to one of the many attractive, well-born ladies surrounding him at Court. It had happened to the Tsar as a young man, so he was aware of the possibility and sympathetic, to a point.

Princess Marie Elimovna Mescherskaya, one of the Tsaritsa's younger maids-of-honour, was particularly beautiful: 'There was something Oriental about her whole person, and especially about her great dark velvety eyes, which fascinated everyone', a friend remembered.[22] She brought out the gentle side of Alexander and he found her easy to talk to: their relationship appears to have been well established at the time of Nikolai's death. Then, it was made clear that one of his new duties was a suitable marriage – to Dagmar, whom he had met for the first time over his brother's deathbed. By early July, as his parents put pressure on the Danes to send Dagmar to Russia, Alexander resolved to break all contact with Marie. But it was very hard. The maid-of-honour's absence hurt, because he was used to seeing her every day. He enjoyed their conversations and looked forward to them: given his awkwardness in company it was probably unusual for him to find talking easy, just for its own sake.[23] Nonetheless, he did his best to think of marriage, Dagmar and duty.

After a few months, though, his resolve wavered. Marie was hard to avoid, and through the spring and autumn of 1865 their love deepened. As the year of mourning drew to its end the following spring, Alexander knew that decisions would have to be made. His father had told him that once mourning ended he must go to Denmark, and the arrangements were in place. In early April Alexander confided to his diary, once again, that his meetings with Marie must stop. 'I will say goodbye to M.E., whom I loved as I have loved no one before, and I am grateful for all that she has done for me: good and bad.' He was unsure of her feelings, certain of his own, and he looked back on the conversations thay had shared, known only to themselves, and the difficulties they had endured, with nostalgia and longing.[24] Once again, it took only a few weeks for him to realize that this was a tie he could not break, and by the end of May, with the visit to Denmark looming, he reached a very different decision. He wanted to break free from the walls that were closing around him. He could raise no love for Dagmar, and was beginning to feel that his only escape would be a complete renunciation of his right to the throne. 'I feel incapable of ruling. I have too little respect for people and get fed up with everything that concerns my position.' He wanted the undemanding life of a younger brother again, and he wanted to marry Marie.[25]

Somehow word of this reached the newspapers, and reports that Alexander loved Princess Mescherskaya were published in Denmark where they caused understandable concern. The Tsar sent for his son and asked him if the reports were true and Alexander, faced with a direct question, admitted that he did not want to marry Dagmar. He was given a day to think. On 19/31 May, with his departure for Denmark imminent, he took a walk with both parents, spent time alone with his mother, then went to face his father. He announced that he would not go, and, pressed on his reasons, and on his feelings for Marie, he abandoned all caution and said that he had decided to renounce his claim to the throne.

This caught the Tsar at a vulnerable moment. A few weeks earlier Alexander II had narrowly escaped an attempt on his life, which left him shaken. His eldest son was dead, his wife absorbed in her grief, and for almost a year he himself had been obsessed with the young Princess Dolgorukaya, who was still resisting his advances. Faced with a situation which, in all conscience, he should have understood, he lost his temper completely and told his son that he too held a position he had never wanted. Duty bound him as it would bind Alexander. He was no longer prepared to be patient; his sympathy for his son's plight was at an end and he ordered Alexander to go to Denmark, making it clear that Princess Mescherskaya would not be at Court when he returned.[26] Guilt probably intensified the Tsar's anger. He would hear no appeal, and Alexander was dismissed in abject misery.

The next day, Alexander boarded the imperial yacht for Denmark with his brother Vladimir. It would be hard to imagine less favourable circumstances than these, but a few days after his arrival he wrote home with welcome news: he believed that he could come to love Dagmar in time after all. Characteristically, he was unsure of her feelings and this worried him, but he was prepared now to move forward with hope. The key to his change of heart seems to have been the love and grief for Nikolai that he and Dagmar shared, and the sense that she was already part of his family. It took him a few more days to build up the courage to mention marriage, then the understanding was instant: he had barely finished speaking before Dagmar flung her arms around his neck and they both broke down in tears. At that moment their thoughts and words were all of Nikolai. Alexander assured her that his brother would be happy for them, and asked if she could accept him in Nikolai's place. She told him she would love them both, and they embraced and talked of Nikolai, exchanging the memories that were still so fresh in their minds.[27]

The engagement was announced, and Alexander returned to Russia. At first the wedding was planned for the following spring but soon the Tsar and Tsaritsa changed their minds, insisting that Dagmar must arrive in Russia in the autumn for a November wedding, and over-ruling all objections. Perhaps they felt that their son's resolve might weaken without Dagmar, or that being in Russia alone might revive memories of his former love. Perhaps they were troubled by his continuing inability to adapt to his public role. Whatever the reason, Dagmar left Denmark on 22 September, making a ceremonial entry to St Petersburg with her brother on 17/29 September. She had a month to prepare for acceptance into the Orthodox Church under the guidance of the Archpriest of the Great Chapel of the Winter Palace, and it cannot have been easy, surrounded as she was by reminders of what might have been. Nikolai's rooms in the palace and at Tsarskoe Selo were preserved, his face looked out from a thousand picture frames, and he was buried on the opposite bank of the Neva, within sight of the palace. Years later she would still cry when she talked about him. During those first weeks she threw all her energy into parties and balls, until her father sent a gentle warning that so much activity could be harmful to her health and her looks.

On 12/24 October the Princess was anointed, setting aside her childhood names and becoming 'Maria Feodorovna' – though in the family they would continue to call her 'Minny'. The wedding took place fourteen days later. Shortly after midday guns were fired, and within the palace the processions began. The Tsar and Tsaritsa led, walking slowly through the Chapel to the pool of light under the cupola where the Archbishop Metropolitan of Novgorod and St Petersburg was waiting to receive them, holding a cross which each kissed in turn. Alexander followed his parents, next came the bride, then the Prince of Wales and the Crown Princes of Prussia and Denmark. Behind them came Alexander's younger brothers and sister and other members of the imperial family, and onlookers noted that the Metropolitan was especially gentle with the children, bowing low to help them reach the cross. The splendour must have been almost overwhelming, and at the day's end the Minister of the Interior, Peter Valuyev, noted in his diary that he had seen the new Grand Princess look tired that day for the first time. He believed she had momentarily lost the will-power that had already carried her through so much.[28]

She would regain the energy, and the power to charm. From the first, she and Alexander were openly affectionate – and at times openly irritable with one another – though King Christian was pleased to see that their disagreements only seemed to lead to greater displays of affection.[29] It was as well that their private understanding was so good, because Alexander continued to find his public role difficult to accept. He resented the need to be seen, even by simple people who had travelled miles for a glimpse of him. He would refuse and become surly and difficult if forced to appear in public, and his temper afterwards was terrible. But Maria Feodorovna had the social graces he lacked and, fortunately, even when his moods hurt her, she seemed to understand his deepest motivation, and so to carry on. In time, her example and her strength helped him to adapt and, if he could be said to have been one of Russia's most admired Tsars, the achievement was as much hers as it was his. At the end of 1866, the year that had been so momentous for them both, Alexander turned to his diary to confide the sense that he was not yet worthy of his wife, and the determination to be worthy. He understood how much she had done for him already and looked forward to increasing happiness. The rapid pace of events, which had thrown him out of the shadows and into the empire's second position, as heir to the throne and as husband to the woman his brother had loved for years had left him bemused: 'I hardly think that anyone has ever been through or ever will go through the changes I've seen.'[30]

6

A Tale of Two Women

THE WIVES OF ALEXANDER II

Dagmar and Alexander were young and could rebuild their lives after Nikolai's death, but for his mother it was an enduring agony. So many of her hopes had focused on Nikolai. It was said that she had followed his studies so closely that she read the books he was given in order to discuss them with him, and in time she herself would admit that she neglected her other children for his sake. But this was just one of a series of sorrows, which ensured that later generations would remember Maria Alexandrovna for her sadness alone, when other aspects of her story and her personality were long forgotten.

In the 1890s the last Tsar and his wife employed an Irish nurse for their little daughters. Margaretta Eagar was fascinated by the supernatural, and she believed that the spirit of Tsaritsa Maria Alexandrovna haunted the Winter Palace. As soon as her head touched the pillow at night, she said, she heard the voice of a woman, crying bitterly and complaining of her husband's infidelity. Tsaritsa Alexandra told her that the bed she was using had been the one in which Maria Alexandrovna died, and she recognized the story the nurse related as that of her husband's grandmother. On a number of occasions Grand Princess Olga, who was only three, told Miss Eagar about an old lady in a blue dress, whom she had seen in her room. The nurse saw nothing. Then, as they walked through the Rotunda on the first floor of the palace, the child pointed to a portrait of Maria Alexandrovna and identified her as the old lady. Stories like these show how deeply the idea of Maria Alexandrovna's unhappiness had penetrated the memory of the Russian Court, which never quite accepted her as one of its own.

The unhappiness began early. The future Tsaritsa was a child of eleven when her mother died, leaving her as the only woman in her family, apart from a sister-in-law who was new to the Hesse Court. She was a timid, clever little girl who took life very seriously: the mere idea of having her ears pierced gave her nightmares for weeks, and the operation had to be postponed until she felt able to face it. She was very close to her mother and it was whispered, and widely believed, that the Grand Duke of Hesse was not really her father at all. The story has been told so often that fact and legend are irretrievably interwoven. Her parents, Prince Ludwig of Hesse and Princess Wilhelmine of Baden, were first cousins who married at Karlsruhe in 1804, during an interlude of peace in the Napoleonic Wars. Wilhelmine was a pretty, charming fifteen-year-old while Ludwig was twenty-six, and so shy and withdrawn that most people found him unapproachable. The early years of their marriage were set against a background of war: their first child, a son, was born six months after the battle of Austerlitz. Two more sons followed, one of whom was stillborn, then eleven years went by before the birth of the next child, Elisabeth. She was followed by a second, stillborn daughter. In the following year, 1823, Wilhelmine had another son, Alexander: Maria was her youngest child, born in Darmstadt on 8 August 1824 and christened Maximiliane Wilhelmine Auguste Sophie Marie.

The difference in age and temperament would have been enough to explain any problems in Wilhelmine's marriage. Moreover, for the first five of her childless years Ludwig was often away leading Hessian troops in the field. But the gossips whispered that Wilhelmine's younger children, Elisabeth, Alexander and Marie, were not fathered by Ludwig at all but by the Court Chamberlain, Baron Augustus Senarclens von Grancy. The idea persists to this day and is often taken as fact: many believed it at the time too, though it seems unlikely that Ludwig's father, Grand Duke Ludwig I, would have allowed his daughter-in-law to conduct an affair openly for so long, while still keeping the Chamberlain in his Household. Officially there was no question but that all three were true Hesse children: their names were recorded in contemporary volumes of the *Almanac de Gotha*, and when Alexander was born he had his uncle, Tsar Alexander I, for a godfather: a sign of acceptance at the highest level.

Elisabeth died of scarlet fever at Lausanne in 1826, when she was five. She was buried in the Hesse mausoleum on the Rosenhöhe in Darmstadt, and the whole family mourned, but gossip can slide under even the strongest defences. Ludwig may have heard the rumours and wondered about the children: for this, or for other reasons, there does seem to have been a short period of estrangement between him and Wilhelmine. The Dowager Tsaritsa mentioned it in a letter to her daughter in 1827, and her sympathies were all with Wilhelmine. In 1828 the estate of Heiligenberg was bought for – some say by – Wilhelmine and she moved there with Alexander and Marie. The scandal took wings and all Europe was intrigued – though the following year Wilhelmine and Ludwig celebrated their silver wedding in apparent harmony.

But, true or false, the rumours had spread, leaving a trail of misery. Marie spent the best part of her childhood at Heiligenberg and when her mother died of tuberculosis in 1836 the little girl was left painfully alone. She was not used to her father's Court and those who had whispered against her mother were unkind to her as well. She adored her elder brothers, but they were grown men, and her only close companion in the family was Alexander. The two children had been educated together, but by the 1830s Alexander was considered too old to share his schoolroom with a girl. So, after her mother's death, Marie's education and care were entrusted to a lady-in-waiting, Mlle von Grancy, a sister of the Baron, and she continued to spend the greater part of each year at Heiligenberg, where she felt most at ease.

When the Tsesarevich made his unplanned stop in Darmstadt in March 1839, his heart was touched by this sad fourteen-year-old, wearing her mother's pearls. Unwittingly Marie had caught one of the most prestigious prizes in Europe – to the disappointment of many an older princess – and the tongues began to wag. From Berlin particularly the old scandals were spread: the Hohenzollerns had grievances against the Hesse family and never missed a chance to stir feelings against them, and the Tsaritsa Alexandra, a Hohenzollern herself, probably shared their prejudice. The Tsar knew the stories about Marie's origin, but he took a very down-to-earth view. The Austrian Ambassador in St Petersburg reported home in April that Nicholas I 'is well aware of what is said about her birth but . . . if the Grand Duke of Darmstadt chooses to ignore it, he finds it presents no obstacle. His son, despite only spending one day at Darmstadt, found his attention drawn to the Princess because she was not very well treated, and the Emperor quite understands how this would heighten the interest his son already felt for her; that he would feel the same way in his son's place.'[1]

Marie was overwhelmed and terrified by the new turn in her fortunes. She liked Alexander enough to accept his proposal, but if Darmstadt seemed grand to her, how would she cope with St Petersburg? In June 1840 she had her first meeting with Nicholas I and his wife at Frankfurt, and two months later they took her back with them to Russia, where she was to spend almost a year learning the language and preparing for her conversion to Orthodoxy. She was sixteen. Recognizing her shyness, the Tsar invited her brother to go with her. This was something of a family tradition: once, long before Marie or Alexander could remember, their great-aunt Wilhelmine of Hesse had gone to Russia as a bride, and she too was accompanied by her brother. Mlle von Grancy went as well, and remained in Russia with Marie.

The first months were an ordeal. Marie was homesick and bewildered, and in later years she told one of her ladies-in-waiting that she had often been forced to hide her tears, opening the ventilation slats in the window so that the cold air of the Russian winter would take the redness from her eyes. As shy as her father, she was too withdrawn to make a good impression at a Court where social skills were all-important. Fortunately she found a sympathetic ally in her husband's aunt Elena, Grand Princess Mikhail, and a lasting friendship grew between the two women, who were seventeen years apart in age, but very similar in character and in their approach to life.

In one respect, though, Marie was much luckier than her new friend. The Tsesarevich was everything she could have wanted in a husband, and after the wedding she and Alexander were partners as well as lovers. She mastered the Russian language remarkably quickly – as quickly as Catherine the Great, people said – and she shared her husband's dream of enacting real reform in the country. She was intelligent and thoughtful, and Alexander trusted her judgement. They built up their own circle of friends, and as Alexander relied on Marie, now Maria Alexandrovna, to support him in his work, so she relied on him to guide her into society, and give her confidence. The Russian historian Tatitchev described these as 'years of untroubled family happiness. . . . There were almost daily gatherings at the young court . . . there would be reading aloud, music, cards . . . the host and hostess charmed everybody by their manner.'[2]

The young couple was given a suite of rooms in the south-west block of the Winter Palace, and another in the Zubov wing of the Catherine Palace at Tsarskoe Selo; here their first child, Alexandra, was born in 1842. Their family grew rapidly. To mark each birth, Alexander and Maria planted an oak tree in their private garden at Tsarskoe Selo, where skittles, swings and slides were provided for the children. A set of ship's masts made a climbing frame for the boys and they had a miniature railway and a farmhouse, and their own vegetable garden. Maria imported lilies of the valley and cowslips from her German home and tended them carefully. Indoors she played the piano with the children, created tapestries, and even indulged in some interior decorating. One ceiling in the Winter Palace with delicate loops of pale blue flowers and green foliage is still pointed out as her handiwork.

It was the best of times for them all, but there were still problems. It had meant a great deal to Maria to have her brother close by. Prince Alexander had grown into a tall, handsome man with a good mind; he got on well with the Tsesarevich and his sister worshipped him. The Prince served creditably with the Russian army in the Caucasus. 'It is worth a great deal to a soldier to have looked death in the face so often', he told his sister. 'You feel that you have more right to wear the uniform.'[3] With the Tsar's favour a glittering career lay before him; there was even talk of a marriage with Grand

Princess Ekaterina Mikhailovna, Elena's daughter, but things turned sour when he fell in love with his sister's lady-in-waiting, Julie Hauke. Nicholas I would not allow him to marry morganatically and remain in Russia, so in 1851 he resigned his commission and left. Eventually he settled at Heiligenberg with Julie, who became Princess of Battenberg, but Maria missed him terribly.

There were other sorrows. The death of little Alexandra Alexandrovna in 1849 was not so public a loss as Nikolai's death would be, but it was devastating for both parents. Twenty-four years later Maria visited her nephew's wife Alice, Princess Louis of Hesse, who had just lost a child, and the pain was still clear to see. 'Aunt Marie was so sympathising, motherly, and loving; it touched me much', Alice told her mother, Queen Victoria. 'At such moments she is peculiarly soft and womanly, and she loves her own children so tenderly. She cried much, and told me of the sad death of her eldest girl. . . .'[4]

Maria's answer to sorrow was to withdraw, finding strength in the religion she had been forced to adopt for her marriage. It was not in her nature to convert as a formality; she took the Orthodox faith to heart with an intensity that puzzled many who had been Orthodox from birth. With the religion came a growing fascination for the country and its ways. It was a sad irony that Maria and her great-niece Alix, the two Tsaritsas who fell in love with Russia when they married and longed to be at one with its culture, were the two who found the least acceptance in society. Within the family though, things were different – for Maria at least. After Alexander's accession he began to call all adult members of the imperial family together under his roof each week for a Sunday meal and this became a tradition, ensuring that the Romanovs came to know and love his wife for her gentle friendliness. But outside the family circle people found her too serious and misunderstood her reserve, thinking her cold and unyielding. She was never really popular.

She was still Tsaritsa, though, and could at last help her husband with the reform programme they had discussed for so long. An eyewitness described their coronation in the Cathedral of the Assumption in Moscow on 26 August/7 September 1856. Alexander took the crown and placed it on his own head, then 'it was the turn of Empress Maria Alexandrovna. She knelt before the Emperor, who took off his crown and lightly touched her head with it; then he placed the small crown on her head and put the robe and the diamond chain of the Order of St. Andrew round her shoulders.' They came out onto the Great Steps of the Kremlin, and 'no description can convey the solemnity of that moment when, surrounded by the monuments of old Russia . . . those two heads, their crowns reflecting the rays of the sun as an outward and visible sign of their grandeur, bowed before the love and trust of the state. The cannon fire and sound of the bells could no longer be heard above the clamour of the crowd.'[5]

The ending of serfdom and other abuses were causes that the imperial couple shared but, encouraged by Grand Princess Elena, Maria would also use her position as Tsaritsa to develop a reform programme of her own. She was profoundly interested in anything that concerned the lives of women, particularly in their education and health, and she played an active part in the foundation of many new girls' schools and colleges. She was interested in medical services too and, taking her lead from the work Elena started during the Crimean War, in 1877 Maria went on to establish the Red Cross in Russia, with the motto, 'Strength does not lie in power, but only in love'.

But that lay a long way in the future, and as the new Tsar and Tsaritsa turned to their serious public work they faced an immediate private anxiety. As the 1850s drew to an end, Maria's health began to deteriorate. Like her mother, she suffered from tuberculosis; when she was twelve the disease had almost killed her, and the combined effects of the damp and cold climate of St Petersburg and her rapid succession of pregnancies were more than her body could bear. On a growing number of occasions she was too ill to appear in public, and she became painfully thin. Alexander worried and consulted various doctors; nine months after the coronation, in May 1857, Maria gave birth to her seventh child, Sergei. The Tsar wrote to his brother Konstantin shortly after the birth, 'Maria is fully recovered, thank God, but the doctors are sending her to Kissingen, and I am inclined to accompany her.'[6]

This was to be the first of many trips to the European spas, which did little to halt the Tsaritsa's slow decline but did give her a chance to revisit her old home. She and Alexander set out on 28 June, taking their three youngest children, and went first to Darmstadt, then to Wildbad and Kissingen; at Bad Brückenau she was delighted to welcome her beloved brother and his family. Prince Alexander's eldest child, five-year-old Marie, her goddaughter, retained vague memories of 'a hotel or kurhaus; and the grave, loving face of a distinguished-looking woman whom everyone addressed as "Majesty".'[7]

This was only the first of a series of family reunions that saw the Tsaritsa at her liveliest – and perhaps her happiest too – and surviving glimpses of the Heiligenberg reunions are valuable because they show a Maria Alexandrovna very different from the tragic figure remembered in Russia. In July 1864, almost four years after the birth of Pavel, her youngest child, the doctors sent her to Germany again, to take the waters at Schwalbach. The eccentric young King of Bavaria was there; he took a fancy to Maria and showered her with daily bouquets of flowers. On Tuesday 23 August, under a steady downpour of rain, her train drew into the station at Bickenbach, near Heiligenberg, accompanied by her three youngest children and thirteen carriages of attendants and luggage. The entire Heiligenberg household had crammed itself into one small wing of the house to make way for them, and most of the Russian suite would actually sleep in the nearby village of Jugenheim. After a week the Tsar arrived with his sons Alexander and Vladimir. Three days later Louis and Alice of Hesse and their baby daughter Victoria joined them, and the party was completed when the Tsesarevich Nikolai arrived with his brother Alexei, alive with the news of his engagement to Dagmar.

This was not the only celebration. The Tsar's birthday fell on 11 September and an Orthodox service was held, followed by a dinner party and parlour games. The next day the Battenberg children decided to show their cousins one of the local beauty spots. They set off on donkeys, but were caught in heavy rain that forced them to take refuge in the hut of an obliging forester, who provided food, coffee and dry clothes. 'The Tsar, the Tsarina and all the company were already at table when we got back, and all ran out laughing into the courtyard to welcome us. It was a delightful party.' The holidays ended with a flourish when both families set out to commemorate the fun they had shared. 'Before breakfast we all went . . . to the great beech-tree that stands on the road leading to Felsenberg, in order to bestow on it the new name of "the Tsar's Beech". On the trunk hung a white shield, on which was inscribed "The Tsar's Beech, 14th September, 1864". We formed a chain and danced round the tree three times, and then went back to the house to drink coffee.'[8]

But when the fun was over, Maria was too ill to return to Russia with her husband and she had to be carried to the station, on her way to spend the winter in Nice. It was to be a sadder winter than anyone had dreamed possible, dominated by Nikolai's last illness. After his death the imperial family made their way back to Heiligenberg, where their days were quiet and solemn. One day Marie of Battenberg found her cousin Alexander, the new Tsesarevich, crying on the drawing room sofa because he could not face his transformed future – a scene that would be repeated twenty-nine years later when his son Nicholas faced the prospect of ruling Russia. Maria herself was broken, physically and mentally, and her nephew Louis feared that she would never survive. Only his father, Prince Karl of Hesse, was able to comfort her. He had just lost an only daughter so he understood, and they talked about their children together. 'Aunt Marie talked for a long time yesterday evening about her son, about his education and so on', Princess Alice told her mother. 'Nix was her whole life, she worked and lived for him, to make something of him, knowing what he must be in the future.'[9]

That future was gone. As far as she could, Maria devoted herself to her youngest children and to her favourite causes. In April 1866 she and Alexander celebrated their silver wedding anniversary. Rumour would have it that he had already had several affairs: nonetheless, he and Maria were still a loving couple who had come a long way together, though the tensions were mounting around them. By the mid-1860s the Tsar's life was under increasing threat from terrorists, and each assassination attempt made Maria more nervous for him.

Echoes of the old family life lingered longest away from Russia. In 1868 the imperial couple returned to Heiligenberg with Maria, Sergei and Pavel, their visit eagerly anticipated by the local people who had gained a great deal from the Tsaritsa's generosity to her old home. The villagers put up a triumphal arch, and on the morning of 24 October a steady procession of luggage and servants climbed the hill to the house: that evening Prince Alexander and his family drove down to the station to meet their guests. There was a new waiting room and forty carriages were lined up outside, but, despite all the trappings of royalty, the imperial family was as full of excitement as any other family might be, and as the train pulled into the station the Russians were hanging from the windows. 'The Tsarina wept for joy and the Tsar was very cordial; after them came Marie, Sergius, and Paul, the ladies-in-waiting, and the whole court entourage. Then they all took their places in the waiting carriages, and we drove off. A halt was made at the triumphal arch, where the Russian National Anthem was sung by the choral society, and flowers were scattered.'[10]

No shadow darkened the holiday and each day was more riotous than the last. Even Maria was well enough to join in the fun. Her niece remembered a particularly exciting evening spent in a ruined convent close by the house. 'It was pitch dark and we were thoroughly frightened, especially the boys, who gave vent to the most ear-splitting shrieks all the time. In the ruins stood "Pirenpinker", a colossal white figure; mysteriously lighted up by the moon, it made one shudder. Whenever the ghost moved we all started back screaming. . . . Then all sorts of other ghosts appeared, a white nun in the hollow lime-tree (it was the Tsarina); the Tsar, too, frightened us several times when he stood absolutely motionless in a dark corner of the ruins, his light clothing showing white in the moonlight in a very ghostly fashion . . . we stayed in the ruins till ten o'clock.'[11]

The morning of the Tsar's birthday dawned fine and bright – which was fortunate, because a special tent had been erected on the terrace to accommodate all the guests who would come to the

Orthodox service in his honour. Cossacks mounted guard and it was a huge occasion, but once the visitors had gone the family took over and held a special concert in which they were both performers and audience. Fireworks brought the party to an end, and when the time came for the Russians to leave a week later, there were tears all round. 'For the Tsar it seemed specially hard to tear himself away from these peaceful hills, where he spent such tranquil days in safety. He was so moved . . .' his niece noticed.[12] There would be more big Heiligenberg reunions, in 1871, '74, '75 and '76, but as the children grew and embarked on their own lives things would never be quite the same.

Things would never be the same for another reason, too. During the family party of 1876, Princess Marie was puzzled by a comment someone made about seeing the Tsar walking in the valley with a young woman and a little boy. Not until the visitors had gone did she learn from her mother what St Petersburg had known for nearly nine years. Alexander II had a mistress. Though he still lived with his wife, travelled with her, and showed her every kindness, in the shadows another woman followed, as a closely guarded secret known to them all.

The steps along the road were simple enough, even predictable. When Maria Alexandrovna's health first started to make a serious dent in her official programme, Alexander attended functions on her behalf. He visited the Smolny Institute, which had been under the patronage of the tsaritsas ever since its founding in the time of Catherine the Great. The Smolny provided an education for the daughters of the nobility and among its pupils in the early 1860s were two sisters, Princesses Ekaterina and Marie Dolgorukaya, whose father had died leaving only debts for his children to inherit: the two girls and their four brothers became imperial wards. Seeing Ekaterina reminded Alexander of an earlier meeting in the autumn of 1857 (some say 1859), when he stayed at her father's house near Poltava in the south. Then, she had been a mischievous little girl. Now, she was fourteen or fifteen years old, strikingly beautiful, and very unhappy. She was a country child who had known only freedom and the Smolny, with its uniform and strict rules, felt like a prison.

It was history repeating itself. In Darmstadt in 1839, Alexander had been captivated by a pretty fourteen-year-old who was obviously unhappy and out of place. Now he felt the same awakening interest in another unhappy teenager. Like Maria, Ekaterina was serious and reserved. Early photographs of her show that at this age she even looked rather like the Tsaritsa, and the combination of youth, beauty and unhappiness was something Alexander could not resist. By this time Maria's poor health would have made a physical relationship between them difficult, if not impossible – and he was a man who needed physical love. His visits to the Smolny became more frequent, and he paid especial attention to his young wards. When she was seventeen, Ekaterina left the Smolny and went to live with her brother and his wife in a house in the city. Her path crossed Alexander's at balls and receptions and one day, walking in St Petersburg's Summer Garden, he chanced to meet her, walking with a maid. He drew her aside and told her that he loved her, but she simply curtsied and walked on.

This stand-off continued for a year. Ekaterina was not born to be a mistress; her lineage was longer and prouder than Alexander's own, and it was not in her nature to love lightly. She did not meet the Tsar alone as he wanted until July 1866, when she went to him at the Belvedere Pavilion at Peterhof. It is said that she was frightened into submission by Dmitri Karakozov's attempt on Alexander's life, by the gates of the Summer Garden. Like Maria, she feared for the Tsar's life. They made love in the Belvedere that day, and Alexander promised that he would marry her if ever he could. He called her his 'wife before God', and their meetings continued in secret until, at the start of 1867, the secret was broken. Shocked, Ekaterina's sister-in-law insisted on taking her to Italy, and neither Ekaterina nor the Tsar made any protest. Her stay in Italy lasted five months, but she exchanged passionate letters with Alexander. In June 1867, at his request, Ekaterina rejoined him in Paris and then returned to St Petersburg. In 1869 he provided her with a home of her own on the Millionnaya, one of the most exclusive streets in the city close by the Winter Palace. It was the first of several apartments they would share.

Officially the affair was not discussed, but it could never really be hidden. Infidelity was part of the mythology of tsardom; society was certain all tsars had affairs whether they did or not, but this affair left people feeling cheated. There was no juicy gossip to be had. Ekaterina never tried to gain any advantage from the fact that the Tsar loved her. She never offered favours to her friends, indeed, she had very few friends. She cut herself off completely, retreating into the little island of domestic bliss that she had created for her lover, and it became apparent that the Tsar was taking the whole thing far more seriously than convention allowed. Some of his meetings with Ekaterina took place in the Winter Palace itself: her first child, Georgi, was even born there in 1872 with an imperial doctor in attendance. Defying convention still further, no convenient husband was found for the baby's mother, to give him a name. Georgi and his attendants moved into apartments of their own in the house of Alexander's friend, General Ryleev, so that, officially at least, the pretence that Ekaterina was a maiden lady would be maintained. When the baby was eighteen months old a second child, Olga, joined the secret household. Each afternoon at three, when the Tsar was in St Petersburg, he would visit Ekaterina and the children would be taken to join them: in their company Alexander rediscovered the untroubled happiness he had known with Maria when their own children were small. He adored his second family, but for Ekaterina it must have been a strange existence. Her whole life was concentrated in those few snatched hours, and outside these she could not even be seen with her children.

Private letters exchanged between the lovers show that the Princess could be difficult, and she was often jealous. This was probably inevitable given the restrictions the relationship placed on her life. But Alexander was too deeply in love to mind, and he trusted her enough to confide the concerns of his office. Gradually, she came to provide him with a continuation of the support his wife had given before tuberculosis took hold. Ekaterina was less intelligent than Maria and not so well educated: she listened and encouraged with the uncritical fervour of a lover. Her presence became increasingly important to the Tsar, but the gain for him was bought at a terrible price. Maria knew about the relationship and was aware that everyone around her knew and waited for her reaction. She showed none. She continued with her duties and her marriage, as far as her health would allow, with quiet dignity, keeping her pain to herself.

Other people's needs absorbed her mind. In 1875 the Prince of Montenegro entrusted his elder daughters to her care and she found places for them at the Smolny. When she heard that the younger of the two, Militsa, had typhus she went straight to her and summoned the best doctors. She sat by the girl's sickbed herself, sending daily messages to the Prince. Often her own illness took her far from Russia, and if her travels were sometimes prolonged, who would blame her? Her daughter Maria married Queen Victoria's son Alfred at the start of 1874 and in December the Tsaritsa went to England for the christening of their first child. 'I thought her very ladylike . . . and very kind and amiable', the Queen told her eldest daughter. 'We were at ease at once, but she has a sad expression and looks so delicate. I think we should get on very well together. Poor thing I pity her much.'[13]

Across the Courts of Europe there was pity for Maria Alexandrovna, sometimes with a patronizing edge. Everyone discussed the scandal. Some condemned her for remaining with the Tsar at all. She disdained to react, and gave all the time she had to her children, her faith, and her work. As the 1870s drew to an end, political events imposed a new strain on her already troubled marriage. For the first time, Alexander II and Maria Alexandrovna, who had begun in such harmony and survived so much together, were to find themselves on different sides – but even a war, though it injured their relationship, could not finally separate them. There was an enduring strength in their marriage, as events in the final years would show.

7

A Tsar at War

On 23 December 1877 Alexander II entered St Petersburg in triumph. After months of defeat and disappointment his armies were successful against the Turks in Bulgaria and Armenia and seemed poised to achieve the dream of freedom for the Christian peoples of the Balkans and, perhaps, the more ancient dream of extending Russian influence all the way to Constantinople. The imperial family and the highest officials of Court and government welcomed him in the square outside the Nicholas Station and thousands lined the streets to cheer him and to join in the celebration. They hailed him 'Liberator Twice Over', of the serfs and now of the Balkans, and at times his carriage could scarcely move for the enthusiastic crowd. Few people in that crowd would have been near enough to see the effect the war had had on the 'Tsar Liberator', but one eyewitness noticed with horror, 'his muscles were relaxed, his eyes dull, his figure drooping, his whole body so thin that he seemed to have no flesh on his bones. A few months had sufficed to make an old man of him.'[1] As soon as the official celebrations were over Alexander fled to the one place where he felt at ease: the house on the English Quay that he had rented in 1874 for Ekaterina.

Three years had passed since Turkish repression of the Balkans began to alarm the governments of Europe. A riot in Nevesinye, near Mostar in Herzegovina, was put down with terrible cruelty. The unrest spread across Serbia and Bulgaria and stories of Turkish atrocities multiplied. It was hard to ignore what was happening, but the Great Powers had their own conflicting plans for the Balkans and were unlikely to act together. Austria hoped to extend its own empire while Britain wanted to protect the status quo and to avoid any risk of a growth in Russian influence. Russian Pan-Slavists had sought closer links with Orthodox Christians in the Balkans for years, and some Russian intellectuals hoped that a war for liberation in the Balkans would be followed by demands for liberation at home.

In January 1876 the Powers sent an official protest to Turkey, which had no effect at all. Russian volunteers headed south in their thousands and it was even rumoured, falsely, that the Tsar's son Vladimir had offered his services to the Prince of Serbia. As the crisis deepened and the war movement in Russia gained strength, Alexander II toured Europe desperately advocating peace to anyone who would listen. He spoke to his uncle Kaiser Wilhelm I and to Bismarck, the German Chancellor, and appealed to Queen Victoria through her daughter Alice, who reported that he had tears in his eyes when he spoke of the need for peace. He tried to call a European conference. In July the Turks massacred the inhabitants of Batak in Bulgaria after promising safe passage in return for surrender. The fighting intensified and Alexander went home.

The Tsar had no appetite for war. He had seen the damage the Crimean conflict had done to his country and he knew that Russia was in no condition to take on another war. The reforms he had tried to bring to the armed forces had not had time to take effect, but within the country the clamour for war was so loud that no one could hear him. Despite an official ban, Balkan appeals and recruiting drives were taking place all over his empire and even his own family was deeply committed to the cause. He arrived home to find Maria Alexandrovna, urged on by her confessor Father Bajanov, financing and equipping hospital trains. She was firm in her enthusiasm for war and, after years of working together, Alexander and his wife found themselves on opposing sides. His brothers and sons were keen to join the fight and the Tsesarevich Alexander was allowing soldiers from his regiment to volunteer for the Balkans. The European governments would not believe that the autocratic ruler of all the Russias had so little control and they doubted his sincerity. The asthma that Alexander had suffered from periodically all his life was worsened by the strain, and he was hurt by attacks in the foreign press. He placed all his hopes on a peace conference that was planned for December but Lord Beaconsfield, the British Prime Minister, soured the atmosphere with a speech on the inviolability of Turkish possessions which caused outrage in Russia.

There was a real danger that if Alexander did not take his country into the war they would go without him so, to cries of duplicity from abroad, he ordered a partial mobilization.

In March 1877 the Great Powers ordered Turkey to reduce the strength of its armies and promise reforms. Turkey refused. Alexander left the Winter Palace and walked alone to the Kazan Cathedral to pray. His decision was made: on 12 April Russia declared war on Turkey and amid scenes of general rejoicing the troops were ordered south. Alexander followed, though he had entrusted the supreme command to his brother Grand Prince Nikolai Nikolaievich. His youngest brother Mikhail Nikolaievich, who commanded the army of the Caucasus, was to open a second front east of the Black Sea. Only one person offered the Tsar uncritical support: Alexander wrote to Ekaterina, 'you will understand better than anyone else what I feel at the beginning of a war I so much wanted and hoped to avoid. . . . It is a nightmare.' His address to the army was equally doom-laden and honest: 'most profoundly do I regret having to send you on such a business. As you may know, I kept trying to avoid it until the very last hope had gone. Now I can but wish you success.'[2]

Heavy rains impeded the army's march across the Wallachian plain and made the Danube, which formed the border between Romania and Bulgaria, impassible for weeks. Alexander travelled south with his sons, Alexander, Vladimir and Sergei. His fourth son Alexei was commanding a naval company on the Danube and his nephews Nikolai Nikolaievich the younger, who would rise to supreme command of the Russian Army in 1914, and Sergei of Leuchtenberg, were also with the army. Another nephew, Alexander of Battenberg, had received special permission to leave his regiment in Berlin and join the Tsar's retinue. He was awarded the Vladimir Cross for his part in the crossing of the Danube, which was achieved on 27 June at enormous cost. The Tsaritsa had provided five luxurious hospital trains with six hundred beds, but in the early days of the war there were thousands of casualties every day who had to be taken from the battlefield in carts, on gun carriages or in cattle trucks.

Alexander established his headquarters at Sysov in Bulgaria, while Russian engineers hurried to build permanent bridges across the river. The Tsesarevich was given command of XII and XIII Corps with orders to hold a fifty-mile line along the River Lom, to protect the left flank of the army and threaten the Turkish forces at Rustchuk, Shumla, Varna and Silistra. He was no military genius, but he held his position with dogged courage against a much stronger army, and developed a horror of war that would last for the rest of his life. He wrote daily letters to his wife, the Tsarevna Maria Feodorovna. She was busy in St Petersburg with charity work for the wounded and for soldiers' families, and the story that she slipped away from the city disguised as a nurse in order to visit him persisted for many years.

The Tsar was also writing daily letters, but not to his wife; while Maria Alexandrovna was so convinced in her support for the war Alexander could not be open with her, and only to Ekaterina could he confide his real feelings about what was happening, and his anxiety about the attitude of foreign governments, particularly the British. He felt humiliated because his health did not allow him to fight and he worked an impossibly long day, devoting as much time as he could to the men in the hospitals. He suffered from insomnia and his asthma became acute; Dr Botkin urged him to return to the north but he refused.

At first the army did well, capturing Tyvorno and Plevna, but the strain of war soon revealed serious weaknesses in high command. After making an epic crossing of the Balkans through the Khaïnkioy Pass, and successfully taking Shipka, General Hourko's division was forced to retreat because no one had thought to arrange reinforcements for them. Tyvorno was held to have great symbolic importance because it was the ancient capital of Bulgaria, but the Russian commanders did not see the strategic importance of Plevna, which stood on a vital crossroads. Left without adequate defence the town soon fell to the Turks, and after a series of reverses Alexander had to move his headquarters to Gorny Studen, to the west of Tyvorno.

In the unbearable heat of summer, with inadequate and sometimes non-existent supplies, Alexander kept up his punishing workload. An old opponent of his policies, Prince Cherkassky, visited Gorny Studen in July as commandant of Maria's newly formed Russian Red Cross. He was dismayed by the incompetence of the staff, but for Alexander he had only praise. 'In this vortex', he wrote, 'I cannot but admire the Emperor, who maintains his calm in spite of his deep mental anguish, who alone of all the people here seems capable of grasping matters of real moment. When you see him, tired and unwell as he is, visiting hospitals, entering into the men's interests and needs, bearing himself with a sovereign's dignity and a friend's compassion . . . you cannot but love him as a man.'[3]

Realizing too late that they needed Plevna, the Russians attempted to retake the town; a first assault on 20 July floundered with the loss of thousands. The attackers were outnumbered by three to one, and if the Turks had followed their retreat Russian hopes might have ended that day. Ten days later a second assault failed. Gorny Studen was no longer safe, and Alexander's headquarters was moved again. In vain his sons urged him to leave Bulgaria. In the east Grand Prince Mikhail's army was shattered by the Turks at Kizil Tépé; morale could hardly have been lower and Alexander was forced to request help from Prince Carol of Romania, who brought in an army of 50,000 men and 180 guns. The Tsar also recalled General Totleben, who had made his name through the defence of Sevastopol in the Crimean War. In early September a third assault on Plevna failed, with the loss of 25,000 lives. The Romanians fought with immense bravery and steadiness, which won the admiration of all, but an English officer described the chaotic state of the Russian army: 'the negligence and want of arrangement (for the wounded) is quite astounding. One day at Plevna three thousand Russians, wounded in the head and arms and chest, had to march twenty miles to the rear as there were only bullock carts for those who could not stand!'[4] 'God help us to bring this war to an end,' Alexander wrote to Ekaterina, 'it dishonours Russia and Christianity. This is the cry of my heart, and none will understand it better than you, my treasure and my life.'[5]

In Russia too morale was low. People had imagined a quick victorious war with lots of dash and glory and they were not prepared for this. The Grand Princes were criticised, the Tsar was accused of cowardice for not taking part in the fighting, and of neglect of duty for not returning to St Petersburg – someone had to be blamed for the shambles. There were calls for a National Assembly and revolutionary activity was rife. On 13 September a Council of War was held at headquarters. Fearing that with the onset of winter supplies would fail altogether, Grand Prince Nikolai urged a retreat across the Danube to the safety of Romania and his commanders agreed. Only Milutin, the Minister of War, opposed them, arguing that Russia could not afford to abandon the foothold that had already cost 60,000 lives: Plevna commanded the road south so Plevna must be taken. There was uproar until the Tsar stood up. 'There is to be no retreat, gentlemen', he said, and he left with Milutin and Totleben.[6]

Alexander had taken control, and the effects of his decision were far-reaching. Totleben took over the siege of Plevna and he refused to waste another life on a frontal attack, concentrating instead on cutting off every supply road to the town. As winter set in, Dr Botkin again urged Alexander to go home, so badly was he suffering from asthma, insomnia and the stress of the campaign. 'All these sights', he told Ekaterina, 'make my heart bleed and I find it hard to keep back my tears,' but he would not leave until Plevna fell.[7]

On 24 October his nephew Sergei of Leuchtenberg was killed in action. Sergei was with the Tsesarevich's XII Corps, who had been ordered to advance towards Basarbowa and Iovan-Tschiflik after small advance parties had succeeded in pushing the Turks back. By Basarbowa the fighting became intense: Sergei was leading a reconnaissance when a Turkish bullet caught him on the temple and killed him. He was twenty-six. In distant Berlin the Crown Princess of Prussia lamented his death, though she said he was 'as wild as possible', but those who knew him better took a kinder view. Sergei was a cultured, clever young man who had spent long periods in Italy. Twelve years earlier, in Florence, he had done his best to comfort his dying cousin Nikolai by describing the wonders of the city he knew so well. His friend Princess Kurakin met him at his sister's house before he left for the front. 'He was a thorough West European,' she remembered, 'an artist, elegant and clever. All his sympathies were with Italy, the home of art, science and culture, "but for these Bulgarians, Serbs and other Slavs," he said to me, "I have not the slightest sympathy."'[8] The war had claimed one of its few opponents.

The first breakthrough came in the east in November, when General Loris Melikov, Grand Prince Mikhail's Chief of Staff, took the town of Kars. Plevna itself fell on 10 December, after a few hours of fighting when the Turks made a last attempt to breach Russian lines. Alexander attended a Te Deum in the captured town before returning to St Petersburg as he had promised. He arrived at 10 a.m. on 23 December and was greeted by cheering crowds.

After Plevna the Turkish resistance fell away. As Alexander entered St Petersburg, General Hourko's division was repeating its crossing of the Balkans; this time it captured Shipka and advanced towards Sophia. A few weeks later General Skobelev, brother-in-law of Evgeni of Leuchtenberg, Sergei's elder brother, took Adrianople without a shot being fired, and in February a truce was signed and treaty negotiations began. The Treaty of San Stefano established a large autonomous Bulgaria – autonomous in name but in reality under Russian control – and full independence for Romania, Serbia and Montenegro, with indemnity payments and territory to be given to Russia. Its provisions were less than generous to the Prince of Romania, whose army had provided vital support when Russia was at its lowest ebb.

The Great Powers were alarmed and determined that Russia should not profit so much, and the Balkan countries were equally uneasy. Constantinople lay open to the Russian armies. Alexander thought of ordering the occupation of the city, then wavered. His troops were suffering from typhus and there was no money left to pay for a prolonged war. The British sent a naval force into the Black Sea to discourage him; Princess Marie of Battenberg described the anxiety she felt in the weeks that followed, with her brother Alexander in the Tsar's army and her brother Louis on one of the British ships.

The Tsar had no choice but to back down, but his country would never forgive him. The terms of the Treaty of San Stefano were modified by an international congress in Berlin, where the other Powers stepped in to take their share of the spoils. Even so, Russia had succeeded in freeing the Balkan countries from Turkish rule and in establishing the new state of Bulgaria. On Alexander II's birthday in 1879 his nephew Alexander of Battenberg became Bulgaria's first reigning prince.

But within Russia the effects of the war were as bad as the Tsar had known they would be. The terms of the new settlement were extremely unpopular, there was widespread unrest, and terrorist groups flourished as never before. Political murders multiplied and powers to contain the situation were given to the heroes of the war, Hourko, Totleben and Loris Melikov. Urged on by Loris Melikov and by Grand Prince Konstantin Nikolaievich, Alexander began to look at a renewed programme of constitutional reform as the only way to ease the disturbances in the long term: in private he was ill, disillusioned and very tired. His emotional dependence on Ekaterina Dolgorukaya was complete now and he horrified his family and Court, society and the rest of Europe, by bringing her and her children into the Winter Palace to see him while his wife lay sick in her rooms on the floor below. For the rest of his life, Alexander II would exist under a state of siege, in public and in private.

But no one will ever really know what passed between the Tsar and his wife on the subject of Ekaterina, once the time for secrecy and evasion was over. In July 1878 Maria Alexandrovna suffered a crisis in her illness and appeared to be dying, but she revived and remained with her husband, sharing their day-to-day concerns as they had always done. The idea that their marriage existed in name only after the affair with the Princess began is no more than a guess, and the truth may be quite different. Vera Borovikova, the maid who looked after Ekaterina's children, described an occasion in these final years when little Georgi and Olga visited the Winter Palace. Alexander took them himself to the Tsaritsa's room, Vera said, and introduced Maria to them as 'Aunty': as Maria kissed and blessed her husband's children by his mistress, the couple were both in tears.[9]

There are depths in every relationship which the outside world simply cannot comprehend. To the very end, when Maria was at the point of death, Alexander did not forget what they had meant to each other. In February 1880 a terrorist bomb shattered the room in the Winter Palace where he was about to have dinner and several soldiers on the floor below were killed. Maria had only just returned from Cannes, at what must have been the very worst time of the year for someone in her condition, and his first impulse was to hurry to her room to make sure that she was unharmed. When he found her still sleeping he sat by the door so that he could be the first to tell her what had happened and to reassure her. For fourteen years he tried to be a husband to two women and a father to two families, without causing anyone pain. This was a circle that even a Tsar could not square.

8

The Admiral-General

GRAND PRINCE KONSTANTIN NIKOLAIEVICH

The bomb at the Winter Palace was only one of many assassination attempts, and they gave rise to some very wild rumours. It was even whispered in St Petersburg that Grand Prince Konstantin Nikolaievich conspired against his brother's throne, and gossips saw his hand in every move against Alexander's life. Nine years younger than the Tsar, Konstantin saw only the need for change in Russia, never the difficulties, and he pushed his brother on with absolute confidence. There was a strong vein of arrogance in him: his manner could be abrasive and many would have longed to see him fall, but when that fall came it was Konstantin, not the gossips, who brought it about. He left behind him a close and loving family, utterly loyal to the dynasty while its rule endured . . . and one very black sheep.

You can imagine our happiness! Everything went well and fairly quickly. I am happier than I would have dared to believe, and I give thanks to God from the depth of my soul.'[1] Nicholas I loved all his children, but after nine years of daughters he was overjoyed when his wife gave birth to a second son, in September 1827. The little Prince was a few months old when his father described him in a letter to his aunt in the Netherlands as 'a big, fat handsome fellow, so quick and heavy that I cannot hold him: he seems really to belong to the family as the only thing he hears with pleasure is the drum.'[2] By the time he was five Konstantin had become too wilful and difficult for a governess to handle, so his father decided to appoint a male tutor. It was the first sign of the temper that would become the Grand Prince's least attractive feature in adult life.

The Tsar intended that Konstantin would one day be Admiral-General of the Russian Fleet, and he chose a tutor with this in mind. Frederick Lütke had circumnavigated the globe at the age of twenty and he trained the boy in naval sciences and filled his head with tales of the sea. In the hall of the Winter Palace that served as a games room for the Tsar's younger sons there was a scale model of a ship, large enough for the boys to scramble up the masts and learn the rudiments of seamanship on dry land. Young Konstantin would not be allowed to forget his destiny, and he grasped it eagerly: 'the hours of my first interview with the animated boy passed as quick as lightning,' Lütke recalled, 'in tales about Vesuvius, Rome, and sea voyages, and I at once felt that my undertaking was likely to bring forth good fruit.'[3]

But however keen Konstantin was, his naval training proper would not begin until he was twelve and first he had other things to learn. His parents and tutors agreed on a structured programme far less academic than Zhukovsky's timetable for the Tsesarevich. Only three hours a day were spent in lessons; the rest of the time was devoted to walks and exercises and, being musical, Konstantin also learnt to play the piano and cello. French and German were added to the Russian and English of his nursery and he became an enthusiastic reader. Lütke was also determined to teach his pupil about the world outside the palace walls. A friendship grew between them that lasted for the rest of the sailor's life, but as he grew older Konstantin found greater intellectual stimulus in the home of his aunt Elena Pavlovna. She broadened his tastes in literature and music, introducing him to the best new work. She showed him the latest ideas in science too, and encouraged him in the political idealism that shaped the course of his life.

Konstantin lived at speed. Before he was twenty-one he had become engaged to Alexandra of Saxe-Altenburg: it was said that she looked so like his sister Alexandra, who had died in childbirth, that his mother burst into tears at their first meeting. The Princess of Saxe-Altenburg was in St Petersburg to witness Konstantin's coming-of-age, when he swore the Oath of Allegiance to his father and elder brother in the ceremony his father had instituted to ensure that the succession could never again be surrounded by confusion and violence. The future Alexander II was first to take the oath in 1834, when he was sixteen. Now, in the winter of 1847, the Tsar led his second son into the chapel of the Winter Palace, 'and after making the sign of the cross and kissing the Bible, the latter read the oath in clear voice, with his hand upraised. He seemed very much impressed, and as soon as he had read the oath, he was blessed and embraced by his father and mother, who were both much affected. He then embraced his brothers and sisters, and his betrothed.' The entire company then moved in procession to St George's Hall, where the Grand Prince repeated the oath in front of selected officers and representatives of the army.[4]

In September 1848, nine months after his coming-of-age, Konstantin and Alexandra were married; she joined the imperial family as Grand Princess Alexandra Iosifovna and a year later, on the death of Grand Princess Elena's husband, Grand Prince Mikhail Pavlovich, the young couple inherited Pavlovsk, one of the loveliest of the Romanov palaces. The greater part of their married life would be spent at Pavlovsk, in the Marble Palace in the city, and at Strelna, near Peterhof.

Alexandra Iosifovna was a princess to her fingertips, with innate dignity and a profound respect for traditional values. In later years it amused her to hear the expectations of her granddaughters and younger ladies-in-waiting, and she liked to let them know how times had changed. She recalled the engagement of her eldest sister Marie to the Crown Prince of Hanover. Marie had met the Prince only once, and when he arrived at her father's palace for the official announcement her mother sent all four daughters to him, dressed identically in pink with roses in their hair. The Prince, who was almost blind, turned his head from one to another in bewilderment. The prospective bride blushed and almost burst into tears and Alexandra, then only twelve years old, piped up helpfully 'it isn't me'. An aide-de-camp pushed the Prince towards Marie, '"to whom he ceremoniously handed his flowers, thanking her for the honour she had done him. . . . My sister curtsied: they were engaged. That was courting in my day", she laughed.'[5]

Her own courtship was probably more considered: certainly she and Konstantin were well matched and their marriage began happily. Their first child, Nikolai, was born in St Petersburg in 1850, to be followed nineteen months later by a daughter, Olga. Konstantin was a loving father and his diary and letters to his elder brother bear witness to the private harmony of the early years. The brothers hardly ever refer to their wives without using phrases like 'your angel', or to their children without mentioning how sweet, good, or beautiful they are; adjectives that echo with affection and the pride of parenthood. Both men were wholeheartedly involved in the most intimate details of childbirth and infant care – matters that most men of their generation would have left to the women and the servants. 'I write you a few words, dearest Sasha,' Konstantin wrote from Strelna in the summer of 1858, just after the birth of his second son, 'in order to let you know that everything here is going satisfactorily, thank God. Today is the third day. My wife's milk is beginning to appear, her breasts fill and swell a good deal, and this is giving her much discomfort but, thank God, there is still not the slightest sign of fever. Unfortunately her old insomnia still troubles her. Little Kostya is also doing well, and lies in bed with his mother the whole day. Our Mama is invaluable, she is with us every day, and is pleased to stay for a long time. Yesterday she had dinner with me.'[6]

In November 1859 Nikolai became ill, and his parents were beside themselves with worry. 'Our poor Nikola is not good,' Konstantin confided to his diary on the fourth day, 'the fever has not broken, he is getting weaker, and the doctors, it seems, begin to fear typhus, although they dare not yet say so openly. We are greatly worried. God is our only hope.'[7] He and Alexandra sat by their son's bed that night and through the next day, and they were delighted when the child began to show signs of improvement as evening came. They adored Nikolai – too much, perhaps, as later events would show.

Plans for naval reform absorbed Konstantin's attention at the start of his brother's reign and tested his talents to the full. Visits to England and France in 1857 had shown him what a modern navy should be, but he inherited just 200 poorly maintained sailing ships, an overstaffed bureaucracy which obstructed his every move, and no funds. Konstantin wanted the country to have its own shipyards, to free the navy from dependence on overseas orders, but it was an uphill struggle. 'I want shipwrights and sailors, not crowds of clerks', he was heard to say. To a friend he explained his long-term ambition: 'I am about to create a Navy. We have not got one and we must have it. Our first duty is to work hard and not expect any brilliant results . . . work not for our day but for the future.'[8] Nothing put him off, not even the treaty obligations imposed on the country after the Crimean War which forbade the placing of a Russian naval fleet in the Black Sea.

The Grand Prince was energetic and determined, and as he pushed forward his plans for the navy he was also involved in the reform of the naval and military colleges, in a thorough investigation of corruption in the army, and in the revision of the country's stringent censorship laws. He sponsored expeditions to explore and map remote parts of the empire. He was the Tsar's secret weapon. Abrupt and quick-tempered, utterly contemptuous of anyone who opposed him, he could forge through problems that daunted his more sensitive elder brother. Emancipation of the serfs, the most important reform of all, was not a popular policy. When the committee appointed to bring it about dug in their heels and made difficulties, Alexander brought in Konstantin. His manner made enemies but he pushed the business forward, although it proved to be a nightmare for him. After twelve stormy months he lost patience and left for a long cruise in foreign waters, 'disheartened and frustrated by everything said about him here'.[9] He returned to his post almost a year later. When the emancipation finally became law in 1861, Alexander II publicly thanked his brother for the contribution he had made.

The same year, 1861, saw events that would bring an important change to the life of the Grand Prince and his family. The Russian sector of Poland, partitioned since the previous century, was disturbed and under martial law, and the old Viceroy, after pleading to be released from his office, had died of heart failure. As the unrest increased, Alexander saw the need for a Viceroy he could really trust and he appointed Konstantin. It was early in 1862 when the Grand Prince arrived in Warsaw, and almost immediately he was shot in the shoulder by a tailor's apprentice. The Tsar summoned him home but he refused to go, and his wife and family stayed with him. As soon as he could, Konstantin appeared in public and pleaded for an end to the violence.

He had some sympathy for the Poles and, ignoring the advice of his brother's generals, he ended martial law and embarked on a programme of liberalization. Polish was reinstated as the official language, the Grand Prince appointed Poles to administrative positions and gathered a distinguished court of Poles and Russians around him. Years later Countess Marie Kleinmichel, whose father Count von Keller was one of Konstantin's ministers, described the short-lived brilliance of it all.

A child herself, Marie was often invited to play with the Grand Prince's children. Olga had grown into a gentle, timid little girl, too easily moved to tears. The younger daughter, Vera, spent long periods in Germany with their childless aunt Olga Nikolaievna, Queen of Württemberg. Marie was closest in age to Nikolai who, at twelve years old, was dark and attractive and very much his parents' favourite, overshadowing his little brothers, four-year-old Konstantin and baby Dmitri. With Marie he shared his obsession for a popular book, *The House of Ice*, which described the struggles of the hero Artemi Volinsky against the evil statesman Biron, in the reign of the eighteenth-century Tsaritsa Anna Ivanovna. The boy imagined himself as Volinsky and dreamed up great schemes with himself as the hero. He had inherited his father's idealism, but also his pride and his unpredictable temper.

In July 1862, Grand Princess Alexandra gave birth to a sixth child in the Lazienki Palace in Warsaw. As a compliment to the Poles, she and Konstantin decided to name him Vacslav, but this was an unfortunate choice. The Russians at Court insisted on using the Russian form of the name, Viacheslav, which caused a lot of unnecessary bickering and bad feeling. Nonetheless, baby Vacslav, or Viacheslav, was christened in great style. His uncle Grand Prince

Mikhail Nikolaievich and his wife, and one of the daughters of Maria Nikolaievna, Duchess of Leuchtenberg, travelled to Warsaw with their suites, and the Tsar sent his second son, Grand Prince Alexander Alexandrovich, to hold the baby at the font. At seventeen Alexander was large, lumpish and awkward. Lacking the polished manners of his elder brother the Tsesarevich, he was noisy and boisterous at the wrong moments, knocked over furniture and showed his embarrassment in formal situations; 'Sasha with a bear's paws' his cousins called him.

During the week of festivities that marked the christening, keen-eyed observers might have noticed the seeds of trouble to come. Grand Prince Konstantin was not a tolerant man. He had known his brother's children from birth and enjoyed an especially close relationship with the Tsesarevich. When Nikolai Alexandrovich began to show an interest in serious music, Konstantin recorded this delightedly in his diary and he watched his nephew's progress with pleasure. He had never been able to feel as fond of Alexander, and the boy's awkward performance in Warsaw filled him with disgust. In the course of one formal dinner party Alexander knocked over a decanter of red wine: 'See what a pig they have sent us from Petersburg', Konstantin boomed down the table. Alexander said nothing but he scowled at his uncle, and there was bitterness in his eyes.[10]

As Viceroy, the Grand Prince had done his best to appease the Poles but it was autonomy they wanted, not reform, and their well-laid plans for an uprising came to a head when he called a conscription levy in 1863. The resulting Polish mutiny brought Konstantin's rule to a savage end, and he returned to St Petersburg with his family and took up again the work of naval reform, concentrating on Russia's need for a Black Sea fleet. The abolition of corporal punishment in April 1863 had made his work easier, and the official reports of the Naval Ministry began to record instances of officers dismissed and disciplined for cruelty to the lower ranks. In recognition of his varied services to the country, Alexander II raised Konstantin to the office of President of the Council of State.

By the mid-1860s the children were growing up. In 1867 Olga became engaged to King George of the Hellenes, whose sister

Dagmar had become the Tsarevna Maria Feodorovna in the previous year. She worked hard to make the engagement happen for her brother against determined opposition from the Konstantins: somehow she managed to persuade them both to think again. Their hesitation was understandable. Olga was only fifteen, a child still, and the wedding took place a few weeks after her sixteenth birthday. She left for Greece with all her dolls and toys and found the welcome in Athens overwhelming. Even the language was strange. Before one reception she disappeared, and after a long search they found her hiding under the stairs crying into the fur of her favourite stuffed bear. She settled in time, but never lost her love of Russia and returned whenever she could. In July 1868 her first child was born and named Constantine after her father, by popular acclaim.

Konstantin and Alexandra should have been able to share their delight in becoming grandparents, but the beginning of the new family coincided with a crisis in the old. Around 1866, the year Alexander II began his relationship with Ekaterina Dolgorukaya, Konstantin began to pursue a young dancer from the St Petersburg Conservatoire. Anna Kousnetsova was twenty years younger than the Grand Prince and she resisted him for years, but he knew how to get what he wanted. In 1873 she gave birth to their first child, Sergei; four more would follow, and the Grand Prince maintained separate establishments for his mistress and her children at Pavlovsk and in the Crimea. He is even said to have asked for permission to divorce his wife, which the Tsar refused to grant.

For Alexandra this was a bitter blow. She and Konstantin had been happy together and she was a proud woman. She became increasingly obsessed with her appearance. There was something defiant and rather sad in the insistent comparisons she made between herself and the Empress of Austria, reputedly the most beautiful woman in Europe: many an envoy stood tongue-tied by her questions, fearing to give offence by an honest reply. In later life she is reputed to have worn corsets and shoes in bed to preserve her tiny waist and feet. Not for her the quiet self-sacrificing love of Maria Alexandrovna; faced with Konstantin's disloyalty she withdrew from him and from the Court, taking refuge in the company of her younger children.

Alexandra was preparing to leave Russia for the wedding of her younger daughter in 1874, when she discovered that three valuable diamonds had been stolen from an icon given to her by her father-in-law Nicholas I, which she kept in her bedroom. A second icon had been damaged. She showed Konstantin and the police were called, while she herself left for Stuttgart, where twenty-year-old Vera was due to marry a distant cousin, Duke Wilhelm Eugen of Württemberg. Two days later the diamonds were found in the possession of Captain Varpakhovsky, Nikolai Konstantinovich's aide-de-camp. The Chief of Police, Count Schouvalov, informed Konstantin that his eldest son was the thief.

Twenty-four years of adoration from both parents had turned Nikolai Konstantinovich into the very worst type of autocratic prince. Attractive, cultured and intelligent, he liked to pose as a liberal revolutionary, but in reality he cared for no one but himself. He often told stories of the unreasonable strictness, almost brutality, of his upbringing, but those who had watched him grow remembered a spoilt teenager beyond all control, who was quite capable of securing the dismissal of any tutor he disliked. He had no respect for the ordinary standards of behaviour: he was sixteen when Marie von Keller saw him torturing a lamb he had tied to a tree, and he laughed as it died. Sex became an obsession, and his mother's attempt to settle him down in marriage to her sister's daughter, Princess Friederike of Hanover, failed because Nikolai was already involved with a number of mistresses. Now, when questioned by his father and Count Schouvalov, Nikolai showed no fear and no sign of remorse: the theft turned out to be one of many and both men were shocked by his attitude. With the Tsar's agreement it was decided that he would be declared insane and placed under medical supervision: privately, as Konstantin recorded in his diary, 'to punish Nikola he will be shut in an isolated cell under strict surveillance, and his medals and epaulettes will be taken away. This is just for us, and not for the public.'[11]

But even in confinement Nikolai Konstantinovich continued to cause trouble. At first he was sent to Oreanda in the Crimea, where the surveillance was not nearly so strict as his father expected. A young woman, Alexandra Demidov-Abaza, gained access to him, and when she wrote to the Tsar claiming to be pregnant and requesting legal recognition for her baby, Nikolai was moved to the Ukraine, then back to the Crimea, where she followed. Once again Nikolai was moved, but in September 1876 Alexandra was found to be living secretly in his rooms. She was pregnant again. The General charged with the guardianship of the Grand Prince asked to be relieved from his duties, and in May 1877 Count Rostovtsev arrived to replace him and took Nikolai to a new place of exile in Orenburg. He would never see Alexandra or their children again.

In Orenburg, Nikolai began to show a different side to his character. He took great interest in Central Asia, pouring hours into serious reading and research. In the autumn of 1878 he organized the first of a number of fact-finding expeditions, and afterwards wrote articles for scientific journals. Improving conditions in Turkestan, particularly by the introduction of workable irrigation schemes, became his new passion but his other passions had not subsided. The Tsar was exasperated to learn that on 15 February 1878 Nikolai had contracted a marriage in secret with Nadejda Dreyer, the daughter of the local police chief. He had used the name 'Colonel Volinsky', recalling his childhood hero. He tried to paint himself as a revolutionary and claimed that the people would rise up to support him: it was no wonder that his father and uncle lost patience and it seems to have been at this time that his name was removed from published lists of the imperial family. Officially he ceased to exist.

Privately, of course, he remained a problem to be dealt with. His embarrassed guardians tried to throw the blame on one another, and by the autumn of 1880 life in Orenburg had become unbearable. Nikolai refused to take any further orders from Count Rostovtsev and a representative sent from the Tsar showed some sympathy for his position. In November he was moved to a small property near to St Petersburg and the supervision around him was relaxed.

Early in February 1879, Grand Princess Alexandra was walking in a gallery at Pavlovsk when she saw a terrifying apparition of a white lady, floating towards her. She believed this to be an omen, and her fears were confirmed the next day when her son Viacheslav was taken ill. He died within the week. Now she was more alone than ever, watching with sadness and anger as her husband and his brother devoted themselves to their mistresses. She was annoyed with Konstantin for supporting the Tsar in his affair with Ekaterina, and furious when their illegitimate son Georgi was given a temporary home at Pavlovsk, in the summer of 1872. On 22 May/3 June 1880, Tsaritsa Maria Alexandrovna died alone in her room at the Winter Palace. The widowed Tsar took steps almost immediately to fulfil his promise and make Ekaterina his wife. To his sister Olga, Queen of Württemberg, he explained, 'I would never have married before a year of mourning if not for the dangerous time we live in. . . . Ekaterina Dolgorukova preferred to refuse all the pleasures and gaities of society which means so much to a young woman of her age in order to devote her entire life to love and care for me. Therefore, she has a full right for my love, esteem, and my thankfulness.'[12] He hoped that the family would understand and support him but most of them, particularly the women, were horrified. Alexandra Iosifovna refused even to meet Ekaterina, defying an imperial command. Konstantin tried to reason with her but she was adamant, and only gave way at the last moment, moved, despite herself, by an illness of Ekaterina's elder daughter which appeared serious. But she still remained defiantly loyal to the memory of the Tsaritsa, who had been her friend.

She would not have to endure the situation for long. Shortly after midday on Sunday 1/13 March 1881, Alexander II left the Winter Palace to attend his customary military parade in the Mikhailovsky Riding School, disregarding the terrorist threats which had become part of his life. He responded to them with the same resolute courage that he had once shown to his grandson Nicholas, in the Gothic Chapel at Peterhof. Besides, on this occasion his nephew Dmitri Konstantinovich was to ride beside him as aide-de-camp for the first time, and he would not have wanted to disappoint him by cancelling the parade. Once it was over, the Tsar went on to visit his cousin Ekaterina Mikhailovna at the Mikhail Palace. He was on his way home when two deafening blasts shook the city. In the silence that followed, a hushed and frightened crowd gathered around the Winter Palace to hear their fate. The Tsar had been struck by a handmade bomb on the embankment of the Catherine Canal, and though his brother Mikhail rushed to his side and he was hurried back to the Winter Palace, his injuries were terrible. He died within hours, and the tragedy would tear his family to its foundations.

In the last year of his reign Alexander had set in train discussions that were intended to lead to constitutional reform. Konstantin was one of the prime movers and, as President of the Council of State, he helped to prepare the proposal for a limited elective assembly which Alexander was due to approve on the very day of his death. For Konstantin and his fellow reformers, hope ended within months of the new Tsar's accession. At first it seemed that Alexander III might continue his father's policies, but behind their backs he gave ear to the conservatism of his former tutor and drafted a manifesto ruling out all hope of reform. When the reformers heard this, they were left with no choice but to resign. For Konstantin the dilemma was personal as well as political, for the new Tsar was 'Sasha with a bear's paws', the nephew he had disliked and humiliated. That distant incident in Poland must have been one of many, and Alexander III made it clear that his uncle would no longer be welcome at Court. He was kind to Alexandra but refused her appeals for clemency for her beloved son Nikolai, certain in his own mind that his cousin could not be trusted either. The surveillance was tightened once again and Nikolai was transferred to Pavlovsk before finally being consigned to internal exile in Tashkent. The new Tsar's obvious dislike of Grand Prince Konstantin and his son was noticed, and the rumour that Konstantin was implicated in his brother's murder spread through the Courts of Europe.

With nothing left to do, the Grand Prince retired to Pavlovsk. His chess problems were published in international journals, but that was no substitute for the position he had once held at the centre of affairs. In 1883 he visited his daughter and her family in Greece, and he looked forward to their visits to Russia: he was fond of the Greek children, and used to amuse them by bellowing at unsuspecting servants. Some became so used to this trick that they hardly reacted, but it delighted him if he could make them jump – an indication of his boredom and increasing bad temper.

Konstantin suffered a slight stroke during the wedding of his granddaughter Alexandra of Greece to his nephew Grand Prince Pavel in the summer of 1889, and a second seizure soon afterwards left him paralyzed in the legs and unable to speak. His attempts to communicate reached the outside world as a series of unintelligible noises. Dependent now, the Grand Prince was cared for by his wife, who gained a sort of revenge for his unfaithfulness. Anna Kousnetsova and her children still lived in the nearby house that Konstantin had provided for them, but Alexandra Iosifovna made sure that his attendants never took him there, and he could not take himself. His grandson Prince Christopher of Greece witnessed the aftermath of one of his attempts to visit: brought home by attendants who knew perfectly well what he wanted but could not obey, the Grand Prince grabbed his wife's hair and beat her with his stick before anyone could intervene. It must have been a miserable situation for them both.

In January 1892 Grand Prince Konstantin Nikolaievich died at Pavlovsk. In later years he had become a figure of mystery, suspected of involvement in all manner of plots that he would never have touched in life, for, although he was a difficult man, and often unpleasant, he had worked tirelessly for his brother and his country. His serious contribution was the one thing few people remembered.

9

This Gloomy Castle

GATCHINA

Alexander III was profoundly affected by the murder of his father, and came to believe that the late Tsar's attempts to reform the government of the country had unleashed the dangerous tide of unrest. Concessions to his opponents would not be the new Tsar's way: he preferred to rule from a position of strength, as his grandfather Nicholas I had done. Years later, exiled Russian liberals would blame Alexander III's change of direction in policy for the Revolution, but there were others who looked back on his rule as a golden age: under Alexander III the country was at peace – with the outside world, if not with itself. Alexander was his own man and a man of paradox; ill at ease in society from his boyhood, yet well able to preside over the most glittering social occasion; a man whose bare hands could bend an iron bar yet still handle the most delicate creations of Fabergé with subtlety and care. He never wanted to be Tsar. At heart he liked nothing better than to roam the countryside with his children, and of all the places in Russia connected with the imperial family, the place that recalls him best is Gatchina, his chosen residence, for Gatchina too is a place of paradox.

'Gatchina is almost visible from this height, Kissing you tenderly, Your Misha.'[1] In September 1913 Grand Prince Mikhail Alexandrovich, the youngest son of Alexander III, stood at the top of the Eiffel Tower and wrote these words on a postcard to the woman he loved. To marry Natalia Sheremetevskaya he had accepted exile, and though there was humour in the message there was also sadness. He longed for Gatchina, where he and Natalia had met and where, as a child, he had followed his father through the snow-laden park. Gatchina was his home, and in five generations of his family few people had had the chance to know and love it quite so well as he did. Some hated Gatchina and others even feared it; for over three hundred years the palace has abounded with contrasts. They say that even the stone changes colour with the changing light.

Contrast was in the mind of Gatchina's creator, Grigori Orlov, one of the lovers of Catherine the Great. He wanted a building whose austere façades would hide a rich interior, and the Tsaritsa found an architect who could bring his ideas to life. The original house was two storeys high, joined by open, semicircular galleries to two identical squares, one on each side, housing the kitchens and the stables. The overall effect came somewhere between a castle and a barracks. Behind the building were two lakes, and the surrounding park was carefully landscaped. When Orlov died the Tsaritsa bought the estate from his heirs and gave it to her son, to celebrate the birth of his first daughter. Grand Prince Paul hated his mother but he welcomed the gift, and his personality became interwoven with the story of Gatchina.

Paul was twenty-nine when he took over the estate. Resenting his exclusion from government, he turned Gatchina into his own small kingdom, developing a Court to rival his mother's and imposing a system of rigid military discipline. He had an army of two thousand men in Prussian-style uniforms and rose at dawn to superintend their drill. People complained that all this was too foreign; they called Gatchina a Russian Potsdam, and over the years Paul's obsessiveness grew. He trusted no one and enforced rigid security, but his influence was not all bad. In the little town of Gatchina, where estate workers and soldiers' families lived, the Grand Prince built a church for Catholic and Lutheran worship and endowed a hospital, a school and an orphanage. He set up factories and workshops, controlled rents, and even tried to provide a kind of poor relief.

Gradually, under Paul's hands, the original house took on grander form. He commissioned the architect Brenna to enclose the semicircular galleries and build an upper floor to each of the service wings, placing a chapel above the kitchens and turning the former stables into living quarters, with a library, a theatre and an armoury.

To this day it is known as the Arsenal, or Armoury, Square. After Paul's accession in 1796, Gatchina gained new importance as an imperial residence and its furnishings were upgraded accordingly, with the addition of throne rooms and works of art from the Hermitage collections. Formal gardens were created, and a huge project began to record every aspect of the palace and its four parks in watercolour. It was a last flowering. In 1801 Paul was assassinated, with the cooperation, some said, of his elder sons, and Gatchina was left to his widow.

For the next forty years history passed Gatchina by. Maria Feodorovna made occasional visits, but she preferred her own palace at Pavlovsk. She tried to interest her elder sons in Gatchina, but they fought shy of anything so intimately concerned with their father. Their mother watched their ways with concern and in the winter of 1810, disapproving of the lives they led in the city, she decided to take her younger sons, Nicholas and Mikhail, to Gatchina to complete their education away from the distractions and temptations of St Petersburg. They were fourteen and twelve years old and they came to hate the palace, associating it with three years of absolute boredom.

Once they were older, though, things changed. Autumn hunting parties at Gatchina drew the family together and Nicholas's wife Alexandra Feodorovna, who at first had found the palace gloomy, wrote of her delight 'in this country house and in the sporting life we led there. We were gay, we were talkative, we were agreeable, each one in his own way, and we parted very pleased with one another.' In the evenings the family gathered for readings from the novels of Sir Walter Scott and Fenimore Cooper. The hall of the Arsenal Square was equipped with a stage for acting and charades, a slide large enough for adults to play on, and other indoor games. Alexandra noticed 'the freedom from stiffness which prevailed there compared to other places. . . . The games made things lively. I there tried for the first time to slide, standing, down a wooden mountain.'[2]

In 1828 the Dowager Tsaritsa died, leaving Gatchina to Nicholas. For twenty-seven years she had carried relics of her murdered husband wherever she went: she left instructions that these things, Paul's uniform and linen, his sword, his stick and the bed he slept in on the night of the murder, should be placed in his rooms at Gatchina. In time this gave a ghoulish fascination to the apartments and corridors of the central block, and people came to believe that Paul had actually died there. But Nicholas I felt only the tenderness of a son, and he decided to preserve his parents' apartments as a family museum. Even the bed where his mother died was moved from the Winter Palace to Gatchina.

If these old apartments were not to be used, new ones would be needed for the imperial family and their suite. Nicholas ordered a complete rebuilding of the squares, though he commissioned a young artist, Konstantin Ukhtomsky, to make paintings of favourite rooms before they disappeared. In future the upper floor of the Kitchen Square would house the suite, staff and guests, as well as the chapel, while the main focus of life at Gatchina shifted to the Arsenal. The imperial couple and the Tsesarevich and Tsarevna would have their apartments on the ground floor, the younger Grand Princes and Princesses and senior ladies of the suite on the floor above, and a low-ceilinged 'entresol' between the two floors was left for the servants. The hall was completely redecorated, and a brightly coloured swingboat joined the collection of games. Works of art from the palace were taken to the Hermitage for cleaning and restoration, and on 1 August 1851 Gatchina reopened with a flourish. At the climax of the celebration Nicholas unveiled a new statue of his father on Palace Square.

Twice a year, in the spring and again in October, the Court descended on Gatchina, and for a few weeks the palace buzzed with life. They came to relax, but the presence of the Tsar guaranteed a constant stream of ministers, ambassadors and officials, and his own family was large and lively. There were games and charades in the Arsenal, musical evenings, carriage drives, picnics and hunts in which, unusually, even the ladies took part. It was all good fun but many members of the suite found Gatchina's charms elusive. The lady-in-waiting Anna Tiutcheva described her reactions to the palace:

I am at Gatchina for the first time and am already finding my bearings, with difficulty, around this vast palace with its endless staircases and corridors. The palace is made up of two huge dwelling blocks joined by a semi-circular building. . . . I live in the right-hand block, and so it falls to me to pass through halls of the central building three or four times a day in order to reach the Arsenal, where it is laid down that all the company will have breakfast, dinner or tea. Often I go through these rooms at night, with only the dim light of a flickering lamp, past Emperor Paul's room and past his throne with its old faded cloth covering. I confess that my heart thumps and my pace quickens, and I am terrified all the time that the sinister figure of Emperor Paul will suddenly emerge from the dark corners. . . .

In the park near the lake a cavern can be seen, closed off with iron railings. They say that this is the exit to underground tunnels which the Emperor had made from his rooms, to give him a chance to escape from assassins. A useless precaution which did not save him from the death which he so feared, and realised, perhaps, that he deserved. All of these recollections make the stay at Gatchina very gloomy and unpleasant. I don't understand why they choose Gatchina when they want to enjoy themselves. . . . The park is vast; in summer it might be beautiful, but now the bare autumnal countryside, with its darkening dry branches and swampy ground covered in puddles presents a melancholy scene.[3]

Clearly someone had been filling Anna's head with horrors, but her first visit had also come at a tense time. Far away in the Crimea enemy forces were closing in around Sevastopol, and there could be no real joy in the games at Gatchina that autumn.

On Nicholas I's death Gatchina passed to his eldest son, on condition that the palace, the park, and all the charitable foundations in the town were maintained. Alexander II added some of his parents' rooms to the family museum and moved the imperial hunt from Peterhof to Gatchina, otherwise things remained as they had been in his father's time. He commissioned a further series of paintings to record the interiors of the palace and the park: the artist Eduard

Petrovitch Hau was given his own rooms in the Kitchen Square and produced a series of fifty-eight paintings in eighteen years.

In 1881 assassination changed Gatchina's fortunes as decisively as it had done eighty years before. After the murder of Alexander II, his son accepted General Loris Melikov's advice to move away from the city and make Gatchina his permanent home. It was all done in a rush; the new Tsaritsa, Maria Feodorovna, told her parents that there had not been time to prepare Gatchina and the rooms were full of workmen. It was midwinter and the palace felt cold and empty and, to make matters worse, in their hurry to leave the city the imperial couple had been forced to leave their younger children behind: the baby, Mikhail, had a chill and had to remain indoors. Maria missed her homely, familiar rooms at the Anichkov and confessed that she had often been reduced to tears. But she added that her husband was glad to go, and that she too was beginning to find her new surroundings comfortable, and to enjoy the unaccustomed peace.[4] Once again Gatchina had become the centre of the Russian empire, guarded as closely as it had been when Tsar Paul held sway. Special passports were needed even to enter the town, where the Blue Cuirassiers and the Combined Regiment, which provided the Tsar's personal bodyguard, had their barracks. In time the soldiers became friends to the imperial family and the Tsar's children liked to sneak out to the barracks to hear the men singing, and perhaps be swung into the air by a pair of strong arms.

Alexander III enforced rigid controls on the country but there the resemblance between him and his great-grandfather Tsar Paul ended. In person Alexander was extremely down to earth, disliking all forms of ceremony. He chose to live in the small, low-ceilinged rooms of the 'entresol'. He rose early, dressed himself and made his own coffee, and settled to work until his wife was ready for breakfast. When there were no guests the family dined together in the ground-floor room that had been his grandmother Tsaritsa Alexandra's bathroom; the bath was filled with azaleas, and in summer the doors could be thrown open to the gardens.

If Gatchina was now the centre of government, it was also a family home. Alexander treasured memories of his childhood; in his study he kept a hidden collection of miniature glass animals and drawings of the make-believe world of 'Mopsopolis', which he and his brother Nikolai had created when the Crimean War was at its height. They were strange treasures for a lumbering, tough man, but Alexander liked nothing better than to share them with his children. He was most at his ease with the youngest members of the family. On one occasion he took his sons on an expedition to the deer park at Gatchina to collect two donkeys to add to their menagerie of pets; over the years they had dogs, a parrot, an albino crow, a tamed hare and a wolf cub.

Olga, the youngest of the children, remembered the special magic of outings with her father and Mikhail, the brother closest to her in age: 'We would set out for the deer park – just the three of us – like the three bears in the fairy tale. My father always carried a big spade, Michael had a smaller one, and I had a tiny one of my own. Each of us also carried a hatchet, a lantern, and an apple. If it was winter he taught us how to clear a tidy path through the snow, and how to fell a dead tree. He taught Michael and me how to build up a fire. Finally we roasted the apples, damped down the fire, and the lanterns helped us find our way home. In the summer he taught us how to distinguish one animal spoor from another. . . . He so wanted us to read the book of nature as easily as he read it himself.'[5] Olga and Mikhail were Gatchina's children and their memories were full of its pleasures. Once they stole out onto the roof at night to see the park by moonlight. Even the ghost of Tsar Paul held no terrors; Olga longed to see him, but she never did.

It was a strange existence, caught between simplicity and splendour. They were country children who slept in camp beds with only the plainest furniture, yet their tutors wore tailcoats. Olga had the grandest rooms in the family because her nurse, Mrs Franklin, thought that the cramped and airless 'entresol' was too unhealthy for a child. Her nursery suite was on the upper floor of the Arsenal, with Biblical tapestries covering the walls. The children played hide-and-seek in the Chinese gallery, where the priceless vases were large enough to conceal a child, and on Sundays Mikhail and Olga were allowed to invite parties of friends to play in the state rooms. Their toys were beyond the dreams of other children; a particular favourite at Gatchina was the miniature electric railway donated by a firm of contractors. 'Its coaches and trucks were exact copies of the real ones, its engines attained a speed of four of five miles an hour; its lines were equipped with stations, tunnels and railway bridges calculated to delight the heart of any child.'[6]

The enchantment ended all too soon. Olga was walking with her father in the park at Gatchina in the spring of 1894 when she realized that he was ill; he died before the year's end. The palace passed to his widow, who ordered that nothing in his rooms, not even his handkerchief, was ever to be moved again. She still used Gatchina, but had never loved country life as Alexander had and preferred to prolong her stays in the city. Her son, Nicholas II, still enjoyed the winter hunts at Gatchina, and he and his wife made frequent visits in the early days when his mother was in residence.

Tensions grew imperceptibly between the Courts of the Dowager Tsaritsa and the young Tsaritsa. A maid-of-honour from Tsarskoe Selo described her first visit to Gatchina with the young Tsaritsa, one evening at the end of 1904. Sophie Buxhoeveden found the atmosphere as oppressive as Anna Tiutcheva had, fifty years before. The drawing room into which she was taken seemed like 'the fancy of a decorator in a deeply depressed mood', and the elderly ladies-in-waiting bombarded her with questions, tutting and sighing over the way things were done in the young Court. She felt increasingly uncomfortable, and upstairs with the Dowager Tsaritsa her mistress fared no better. Alexandra Feodorovna found it almost impossible to breathe in her mother-in-law's stuffy, overheated rooms and was as eager as Sophie to get away.

But the evening had an amusing end: Alexandra thankfully accepted Grand Prince Mikhail's offer of a moonlit ride in his sleigh through the snow-covered park. Just as she and Sophie were beginning to unwind, and to enjoy the enchanted landscape, the sleigh skidded and they both were thrown out. The snow was deep enough to cushion their fall, and after hours of tension the young Tsaritsa simply couldn't stop laughing. '"What <u>would</u> the old ladies say if they heard this?" she gasped. "They must never know about it: they would think it too dreadful for words." I helped her to her feet, and we flicked the snow off each other's capes with our handkerchiefs and got back into the sleigh.'[7]

Gatchina was quieter in these days than it had been, but each Christmas the Dowager Tsaritsa and her younger children held parties in the Banqueting Hall for the officers of the guard. The little gold-wrapped sweets and gifts from the Christmas tree, which the men received from Maria Feodorovna's own hand, were treasured for years in many families. More often, though, it was Mikhail who spent time at the palace. He commanded the Blue Cuirassiers, one of the Gatchina regiments, and first met Natalia at a reception for officers and their wives. Theirs was not the only love story that started within sight of the palace. Mikhail was one of the very few people who knew that in 1903 his sister Olga, who was miserably unhappy in a loveless marriage, met at Gatchina and fell in love with Nikolai Kulikovsky, an officer in his regiment. It was a secret they kept for thirteen years.

Like her brother, Olga continued to love Tsar Paul's 'gloomy castle' and to think of the past. When her indomitable old nurse Mrs Franklin died in the spring of 1913, during Mikhail's years of exile, Olga had her buried in the park at Gatchina, under a favourite tree where she had often sat to watch the children at play.

With the outbreak of war in 1914, Mikhail and Natalia were allowed to return to Russia. Mikhail was often away at the front, but his wife settled in Gatchina town and established a military hospital. She would never be accepted by her husband's family, and had little time for them. Sociable by nature, she continued to hold parties at Gatchina even after the February revolution and Mikhail did not interfere, though he could not share her pleasure. A friend later described one evening when he and Mikhail avoided the company: 'he did not wish any light, though dusk had come early and we faced each other in the twilight. Lying on a couch, shivering from fever, he talked in a sad voice about the difficulty of living among the sorrows, wickedness and deceitfulness of men, and that God was far away. . . . Michael was afraid of the future. I tried to console him, but could not find words equal to the intensity of his grief. Tears choked his voice. It had become quite dark. When I turned on the light I was shocked by the utter despair on the pale face before me and had the distinct feeling that we all stood on the threshold of great misfortune.'[8]

They did, of course, and once more the spotlight of history lurched back towards Gatchina. Nicholas II abdicated in Mikhail's favour and for a few hours the palace was seen as the residence of the last Tsar. Later Kerensky moved into Gatchina Palace in a final attempt to save his failing government. As a Bolshevik mob approached the palace he escaped through the park: some accounts claim that he used the very tunnel which inspired Anna Tiutcheva's gloomy reflections. Mikhail and Natalia stayed in Gatchina town until the spring of 1918, when Mikhail was ordered away to exile and death in Perm. Natalia and her family escaped to the West, and the palace was left to its memories.

Today Gatchina is being restored, after years of neglect. The Revolution caused some damage and valuable items were stolen or vandalized, others were lost in the Soviet art sales of the 1920s, but photographs taken in 1940 show Mikhail's rooms in the Arsenal as cluttered and as full of life as if the owner had just stepped outside and could be expected to return. A few kopecks could buy the visitor access to the state apartments, to the private rooms of Tsar Paul where the ghost used to walk, and to all the family rooms in the Arsenal. It was the Second World War that came close to destroying everything: when the Germans retreated in 1944 they left a burned-out shell, and the treasures that had been saved were taken elsewhere. Gatchina town was in a closed military area until 1977, when the restoration began, using the paintings of Ukhtomsky and Hau as reference. The work is slow but the skill of the restorers is astonishing, and one day the whole palace will live again. Perhaps even the ghosts will return. There were some who hated Gatchina but others belonged there. Exiled in Perm in the spring of 1918 Grand Prince Mikhail wrote; 'it is terrible not to be in our dear Gatchina at this lovely time of the year. I was used to spending the spring there and have so many perfect and delightful memories of my childhood there, and also of the later years. It always seems that only there is it really spring.'[9]

Nannie Fry and Dmitri Mrs Orchard, Mrs Franklin Miss Eagar and Anastasia

10

Far From Home

NURSING THE TSAR'S CHILDREN

The remains of Elizabeth Franklin must still rest somewhere in the park at Gatchina, beside one of the countless trees. It was an unconventional grave, more like the burial place of a pet dog or cat, and very far from home. But Mrs Franklin was not the only English woman who ended her days in Russia after years of loyal service to the imperial family, and other nurses brought up one or two families of Romanov babies before moving on to royal nurseries in different countries. For at least a century the Tsars and Grand Princes and Princesses of Russia grew up speaking English as their first language and learning the habits of the English nursery. It was a situation no one questioned; all over Europe nursery English ruled, along with porridge, mutton, cold baths and bracing fresh air.

English nurses had already reached Russia in the eighteenth century, long before the invention of the railway. They must have been brave and resourceful women to have risked the dangers and discomforts of so long a journey, alone across a continent with no transport but the sailing ship and the horse-drawn carriage. Few nurses even bothered to learn a second language: it was a matter of pride for them to believe that English, spoken firmly and clearly, would always be understood. Their very toughness must have added to their popularity, for a woman who had overcome so many difficulties was unlikely to be daunted by a troublesome toddler. The English were seen as phlegmatic and reliable, safe from unsuitable entanglements and romantic adventures, and in foreign Courts the distinction between the different races of Britain was never understood. Scottish and Irish nurses were considered equally 'English' and therefore desirable.

Grand Prince Nicholas Pavlovich, the future Tsar Nicholas I, had a Scottish nurse, Miss Lyon. 'My beautiful lioness', he called her fondly in later life. She was strict but not so strict as Mrs Kennedy, his brother Mikhail's nurse, whose name might suggest Irish descent; she was renowned for her quick temper.

The formal structure of the imperial nurseries hardly changed through the nineteenth century, though many more people were employed in the early years. A senior lady of the Court had overall charge of each generation of children; her role would have been little more than supervisory. Beneath her came a head nurse, or nursery governess, almost invariably an 'English' woman, and the required number of under-nurses, often English girls in training. Then there were general servants, men and women, and Russian nursery maids, who gave the children an exciting glimpse of the food, music, customs and folk tales of their native regions, and often wore regional dress. Nicholas I wrote a memoir of his childhood at the turn of the nineteenth century: in his generation an establishment like this was employed for every child. He and his brothers and sisters had one nursery governess, two night maids, four chambermaids, an under-nurse, two valets, two footmen, eight domestic servants and eight drivers each – and he believed that his upbringing was like that of any other child.

In Nicholas's day, the imperial children lived for much of the year in a suite of rooms on the first floor of the north-western side of the Winter Palace. When they were tiny and learning to walk, the lower walls and floor were given a temporary padding of cushions, covered in green woollen cloth. The children slept in iron beds, each with its own white curtain, with two horsehair mattresses, and with huge white bolster cushions on either side, presumably to stop them from rolling out. They wore long nightgowns in bed but Nicholas and his brother hated their cotton nightcaps and refused to wear them. Their bedroom had two wood-burning stoves and he complained of the heat. In later years this same room became the study where Alexander II died. It was preserved in grief and respect by his family until the Revolution but had had no sacred associations for Alexander's father: Nicholas remembered how the fine marquetry floor had been damaged by his elder brothers with their rifle butts and spurs. He and his younger brother enjoyed adding to the damage, cheerfully blaming it all on their elders.[1]

Nicholas grew up and married and, as a reaction, perhaps, to the overstaffed nursery of his childhood he and his wife employed fewer attendants for their own children. All seven were cared for by the same English (or, at least, Scottish) head nurse and her subordinates. Her name is not recorded, but she was appointed in time for the birth of the future Alexander II and she nursed each of his sisters and brothers in turn. The children were carefully protected from the splendour of the Court. They wore simple clothes and ate out of plain wooden bowls, and the servants were instructed to call them by Christian name and patronymic in the Russian fashion, never using their formal titles.

An island in one of the lakes beside the Alexander Park at Tsarskoe Selo was set aside as a playground for Nicholas I's children: on the 'Children's Island' they had a cottage where the girls learnt to cook and keep house, a garden tended by all the children, and a fortress for the boys. Visitors were sometimes taken there to watch them at play, and others had informal glimpses of the children within the family circle; this was a deliberate policy pursued by their father. Nicholas I was keen to protect his children from life at Court, but allowing them to be seen by public and visitors alike helped to project an image of happy domesticity within the imperial house. On fine evenings at Tsarskoe Selo crowds would gather to see the Tsar and Tsaritsa and their children amusing themselves in the park. One Saturday evening in September 1836, Lady Londonderry and her husband were invited to dine with the imperial family in the Alexander Palace. After the meal, as she noted in her diary, the Tsar's youngest sons Nikolai and Mikhail, then aged five and four, joined the company 'dressed in the Russian costume – a sort of loose red and gold shirt buttoned up on one side without a collar and with a sash. They seemed very happy, quite at their ease rolling on the floor. Their attendants were all English. An old Scotch nurse made acquaintance with me and spoke of the whole family with enthusiastic affection.' The nurse told the visitors that she had worked for the family for nineteen years and that they relied on her completely, even trusting her with their money and jewels. 'This old lady', Lady Londonderry remarked, 'seemed quite a character.'[2]

The Tsesarevich was eighteen years old at the time of Lady Londonderry's visit, and it would not be long before he married and had children of his own. He and his wife were still very young when Grand Princess Alexandra Alexandrovna was born, and they were likely to have been guided in their choice of nurse by Alexander's mother. They employed a Miss Hughes, who may even have been the old Scottish nurse. A year later a 101-gun salute marked the birth of the Tsesarevich Nikolai, the most important baby in Russia, and he also came under Miss Hughes's care, but she died while he was still in the nursery. A Miss Isherwood nursed the children for a time, but after she too had died in service, 1845 saw the appointment of a woman who would become a permanent fixture at the Russian Court.

On 26 February/10 March 1845, the Tsarevna gave birth to her third child, the future Alexander III. The baby was appointed Colonel-in-Chief of the Astrakhan Carbineers and added to the lists of three regiments of the imperial guard and Miss Kitty Strutton moved into the palace on the day of his birth to nurse him. When the next child, Vladimir, was born in the spring of 1847, his uncle Alexander of Hesse commented that he squawked like a rook, but the sound of another imperial baby must have been music to the nurse's ears for it promised her continuing employment. She cared in turn for each of Alexander's four younger brothers, and for his sister Maria.

The children were raised with the same carefully studied simplicity as the previous generation. When they were small, the boys wore Russian-style tunics like their uncles before them: there is an early portrait of Nikolai, the eldest, in a light Russian blouse with braided edging. But children's fashion, like the culture of their nurseries, was becoming universal. Winterhalter painted the little Prince of Wales in a similar Russian costume several times in the 1840s and in the 1860s Nikolai's youngest brother, Pavel, was photographed in a full-skirted dress of Scottish tartan. The family came to regard Kitty Strutton almost as one of their own. When

Grand Princess Maria married Prince Alfred, the Tsar himself praised her nurse to representatives sent from England for the wedding: the year was 1874 and Kitty, whose first family of charges had long since grown out of the nursery, was living in a little house in Tsarskoe Selo. The imperial family had also given her rooms in the Winter Palace as a reward for her years of service.

But what had she done in the meantime? Grand Prince Pavel would have been too old for a nurse by about 1865, twenty years after Miss Strutton's arrival in Russia. She may have reached retiring age by then, but if not, a new generation of imperial babies was about to appear and they too would need nurses. In 1866 the Tsesarevich Alexander, Kitty's first Romanov baby, was married, and his eldest son, the future Nicholas II, was born in the Alexander Palace at Tsarskoe Selo two years later. 'The birth of children is the most joyful moment in one's life', the Tsesarevich told his former tutor, 'and it is impossible to describe it because it is a very special feeling, unlike any other.'[3] Like his father and uncle, Alexander was closely involved in the business of childbirth and both he and the Tsar held the Tsarevna during the birth. The new-born baby must have had a nurse, and it might have been Kitty Strutton. She was certainly in the right place at the right time, and in later years Nicholas knew her well.

The Tsesarevich's philosophy on child-rearing was simple: the children were to pray hard, work hard, play and have fun. Mischief and squabbling were normal, and the only crimes in the nursery were to be idleness and tale-bearing. In 1875, when Nicholas was seven, his education was taken over by a governess, Alexandra Ollongren, but the same year his mother gave birth to her first daughter, so the household still needed a nurse. By coincidence, also in 1875, Kitty Strutton's second charge, Vladimir, wanted a nurse for his first child and, being unable to take the position herself, Kitty brought her niece, Millicent Crofts, to Russia.

Miss Crofts went on to look after five children, one of whom died in infancy, in the sumptuous nurseries of the newly built Vladimir Palace. The setting later amazed another Englishwoman, Kate Fox, who visited Russia with the next generation of children: 'Everything is exquisite', she wrote. 'My nurseries consist of eight beautifully furnished rooms; dining-room, two saloon ante-rooms, night nursery, dressing-room, bathroom and so on . . . there must be a regular army of servants here.'[4] But behind the splendour, Miss Crofts' life cannot have been easy. In the spring of 1886 the painter Henry Thaddeus Jones spent some time with the Vladimirs in Cannes, and was asked to paint the couple's only daughter Elena, then a child of four. He noticed that she was not in the best of moods, 'evidently nurturing some grievance against the nurse. Whilst peacefully painting I tried to pacify her, when suddenly she seized a large paper-knife from a table near and made a lunge at the nurse, who, retreating before the onslaught, took refuge behind me. The little lady then transferred her attention to me, her black eyes ablaze with fury. Before I realised her intention, over went the picture and easel, and, quite unprepared for the impetuous charge, I nearly went over myself as well. I caught her up, she still furiously stabbing, took the paper knife from her chubby little fist, and eventually restored peace. It was, however, a revelation of passion in one so young.'[5] Elena probably needed to be a tough little character as she had three elder brothers: on one occasion they hoisted her up a pole like a human flag. But when their childhood was over the eldest boy, Kyrill, remembered Miss Crofts with great affection: 'Milly was with us from our earliest days, and it was through her that the first language we talked was English. I remember her singing nursery rhymes to us; later she introduced us to the works of English literature, the first of which were Barnaby Rudge and Oliver Twist.'[6]

It is hard to believe now that young members of the ruling family of Russia learned English as their first language without a word of complaint from their parents, but the same was true of young Germans, Greeks, Belgians, and well-to-do children from across Europe: from the Balkans to the Atlantic nursery English ruled, along with the strict régime that English nurses favoured. Children were drawn into an international culture, only seeing their own country and its customs through the eyes of the nursery maids and servants. Kyrill's cousin, Grand Princess Marie Pavlovna, remembered how her own nurses, Nannie Fry and Lizzie Grove, 'brought to Russia all the habits of their native country; they ruled the nursery according to their own ideas and principles, and enjoyed an absolute sovereignty not only over my brother and me but over an innumerable retinue of Russian chambermaids, valets and assistant nurses. Until I was six years old I hardly spoke a word of Russian.'[7]

Despite their prejudices and limitations the nurses were loved, and deservedly so, because a good nurse could make the difference between life and death – quite literally – for the children in her care. The brother mentioned by Grand Princess Marie, Dmitri Pavlovich, was born prematurely in 1891. The midwife thought that he was dead, or dying, and he was put aside on a chair in a heap of discarded blankets while everyone attended to his mother: it was only the nurse, Nannie Fry, who noticed that, tiny and feeble though he was, Dmitri could be saved.

Kitty Strutton died in her rooms in the Winter Palace on Alexander III's birthday in 1891, forty-six years to the day since she had first taken him into her arms. She was buried in St Petersburg, and the Tsaritsa sent her son Nicholas an account of the funeral: 'The dear old soul was lying in her open coffin, looking so calm and beautiful. The clergyman said a few prayers and then they closed the coffin and bore her away from the palace where she had spent forty-six years. Only ourselves and her nephews and nieces attended – all was very simple and moving. Papa and the uncles followed the coffin on foot and we in carriages, to the English Church where a very beautiful service was held. Papa and his brothers then accompanied her to the cemetery. . . .'[8] There could be no more eloquent tribute to the power of a good nurse than this; that Tsar Alexander III and his four brothers, five of the grandest and most powerful princes in the world, walked through the city streets behind the coffin of an ordinary English woman because she had cared for them in childhood.

Many royal children became closer to their nurse than they could ever be to their mother. Grand Princess Olga Alexandrovna, Alexander III and Maria Feodorovna's youngest child, was a delicate baby, born after Miss Strutton's retirement, and her aunt, then Princess of Wales, advised her mother to employ another English nurse. This was the need that brought Elizabeth Franklin into the family. She was 'capable, courageous, tactful', as her charge remembered, and she stayed in Russia long after Olga had outgrown the nursery.[9] When Olga was in her late teens, her mother decided to replace Mrs Franklin with a lady-in-waiting. She could hardly have anticipated the reaction; Olga was horrified. 'What shall I do without Nana? If you send her away I will run away myself. I will elope with a palace sweep. I will go and peel potatoes in someone's kitchen, or offer myself as a kennelmaid.' The Tsaritsa gave way, with bad grace, and Mrs Franklin stayed with Olga until her death. To Maria Feodorovna she was always 'that odious woman'.[10]

Mrs Franklin found an ally in another long-serving and devoted nurse. Mary Anne Orchard arrived in Russia in 1894 with her 'baby', Princess Alix of Hesse, who was twenty-two years old and engaged to the Tsesarevich Nicholas. Mrs Orchard had been chosen as nurse to the Hesse family by Queen Victoria almost thirty years before and Princess Alice, the children's mother, was delighted. 'I can't praise Orchard enough', she told the Queen. 'Such order she keeps, and is so industrious and tidy, besides understanding so much about the management of the children's health and characters.'[11] To Alix, who lost her mother when she was six, 'Orchie' was like a second mother. The two old nurses soon became firm friends, having little to do but exchange stories over the teacups.

But Mrs Orchard's working life was not over. When Alix's first child was born it seemed natural that her old nurse should supervise the nursery, with an assistant to do the physical work. The arrangement proved to be a disaster. Mrs Orchard had become set in her ways and she argued endlessly with the nursery staff. She expected everyone, even the Tsar, to do as they were told and simply refused to see the Tsaritsa as a grown woman. No nurse would work under her for long and the nursery was plagued by a succession of horrors. Baby Olga was five weeks old when the first nurse arrived from England and made a terrible impression from the start. She had been at the palace a day when the Tsar told his brother, 'she has something hard and unpleasant in her face and looks like a stubborn woman. In general she's going to be a lot of trouble and I am ready to bet that things are not going to go smoothly. For instance, she has already decided that our daughter does not have enough rooms, and that, in her opinion, Alix pops into the nursery too often. How do you like that?'[12] He envied the excellent English nurse employed by his sister Ksenia and her husband, and was delighted when his daughter's nurse left after only four months. But the nursery gremlins did not leave with her. One of her successors was found in bed with a Cossack and dismissed on the spot, and when Nicholas and Alexandra visited Balmoral in 1896, Alexandra's main topic of conversation was her problems with nurses.

It was an English relative who found the answer in Margaretta Eagar, who was appointed late in 1898. She arrived in St Petersburg in February 1899, speaking not a word of Russian and clutching a sealed bag from the Embassy in Berlin, which she had been asked to deliver into the hands of a courier. Unable to understand what was being said to her, she refused to part with the bag even for a second, but the rest of her luggage was minutely examined at the Russian border for sixpence a trunk – even the linings of her shoes and gloves were removed. After this awkward beginning, Miss Eagar established herself quickly and the nursery settled to an unaccustomed peace. 'It is real paradise', the Tsar commented to his mother, 'in comparison with the dismal past.'[13]

Miss Eagar was not English but Irish. A lively, intelligent woman with an opinion on everything, she took great interest in her surroundings. With the Tsaritsa's agreement she began to write short articles for magazines at home describing aspects of life in Russia. The two women understood one another well, and Miss Eagar was given a controlling hand in the nursery. There were two children when she arrived, three-year-old Olga and baby Tatiana, and Miss Eagar saw the family grow and the nurseries expand to make room for them. The under-nurses deferred to her in everything: they would even tell her if a man showed interest in them, so that she could make enquiries and find out if he was suitable. There would be no uninvited Cossacks in her nursery. But though Miss Eagar had taken charge of the children, Mrs Orchard was still on the scene, and despite all that had happened the Tsaritsa would not part with her old nurse. Mrs Orchard lived and travelled with the family. At Livadia in 1900 the Tsar almost died of typhoid and Mrs Orchard helped to nurse him, and to support 'her baby' through the ordeal. 'Orchie would wash his face and hands in the morning', Alix wrote, 'and bring my meals in always.'[14] In later years the old lady's mind failed, and the Tsaritsa cared for her until she died. Her room in the Alexander Palace was preserved exactly as she left it, and was known as 'Orchie's room' until the Revolution.

Miss Eagar's appointment ended after six years. The Tsar, who had liked her so much at first, suddenly became determined to see her go. In October 1904, three weeks after the infant Tsesarevich's haemophilia first became apparent, Nicholas noted in his diary that 'after many weeks of wavering Alix, strongly supported by myself and Princess Golitsina, at last decided to dismiss the Englishwoman, the children's nurse Miss Eagar'.[15] All sorts of explanations have been given for this change of heart. It is sometimes said that the children were speaking English with broad Irish accents, or that it was not thought proper for the baby Tsesarevich to be raised by a foreign nurse. The discovery of the baby's haemophilia may have had something to do with the dismissal, but the children's aunt believed that Miss Eagar was more interested in politics than she was in her job. It was whispered abroad that Miss Eagar had been dismissed for spying, and the nurse reacted angrily to this. She sent a letter to *The Times*: 'so far from being ignominiously dismissed', she wrote, 'I received from the Empress a handsome money present, and a pension for life was settled upon me. At Christmas I was the recipient of letters, cards and gifts from the Empress and the Imperial children.'[16] Whatever the truth, Miss Eagar remained fiercely loyal to the Tsaritsa and wrote an interesting account of her years in Russia.

Times were changing and little Alexei was unusual among his contemporaries, both in and outside Russia, in that he was nursed exclusively by his own nationals. He was eight years old before he really spoke English. Outside his nursery English nurses still held sway and the accounts of Russians fortunate enough to escape the Revolution include many tributes to the loyalty and courage of these women. But perhaps Alexei's upbringing signalled the beginning of a wider change, and it is hard now to realise how hopeful that beginning seemed. Miss Eagar was still in service at the time of his birth. She attended the christening and wrote: 'He is a very beautiful boy. In the middle of the baptismal ceremony, when he was being anointed for the first time, he raised his hand and extended his fingers as though pronouncing a blessing. Of course, everyone said that it was a very good omen, and that he would prove to be a father to his people. God grant it, but not for many years to come. . . .'[17]

11

Behind the Empress

GRAND PRINCESS VLADIMIR

At the start of the nineteenth century, Russia was not used to having a royal family. Paul was the first Tsar since the 1600s to father a large family of children, and it was he who laid down the Family Statutes that defined the order of succession, the religion and marriages of his descendants – and caused endless heartache for them. The Decembrist Rising gave the Statutes their first severe test: after this experience of uncertainty over the succession, Nicholas I was determined to bind his children together as a disciplined unit, in service to the Crown. One by one as they came of age, his sons were called on to take the Oath of Allegiance, announcing their loyalty to the Tsar before representatives of the government, the church and the army – and they meant it. Nicholas created a unified family by imposing his authority. Alexander II strengthened the bonds between himself and his brothers by instituting regular family meetings, which gradually drew a new generation into the 'firm'. He also made a point of befriending his brothers' sons. But the women who married into the family were much harder to bind: Alexander's affair and second marriage alienated them all and there is no telling how relationships within the family would have developed if his death had not followed so closely upon the wedding. But that death itself brought a more important change. For the first time, there was an older generation of Romanov princes, bound by oath to obey and look up to a younger nephew. Alexander III's reign saw the cracks begin to open in the unity his grandfather had forged. His own treatment of Grand Prince Konstantin Nikolaievich showed an unwillingness to trust his uncles, and more damaging, in the long term, was the question mark that hung over his relationship with his brother Vladimir. Vladimir was clever and ambitious, said by some to have been his father's favourite. Even in childhood there had been a sense in the family that Vladimir was destined for something special: the potential for jealousy and resentment was always there, but it flowered when Vladimir married a princess whose ambition matched his own. In a somewhat breathless recollection of the

118

*Court at St Petersburg, Marie of Romania captured the glamour which made her
aunt 'Miechen', Grand Princess Vladimir, unforgettable:*

*Close behind the Empress stands Aunt Miechen. More gorgeous than the sunset
is her gold-embroidered orange gown. Each time she moves the pear-shaped pearls
of her diadem sway gently backwards and forwards. She is not thin enough for
classical lines but she wears her clothes better than any woman present; her
shoulders are superb and as white as cream; there is a smartness about her that no
one else can attain.[1]*

*The most telling words in this description are 'behind the Empress'. It was a
position the Princess held and resented for most of her adult life. Some people
seem born to fill a wider stage than fate allows them; when they sense this
limitation themselves, the results can be disastrous. Grand Princess Vladimir was
one of those people. Strong-willed, intelligent and imperious, she would have
made an outstanding empress.
She was never cut out to be the wife of a younger son.*

'Miechen' began life as Duchess Marie of Mecklenburg-Schwerin, in the spring of 1854. She was born at Ludwigslust, a country residence to the south of the grand-ducal capital. The duchy was a quiet, rural place on the north German coast; in later years Marie's half-sister-in-law, Queen Wilhelmina of the Netherlands, described it as 'thinly populated, rich in hills and lakes, cornfields and forests'.[2] The Mecklenburg-Schwerin Wilhelmina knew was hostile to its Prussian neighbour, but in Marie's childhood Prussian influence dominated. Small wonder, when the real power in Schwerin was the formidable Dowager Grand Duchess Alexandrine, whose brother was the Prussian King. Alexandrine ruled her son, Grand Duke Friedrich Franz II, and provided stability for her granddaughter, whose childhood was rocked by a series of tragedies. In many ways they were alike. Alexandrine was a proud woman, blessed with absolute confidence in the rightness of her own views. She could be charming, but to anyone who crossed her, she was vicious.

Marie was the Grand Duke's first daughter; he and his wife, Auguste Reuss Köstritz, had two elder sons, Friedrich Franz and Paul Friedrich, and two more boys were born after Marie, one of whom died in infancy. Marie lost her mother when she was only seven. Gossip said that the Grand Duke got over his grief remarkably quickly, and soon he was looking for a new wife. It seemed as if his children might have Princess Mary of Cambridge, later the Duchess of Teck, as a stepmother, but the moment passed, and in May 1864, two days before his daughter's tenth birthday, the Grand Duke married Princess Anna of Hesse-Darmstadt, Tsaritsa Maria Alexandrovna's niece.

Like Marie, Anna was the only girl from a household of boys. They adored her, but she had little chance to make an impact on her new family. She died in childbirth eleven months after the wedding, and four more years would pass before the Grand Duke found another mother for his children. These were eventful years for Germany. While many of the German princes supported Prussia with great reluctance in the Austro-Prussian war of 1866, or refused to support her at all, Friedrich Franz was eager to see Germany united under Prussian rule. This was resented by his neighbours, but being on the winning side preserved his duchy and gave his family new confidence and a new standing. In the summer of 1868 he married for a third time, choosing Princess Marie of Schwarzburg-Rudolstadt, who was only four years older than his daughter.

The new Grand Duchess was kind and easy-going. Lacking both the pride and the self esteem of her mother-in-law, her tastes were simple, and she made few rules for her household. There is no evidence of her feelings for her stepchildren or theirs for her, but her coming into the family almost decided Marie's future. Early in 1871 the Crown Princess of Prussia visited Schwerin and noticed interesting negotiations in progress between the Mecklenburg and Schwarzburg families. She wrote to Queen Victoria on 27 May: 'Marie of Schwerin you have no doubt heard – is engaged to that stupid George Schwarzburg. . . . it is officially announced – it was her own doing, he is a greater goose than ever.'[3] The 'great goose' was the reigning Prince of Schwarzburg-Rudolstadt, a second cousin of Marie's stepmother. He was thirty-three and Marie barely seventeen.

The events of the next few years made Marie a talking point all over Europe. It was her own idea to marry George of Schwarzburg, but within weeks she broke off the engagement because a better prospect had come into view. Grand Prince Vladimir Alexandrovich, the Tsar's third son, was twenty-four; cultured, intelligent and very wealthy indeed. Too keen a taste for the finer things in life had done Vladimir's waistline no favours, but he was attractive still, and in June he visited Germany with the rest of his family. Marie was impressed: poor George of Schwarzburg would remain single for the rest of his life.

The Dowager Grand Duchess may have played some part in this: if the Crown Princess was right, George was not much of a catch. Alexandrine was ambitious for her family and fiercely pro-Russian, and she was also Vladimir's great-aunt, his grandmother's sister. But breaking the engagement was a dangerous move. It became common knowledge that Marie wanted Vladimir, yet the months passed without an announcement.

As the year turned, the young Duchess was once more considered 'available'. In January 1872 Queen Victoria found this idea worrying as her favourite son, Prince Arthur, was about to set out on a visit to Germany to meet suitable princesses. Was he safe? The Queen gave his governor very clear instructions: Marie, she told him, was 'said to be vy pretty but a <u>gt. coquette</u> – who has thrown over <u>one</u> Pce. she was engaged to – for one of the Russian Gd. Dukes, and who might vy possibly <u>try</u> to catch Pce. Arthur. <u>She must not</u> be <u>thought of</u>.'[4] Spring came, and then summer; still there was no engagement with Vladimir, though he was as keen to marry as Marie was. In November Princess Alice told the Queen why: 'the Empress of Russia has just written that the engagement with Marie of Mecklenburg is quite impossible, because she will not change her religion. I hope that all other German princesses will follow her example.'[5]

The assertiveness which marked Marie out in later life was already being felt. She had thrown over the chance to be a reigning princess, albeit a minor one, to win Vladimir, but would accept him only on her own terms. She held out for almost two years: 1873 came and went and a settlement seemed as far away as ever, but as spring returned the walls finally tumbled. Alexander II wrote to Grand Duke Friedrich Franz giving permission for Marie to marry his son. In a relaxation of the Romanov Family Statutes he said that she could keep her Lutheran faith and Vladimir would not lose his right to the throne. (This is contested by some members of the Romanov family today, who were told by their elders that Vladimir signed a secret renunciation which was kept under the altar at Tsarskoe Selo: so far no evidence has emerged to support the story.) The engagement, announced in April 1874, was welcomed all over Germany as a victory. Queen Victoria's elder daughters agreed, but they sounded a note of caution. Alice had discussed the matter with Vladimir's mother and was sure that the Tsaritsa had given way to the engagement against her wishes. The Crown Princess predicted conflict. 'I do not think the marriage of Marie of Schwerin & Vladimir promises to be a happy one,' she wrote, 'and being of another religion in so bigotted a country will no doubt make it difficult for her to get on.'[6]

Even the Tsar may have had misgivings. His decision was not popular with his family or in society; no one was willing to see their cherished customs overturned by a young foreigner. Vladimir and Marie were married in the Winter Palace that August, and it was probably no accident that the ceremony took place at the height of summer. 'At this season of the year', the British Ambassador, Lord Augustus Loftus, reported, 'this town is a desert and therefore only those came who were obliged to come.' Seven months earlier Vladimir's sister had married and Lord Augustus compared the two weddings rather unfavourably; even the Protestant service, for which Marie had fought so hard, 'fell very dull after the magnificent Russian service. Fortunately it was <u>short</u>.'

But the Ambassador was full of admiration for the new member of the imperial family. 'The young Grand Duchess is a superior person, not actually pretty but very intellectual and with a graceful and dignified deportment. At the Te Deum on the Emperor's Birthday she stood erect when the others were genuflecting and crossing themselves. It is a matter of surprise here for a Foreign Princess married to a Grand Duke to retain her own religion but it is a process to which they will have to accustom themselves or they will find no wives for the Russian Grand Dukes. I think it a healthy practice and it will do them good.'[7]

Marie had gone to St Petersburg determined to meet hostility head on. There was a note of defiance even in the patronymic she chose: 'Pavlovna' recalled not only her grandfather, Grand Duke Paul Friedrich of Mecklenburg-Schwerin, but *his* grandfather, Tsar Paul of Russia. The name was a constant reminder that Marie was a direct descendant of Russia's most powerful sovereigns; she considered herself the equal of her husband's family and enjoyed saying that she was more truly Slav than they were, because of her own family's Slavonic origin. According to her friend Prince von Bülow, she even found fun in the old story that her husband and his brothers and sisters were really the grandchildren of a Hesse court official, and therefore only three-quarters royal.[8]

The marriage itself, though, had been worth fighting for. As a single man Vladimir was a notorious playboy, but he and Marie were ideally suited and no breath of scandal ever touched their relationship. They were happy, and Marie adopted her husband's wealthy lifestyle with relish: Vladimir was the first Grand Prince ever to take his wife straight into a purpose-built palace. On the Neva embankment, the most prestigious site in St Petersburg, the Vladimir Palace was a luxurious new building with the latest equipment and fittings, decorated in the grand manner. Within weeks Marie had ordered elaborate new scarlet summer uniforms for the servants.

Christmas found the young couple at Tsarskoe Selo, where they stayed for a while before returning to the city for the round of parties that filled the year until Lent. Marie was in the early stages of her first pregnancy, and in July her grandmother made the journey to St Petersburg. The baby, a boy, was safely delivered at Tsarskoe Selo at the end of August, and was given the name Alexander for his grandfather the Tsar. While many in the family remained cold to Marie, Alexander II treated her with unfailing kindness, and this was something she would never forget.

In October 1876 she gave birth to a second son, Kyrill, but tragedy followed the turn of the year: little Alexander died in March 1877. In silent sympathy the Tsar made Marie head of the 37th Regiment of Infantry, as a mark of his favour. She was an accomplished rider and enjoyed the chance to participate in troop reviews with her husband. Before the year was over, they had a third son and two years later, a fourth. Their only daughter was born in 1882. Kyrill, Boris, Andrei and Elena were attractive children and their parents were fiercely proud of them. They took them to Schwerin every second or third year; Kyrill remembered one occasion when Grand Duchess Alexandrine put on full evening dress complete with orders to attend nursery dinner, treating him and his brothers and sister like visiting monarchs. Marie strengthened the ties between her two families by introducing her elder brother Friedrich Franz to Vladimir's cousin Anastasia Mikhailovna; they married in 1879.

She must have felt isolated in Russia at times, but it was not in her nature to let it show. Instead she threw lavish and expensive parties, and found friends among the diplomatic community and other foreigners living in the city. She was the first lady of the imperial family to welcome divorced people into her salon; the *nouveau riche*, the fashionable, and the actors, artists and writers whom Vladimir encountered in his capacity as President of the Imperial Academy of Art all found a ready welcome at her table, where the conversation was witty and amusing, and often had a spiteful edge.

Within the imperial family, Marie adopted her husband's resentments and made them her own; no one could ever accuse her of being a peacemaker. Vladimir envied his elder brother for being Tsesarevich and having the prospect of power. Shadows of this ran right back into their childhood. In March 1855, a few weeks after her husband's accession, Maria Alexandrovna told one of her ladies-in-waiting about a worrying conversation she had had with her children. She overheard the Tsesarevich Nikolai say to five-year-old Vladimir, 'When you are Tsar . . .'. She interrupted him, 'You know perfectly well that Vladimir will never be Tsar.' 'No, he will,' Nikolai replied, 'his name means "ruler of the world".' His mother explained that the succession was about order of birth, not about names, but Nikolai would not give way: 'Grandfather was a third son, and he became Tsar. I will die, then Sasha will be Tsar. But Sasha will die too, then Vladimir will take over.'

This was just children's talk but the Tsaritsa found it chilling to hear the words spoken by one so young.[9] The idea took a more adult form when Nikolai did die and Alexander became Tsesarevich in his place. He had come within a hair's breadth of renouncing his claim to the throne in order to marry Marie Mescherskaya: if he had followed his heart, Vladimir would have taken his place as Tsesarevich and, after that, as Tsar. Vladimir might well have resented his ill-luck, and his gradual slide down the order of succession as Alexander produced sons would not have made the disappointment easier to bear. So there was a perceptible crack in the relationship between the brothers, and when Marie joined in the crack became a chasm. Alexander's wife, Maria Feodorovna, was the only other young woman in the Tsar's immediate family since his daughter had left Russia. She was six years older than Marie, well established and popular, and she did not like Germans. Before long the two young women, the second and third ladies in the country, were beginning to be seen as rivals.

While Alexander II lived all rivalries were held in check, but unease between the brothers was brought to the surface by the assassination: as the Tsar lay dying in his study, it was Vladimir who took command and gave orders, for in the immediate aftermath of the tragedy the Tsesarevich seemed stunned. Throughout their boyhood Vladimir had dominated Alexander and perhaps he thought this domination might continue. He was mistaken. As Alexander III assumed power and the dust settled, it became clear that things had changed forever.

The new Tsar imposed his will on the family by introducing a series of changes to the Family Statutes to redefine their rights, their titles and even their incomes. There was sense in this and many supported him. Vladimir did not. Alexander demanded loyalty and got it – in words at least – but a brother is less easy to obey than a father. On the day of Alexander's accession Vladimir was made commander of military forces in the St Petersburg area, though he had no particular love for the army. Without open dissent on his part, the uncomfortable relationship between the second couple in Russia and the first soon became obvious.

Ultimately the rift would contribute to the dynasty's fall, but in the 1880s it was simply an amusement for Court gossips. In 1888 the imperial train crashed at Borki, and the Tsar and his three sons narrowly escaped death. As Alexander climbed from the wreckage he is supposed to have said 'imagine Vladimir's disappointment'.[10] A year later a scandal erupted over the disappearance of funds collected by public subscription to build a church in memory of Alexander II. For five years Vladimir had presided over the official commission that supervised the building, and he was suspected of complicity in the loss. People pointed at expensive redecorations underway in the Vladimir Palace and whispered. Over his brother's head, Alexander III ordered an enquiry which found the commission's secretary guilty of embezzlement, despite Vladimir's attempts to protect him. From the sidelines Maria Feodorovna and Marie Pavlovna egged their husbands on, and shared their sense of outrage.

Their differences were not political. Vladimir was no closer to his father's politics than Alexander, and Marie was certainly no liberal. It was more a matter of style and temper. The imperial family, Russia's oldest aristocratic families, and all those with a tradition of service at Court gravitated towards Alexander III and Maria Feodorovna. The Vladimirs were more daring and more fashionable. On visits to Paris and the Riviera, Marie had developed a taste for gambling, and she had a roulette wheel fitted in her private rooms. Her parties were fabulous, involving vast expenditure and long preparation. For one celebrated costume ball in the 1880s she ordered source books from the Art Academy Library months ahead, and expected her guests to dress in authentic old boyar costumes. She hated walking, but was an enthusiastic and graceful dancer, and needed always to be at the centre of things. While people were admiring her, she was happy. When she could take a younger, humbler, or less experienced person under her wing and guide them, she was kindness itself. Grand Princess Olga Konstantinovna's younger daughter Princess Marie of Greece, who first visited Russia as a child in the 1880s, remembered her as having 'the greatest charm any woman ever possessed'.[11]

Critics said that Marie cared only for pleasure, but no one had offered an outlet for the serious side of her nature. Her correspondence with diplomats and politicians from all over Europe only led her into further trouble. Alexander III shared his wife's dislike of Germany, while the Vladimirs were seen as pro-German. When the secret police discovered that Marie wrote to Bismarck, the Tsar was furious and ordered her to stop. Vladimir was outraged on her behalf, but the suspicion that she was disloyal, perhaps a German agent, would cling for many years, and it was not only the Russians who believed it. In 1884 her second cousin Wilhelm of Prussia, the future Kaiser Wilhelm II, visited St Petersburg and reported to his grandfather; 'the Grand Duchess Vladimir . . . works magnificently for the German cause'.[12]

After ten years, Marie was still seen as an outsider. She appeared to enjoy opposition and return it in full measure, but there is one hint that her isolation really hurt. Not even Vladimir could share her religion. She attended the Protestant church in St Petersburg defiantly, on her own, but 1884 brought her two potential allies. Elisabeth of Saxe-Altenburg and Elisabeth, 'Ella', of Hesse-Darmstadt both married into the Romanov family that year, and both refused to convert.

It must have meant a great deal to Marie to welcome these two, and to feel that they were following her lead. Ella was closest to the Vladimirs; she was a niece of Marie's short-lived stepmother Anna, and a great-niece of Maria Alexandrovna, and she had known Marie and Vladimir all her life. She may have remembered how strongly her own mother, Princess Alice, had defended Marie in her refusal to convert. But Ella was deeply attracted to the Orthodox Church. In 1891 she decided to convert after all, and was particularly worried about Marie's feelings. She appealed to her father to keep the news to himself until she had told her, for 'I am afraid she will feel it very much, but I wish her to know it before there is a chance of its being talked about, so as to hurt her as little as possible.' Marie was hurt, though, and felt betrayed; she never forgave Ella.[13]

It was rare for the Grand Princess to appear this vulnerable. The wilful teenager who toyed with poor George of Schwarzburg had become one of the most dynamic and interesting players on the royal stage, with contacts all over Europe. As Russia's second lady she stood behind the Tsaritsa on official occasions, and her Court was the fashionable place to be. But by the 1890s change was in the air. The Tsar's three sons, Nicholas, Georgi and Mikhail, were growing up, and in the natural course of events they were likely to marry. When they did, Marie must lose her pre-eminence, becoming the third lady, and then the fourth, and the fifth, as younger women came into the family. It would be the most painful adjustment she had ever had to face.

Unless. . . . Maria Feodorovna was a possessive mother who would not enjoy sharing her sons when the day came for them to marry. If, in the future, Marie could draw the Tsesarevich Nicholas's wife into her own circle, guiding her first steps in Russian society, she might one day give the words 'behind the empress' a whole new meaning.

12

Think of Coburg

THE ENGAGEMENT OF THE SECOND NICHOLAS AND ALEXANDRA

The Tsesarevich Nicholas came of age on 6/18 May 1884, his sixteenth birthday, and swore the Oath of Allegiance in solemn grandeur at the Winter Palace. 'The Czarevich wore the blue Cossack uniform of the Guard, as Hetman of all the Cossacks', The Graphic reported. 'He looked very young and small to be the principal personage in such a ceremony, but he has a bright, intelligent face, and is very like his mother. Most of the members of the Romanoff family being tall and stalwart, his short stature appears exceptional. In the church he boldly walked up alone to the altar, and, holding up his right hand over the bejewelled Bible and golden cross, repeated audibly and firmly, after the priest, the form of oath, beginning: "In the name of the Almighty and upon His Holy Word, I swear and promise to serve well and truly His Imperial Majesty, my all-gracious parent," and ending "My heart be in Thy hands, Lord. Amen!"'

Just a few weeks after the ceremony, Nicholas met the girl he would marry. Princess Alix of Hesse was twelve years old, and visited Russia for her sister Elisabeth's wedding to Nicholas's uncle, Grand Prince Sergei Alexandrovich. She and Nicholas were attracted to one another, and the childish attachment blossomed on a later visit, in 1889, when the Tsesarevich set his heart on marriage to Alix and discussed his hopes with his father. His mother would have preferred to see him married to a French princess but he would not hear of it. Seeing his determination, both parents agreed and, as the months and years went by, only one obstacle to the marriage remained.

In the spring of 1894 came the critical moment when the couple's future had to be decided, one way or another.

The year 1894 began quietly for the imperial family, with no hint of the changes that lay ahead. Alexander III was ill but no one worried unduly, and the New Year celebrations continued as usual. The Tsesarevich went drinking with his uncle Vladimir one evening in January, and a few weeks later enjoyed one of Marie Pavlovna's famous all night parties. The Vladimirs may have known of their nephew's private unhappiness; for nearly five years he had tried to persuade Alix of Hesse to marry him but she could not face conversion to Orthodoxy. For Nicholas's wife, a future Tsaritsa, there could never be the leniency Alexander II had allowed Marie Pavlovna – a Tsaritsa had to be Orthodox. Nicholas knew that Alix loved him, but she had promised her father that she would never convert and his death, in the spring of 1892, had removed all possibility of discussion or change. For her the whole issue raised a tangle of painful emotions which she preferred to avoid altogether. In June 1893 she stayed away from their cousin the Duke of York's wedding in England because she knew that Nicholas would be there. In November she sent Nicholas her final refusal, but he was not ready to give up and pinned all his hopes on a personal meeting. Alix's brother was due to marry in Coburg in April 1894, and the wedding was one event she could not miss.

As the wedding day drew near, all Coburg was in a festive mood. The streets were bright with flags, bunting, and garlands of flowers, and two triumphal arches were erected on the route from the station to the Schloss Platz, as the little town prepared to play host to a family party on a grand scale. The wedding of Duke Alfred of Saxe-Coburg-Gotha's second daughter, Victoria Melita, to her cousin, the young Grand Duke Ernst Ludwig of Hesse, was to draw together royal cousins, uncles and aunts from across Europe.

From Darmstadt came the bridegroom with his uncle, Wilhelm of Hesse, and Alix herself: their three married sisters, Victoria, Elisabeth and Irene, would join them in Coburg with their husbands, who were all related to the bridal couple by blood as well as by marriage. Kaiser Wilhelm II was expected from Berlin, as were his mother, Kaiserin Friedrich, his sister Charlotte and her husband Bernhard of Saxe-Meiningen (whose daughter Feodora was to be one of the bridesmaids), his brother Heinrich, the husband of Irene of Hesse, his cousin Marie Louise and her husband Aribert of

Anhalt. Most of the guests were to stay at Schloss Ehrenburg, the town's main palace, where the wedding itself would take place.

On 16 April the Russian party arrived at Coburg. The bride's mother was Grand Princess Maria Alexandrovna, Alexander II's daughter; that in itself would have ensured a large turnout of Romanovs among the guests. Officially the visiting party consisted of Vladimir and Marie, Vladimir's two youngest brothers, Sergei and Pavel, and Elisabeth. The Tsesarevich was not expected, indeed, he very nearly changed his mind about going. On the day of his departure his sister Ksenia received a letter from Alix, stressing once again that she could not convert and appealing to be left in peace. This came as a terrible blow to Nicholas, but his mother insisted that he must still go to Coburg and take his chance. Sergei and Elisabeth had been encouraging him in his hopes for years, Vladimir and Marie were keen to support him, and the Tsaritsa advised him also to enlist the help of Alix's grandmother, Queen Victoria, who would be among the guests.[1] The party travelled by train in three sleeping cars, crossing the German border in the evening. They were welcomed at the station in Coburg by the Duke and Duchess of Saxe-Coburg and their children, Marie (the future Queen of Romania), Victoria Melita and Alfred, with Ernst Ludwig and Alix, and once the greetings were over they made their way to the Palais Edinburg, the Duke and Duchess's family home. That evening there was a family dinner and an operetta.

The next morning Nicholas had the conversation with Alix which he had longed for and dreaded. She had not expected to see him arrive at the station with his uncles and aunts, and her first instinct was to run, but Grand Princess Elisabeth acted quickly to bring them together. For two hours the family left Nicholas and Alix alone in Elisabeth's rooms, but it was a tearful, unsatisfactory meeting: 'She cried the whole time', Nicholas told his mother, 'and only whispered now and then, "No, I cannot!".'[2] After lunch he went out with Sergei and Elisabeth and later walked with Vladimir: as all Coburg prepared to welcome the most important guest of all, the Tsesarevich's mind was on his own future, and although he described the parting from Alix as 'calmer' in his diary, he must have been disappointed, and unsure of the next step to take.

At 4.30 p.m., Queen Victoria arrived from Italy with Prince and Princess Henry of Battenberg. As her train drew into the station the skies cleared, and the old lady's thoughts turned to the time almost forty years before when Prince Albert had first introduced her to the sights of his home. Now their son ruled in Coburg, and she was about to witness the marriage of two grandchildren her husband had never seen. Duke Alfred met her at the station with his wife and three of their children, including the bride. A squadron of the 1st Dragoon Guards of Prussia had been ordered by the Kaiser to form his grandmother's guard of honour, and ladies in white showered the royal carriages with flowers as they drove through the streets. The party paused for a civic welcome from the Burgomeister and a march past outside the Palais Edinburg before their arrival at the Schloss, where many of the guests were assembled to meet the Queen. Nicholas was there in full uniform, and was presented, but this was not a moment for private conversation. In any case, his mother's belief that the Queen would help him was sadly misplaced. Much as she liked Nicholas as a person, Queen Victoria had profound misgivings about Russian marriages and always advised against them.

The next morning Nicholas took an early walk with Vladimir up the 500-ft path to the armoury museum in the Veste, the ancient castle where Martin Luther once sheltered from his enemies. He was preparing for another meeting with Alix after morning coffee. Still raw from the previous day's encounter, he tried to touch on the subject of marriage as little as possible, though he handed her a letter from his mother, which he hoped would sway her feelings. She was coming under increasing pressure too from other members of the family. Her brother encouraged her to agree to a private talk with Marie Pavlovna, and he and others gave so much reassurance to Nicholas that the disappointed lover began to feel sure that something must go wrong.

The afternoon brought much-needed relief as the party went to the Rosenau, four miles outside the town, for a relaxing afternoon ending in a tea party. 'We had a good laugh when the chief footman was at last persuaded to sing two or three songs;' Nicholas wrote, 'he started in the tower and ended behind the bushes.'[3] The Kaiser arrived that evening and settled into rooms at the Palais Edinburg. He sat up until the early hours with Nicholas, and he too was firmly behind the wedding plan. He suggested that matters might be made easier for Alix if the Russians allowed a softening of the ancient formula of renunciation which she would have to go through if she converted.

The wedding morning dawned dull and cloudy, but the skies soon cleared, and the streets thronged with people, eager to see the Ducal family and royalties from the outlying palaces make their way to Schloss Ehrenburg. After his long conversation with Wilhelm the night before, Nicholas was late for breakfast, and had to walk to Schloss Ehrenburg alone through the crowded streets. At eleven o'clock the young couple took their civil vows quietly in their grandmother's room. It must have touched the Queen to see Victoria Melita wearing the veil worn by her daughter Alice, over thirty years before. Meanwhile the non-royal guests and the Prussian guard of honour were taking their places in the chapel, which was decorated with garlands of green fir twigs and white flowers. Shortly before midday the band in the courtyard struck up the German national anthem. This signalled the start of the royal procession, headed by the Kaiser and the Duchess of Saxe-Coburg. When everyone was in place, Duke Alfred led his daughter into the chapel with her two bridesmaids; her sister Beatrice, just a day short of her tenth birthday, and thirteen-year-old Feodora. There were five local clergymen in the chapel, but the most important part of the service was taken by the elderly Court Chaplain from Darmstadt, Dr Müller. Onlookers noticed that he was moved by the occasion and he became quite emotional when pronouncing the blessing.

After the service the guests enjoyed a wedding breakfast in the Throne Room, and at 3.30 p.m. the patience of the waiting crowds was rewarded when a carriage decorated with flowers drew up in the Schloss Platz, ready to take the young couple to the station. A relaxed and happy royal party saw them off, laughing and cheering amid showers of rice, and nobody objected to requests from local photographers: the Prince of Wales even formed an impromptu line-up with his brothers. Ernst Ludwig took his new Grand Duchess home to Darmstadt, where they made their triumphal entry the next morning, driving in an open carriage through streets decorated with flags and garlands of flowers. The celebrations continued there for days; almost sixteen years had passed since the death of Alice, Hesse's last Grand Duchess, and the future looked bright.

In Coburg too the family party continued, and tension was mounting for the Tsesarevich. Throughout the service, he had not been able to take his mind off Princess Alix, who was sitting two rows behind his place near the altar. The emotional charge at weddings always runs high: for Nicholas, veering as he was between hope and despair, Dr Müller's sermon 'went straight to the heart of my own problem. At that moment I terribly wanted to be able to look into Alix's soul!'[4] He probably did not realise that it was this very clergyman, the chaplain to Alix's family, who had impressed on her again and again the sinfulness of changing her faith. That afternoon Nicholas and Vladimir walked up again to the Veste and spent a long time exploring the armoury. They had a small family dinner at the Palais Edinburg and afterwards went to the theatre on foot, running to escape the teeming rain.

On 20 April, the next morning, the heavy guns were brought to bear on Alix. The Kaiser, her cousin, had a private talk with her before escorting her to the Palais Edinburg to see Grand Princess Vladimir. It would be hard to imagine a situation more ironic than this one: Kaiserin Friedrich was highly amused by her son's part in the affair because, just a few years earlier, he had treated his sister Sophie's conversion to Orthodoxy as a mortal sin. Marie Pavlovna had been equally outspoken in trumpeting her own refusal to convert as a victory over Romanov family customs. But neither of them was blessed with the ability to laugh at their own inconsistency: in this situation they both wanted to be on the best possible terms with the young man who would one day rule Russia and his future wife, and this was the only imperative they could see. At ten in the morning the Kaiser left Alix with Maria, and shortly afterwards the two women joined the rest of the Russian party: then, everyone withdrew to the next room, leaving the couple alone. At last Alix gave way and accepted Nicholas.

The tension of the past few days evaporated on the spot. 'The whole world is changed for me,' Nicholas wrote, 'nature, mankind, everything; and all seem to be good and lovable and happy. I couldn't even write, my hands trembled so.'[5] Every detail of the day remained clear in their minds, to be recalled in later years:

'You know I have kept the grey princesse dress I wore that morning?'

'As far as I remember, there was a concert in Coburg that evening and a Bavarian band was playing; poor Uncle Alfred was rather exhausted by the dinner, and constantly dropped his stick with a clatter. Do you remember?'

'I feel still your grey suit, the smell of it by the window in the Coburg Schloss. How vivid I remember everything; those sweet kisses wh. I had dreamed of & yearned after so many years & wh. I thought, I should never get.'

'Think of Coburg, and all we went through.'[6]

One person had no idea that all this had been happening, and if Alix had really wanted to refuse Nicholas she could have gone straight to her grandmother for help. Queen Victoria had done her utmost to find an English or German husband for her granddaughter. She was stunned when Grand Princess Elisabeth came into her room shortly after breakfast with news of the engagement, and ushered in the happy, though still rather tearful, couple. But despite her misgivings, the Queen accepted what had happened and was quite touched by Nicholas's attitude and his obvious pleasure. Journalists met the Kaiser walking through the Schloss Platz on his way to see the Duke and Duchess of Saxe-Coburg; he too 'beamed with delight' as he broke the news to the Secretary to the British Legation.[7] Once the interview with the Queen was over, the young couple returned to the Palais Edinburg for a family lunch, and a service of thanksgiving in the private chapel of the Duchess of Saxe-Coburg, who had remained Orthodox after her marriage to Prince Alfred.

The morning's events must have overshadowed the other celebration of the day. It was Princess Beatrice of Saxe-Coburg's tenth birthday and an afternoon ball had been arranged at the Rosenau, which almost all the guests attended. Nicholas was there, though he preferred to miss the dancing and walk alone in the gardens with Alix. Photographs were taken to celebrate the engagement, both of the couple alone and of all the guests, looking particularly relaxed and jolly.

Now the days passed quickly in a whirl of dinners, concerts and walks and, for Nicholas and Alix, a mountain of telegrams to answer. The Kaiser left on the day after the engagement, but not before a further series of group photographs had been taken in the garden of the Palais Edinburg, with his mother and grandmother at their centre. When the Queen was in Coburg, her thoughts were never far from Prince Albert, and she had found time to revisit the places she had first seen with him. Also, before the party broke up, she gave a dinner party and a concert for three generations of her descendants, most of whom Albert had never known. The 22nd saw yet another family celebration: it was Grand Prince Vladimir's name-day, and the Russians gave him presents in the morning before he and his wife set off for St Petersburg, triumphantly bearing letters from Nicholas and Alix for the Tsar and Tsaritsa.

In Russia news of the engagement had been received with joy, and an overwhelming sense of relief. 'Words cannot express with what delight and great joy I received this happy news!', the Tsaritsa wrote to her son, 'I almost felt faint I was so overjoyed! . . . We had parted with such a bad and desperate feeling on the evening of your departure that my heart bled as I saw you go and my thoughts and prayers never left you.'[8] The Tsar also wrote a few days later: 'I have to admit that I did not believe the possibility of such an outcome and was sure your attempt would fail completely, but the Lord guided you, gave you strength and blessed you, many thanks to him for his mercy. If only you had seen the happiness and rejoicing with which everyone greeted the news.'[9] His cousin, Grand Prince Konstantin Konstantinovich, attended the Palm Sunday service at Gatchina on 10/22 April and noted in his diary, 'I had not seen the Empress so radiant in a long time. Nicky's betrothal has delighted all Russians, who have been waiting for a long time for him to settle down to married life.'[10] Everyone was eager to see the Tsesarevich again, to congratulate him in person, but unlike his uncle and aunt he was not returning directly to Russia.

After all the emotions of the past few days, Alix was longing to see her brother and her home, so, at 4.30 on the afternoon of 22 April, she and Nicholas took the train for Darmstadt with her sisters and her brothers-in-law, Grand Prince Sergei and Prince Louis of Battenberg. 'There was a triumphant welcome,' Nicholas wrote, 'Ducky [Victoria Melita] and Ernie were our hosts for the first time. A guard of honour, a four-in-hand escort, illuminations and crowds of people. As soon as we reached the palace, we sat down to supper as we were very hungry.'[11] The stay would be a short one. The next morning the family had coffee together, and Alix and Nicholas sat down to answer more telegrams. They visited the family mausoleum at the Rosenhöhe, where Alix's parents were buried, and after lunch sat for another round of group photographs before taking the train back to Coburg.

The couple would spend just over a week more together, surrounded by the family. At first the weather was fine, and there were walks and rides, quiet visits to the Rosenau and meetings alone with the Queen, and, for Nicholas, all the services and traditions of the Orthodox Easter. His aunt allowed him to move out of the palace into a smaller residence, nearer to Alix, and they saw as much of one another as they could. Beside his happiness, he confided a new feeling to his diary, 'it is so strange to be able to drive and walk alone with her, without feeling at all embarrassed, as if there was nothing unusual in it.'[12] But all things have to end. Queen Victoria left for England on 28 April, at six in the evening, and on 2 May the time came for Alix and Nicholas to part. She left Coburg just after noon, heading for Darmstadt and ultimately for England, to join her grandmother. He spent a few more hours with his family before catching the nine o'clock train bound for the Russian border, the last of the wedding guests to leave. They went away, each with his or her own memories, hopes and plans, but one thing was certain: they would all think of Coburg for a very long time to come.

13

This Garden of Eden

THE ROMANOVS AND THE CRIMEA

Alexander III's family enjoyed two celebrations before 1894 was more than a few months old. The Tsesarevich's engagement was preceded by that of his sister Grand Princess Ksenia to their father's cousin Grand Prince Alexander Mikhailovich; if nothing else had happened, this would have been a year to remember. But events were about to take a much sadder turn. The Tsar was dying. A big, strong man, not yet fifty and apparently in the prime of life, Alexander III might have been expected to live into the 1920s, but even the strongest man can be laid low by illness. Kidney disease, unrecognized and untreated, began to affect the Tsar in the summer of 1894, and the last act of his life was played out at Livadia in the Crimea – a place with many associations, both good and bad, for Russia and its ruling family.

I cannot describe the grandeur of the scenery; some parts so wild, huge mountains towering over us with eagles flying over them. . . . We drove over some of those mountains then down into lovely valleys. After climbing up and up for the last time we went through an old archway, then suddenly the whole of the Black Sea spread before our eyes. It is the most beautiful and startling sight one can imagine. Almost every kind of fruit flourished in the valleys, and in spring the wealth of blossoms, pink and white, of apples, cherries, peaches, almonds, made the whole countryside a perfumed garden, while in autumn the masses of golden fruit were a wonder to behold. Flowers bloomed as though they were the very soul of the fair earth. Never have I seen such roses. They spread over every building in great vines as strong as ivy, and they scattered their rich petals over lawns and pathways in fragrance at times almost overpowering.[1]

In memoirs of the old Russia, the Crimea is recalled as a place of unearthly beauty and peace. The peninsula was remote; even in later years the 1,400-mile train journey from St Petersburg took six days and the railway went only as far as Sevastopol, leaving several hours of travel by sea or road to the imperial houses dotted along the coast. The Tsars were determined to keep their paradise unspoilt. They shared its delights with some of Russia's wealthiest families – Vorontzov, Yusupov, Dolgoruky, and so on – who built their own Crimean houses beside small Tatar villages where the silence was broken only by the daily call of the muezzin. Here, they too enjoyed an idyllic lifestyle, far from the northern cold. There were shadows but the exiles wanted to remember the Crimea only for its sunshine.

Catherine the Great visited the peninsula in the 1780s, but another forty years would go by before the purchase of the first imperial estate. In 1825 Alexander I acquired Oreanda, a little way to the south-west of Yalta along the Black Sea coast, and that autumn he took his wife south for a change of air: Tsaritsa Elizaveta Alexeievna, like so many members of the imperial family, suffered from chronic lung disease. The couple stayed first at Taganrog on the shore of the Sea of Azov. Then, after several weeks, Alexander went on to the Crimea and Oreanda. He told his mother that he thought the climate there treacherous, because the unusually warm days gave way to very low temperatures at night. He caught a chill. 'These little fevers are very common in Crimea and are not really serious if they're looked after properly', his mother remarked to her daughter Anna, but shortly after his return to Taganrog, Alexander died.[2]

His brother Nicholas I visited Yalta in 1837 and made plans for the development of the little town: both he and his wife were taken with the beauty of Oreanda. Nicholas commissioned the German architect Karl Friedrich Schinkel to design a palace there for Alexandra Feodorovna, but when the blueprint was submitted it proved to be so ambitious and so costly that the Tsar was forced to call on Andrei Stackenschneider, the architect of several of St Petersburg's palaces and churches, to scale the project down. Still, the white palace at Oreanda, which was completed in 1852, was a magnificent building that the Tsar and his family might have expected to enjoy for many years.

In fact, they visited Oreanda only once, in the autumn of 1852. In 1853 the Crimean War began: the first enemy troops landed on the peninsula in 1854 and although the actual fighting happened many miles to the west, it was neither the time nor the place for a restful autumn holiday. After Nicholas's death in 1855, Alexandra never saw the Crimea again. On her own death in 1860, Oreanda passed to her second son, Konstantin Nikolaievich. He visited for the first time in August 1861, and celebrated his son Konstantin Konstantinovich's third birthday on Oreanda's terraces. The elder Konstantin loved Oreanda and its dramatic setting, so different from his northern home. A metal cross on the summit of one of the mountains that towers above the site of the old palace still marks one of his favourite climbs: he is said to have planted it there himself.

But the focus of imperial interest in the peninsula was soon to move eastwards. As Konstantin Nikolaievich established himself at Oreanda, Alexander II turned to the Crimea in the hope of finding a cure for his wife, whose physical weakness was causing grave concern. For her sake, the Tsar had introduced himself to Sergei Petrovich Botkin, the respected professor of St Petersburg's Academy of Medicine. Botkin would go on to become Alexander's personal physician, accompanying him to Bulgaria in the war of 1878, but the appointment almost ended at the first consultation. Following the etiquette of generations, Maria Alexandrovna would only agree to be examined through her clothes. The doctor threatened to resign and it was left to the Tsar to resolve the problem, quietly and simply, by setting the old scruples aside for ever.

The doctor's recommendation for the Tsaritsa was a prolonged visit, perhaps many, to the Crimea. He was already using the southern climate to aid the treatment of tubercular patients and, on his advice, Alexander II bought an estate between Oreanda and Yalta, where the pine woods were thought to exude particularly healthy vapours. The property's original owner, Colonel Feodosy Revelioti, the Commander of the Balaklava Greek battalion, had named the estate 'Livadia' in memory of his home: 'Livadia' comes from the Greek word for a meadow. Alexander presented Livadia to Maria as a gift and placed it entirely under her administration.

Livadia welcomed its first imperial visitors in August 1861. The Tsar and Tsaritsa, with their children, Alexei, Maria, Sergei and Pavel, made the long journey south to Sevastopol, where they were able to see for the first time the sites made famous in the Crimean War. The town was still recovering from the long siege: Alexander laid the foundation stone of a new cathedral dedicated to St Vladimir, where some of the Russian war heroes would be buried. Then he and his family embarked on the steamship *Tiger* and on 26 August/7 September had the first sight of their new property, shortly before the ship docked at Yalta. They were immediately captivated by the beauty of the setting, as well they might have been, for the scenery around Livadia is breathtaking. The house, as it then was, perched high above the sea against the backdrop of the Jaila mountains, which protect the coast from the northern wind. The family spent this first visit exploring Yalta and the surrounding area, learning its character, its traditions and its folk tales. One of the attractions of the Crimea would always be the lack of ceremony that was possible there; the imperial family was able to talk to ordinary people in the street – something that would be unthinkable in St Petersburg – and they went to local churches and attended a Tatar wedding in one of the villages.[3] For Maria Alexandrovna the place had already become 'my sweet Livadia', and she and the Tsar decided to have new buildings erected to suit their needs.

Another of St Petersburg's fashionable architects was employed to transform Livadia. Ippolite Monigetti produced the Great Palace, a wooden building with long covered balconies, commanding a stunning view of the Black Sea and of a broad sweep of the coastline to the east, with Yalta nestling below its protecting mountains. A smaller palace was built for the heir to the throne and other houses for the suite, and Monigetti gave Livadia its own white stone church in the Byzantine style. The gardens were laid out to a new plan, with the little pavilions, summerhouses and tea houses typical of the period, and, high in the mountains, about an hour's drive from the main palace, the Tsar had a dacha built for his wife. 'Eriklik' was an attractive wooden house surrounded by pine trees, with balconies and terraces where the Tsaritsa could rest in the shade, still enjoying fine views of the plains and the sea. The dacha took two months to build and Maria Alexandrovna is said to have spent only fifteen days there, but her children and grandchildren preserved the house as a favourite spot for picnics and a refuge from the heat.

Visits to Livadia became part of the imperial family's annual migration. Sometimes Alexander and Maria's children were sent to the Crimea alone, and on these occasions the lively youngsters ran wild, playing with tame mountain goats that wreaked havoc among the carefully manicured lawns and flower beds. They were the bane of the gardeners' lives and it was left to the Tsaritsa to smooth ruffled feelings and restore order. In 1867 a party of Americans, including the writer Samuel Langhorn Clemens ('Mark Twain'), anchored at Yalta in the side-wheeled steamship *Quaker City*, and were invited to visit the imperial family at Livadia. They were able to explore the palace and were amazed and delighted by the informality of their reception:

> We assembled in the handsome garden, for there was no room in the house able to accommodate our three-score persons comfortably. The Imperial family came out bowing and smiling and stood in our midst. With every bow his Majesty said a word of welcome. All took off their hats, and our Consul inflicted an address on him. He thanked us and said that he was very much pleased to see us . . . The Empress said that the Americans were favourites in Russia and she hoped the Russians were similarly regarded in America. After this she went and talked sociably (for an Empress) with various ladies in our circle; several gentlemen entered into a disjointed general conversation with the Emperor; and whoever chose stepped forward and talked with the modest little Grand Duchess Marie, the Tsar's daughter. She is fourteen; light-haired, blue-eyed, unassuming and pretty. Everybody talks English. The Emperor wore a cap, frock coat and pantaloons, all of some kind of plain white drilling, and wore no jewellery or any insignia whatever of rank. No costume could be less ostentatious.[4]

This display of family happiness already concealed the uncomfortable fact of the Tsar's relationship with Ekaterina Dolgorukaya, though as yet the Princess did not follow him to Livadia and had to be content with letters. She did not visit the Crimea until the autumn of 1872, when Alexander placed her in a small house on the Livadia estate, about a mile from the Great Palace. But the Tsaritsa was also in the Crimea that autumn and realizing the insensitivity of this arrangement – particularly as Livadia belonged to his wife – Alexander bought a separate house called in the Tatar language, 'Biuk Sarai'. Then each year at the end of August, when the imperial family left for the Crimea, Ekaterina would follow at a discreet distance to her own house, and it was at Biuk Sarai that her two daughters were born.

In July 1880, four weeks after the death of Maria Alexandrovna, Alexander married Ekaterina in secret in the Catherine Palace at Tsarskoe Selo. The time came for him to leave for Livadia, but only a few intimate friends had been told about the wedding; officially no one else knew, and whatever they really did know in fact, the pretence had to be maintained and the presence of a woman and three children with all their attendants, on the way and in the palace, had somehow to be made invisible. For security reasons two identical trains made the long journey, changing position at each large station en route. The Tsar and his suite caught the first train in St Petersburg while the baby and her nurse slipped 'unnoticed' into the second train: meanwhile Ekaterina herself and the older children and servants travelled thirteen miles by troika and boarded the Tsar's train at the small country station of Kolpino. For the rest of the journey Ekaterina and the children remained in their carriage, and the suite had to contend with the awkwardness of reaching the dining car without seeing what should not be seen. The problems were compounded when the party's arrival at Livadia coincided with a memorial liturgy for the late Tsaritsa in the palace chapel. The Tsar and his suite attended the service, while Ekaterina and the children settled into the rooms once occupied by Maria Alexandrovna.

For the couple, too absorbed in one another to notice what those around them were feeling and saying, these three months at Livadia were a blissful interlude of family life, openly acknowledged for the first time. On 4/16 October the Cossacks of the Tsar's escort held their annual parade and Ekaterina appeared beside her husband. Onlookers were surprised to see that their eight-year-old son Georgi, who still lacked both family name and legal status, appeared in Cossack uniform just as if he had been one of the Grand Princes. Courtiers were shocked and concerned for the future, pitying the Tsar who seemed to them to have fallen entirely under the Princess's influence, but for Alexander and his new family the autumn was a time of intense happiness, which would never return.

After his assassination the following spring, Livadia passed to Alexander III. He made his first visit to the Crimea as Tsar in the autumn of 1884, with Maria Feodorovna and their younger children Ksenia, Mikhail and Olga, travelling from Yalta on board the cruiser *Yaroslavl*.[5] From Yalta they made their way to Livadia, never anticipating the awkward situation they would find. 'We set out for Livadia and Papa's house,' the Tsar recorded in his diary, 'where we bumped into Princess Dolgorukaya and her children in Mama's rooms! I could hardly believe my eyes and could not comprehend where I was, especially as Livadia is so dear to our hearts and memories! Every little thing here recalls our dear beloved Mama! Minny and I were utterly confused and dumbfounded. I really cannot call our visit to Livadia cheerful or pleasant; the time dragged and there were various clashes, misunderstandings and delicate explanations, but in the end things worked out for the best, and I hope that now there will be no misunderstandings whatsoever, and that everything will go on as it should.'[6] The meeting must have been very awkward on both sides and afterwards Ekaterina did not appear at Livadia again. In 1892 she sold Biuk Sarai.

The imperial family continued to make regular visits to Livadia, usually in the 'velvet season' of autumn, but it was in spring, in 1886, that Grand Prince Sergei chose to introduce his wife to the Crimea. They stayed a month: Elisabeth told her grandmother Queen Victoria, 'we are very sorry to leave tomorrow. The weather is quite splendid in summer, all is green and covered with roses, glycinias, honeysuckle, which not only cover the houses but one also sees hanging on the trees. What charms me especially is to have the sea reminding me of Osborne and the grand hills of Scotland.'[7]

The 1880s were to see a great deal of development and change in the area, not all of it welcome. On the night of 7/19 August 1881, fire destroyed the palace at Oreanda. It would never be rebuilt. The Konstantins continued to use one of the smaller houses on the estate until the Grand Prince suffered the stroke which took away his mobility and confined him to Pavlovsk. Meanwhile, Alexander III directed all his energies towards Livadia and the east. In 1888 he added the villages of Massandra and Ai-Danil to the Livadia estate and had vineyards planted and wine cellars made. In time Massandra became a centre for the production of Crimean wine: a half-built palace on the estate, constructed for the previous owner, Count Simeon Vorontsov, was brought to completion. It was, and is, a curious sight: a turreted French château, standing proud in a setting quite alien to its concept and design. Local people say that there is something sinister about the building. It was said at the time that the Tsar was preparing the palace for his heir, but his early death took away the need for such a property and, in the event, Massandra Palace was never used by the imperial family, except for occasional visits and tea parties.

But Alexander's plans went beyond the needs of his own children. He ordered rebuilding in Yalta, turning the town into a full-scale port: old houses were replaced on a new street plan, the embankment was reconstructed with a new harbour and pier, and improvements were made to education and welfare services for local people. The year 1891 saw Alexander III and Maria Feodorovna's silver wedding anniversary, and Livadia and Yalta were at the centre of the celebrations.

The Tsar and Tsaritsa, Tsesarevich Nicholas, Ksenia, Mikhail and Olga were accompanied on the journey south by the Tsaritsa's parents, King Christian IX and Queen Louise of Denmark, by her sister Alexandra, Princess of Wales, and the Princess's daughters, Victoria and Maud. The party sailed from Sevastopol on the cruiser *Orel* and were joined at Livadia by the missing member of the family, Grand Prince Georgi Alexandrovich, who travelled from the imperial estate at Abastuman in the Caucasus with his father's cousin Alexander Mikhailovich. The anniversary was on 28 October/9 November. In the morning, family and guests presented their gifts to the couple, and all attended a service in the palace church. It was a beautiful day and they spent most of the afternoon in the garden or on the beach, enjoying a spectacular firework display in the evening.

Alexander III's reign would last only three more years. His sudden decline took everyone by surprise, and even when the doctors recognized that his kidneys were inflamed, they refused to give up hope. They prescribed a holiday in the south: plans were made for him to go to the Crimea, then on to Corfu. The Tsesarevich abandoned his own intended visit to his fiancée in Darmstadt and accompanied his parents, but, by the time they had reached Livadia it became clear that the Tsar could go no further. He settled into the small, 'Maly' Palace and his relatives were summoned to the Crimea. The family continued to hope, and Alexander still made plans for the future. One of his first acts on arriving at Livadia was to complete the purchase of Oreanda from his widowed aunt, Grand Princess Konstantin. He fully intended to have the palace rebuilt.

Days passed and hope persisted. Once the Tsar and Tsaritsa went to Ai-Todor, to visit their newly married daughter Ksenia and her husband Alexander Mikhailovich. The Tsesarevich was given permission to invite his fiancée to Livadia, and she telegraphed her own decision to be received into the Orthodox Church on her arrival. On 10/22 October, he and his uncle Sergei set out to meet her: she had had to make her own way across Europe as an ordinary passenger because, in the mounting tension at Livadia, no one had thought to organize transport for her. The gravity of the Tsar's condition was obvious now. The priest Father John of Kronstadt was at Livadia and his prayers brought comfort, but no miracles. On 20 October/1 November, at about 4.30 p.m., Alexander III died quietly in his chair in the Maly Palace. Few Tsars were able to end their lives in such peace, and the scene had a profound effect on all those present. Even his cousin Nikolai Mikhailovich, who was renowned for his cynicism, returned to St Petersburg calling the widowed Tsaritsa and her children 'a holy family'.[8] Later the imperial family would have a cross set into the floor to mark the place where the Tsar died, and services in memory of Alexander III would become part of their autumn routine.

But for the moment a stunned silence followed the death and the new Tsar came close to despair, because he had absolutely no confidence in the future. Princess Alix was received into the Orthodox Church the next day: Nicholas wanted to marry her immediately while his father's body was still in the house and his mother agreed, but his uncles would not hear of it. This should have given the first inkling of trouble to come in the new reign. Alexander III came to the throne as a mature man and immediately stamped his authority on the family, putting a distance between himself and his uncles and bringing his brothers to the fore. In contrast, Nicholas II was an uncertain 26-year-old, whose uncles were still young, vigorous men accustomed to having their own way: his brothers were little more than children.

The Prince and Princess of Wales arrived from Sevastopol on board the *Orel* on 23 October/4 November and their presence helped to bring calm to a household in increasing disarray. While the Princess comforted her sister, the Prince took charge of the complicated funeral arrangements. The seventh day after the Tsar's death, the body was carried from the palace church down to Yalta by Cossacks and sailors from the imperial yacht, with the family following on foot. They embarked on the ship *Pamiat Mercuria* and sailed to Sevastopol, escorted by six ships of the Black Sea Fleet, before the imperial train took the funeral cortège on its long journey to St Petersburg.

The Crimea did not see the new Tsar again until 1898, when he made the journey south with his wife and their two little girls. The Tsaritsa was in the early stages of her third pregnancy, losing weight, and feeling very unwell, so their three-month stay was not particularly easy. Their next, in 1900, was almost a tragedy. Alexandra Feodorovna was pregnant again: 'It is a pity that the first stage should be spent in beautiful Crimea,' Nicholas told his mother, 'because she cannot go out for drives; we are separated all day and only eat together. . . . Our children are well and bathe in the mornings in warm salt water . . . They have all grown a lot and the small baby can walk beautifully, but falls often, because her elder sisters push her about and when one does not watch them they are altogether inclined to treat her very roughly.'[9] Two weeks after writing this he began to feel ill and took to bed beside his wife. At first the doctor insisted that he had influenza, but the illness was typhoid, and as the days passed anxiety grew. Court and ministers worried about the succession: if the Tsar died, leaving only daughters, should his brother succeed him? What if he did, and the unborn child was a boy? In this crisis the young Tsaritsa showed her quality, as she always would. Forgetting her own discomfort, she took over the nursing personally and refused to give up, or to be persuaded to return to bed. The crisis passed and the Tsar recovered.

The family spent their Christmas at Livadia that year, for the first time ever, and special messengers carried their presents by sledge across the snow-covered mountains. They left in January and did not return until 1902; after this, family events and political developments would keep them away for several more years. The revolution of 1905 was particularly bad in the Crimea, around the bases of the Black Sea Fleet, and the long journey was considered too dangerous. The imperial couple did not see Livadia again until 1909, when they found that the Great Palace had been severely affected by damp: as their visit drew to an end, they decided to have the palace demolished and a new one erected on the site. The local architect, Nikolai Krasnov, was called on to design the building and only two places were considered too sacred to be changed: the Maly Palace, where Alexander III died, and the palace chapel – Krasnov had plans to replace this but the Tsaritsa would not hear of it. Work began as the imperial yacht sailed from Yalta and Monigetti's palace was finally razed to the ground on 3 February 1910. The foundation stone of the new palace was laid and blessed on Alexandra Feodorovna's name-day.

In the years leading up to the First World War, the Crimea blossomed. Not only at Livadia but also along the coast, the imperial estates were developed, changed and enjoyed by the various branches of the family, who had started to establish footholds in the south in the 1860s. While the Konstantinovichi had owned Oreanda, Alexander II's next brother, Nikolai Nikolaievich the elder, bought land near to the dacha 'Eriklik', though in the event he never built on it. It was left to his sons to buy and build: in 1893 his younger son, Piotr Nikolaievich, who suffered from tuberculosis and needed to spend prolonged periods in the south, bought land near Koreis, several miles to the south-west of Oreanda. He commissioned Krasnov to build him a palace of his own devising: 'Djulber', a large silver-white building in Arabic style, completed in 1897, was always considered one of the most beautiful buildings on the peninsula. Five years later Piotr's elder brother, Nikolai Nikolaievich the younger, acquired his own Crimean land near Koreis, which he later presented to his wife. For her, the architect created 'Chair', whose Turkish name means 'a neglected garden'.

The Mikhailovichi were even quicker to appreciate the Crimea. In 1869, Grand Princess Olga Feodorovna, the wife of Alexander II's brother Mikhail Nikolaievich, bought a plot of land at Ai-Todor, between Koreis and Oreanda. 'With the passing of the years,' her son Alexander remembered, 'it became a flourishing country estate covered with gardens, vineyards, lawns and coves. A lighthouse was built on its grounds to enable us to find our way on a foggy night.' Alexander Mikhailovich inherited Ai-Todor and made continual improvements, buying surrounding plots of land whenever he could. Years later he wrote, 'There was something hopeful and encouraging in being able to get up at sunrise and to say to myself, while riding along the bridle-path lined by jungles of wild roses: "This is real. This is mine. This will never turn on me. This is the place where I belong and where I should stay forever."'[10] At the turn of the century, his brother Georgi acquired a neighbouring estate and employed Krasnov to build for him: 'Harax', perched on the cliffs of Cap Ai-Todor, would have looked quite in keeping in an English suburb. The family was still building almost until the end. In 1912 Dmitri Konstantinovich, Konstantin Nikolaievich's third son, had his own Moorish palace, 'Kichkine', built near Oreanda, and soon afterwards the Yusupovs ordered a mansion close to their own estate at Koreis for their son and his wife, Princess Irina Alexandrovna.

So, when the imperial family returned to the Crimea to see the new Livadia palace for the first time, they were surrounded by relatives, and they would come to share Alexander Mikhailovich's intense feelings for their southern home. The new palace was completed in 1911 and the season was particularly joyful, as the Tsar's eldest daughter came of age and a full dress ball was given in her honour.

> The ladies were in rich coloured gowns, the young girls mostly in white tulle, and the gorgeous uniforms seemed to belong to a feast from the eastern hemisphere. The doors at the end of the room opened; instantly a silence fell on the assembly. The Emperor appeared leading the Grand Duchess Olga; she looked pretty in her first long gown and her hair up for the first time. The rest of the Imperial family followed. . . . The Empress as usual was not strong enough to attend but as the guests walked out of the dining room she stood in the hall to greet them. I shall ever remember how beautiful she looked, like a Greek ikon, in a gown of cloth of gold; she had a priceless gold and diamond band in her fair hair, a glorious necklace of many rows of different stones coming down to her waist; she seemed to be a Byzantine picture. The Tzarevitch was next to her, his lovely little face flushed with the excitement of the evening.[11]

The Tsaritsa's friend Anna Virubova was at the ball too and remembered, 'We danced in the great state dining room on the first floor, the glass doors to the courtyard thrown open, the music of the unseen orchestra floating in from the rose garden like a breath of its own wondrous fragrance. It was a perfect night, clear and warm. . . .'[12]

But Alexandra Feodorovna also wanted her children to understand that there was a sadness underlying all this beauty. The area was still a centre for the treatment of tuberculosis: the Tsaritsa established two hospitals and she and her children made items to sell at fund-raising bazaars. On 20 April, 'White Flower Day', they sold flowers in the streets of Yalta. With his haemophilia, the Tsesarevich was no stranger to illness, and he suffered several attacks at Livadia: often the palace chapel echoed to prayers for his recovery. In 1913 he was too weak to attend a performance of Vladimir Dourev's circus at Yalta and, to his delight, the circus came to the palace to amuse him.

The family saw Livadia for the last time in the early summer of 1914. They stayed for two months before leaving on the yacht *Shtandart*, bound for Constanza and a meeting with the Romanian royal family: at Harax, high on the cliffs, Grand Prince Georgi Mikhailovich stood with his family and friends and watched them go, little knowing that this would be their last sight of Nicholas II and the children. 'About four o'clock the Imperial yacht steamed towards us; the Emperor had given orders it should pass as close as possible', one of the party remembered. 'He stood on the top deck, surrounded by the Empress, the four little Grand Duchesses in white and the Tzarevitch. We shouted and then waved our sheets. He and they waved back at us. . . . We waved and waved and could see through our glasses the Imperial family waving back. The last person I saw, although a dim far-away figure, was His Majesty; the rest had gone below, but he remained and I saw him salute and then my eyes filled with tears.'[13] The families had a pact to meet again in the Crimea that October but the war overruled all their plans. The Tsar and his family made a very brief visit to Sevastopol and Eupatoria, on the western coast of the Crimea, in the spring of 1916, and in the same year Dr Evgeni Sergeievich Botkin, the son of the first Dr Botkin, was sent by the Tsaritsa to oversee the establishment of her military hospitals at Yalta and Livadia.

After Nicholas's abdication, his family's dearest hope was to return to Livadia to live quietly in internal exile, but it was not to be. It is said that Kerensky would have allowed the five children to join their grandmother in the Crimea if they had been willing to leave their parents, but for the Tsar and Tsaritsa the south was not even considered. The Dowager Tsaritsa had taken refuge with her son-in-law Alexander Mikhailovich and his family at Ai-Todor after the Revolution, and several other members of the family had escaped to their Crimean estates, where they found themselves interned. At Christmas 1917 the Sevastopol Soviet installed a representative at Ai-Todor and the following February all Romanov prisoners except the Tsar's youngest sister Olga and her husband were moved to Djulber, because the high walls enabled the house to be more closely guarded. There was friction about their fate: the Yalta Soviet wanted to execute them on the spot but their guards would only take orders from Sevastopol, and Sevastopol awaited word from Moscow. Olga was left at liberty because she had married a commoner, Nikolai Kulikovsky, after the breakdown of her first marriage, but she and her husband were allowed no further contact with the prisoners.

The Brest-Litovsk treaty of March 1918 gave the Germans the right to occupy certain areas of Russia including the Crimea, and this precipitated a crisis. Unwilling to wait until the Germans came, the Yalta Soviet prepared a contingent of armed men to capture Djulber and kill the Romanovs. If they had succeeded, almost all the members of the imperial family who made their way to the West would have died in one massacre. Aware of the danger, the commander of the guard offered to take the prisoners to the Vorontzov Palace at Alupka. When they refused, preferring to trust in God and their own high walls, he returned their weapons and allowed them to share in the defense of Djulber. They remained on watch around the clock for a little over a week: then the Germans arrived and the Sevastopol men disappeared into the night. Later it became apparent that in the final hours a band of Bolsheviks had set out from Yalta to kill the prisoners, but in the dark their transport had swerved on a bend and crashed. The crisis was over and the prisoners free, but the Germans were amazed when the Dowager Tsaritsa flatly refused to see them. As far as she was concerned, Germans were still the enemy.

The German occupation lasted only a few months and their withdrawal left a dangerous vacuum that the Red Army was likely to fill. At first, though, there were allied ships in the Black Sea and there seemed reason to hope. Maria Feodorovna, comfortably installed now at Harax, refused to leave the Crimea until April

1919, when the French evacuated Odessa and the Red Army began to advance. Insisting that all her relatives and friends should be evacuated with her, she left from Koreis on 25 March/7 April 1919 on board the British ship HMS *Marlborough*, which flew the imperial standard in her honour. As *Marlborough* finally sailed from Yalta six days later a ship passed very close by – some remembered it as a troopship, others as one of the ships carrying refugees, but all agree that those on board sang the old Russian anthem, 'God Save the Tsar' when they recognized the Dowager Tsaritsa. She stood on deck, making the sign of the cross, as the ship, Yalta and Livadia passed out of sight. This was the last that any of the Romanovs would see of the Crimea.

But now, eighty years after their departure, the Crimea is beginning to remember them. The imperial houses along the coast suffered a mixed fate in communist hands. Some became rest houses for the northern factories, collectives and unions. Livadia was nominated the first sanatorium for peasants. Other buildings, in a parody of their former existence, served as luxury dachas for the new representatives of wealth and power. Then, in 1939, war returned to the Crimea. The peninsula was under Nazi occupation for three years: the population suffered terribly, and among the saddest non-human casualties were Alexander Mikhailovich's main palace at Ai-Todor and the Maly Palace at Livadia. No traces remain. The site of the Maly Palace, where the death of Alexander III was remembered so lovingly by his family, is now a tennis court.

Livadia was opened to the public after the war, but not to celebrate the imperial family. Its displays related exclusively to 1945, when the palace played host to the American delegation to the Yalta Conference and negotiations took place in the White Hall. Not until the '90s did the palace's true owners begin their inexorable return. In 1992 the Yalta Conference still ruled in the lower rooms but upstairs, where the imperial family once had their private apartments, the bare rooms housed a display of Romanov photographs, hastily mounted on cardboard. The chapel opened for worship again. Its paintwork was peeling and rough and the priest had no robes, but the congregation took an obvious pride in the building's revival. By the summer of 1999 Livadia had become unashamedly imperial. The private apartments are decorated and furnished, with photographs in frames, and the display includes many authentic items drawn from a palace archive whose existence no one would have suspected in the past. Other items are returning. An American visitor brought back the carpet which now hangs on the Tsar's Study wall. Originally a present from the Shah of Persia to commemorate the 1913 Tercentenary, it was lost in the Soviet art sales of the 1920s.

Other coastal mansions too are reclaiming their past. Most former rest homes and dachas have to attract customers to survive, so a little history is no bad thing; only Chair remains in government hands. Djulber reclaimed its own name for its centenary in 1997. Harax is still the 'Dnipro' sanitorium, but its brochure recalls both the old name and the original owners. The Yusupov palace at Koreis is now a luxury hotel, proudly retaining both the family history and the suites once inhabited by Stalin and Molotov. In the most curious twist of all, Massandra, which the imperial family never used, has become a palace museum and one of the most attractive reminders of their world.

14

A Russian Enigma

GRAND PRINCE SERGEI ALEXANDROVICH

The sudden death of Alexander III thrust his four surviving brothers under the spotlight. The eldest of them was forty-seven at the time, the youngest thirty-four: out of ambition or arrogance, compassion for their nephew, the young Tsar, or perhaps from a mixture of motives which even they would not have been able to untangle, the sons of Alexander II seemed ready to dominate the new reign. It was a situation the wider family watched with concern – in many cases because they too had agendas for Russia which they wanted to persuade the Tsar to follow. Sergei Alexandrovich, the third of the brothers, was closest to Nicholas II, to whom he was both uncle and brother-in-law. He was, and remains, the most unfathomable of the four.

At Easter 1916 Samuel Hoare, an officer in British Military Intelligence working in Moscow, met Grand Princess Sergei of Russia in the Martha and Mary Convent which she herself had founded. The meeting left a deep impression on him – Ella had always had the power to fascinate men – and he went away determined to understand her life and to investigate the persistent rumours that Grand Prince Sergei, her husband, was a cruel, perverted man whose wife had led a life of misery. The truth that Hoare uncovered contained a tragic twist. Through conversation with those who really knew the couple he became certain that Sergei had been deliberately misrepresented and misunderstood, his reputation destroyed by those who were jealous of his power and jealous of his marriage. The Grand Princess's suffering, he said, was caused by those who professed to pity her.[1]

Hoare was in a minority. To this day most people have accepted the more sensational view of Grand Prince Sergei. As early as 1908, the writer E.A. Brayley Hodgetts repeated the gossip that had intrigued Hoare. 'It is safe to say that he was the least popular of the Grand Dukes', he wrote, 'and the general feeling towards his charming and amiable consort . . . was one of pity that she should be married to such a man, who had been singled out . . . by the scandal-mongers of St Petersburg for general execration, and reputed, by universal consent, to be the victim of unmentionable vices.'[2] General Mossolov, the head of Nicholas II's Court Chancellery, remembered that 'His private life was the talk of the town, and made his wife . . . very unhappy.'[3] Others filled in the small details that can be made to seem so telling. The French diplomat Maurice Paléologue was responsible for the story that Sergei would not allow his wife to read *Anna Karenina*, for fear of the ideas it might inspire. It was Felix Yusupov who first claimed that the Grand Prince wore corsets which could be seen through the fabric of his light summer uniform. In an age of closely tailored uniforms men's corsets were not uncommon, and excessively narrow waists had been the pride of Russian army officers for generations, but the idea has often been used to give credence to suggestions that Sergei was effeminate.[4] His cousin, Alexander Mikhailovich, was the most damning. 'Try as I will,' he wrote, 'I cannot find a single redeeming feature in his character. . . . Obstinate, arrogant, disagreeable, he flaunted his many peculiarities in the face of the entire nation. . . .' Alexander went on to express his admiration for Elisabeth, and his horror that so perfect a woman should have been tied to such a man: 'I would have given ten years of my life to stop her from entering the church on the arm of haughty Sergei.'[5]

Later writers have embroidered the picture and clarified its hints and evasions. The 'unmentionable vices' and 'peculiarities' are usually taken as sadism or homosexuality, sometimes both. Gossip has become accepted fact and the truth Samuel Hoare thought he had uncovered is all but forgotten. But was he really so deceived? Monster or victim, who was Grand Prince Sergei?

Sergei Alexandrovich, Alexander II's fifth son, was born at Tsarskoe Selo on 29 April/11 May 1857. At four weeks old he was christened in the palace chapel: Anna Tiutcheva described the scene as the thirteen-year-old Tsesarevich performed his first official duty before the Court. 'The Heir was godfather at the christening of his little brother and he played his part with great dignity and skill. The godmother was Grand Princess Ekaterina Mikhailovna. There were a great number of godmothers and godfathers besides, but they were not present. The baby cried a good deal when he was plunged in the water, and when he was anointed with myrrh and his hair was clipped. These cries were enough to reassure the Empress, and when the ceremony was over I hurried to tell her that her august son was extremely well.'[6]

As one of the younger children in a large family, the 'august son' enjoyed many happy moments in his early years. Running wild with pet goats across the lawns of Livadia . . . playing at Tsarskoe Selo with his miniature port on one of the canals in the park . . . playing indoors: Grand Prince Pavel owned an exquisitely made version of the nursery game 'Mikado', in which plain wooden spills were replaced with tiny, perfect replicas of household items – a bucket, a parasol, a pitchfork, a saw, a rake. The brothers were inseparable and were brought up alongside their cousins Konstantin and Dmitri Konstantinovich. Sergei was particularly fond of Olga Konstantinovna in childhood and throughout his life he remained close to Konstantin. He was a gentle boy, protective and kind to younger children. In 1864 Princess Alice told her mother, 'we go to Jugenheim today and Baby with us, as little Serge . . . has such a passion for her'.[7] Sergei was seven then and each time his family visited Germany there would be at least one more Hesse baby to play with. He loved them all and would always find it easiest to relate to the very young. 'I will give Serge an extra kiss from you,' his wife told her brother many years later, 'which he will like, as the affection he used to have for you when a baby has remained the same.'[8]

But Sergei was born too late to enjoy the happiest years of his parents' marriage. His birth coincided with the steady decline in his mother's health and, as she was forced to spend longer periods away from Russia, he was one of the small group of children who travelled with her. He and his sister and brother, Maria and Pavel, became extremely close to their mother and to one another. Early photographs show Sergei as a slight, fair boy with a worried expression. He had inherited his mother's shyness and in time would come to share, surely from her example, her intensity of spirit and her devotion to all things Russian. He saw her sadness too: the younger children were with their mother during the agonizing weeks in Nice when the Tsesarevich Nikolai, who had carried Sergei so proudly at his christening, lay dying. Sergei celebrated his eighth birthday at Heiligenberg a few weeks later. 'Yesterday was Serge's birthday,' Princess Alice told her mother, 'we went with uncle and aunt [the Tsar and Tsaritsa] to the Orthodox mass, it lasted over an hour.'[9]

Sergei could hardly help but be affected by these events. On their way home, the imperial family attended a service in the Chudov Monastery in the Kremlin. Afterwards, the eight-year-old's intense questioning of senior clerics attracted attention and prompted his mother to introduce a strong religious element into his education. From the winter of 1865 meetings were arranged for the little Prince and his tutor with Bishop Leonid, Superior of the Savvino Storozhevsky Monastery near Moscow. Leonid was close to the Tsar and Tsaritsa and over the years became both friend and mentor to Sergei, instilling a deep and unshakeable devotion to the Orthodox Church.

The Grand Prince was nine years old when the first attempt was made on his father's life and he grew up against a background of increasing tension. The threat of violent death haunted the family. So did whispers of his father's love for Princess Dolgorukaya: it is said that Sergei found out about the affair and protected Pavel from the knowledge, but he could not escape its effects himself, and unhappiness and anxiety were driven deep into his character. He grew ever closer to his mother and on her death in 1880 she left him Ilinskoe, her estate by the Moscow river, bypassing her elder children in his favour.

From the 1870s the boys were kept in Russia by their studies. They were destined to follow military careers but their tutor, Admiral Arseniev, made sure that they were well versed in artistic subjects too. Both were fluent in several languages. A quiet, bookish boy, Sergei learned Italian in order to read Dante in the original and his interest in Italian art and culture intensified as he grew older. He painted well and was musical, playing the flute in an amateur orchestra consisting of members of the imperial family. He enjoyed acting and steeped himself in the early history, culture and traditions of Russia. In about 1875 his military service would have begun, and at the outbreak of the war with Turkey in the spring of 1877 he left St Petersburg with his father. In later years he wore the medal of the Order of St George, which was only ever awarded for bravery in the field.

At the war's end Sergei returned to St Petersburg. He was twenty and still under the guidance of Admiral Arseniev. Sergei already enjoyed reading Dostoevsky, and in March 1878 Arseniev arranged a meeting with the author over dinner at the Winter Palace, which Grand Princes Pavel and Konstantin and a distinguished historian, Bestuzhev-Rumin, also attended. Talk over the table was serious and intelligent and this was no accident. The meeting was part of the young men's education, and it was hoped that Dostoevsky would have some influence over them. A month later a second meeting was arranged: Arseniev took care to prepare the ground by writing to Dostoevsky, asking him to raise the subject of the Grand Princes' future role.[10] Sergei came to know many of the great names of Russian literature personally and his cousin and brother-in-law Ernst Ludwig of Hesse remembered him as 'amazingly well-read'. 'How many worthwhile books have I been introduced to by him,' Ernst Ludwig mused, in a private memoir written for his sons.[11] Could this be the man who is supposed to have banned his wife from reading Tolstoy? In 1881, after the assassination of Alexander II, Tolstoy drafted an appeal to the new Tsar to show mercy to his father's killers. He chose Sergei as his intermediary.

It has always been said that the Grand Prince set his heart on his future bride when they were still very young. Elisabeth of Hesse was six months old when Sergei first saw her and a letter written by her mother describes the occasion. It was the day after Sergei's eighth birthday: 'We dine at Heiligenberg every day', Princess Alice told the Queen. 'This morning we were also there with our parents and the children, and Aunt Marie [the Tsaritsa] held Ella on her knee for half an hour and played with her, which made the little one very happy, because she is always attentive and charming. Victoria [Ella's sister] romped around with her cousins, Aunt Marie's two and Uncle Alexander's four boys [Sergei and Pavel and their Battenberg cousins].'[12] As the years passed, Sergei's attachment to the Hesse family deepened and there was talk of marriage between him and one of the daughters: at first the eldest, Victoria, was thought to be the one he favoured, while Elisabeth was at one time suggested for Alexei, his older brother. Elisabeth can hardly have reached her teens when her mother began to say that she would not be happy to see a daughter go to Russia: in 1883, when it became clear that there would be an engagement, the Queen told Victoria of Hesse, 'I know how dearest Mama was agst the idea, (tho' personally she liked Serge)'.[13]

Princess Alice died in December 1878. Towards the end of 1880 Queen Victoria heard talk of an engagement between Sergei and Princess Caroline Mathilde of Schleswig-Holstein, but it came to nothing. Russian sources suggest that Sergei was hesitant about marriage. Many would take this as confirmation that he was homosexual, but in the nineteenth century no one felt bound by the rigid definitions of sexuality that dominate our thinking today. Only one sexual relationship was openly accepted, and that was marriage. Any other relationship was illicit, and a profoundly religious young man might well have been disturbed to find himself having sexual feelings of any kind. Both families were keen for Sergei to marry Elisabeth, but she too was unsure. In November 1882 Sergei spent two days with her in Darmstadt and he was happy but cautious, telling his cousin Konstantin, 'everybody here has already married me off. Please, don't believe it.'[14] This may point to his doubts or Elisabeth's – perhaps to a mixture of both – but he must have made at least a tentative proposal.

Early in 1883 Queen Victoria began issuing warnings against Russian marriages, quoting 'dear Mama' as her authority. Elisabeth turned down Friedrich of Baden in March, and appeared to accept Sergei with her father's blessing in June, but by the end of August she had refused him and was said to be considering a Swedish prince. By September Sergei had decided to return to Darmstadt in person. Once again the engagement appeared to be on, despite the Queen's emphatic warnings about the low moral standards of Russian society. In October Elisabeth finally accepted and across the family voices were raised in Sergei's favour. His sister Maria was quick to defend him – 'an exceptionally nice young man, who . . . has excellent principles'.[15] The Crown Princess of Prussia assured her mother that 'Serge will captivate you when you know him I am sure. There is something quiet and gentle, in fact rather melancholy about him, and his appearance and manners have something high bred and distingué which one misses in some of his brothers.'[16] Elisabeth's father told his cousin, Alexander III, 'I did not hesitate to give my consent because I have known Sergei since he was a child. I see his nice, pleasant manners and I am sure that he will make my daughter happy . . . Of course Sergei has not chosen a brilliant match; but he marries a clever, educated lady who will do her best to make his married life pleasant and happy.'[17]

The engagement was formally announced on 6 November. 'I am happy and contented', Sergei told his brother, the Tsar. '. . . You will understand that my first thought, my first prayer was turned to Mama, asking her and Papa to give me their blessing in this important moment in my life.'[18] In the spring he bought a palace in St Petersburg, on the Fontanka Canal. Then he returned to Darmstadt and showered his fiancée with gifts of jewels, insisting that she should try them all on at once. 'I looked like a Christmas tree!' she wrote, 'and we had a terrible time getting them all off, because we couldn't find the clasps.'[19] He told Pavel, 'Ella is, if possible, even more beautiful. We both sit together a lot. In the mornings she is in my room, and I teach her some Russian, which is very funny.'[20] Elisabeth travelled north with her family a few weeks later, and on 3/15 June she and Sergei were married with immense splendour in the chapel of the Winter Palace: she kept her own name, almost, becoming Grand Princess Elizaveta Feodorovna. Soon after the wedding, the couple made their way to Moscow for a quiet honeymoon at Ilinskoe. This was a timeless place, offering the very simplest pleasures to a young couple who could have afforded any luxury on earth. 'Serge and I took a long walk in the fields', Ella wrote one day to her brother, 'and got lots of flowers, chiefly corn flowers. . . . Serge found a nest hidden under the grass with four dear little birds. There are heaps of wild strawberries all over the place, but not yet quite ripe. . . .'[21]

To this point, few people had seen any harm in Sergei. He was an extremely tall and thin young man, with close-cropped fair hair and a neat beard. He stood very straight and had a habit of playing with one of his jewelled rings, turning it around his finger. He was sensitive and felt things deeply, but had been trained to keep his feelings rigidly in check, and many mistook his reserve for pride. Few had had the chance to know him well, but those who did know him loved him. Queen Victoria and her eldest daughter were severe critics of Russian morals but both were careful to exempt Sergei and Pavel from their strictures. Sergei was noted for his sincere adherence to the church. In 1881 he went to Palestine to assist in the founding of a society devoted to the upkeep of Orthodox shrines in the Holy Land and to the service of Russian pilgrims. He became its chairman. He had a connoisseur's knowledge of Russian antiquities and art treasures too and was a keen archaeologist, attending and sometimes chairing meetings of the Archaeological Congress. He hurt no one: in fact, as his brother-in-law would later recall, 'There were many, very many people he helped, but only in the strictest secrecy.'[22]

The marriage itself brought the first change. Ernst Ludwig, who watched the situation develop from the inside, was sure that the whispering campaign that ultimately destroyed his brother-in-law's reputation originated in Berlin. Their cousin Wilhelm, the future Kaiser, had loved Ella and wanted to marry her, and he hated Sergei for having the prize he had missed. Wilhelm was a strange character, and Ernst was positive that he spread gossip to discredit his rival. Nor was Wilhelm the only one; the same envy is clear in the writing of Alexander Mikhailovich. It was Ella's very beauty that drove her many admirers to find fault with Sergei.

After the honeymoon the couple returned to St Petersburg, where society was keen to observe its new Grand Princess. Sergei and Ella became very close to Alexander III and his wife and children, and the Tsar thought particularly highly of his younger brother. In 1886 he appointed Sergei Commander of the Preobrajensky Guard, entrusting him with the sensitive task of introducing the Heir to army life – and Alexander III was a careful man. Often Sergei was asked to represent his brother in public. In 1887 he and Ella attended Queen Victoria's Jubilee. In 1888 they were sent to the Holy Land. This was a real compliment to them both, because the occasion was the consecration of the church of St Mary Magdalene in Jerusalem, built in memory of Tsaritsa Maria Alexandrovna who was revered by her sons. The Tsar would never have entrusted these tasks to a brother who 'flaunted his many peculiarities in the face of the entire nation', but as Alexander III showed more and more favour to Sergei, the whisperers found a growing audience.

For Sergei and Ella, the visit to the Holy Land brought about a profound change. She had opted to remain a Lutheran on marriage and he said nothing, though privately he found it painful to be divided from her in an area of life that was vital to him. Jerusalem, and the service of consecration, gave shape to a longing that had been growing in her mind. At the end of 1890 she began to prepare her family for her conversion to Orthodoxy. Her greatest fear seemed to be that they would blame Sergei. 'Let the people scream about me', she told her brother, 'but only never say a word against my Serge. Take his part above all – <u>tell them I adore him, also my new country and so have learned to love their religion</u>.' She was adamant that the decision was her own, repeating the same assurances about Sergei time and again. 'He was a real angel of kindness . . . never, never did he complain, and only now I know through Paul's wife that there were moments – he was in despair.'[23]

A religious man . . . a kind man, who would let himself be hurt rather than hurt those he loved. This is a world away from the perverted and cruel Sergei of popular myth. Yet there is no ambiguity in Elisabeth's letters. No one reading them could seriously doubt that she loved her husband, but there was a defensive edge creeping into the things she said. She must have been aware that

Sergei had enemies who would twist any event against him, and her love was becoming protective. In the spring of 1891 the Tsar appointed Sergei Governor-General of Moscow and they were touched by the honour, but deeply apprehensive: 'it will be very difficult for us,' Elisabeth told her father, 'since we are really longing for a quiet private life instead of playing such a part. I think that Serge is even sadder than I, for he was hoping to stay another year in the regiment. . . . The officers are really very touching in the way they are devoted to him. . . . It is terribly difficult for my dear Serge; he has become quite pale and thin. How I should love to take him to Darmstadt now, so that he would be able to rest. For they never let him have any peace; he has double the amount to do . . . It makes one's hair stand on end when one thinks how much responsibility is placed on Serge.'[24]

Sergei had been given what amounted to the power of a reigning prince in the Moscow region. This fact alone makes nonsense of recent suggestions that he had been sent to Moscow in disgrace for his part in some unspecified homosexual scandal,[25] but such a promotion was bound to provoke increased envy, and it seems likely that the hostility was finding its centre among Grand Princess Vladimir's circle. There were many reasons why the Grand Princess might enjoy hearing and repeating rumours about Sergei. She was close to Wilhelm of Prussia – her own cousin – and she and her husband were known for their pro-German views. Then there was the religious question: she still took Elisabeth's conversion as a personal slight. The favours the Tsar showed Sergei (he had never got on with Vladimir), the closeness that grew between Sergei and Ella and the Tsesarevich Nicholas, as they encouraged his love for Ella's sister Alix, all these were steady drips that became a flood-tide. Gossip always seems harmless to those who repeat it, and the Vladimirs' circle was renowned for its gossip and intrigue.

To be fair, Sergei was his own worst enemy. He made no secret of the fact that he disapproved of society and its lax ways, and he defied all criticism. He found it hard to cope with opposition and lost his temper too easily. In his home he demanded tidiness, order and discipline, and expected to be obeyed – yet he rewarded those he loved with gentleness and affection. His charm is as strongly represented in the old memoirs as his supposed vices, though those who loved him often felt obliged to apologise for their partiality. So, for example, his niece, Marie of Romania, 'Dry, nervous, short of speech, impatient, he had none of the rather careless good-humour of his three elder brothers . . . But for all that we loved him, felt irresistibly attracted to him, hard though he could be. Few perhaps cherish his memory, but I do.'[26] Or his nephew Kyrill, who credited Sergei with 'the loftiest principles coupled with a character of rarest nobility', and thought him the most remarkable of Alexander II's sons.[27] Or another Marie, Princess of Greece, 'The Grand Duke Serge was not very popular, I am afraid; but I personally liked him, as he was particularly nice and kind to me always.'[28] Meriel Buchanan encountered Sergei in Darmstadt when she was a child. 'The Grand Duke Serge adored children and in spite of the almost forbidding sternness of his face I trusted him implicitly.'[29] But the most surprising witness for the defence is Princess Radziwill. Her gossipy accounts of the private lives of European royalty shook many a reputation but for Sergei she had only praise. He was 'amiable in the extreme', she said, and at one ball in Moscow 'he reminded one, by the grace of his manner, of his father, the late Tsar Alexander II. . . . I remember him well on that particular evening, when representatives from the whole world crowded into his rooms. He had a pleasant word for each one, showed himself an attentive host, and had none of that proud reserve with which he had been credited.'[30]

Moscow brought out the best and the worst in the Grand Prince. He may have quailed before the task of governing, but his interests drew him irresistibly towards Russia's ancient capital and it was not long before he and Elisabeth came to regard Moscow as their true home. Sergei knew and loved every corner and byway of the Kremlin. He was immensely conscientious in carrying out his duties: 'Even in the country when he was supposed to be resting,' his niece remembered, 'he was constantly receiving couriers from Moscow and giving audiences.'[31] He paid extraordinary attention to detail, attending personally to matters that could easily have been left to subordinates and punishing corruption and fraud. At times he would go about the city incognito to see conditions for himself: in private both he and Ella were deeply concerned about the poverty they saw in Moscow and the surrounding countryside, and they discussed ways to improve conditions. The work Ella undertook after her husband's death was the fruit of their shared concern.

But on the negative side, the role of Governor-General gave him the opportunity to be an autocrat. The Tsar trusted his brother to govern sternly, knowing that they shared a belief in strong government and ruthless suppression of dissent. Sergei's rule was popular with the clergy, nobility and merchants in Moscow, all of whom craved order, but it made him even more enemies. He followed the anti-Semitic policies of his brother's government, passing laws in 1892 that expelled Jewish artisans and traders from Moscow. Princess Radziwill defended him from the charge of anti-Semitism, saying that 'he was called on to execute measures – such as the expulsion of the Jews from Moscow – for which he was not responsible', but few would share her view.[32] The Grand Prince's upbringing had taught him that Orthodox monarchy was the only régime for the Russia he loved and he believed in this fervently, as an article of faith. He came to be seen as a brutal reactionary but Ernst Ludwig, who knew him well, told a different story. 'The tragedy of his life', Ernst wrote, 'was that he was too far-sighted. In politics the strict conservative party held him to be much too progressive, because he wished and strove for improvements which were not acceptable to them. The Liberals hated him because they thought he would hinder their attempts to storm forward. He considered many of their wishes to be impractical, or thought that the time was not ripe for them.' Sergei actively encouraged his brother-in-law to make reforms in Hesse.[33]

But the deepest stain on the Grand Prince's career, which no explanation or excuse can cover, was his response to the disaster at Khodynka Meadow during the coronation celebrations of 1896. Sergei looked forward to his nephew's coronation as the crowning moment of his own career, when Moscow would draw the eyes of the world. As Governor-General he had responsibility for the ancient ceremony and he prepared the young Tsaritsa, explaining every detail of the ceremonial to her. Everything was planned: tradition demanded a great popular festival on the Khodynka Meadow with the distribution of commemorative gifts. The arrangements were all made but no one considered how to manage the crowds the event was bound to attract. Through the night of 17/29 May people poured onto the field. The crush became intense but still they came, pressing ever more tightly into a restricted space until a tragedy became unavoidable. By the early hours of the morning over 1,300 people had been crushed to death in circumstances of unimaginable horror, and at least twice that number were injured. Reality did not sink in at first. The field was cleared and the festival went ahead, delighting a crowd of at least 700,000 who cheered to the echo when the Tsar appeared. But the news spread and with it the disquiet; so monumental a blunder had to be paid for in some way and eyes began to turn towards the Governor-General. Sergei did not cause the tragedy personally but the ultimate responsibility was his: as he expected to take credit for the coronation arrangements, so he should have accepted the blame when things went wrong. He should have offered his resignation and cancelled the remaining celebrations, but when the moment came he seems to have panicked. Championed by his brothers, he urged the Tsar to carry on as if nothing had happened, trusting that private gestures of kindness made after the event would ease the city's pain. It was a terrible error of judgement that sealed Sergei's own fate and contributed to the dynasty's fall.

Some still defended him. His niece, Grand Princess Olga Alexandrovna, said that he had offered to resign and been refused: if this were true it would lessen the guilt, but the documents released so far suggest that he threatened to resign some weeks later, when the Tsar wanted to set up a commission of enquiry – and that was quite different. Even those who loved Sergei were appalled. Looking back on the events of coronation week, Konstantin Konstantinovich confided to his diary, 'during the whole of this week Sergei has not acted in the way I consider that he should, rather to the contrary. All these days I have been suffering for Sergei. I love him dearly, we have been friends since childhood, and now I have to listen to condemnation of him from all sides; and yet I am not able to say one word in his defence; I am not able to talk to him: we would only argue.'[34]

After Khodynka, things would never be the same. Superficially the tension eased, and friendly crowds filled the streets again. In 1900 Nicholas II revived the ancient custom of spending Easter in Moscow. The imperial couple carried out an extensive programme of official activities with Sergei and Elisabeth beside them, and Sergei guided the Tsaritsa around the palaces and churches of the Kremlin himself. It must have felt like the personal triumph the coronation should have been. 'My uncle was happy,' his niece remembered, 'the city, for which he was totally responsible, had shown itself worthy of the occasion: there had been every evidence of an impulsive, expansive loyalty on the part of the people; and the political horizon appeared in all ways serene.'[35]

Appeared. . . . But beneath the surface and the reassuring crowds, Sergei had become a focus for serious opponents of the régime as well as for malicious gossips – he had made himself the easiest target in the imperial family and the stories spread as never before. People said that he had too much influence over his nephew. They accused Elisabeth of manipulating the young Tsaritsa, and of being jealous of her. They wove ever more sensational stories about Sergei and Elisabeth's marriage. She knew, and was hurt. In the autumn of 1896 the two couples travelled to Darmstadt together, and after her return Elisabeth wrote to her grandmother,

. . . we thoroughly enjoyed ourselves together at Darmstadt & travelled most pleasantly together home. It must have been a great astonishment as people were saying we did not like each other &c. Well the abominable lies told about us to them [Nicholas and Alexandra] are not eddifying, the intrigues were simply disgusting but one day I trust all the truth will come out & the great thing is to have a clear conscience before God as who can change the unkindness of the world, in this case of a set of jealous intriguers. Our delightful journey freshened us both up although poor Serge looks very thin. People I suppose could not believe that we were harmless & happy so began trying to prove the contrary. Really we want nothing we are very happy we try to do our duty & I must say it sounds vain people here like us & again proved their affection by receiving us most warmly. . . .[36]

The couple were happy in themselves, there can be no real doubt of that. The most telling detail of all regarding their personal relationship occurs in the memoirs of their niece, who lived in their household during the latter part of the marriage: 'They slept up to the last year of their life together in the same bed.'[37] This was extremely unusual at the time, both for royalty and for anyone else wealthy enough to choose their own arrangements. It argues a depth of love and understanding that gives the lie to rumours about the marriage: Elisabeth asked no pity and needed none. She loved her husband. The only lingering unhappiness, for both partners, was their childlessness, in a married life lasting a little over twenty years. Both adored children. Elisabeth gave parties for other people's children and Sergei relaxed in the company of the very young and related easily to them. He was a terrible tease – something which seems quite at odds with his public, adult face. There may be some truth in the suggestion that he was homosexual, in inclination at least, but no evidence has ever been cited and another possibility fits the picture rather better. Elisabeth is said to have told one of her ladies-in-waiting that Sergei was unable to consummate the marriage, a situation she accepted because she loved him.[38] If this were true – and it can only be hearsay – it would go a long way towards explaining his temper and the tension people sensed in his presence. At that time impotence would have been seen as a shameful condition for a man, and it would have been particularly bitter for a man who loved children, and longed to be a father. One thing is clear: by 1892, six years into the marriage, Sergei was already certain that he would never have a family, and this at a time when many homosexual men did father children. He made a will leaving his property to his brother's children after he and Elisabeth were dead. In April that year Alexander III, while thanking his wife for the joys of parenthood, commented, 'Poor Sergei and Ella, I often think of them: for all their lives they are denied this great consolation in life. . . .'[39]

But towards the end, two children did join the household. From the time of their marriage, Sergei and Elisabeth were inseparable from Grand Prince Pavel, living in a threesome that was close enough in itself to raise eyebrows. Pavel married in 1889 and the three became four, until one terrible day in the autumn of 1891 when Pavel's wife went into premature labour and her life could not be saved. It was Sergei who took charge of the frail baby, gently nursing him into health and life with his own hands. After this the children, Marie and Dmitri, were often entrusted to their uncle and aunt and in 1902, when Pavel left Russia in secret to contract an illegal marriage, Sergei requested and was given legal guardianship. It was not an easy situation. Marie adored her father. She knew that her uncle loved her and her brother but resented him, believing that he was trying to take her father's place. She was probably unaware that Sergei and Elisabeth had made desperate attempts to persuade Pavel back to Russia for his children's sake, even making a special journey to Italy to plead with him in person. Marie saw her uncle and aunt through the eyes of an angry child and this perspective stayed with her into adulthood, when she wrote her memoirs. She acknowledged her uncle's love, while emphasizing his strictness, but described her aunt, who had been demonstrative and affectionate to so many other children, as cruelly unfeeling. Perhaps she was right and there were resentments on both sides.

By the end of 1904 the political horizon no longer appeared serene. War with Japan had brought unrest to the surface and as strikes, student riots and mutinies spread across the country the Tsar was forced to make concessions. Sergei opposed the changes themselves and his nephew's manner of granting them. On a Christmas visit to the Tsar in St Petersburg he explained his misgivings, and one of the Tsaritsa's ladies would later recall his words: 'New ideas require new men . . . I am unable to change my views, and if you want to start on a new policy, you must do so with the help of men who are whole-heartedly in support of it.'[40] He resigned from the post of Governor-General and moved his wife and the children into the Neskuchnoe

Palace in the city, which previously they had used only at Christmas. As the weeks passed with no easing of the tension they moved again, suddenly and under cover of darkness, into the safety of the Kremlin. Sergei had barely nine weeks more to live, but he faced the personal danger with the courage once remarkable in his father. Each day he returned unaccompanied to the Governor-General's house to supervise remaining business, refusing to risk the life of his aide-de-camp. On the afternoon of 4/17 February 1905, as his carriage approached the Nikolsky Gate of the Kremlin, an explosion shook the air, rattling every window in the area. Silence followed, and a flock of crows wheeled over the Kremlin rooftops. Grand Prince Sergei Alexandrovich was dead, killed by a terrorist's bomb, and his shattered remains were placed on a stretcher under a soldier's greatcoat and carried to the Chudov Monastery, the historic baptismal place of the children of the Tsars of Russia. He had been hated for the severity of his rule but there was another side, now too easily forgotten. 'There were so many wreaths the coffin was drowned in greenery,' one of his aides-de-camp recalled, 'every day the people were allowed in to pay their respects at specific hours; a hundred people were let in at a time. Services were held from morning to night, without interruption. . . .'[41]

Elisabeth had a memorial cross erected on the site of the assassination with the inscription, 'Forgive them, for they know not what they do', carved in the stone. It was pulled down after the Revolution, reputedly by Lenin himself. The Chudov Abbey was demolished in 1928. In 1990 workmen discovered the blocked-up entrance to the old burial vault under a Kremlin car park, but five more years would pass before Sergei's coffin was finally exhumed and carried in procession to the Cathedral of the Archangel, where a solemn service was held. Afterwards, the procession moved out of the Kremlin and across Red Square to a waiting hearse, which took Grand Prince Sergei's remains on their last journey to the vault of the Novospassky Monastery for reburial. Grand Princess Elisabeth, who suffered a death more brutal even than that of her husband, has been canonized as a saint of the Orthodox Church. In 1998 her statue was erected at Westminster Abbey, with other martyrs of the twentieth century.

Alexandra Georgievna and Elisabeth

15

A Place of Peace and Beauty

Ilinskoe, Grand Prince Sergei's country home outside Moscow, was to play an important part in the final years of Romanov rule because it helped to shape the last Tsaritsa and her view of Russia. More than any other house owned by the imperial family, Ilinskoe came to represent for her the ideal of a peaceful, pastoral land far from the artificial circles of Court and society – a place where the peasants were simple and loyal and at one with their rulers, who cared for them, and worked to ease the hardness of their lot. Benevolent and paternalistic, deeply rooted in the Russian soil and the Russian church, this concept of autocracy was a dream that could never survive in the assertive clamour of the new century – but at Ilinskoe, for a few brief years, the dream seemed enticingly real.

The house was modest by royal standards; a wooden building in an estate of some 2,400 acres on the bank of the Moscow river, about forty miles to the west of Moscow. The nearest railway station, Odintsovo, lay eight miles away; an hour's carriage ride over the only metalled road in the district brought visitors to Ilinskoe through a wide, expansive landscape of wheatfields, grass meadows and forests. Years later one of the house's younger inhabitants, Pavel's daughter Grand Princess Marie Pavlovna, described the last stages of the journey, still fresh in her memory:

Harness bells tinkled gaily. The straight, sandy road passed by the fields. The wheat, still green, was as high as the carriage. A warm breeze stirred the wheat in long waves.

After traversing a pine forest the carriage came out on to a vast meadow from which, beyond the river sunk between its banks and still invisible, you perceived the roof of Ilinskoie drowned in the crests of the trees.

172

At the end of the meadow the coachman slowed down cautiously to cross a wooden bridge which was, because of frequent floods, a floating structure. Hoofs resounded on the planks and the horses breathed noisily.

Slowly now we traversed the village. Dirty children, in small shirts inadequately cut to their stature, played in the dust. Before the tavern stood peasant teams, tied to a trough hollowed out of a tree trunk. The short grass in front of the houses was matted with mud and trampled down by animals. At the left there was a church with a green roof, and just beyond, the wide wooden gates of Ilinskoie, open to receive us.[1]

It was a world away from the surroundings the imperial family knew in and around St Petersburg.

An official ukaze issued from Krasnoe Selo on 27 July/9 August 1864 announced the purchase of Ilinskoe from Princess Golitsina: Alexander II and Maria Alexandrovna were particularly drawn to the estate by its proximity to the Savvino Storozhevsky Monastery, which had had close links with the Romanov family since the seventeenth century. A week after the purchase, Alexander arrived on a tour of inspection with his sons, Alexander and Alexei, and nephews, Nikolai Konstantinovich and Evgeni of Leuchtenberg. They stayed several days, visiting the main house and four smaller dwellings on the estate and viewing the gardens and park. Grand Prince Alexander particularly asked that the small one-storey dacha now set aside for his elder brother be allowed to retain its name 'Nechui Gorya', which in English means 'Feel no grief'.

The Tsar ordered improvements and the following summer he made a brief visit, alone, to oversee the work, returning shortly afterwards with his brother and elder sons. They were received with the traditional gifts of bread and salt and spent some time talking to peasants from the estate before viewing the completed work. The Tsar was pleased with what he saw: on 19 September/1 October the whole family arrived at Ilinskoe. A suite of five rooms had been prepared for the younger Grand Princes and their tutor on the ground floor, facing the Moscow river, while their sister's apartments faced the garden. The Tsar and Tsaritsa occupied twenty rooms on the upper floor.

Like Livadia, Ilinskoe was bought for the Tsaritsa, and she used the estate as a staging-post on her many journeys south, to the Crimea or the European spa towns, and north, returning to the capital. There were palaces in Moscow that she could quite well have used but Ilinskoe was a country retreat far removed from any palace. The Tsar often accompanied her; in the June and early July of 1869 he was at Ilinskoe with her before travelling to Tsarskoe Selo, only to return a few weeks later en route for Livadia in the south – sadly the evidences of his presence are the telegrams he sent to Princess Dolgorukaya. Perhaps this points to one reason why Ilinskoe came to mean so much to the Tsaritsa and to her youngest children who knew her best. Unlike Tsarskoe Selo, Peterhof and Gatchina, which were surrounded by the homes of the wealthy and fashionable whose ears were always open for gossip from the Court, Ilinskoe was miles away in open country, surrounded by the 'real' Russia that attracted Maria Alexandrovna so strongly. When she died on 22 May/3 June 1880, alone in her dark room in the Winter Palace with its windows looking out on bare walls, Ilinskoe, in all its spaciousness and peace, passed to Sergei. She must have known how much he loved it. Visiting him there a few years later, in the summer of 1884, his sister Maria wrote, 'It is such a chance and luck for Sergei that he has got this charming place of his own as none of my other brothers have any country place except near Petersburg. . . .'[2]

Sergei was on his honeymoon that summer. Four years had passed since his mother's death and the house was unchanged: to his sister, it brought back memories of still earlier days. 'The last time I had been here was in '69 when it belonged to Mama and she was so fond of it. Nothing has changed since it has remained exactly as she left it with all her pictures, furniture and small things. The rooms have also been left. It is a very nice old-fashioned house with plenty of rooms besides smaller houses for the suite. I have my old rooms.'[3]

Intended for summer use, the house was built of oak over a stone foundation, on a simple, square pattern with two storeys. The back windows overlooked the river and a broad balcony ran the length of the upper floor, a pleasant place to sit for breakfast, or on long summer evenings. There was a pathway leading down to the river with its wooden landing-stage, boat houses and a tiny changing hut, and an avenue of lime trees shaded the drive to the entrance gates. Beyond the gates was the little green-roofed church and the village. Beyond the village were the meadows, the river itself, and the open stillness of field and forest. If the family wanted company there were neighbouring estates near enough for an afternoon or evening's outing. Usovo, which faced Ilinskoe across the river, had become an imperial property in 1867 but the Golitsins, Scherbatovs and Sheremetievs all had estates in the area. Archangelskoe, which belonged to the Yusupovs, was only three miles away and it was a palace compared to Ilinskoe. The estate had its own picture gallery and theatre; at one time it had even boasted a porcelain factory. 'There are very nice neighbours about the country,' Maria wrote, 'whom we used to know in former days.'[4]

Country life offered the simplest of pleasures; walking, sketching and reading, picnics and carriage drives, picking wild flowers or hunting mushrooms in the woods. Riding, Maria said, 'is the pleasantest exercise here, as the roads are all soft and the woods are shady and cool. The river Moskva runs through the property, which adds to the pleasures of this place as we can go about in boats and bathe.'[5] On one occasion her daughter Marie, Crown Princess of Romania, almost drowned while swimming at Ilinskoe when she was caught unawares by the current: only the quick thinking of her brother saved her from disaster.

In the evenings the family enjoyed music and parlour games. 'This evening we have a small dance and have been making bouquets and wreaths of corn-flowers for all the ladies. There are beautiful wild flowers in the fields and woods, but the hay-making has just begun and they will very soon disappear.'[6] It was an idyllic, peaceful existence tied to the rhythms of the changing year and shared by peasant and prince alike. Family celebrations at the big house drew in people from the villages, who were welcomed and treated with respect. The Duchess of Edinburgh's visit happened to coincide with her brother's name-day, and she told Queen Victoria that after a service in the church and visits from wealthy neighbours, local peasant children gathered in the garden of Ilinskoe to receive gifts of clothing and sweets: in later years the Grand Prince would also organize a lottery for their parents. Sunday services brought all classes together. Prince Yusupov recalled how at Archangelskoe, 'Every Sunday after church my parents received the peasants and their families in the courtyard in front of the château. The children were given refreshments, and their parents presented their requests and grievances. These were always treated with great kindness and their requests were rarely refused.'[7] When saints' days and church festivals brought colour into the life of the village, the household of Ilinskoe would come out of the gates to join the fun, and Sergei and Ella often acted as godparents to the village children.

Their niece described the annual celebration of the feast of the prophet Elijah, who was patron saint of the little church. Preparations began days in advance, as itinerant merchants set up their stalls, fairground rides and games along the main street. The great day began with a service in the church, after which Sergei would declare the fair open. When lunch was over, he set out with his household to walk the village street. 'My uncle and aunt felt obliged to buy from each merchant,' Marie remembered, 'even the most modest. They began the rounds, my uncle on one side, my aunt on the other, continued to the end, met, and began over again. Servants walked behind them carrying enormous baskets which filled rapidly. The merchandise was of no great variety, from year to year always the same: linens, printed calicoes, handkerchiefs and shawls, earthenware, glassware, ribbons, sweets. . . . There were tobacco boxes in enamelled papier-mâché, with portraits of the Emperor and Empress or of my uncle and aunt. . . . In the evening after dinner we returned to the fair and rode on the merry-go-round by the light of the grease-pots and candles stuck in bottles. The crowd was as thick as by day; it became generally rowdy under the influence of drink, and we returned early to the house. The night air carried faintly up to us the sound of accordions, the sticky voices of peasants, and the strident laughter of women.'[8]

Into this picture-book landscape, in the summer of 1890, came

Alexandra Feodorovna, wife of the future Tsar Nicholas I, with her children
Alexander and Maria, *c.* 1820 (Nancy Tryon Collection)

Nicholas I as a young man (Private Collection)

His grandson, Alexander II's eldest son Nikolai Alexandrovich, *c.* 1851 (Nancy Tryon Collection)

The Anichkov Palace in St Petersburg (Private Collection)

Maria Nikolaievna, Duchess of
Leuchtenberg (Private Collection)

Her son, Sergei of Leuchtenberg, who
was killed in action in the Turkish war
(Private Collection)

Olga Nikolaievna, Queen of
Württemburg (Private Collection)

Alexandra Nikolaievna (Private
Collection)

Konstantin Nikolaievich with his
eldest son Nikolai (Private Collection)

Alexandra Iosifovna, Grand Princess
Konstantin with their daughter Olga,
the future Queen of Greece (Private
Collection)

Konstantin (centre), Dmitri (left) and
Viatcheslav Konstantinovich, 1866
(Private Collection)

Alexander II with his dog Milord,
c. 1866 (Private Collection)

Tsaritsa Maria Alexandrovna, *c.* 1866
(Private Collection)

Vladimir Alexandrovich, *c.* 1866
(Private Collection)

Alexei Alexandrovich, *c.* 1866 (Private
Collection)

Maria Alexandrovna, *c*. 1866 (Private Collection)

Sergei Alexandrovich, *c*. 1864 (Private Collection)

Pavel Alexandrovich, *c*. 1864 (Private Collection)

The Tsesarevich Nikolai with his fiancée, Princess Dagmar of Denmark, 1864 (Private Collection)

His brother, the Tsesarevich Alexander, with Dagmar, who became Maria Feodorovna at the time of their marriage in 1866 (Private Collection)

Vladimir Alexandrovich with his fiancée, Marie of Mecklenburg-Strelitz, in 1874 (Private Collection)

The Tsesarevich Alexander (later
Alexander III) (Private Collection)

Tsarevna Maria Feodorovna with
her son Nicholas (the future Nicholas
II), taken in Denmark, *c.* 1869
(Private Collection)

The old palace of Livadia, in the Crimea (Private Collection)

Maria Feodorovna with her children Nicholas (right), Georgi and Xenia, c. 1877
(Private Collection)

Grand Prince Vladimir Alexandrovich (Private Collection)

Marie Pavlovna with their sons Kyrill (left) and Boris, c. 1879 (Private Collection)

Grand Prince Alexei Alexandrovich taken by M.B. Brady in 1871, during the tour of the United States (Nancy Tryon Collection)

Alexander III and Maria Feodorovna
with their children: (l to r), Mikhail,
Nikolai (behind his father), Olga (in
front), Xenia and Georgi, c. 1889
(Private Collection)

Pavel Alexandrovich with his wife
Alexandra Georgievna, formerly
Princess Alexandra of Greece,
1889/90 (Private Collection)

Sergei Alexandrovich and his wife
Elizaveta Feodorovna (Ella), with
their widowed brother Pavel
Alexandrovich and his children Marie
(beside her aunt), and Dmitri, 1892
(Private Collection)

The family at Coburg in April 1894 for the wedding of Ernst Ludwig of Hesse and Victoria Melita: (l to r), seated: Kaiser Wilhelm II, Queen Victoria, behind Beatrice of Saxe-Coburg, Kaiserin Friedrich behind Feodora of Saxe-Meiningen. First row: Alfred of Saxe-Coburg, Tsesarevich Nicholas and his new fiancée, Princess Alix of Hesse-Darmstadt, Victoria of Battenberg, Irène of Prussia, Grand Princess Vladimir, Maria Alexandrovna, Duchess of Saxe-Coburg. Second row: the Prince of Wales, Princess Henry of Battenberg, Princess Philipp of Saxe-Coburg (white cape), Alexandra of Saxe-Coburg, Charlotte, Princess Bernhard of Saxe-Meinigen (partly obscured), Louise, Duchess of Connaught. Behind: Louis of Battenberg, Pavel Alexandrovich (bowler hat), Henry of Battenberg, Philipp of Saxe-Coburg, Count Mensdorff, Sergei Alexandrovich, Marie, Crown Princess of Romania, Crown Prince Ferdinand of Romania, Grand Princess Sergei, Vladimir Alexandrovich, Arthur, Duke of Connaught, Alfred, Duke of Saxe-Coburg (Private Collection)

Nicholas II (Private Collection)

Tsaritsa Alexandra Feodorovna
(Private Collection)

The imperial children Tatiana (left), Olga (right) and baby Maria on the beach at
Livadia with their nurses in 1900 (Private Collection)

Nicholas and Alexandra with their four daughters, Olga, Tatiana, Maria and Anastasia, in 1901 (Private Collection)

The birth of an heir; the four Grand Princesses arranged proudly around their baby brother, the Tsesarevich Alexei, in 1904 (Private Collection)

Alexandra Feodorovna with her son (Private Collection)

The Konstantinovichi in 1903: (l to r), Dmitri Konstantinovich; Konstantin Konstantinovich with his daughter Tatiana; the old Grand Princess Konstantin, Alexandra Iosifovna; Olga, Queen of Greece; Vera Konstantinovna, Duchess Eugen of Württemberg; Ioann Konstantinovich; Elizaveta Mavrikievna, Grand Princess Konstantin; Gavril Konstantinovich; (in front) Konstantin Konstantinovich, Igor Konstantinovich, Oleg Konstantinovich, Prince Christopher of Greece (in sailor suit) (Private Collection)

The daughters of Nicholas II in 1906: (l to r), Olga, Tatiana, Maria and Anastasia (Private Collection)

Ella, Grand Princess Sergei (Private Collection)

Grand Prince Dmitri Pavlovich (Private Collection)

Grand Prince Sergei Alexandrovich (Private Collection)

Above: The Tsesarevich Alexei; Right: Alexei on his third birthday, 1907 (Private Collection)

At play with his sisters (from the left) Anastasia, Maria and Tatiana in the gardens of the Alexander Palace (Private Collection)

Nicholas II on the steps of the Alexander Nevsky Cathedral in Reval with his uncle Alexei (left) and Count Frederiks (right), 27 September/10 October 1904 (Private Collection)

'God Preserve the Tsar': patriotic postcard showing Nicholas and Alexei above the Winter Palace (Private Collection)

The Dowager Tsaritsa Maria Feodorovna
(centre) in Denmark with her sisters,
Queen Alexandra of Great Britain (right)
and Thyra, Duchess of Cumberland
(Private Collection)

Grand Prince Mikhail Alexandrovich
in Denmark (Private Collection)

The imperial children taken in Darmstadt, their mother's old home, in 1910
(Private Collection)

The widowed Grand Princess Vladimir (right) with her daughter-in-law Victoria Melita and grand-daughters Marie (left) and Kyra, 1909 (Private Collection)

Grand Prince Dmitri Pavlovich (Private Collection)

Grand Princess Xenia Alexandrovna and Grand Prince Alexander Mikhailovich with their youngest son Vasili, *c.* 1911 (Private Collection)

The Tsaritsa and her elder daughters,
Olga (left) and Tatiana, as nurses in
wartime (Private Collection)

Tsar Nicholas II in naval uniform
(Private Collection)

Alexei and his dog Joy: a photograph
taken by the Tsaritsa in 1916 and
released for war charities (Private
Collection)

Prince Ioann Konstantinovich and his wife Elena, born a princess of Serbia (Private Collection)

His brother Konstantin Konstantinovich (Private Collection)

Prince Oleg Konstantinovich, who was killed in action in 1914 (Private Collection)

Prince Igor Konstantinovich (Private Collection)

Ella, Grand Princess Sergei, in her nun's habit (Private Collection)

Grand Princess Olga Alexandrovna, the Tsar's younger sister, as a wartime nurse (Private Collection)

Grand Prince Pavel Alexandrovich with his second wife Olga, Princess Paley, and their children Vladimir, Irina and Natalia (Private Collection)

Grand Prince Nikolai Nikolaievich, taken in exile in the 1920s (Nancy Tryon Collection)

The Vladimirovichi in the 20s: (l to r), Elena Vladimirovna, Princess Nicholas of Greece, Grand Prince Andrei, Victoria, Grand Princess Kyrill, Grand Prince Boris, Grand Prince Kyrill (Private Collection)

Maria Feodorovna (centre), taken in Denmark in 1927 with her grandson Vasili Alexandrovich (left), her daughter Olga Alexandrovna (right) and sons Tikhon and Guri Kulikovsky, Olga's children by her second marriage. The others are (l to r) Princess Olga of Cumberland, Thyra, Duchess of Cumberland, Prince Waldemar of Denmark, Princess Max of Baden (Private Collection)

Princess Alix of Hesse, Sergei's eighteen-year-old sister-in-law, with her father and eldest sister. She had been to Russia before, to St Petersburg, but the Moscow countryside was different and it made a profound impact on her mind and memory. In after years, Ilinskoe would remain at the heart of her concept of Russia. She would always believe that somewhere out there, beyond the sophistication and anger of the city, were simple people who lived out their lives in quiet, trusting God and their rulers to care for their needs. For this she has been condemned – even laughed at – but she may not have been so wrong. The Revolution, when it came, was a rising of discontented and badly used soldiers, of educated people and the urban poor. There must have been many remote country areas where the old order was accepted and its people were bewildered and hurt by violent change. She was not the only member of the imperial family to see something uniquely valuable in the old ways. Grand Prince Sergei was one of the most convinced adherents of the old order, and he helped to shape her views. His cousin Konstantin Konstantinovich had an estate in the Moscow countryside some miles to the west, at Ostashevo: he too loved the traditional ways. In describing life in the country to the south of Moscow, Alix's sister-in-law Olga Alexandrovna expressed this attitude to peasant life at its most sincere: 'I went from village to village, nobody interfering with me. I went into their huts. There were hardships and I saw penury too, of a kind I had never imagined to exist. But there was also kindness, magnanimity, and an unbreakable faith in God. As I saw it, those peasants were rich for all their poverty, and I had the sense of being a genuine human being when I was among them.'9

The way of life represented by Ilinskoe was not about rich people pretending to be rural. The house's inhabitants were well aware that life beyond their gates was muddy and harsh, allowing no luxuries and few amenities for the poor. They did their utmost to help. By 1884 every village within reach of Ilinskoe had its own school for children of both sexes: female education was a cause Maria Alexandrovna had held very dear. Her son followed her lead and, though he was inclined to be pessimistic about moves to improve the peasants' lot, he listened to his wife's concerns and made further reforms. On the couple's combined initiative, for example, trained midwives were brought to the villages. Sergei also had a small maternity clinic built at Ilinskoe.

On his own land, Sergei was a great improver. He sunk his resources into new breeds of cattle, imported from abroad, and he financed a stud farm, new greenhouses, poultry houses and vegetable gardens, seeing and expecting little financial return. To lengthen the period he was able to spend in the country he had a brick and stone house built at Usovo with modern heating. In later years the Ilinskoe household would cross the river with the coming of autumn, to settle in the new house.

Twice Ilinskoie provided shelter and peace for a couple on honeymoon. When Sergei and Elisabeth stayed at the house in 1884 they were accompanied by Grand Prince Pavel, who was rarely parted from his elder brother but managed that summer to keep a discreet distance, and occupy his time with long rides and other activities that did not intrude on the couple's privacy. In 1889 it was his turn. He took his new bride to Ilinskoe, and as the months passed the young couple would often return to the house with Sergei and Elisabeth.

When the two couples visited Ilinskoe in the late summer of 1891, unbearable tragedy came in their wake. Grand Princess Alexandra Georgievna, Pavel's wife, was a sweet-natured, quiet young woman who had just turned twenty-one and had a baby daughter. She was seven months pregnant. One sunny day, as she was about to step into a boat from the little wooden landing-stage on the river bank, she collapsed into a convulsive fit, suddenly and without warning. The doctors of Moscow were too far away to reach her quickly and the only help on hand was the village midwife, who delivered a tiny premature baby. He survived, though at first they had thought him stillborn, but Alexandra died six days later without regaining consciousness. The family was devastated and local peasants shared their grief: they carried her coffin on their shoulders for the whole eight miles to the station at Odintsovo, along a road lined with flowers.

Happier times would return, but the house retained its memory of Alexandra Georgievna. Sergei locked the room where she died and it was left untouched, never to be opened again except by him, with a key which he kept. A more visible memory was the baby, her son Dmitri, who was kept alive by his uncle's devoted care and spent most of his childhood summers at Ilinskoe. His sister remembered how Sergei would watch for the children's arrival, leaning over the balcony above the entrance, and would hurry down to welcome them and usher them indoors. Every morning before breakfast he liked to walk them around the farm, then they breakfasted together. Denied children of his own, he lavished attention on Marie and Dmitri and wanted them to see Ilinskoe as their home. Larger house parties were rare, but in 1896 the house played host to the grandest and most important party it would ever see.

The last Tsar's coronation that spring involved long days of solemnity and celebration, cast into sharp relief by the disaster at Khodynka Meadow. A time which must in any case have been physically and emotionally draining, particularly for the Tsar and Tsaritsa, ended with bad feeling and dissension in the family as the reality of Khodynka sunk in. When the official programme of events ended the imperial couple and their baby daughter Olga made their way to Ilinskoe to relax, accompanied by some of their closest relatives and friends. There were so many guests that the house could not contain them all and even the rooms of Usovo were not enough to hold the overflow: some members of the party had to stay at Archangelskoe. For a little over three weeks they rested, walked and played tennis; there were theatrical performances and parties at Archangelskoe, and on 3/15 June everyone celebrated Sergei and Elisabeth's wedding anniversary. The younger members of the party ran wild: the Crown Princess of Romania remembered those weeks as a time when 'Amusement followed amusement, it was a period of buoyant, almost mad gaiety, a giddy whirl of enjoyment. . . .'[10] Only one person, the child Marie Pavlovna, would later say that the tragedy of Khodynka cast a shadow of sadness and foreboding over the holiday. On a human level it is easy to understand why the Ilinskoe party would want to forget, for a time, the drama and tragedy they had seen: historically, one can only hope that they did still remember, and understand.

The party broke up and Ilinskoe settled back to its accustomed peace. Life there in the opening years of the new century is remembered most vividly by the children, Marie Pavlovna and her brother's friend Felix Yusupov, from nearby Archangelskoe. Marie wrote that 'the most beautiful, the gayest memories of my childhood attach to Ilinskoie', but her memories were nonetheless marred by a vein of resentment, for the separation from her father and the guardianship of Ella and Sergei.[11] The Ilinskoe she described was a stiff and quiet place ruled by the clock, but Felix Yusupov saw things rather differently, recalling that Sergei's household 'was composed of the most heterogeneous elements; it was very gay and the most unexpected things happened there'.[12] He went on to describe some of the personalities of the Grand Prince's court; a Princess with the build and manners of a drum-major, who liked to lift grown men into the air to demonstrate her strength; a gentle and rather deaf old general who satisfied the custom of kissing icons by blowing kisses to those he could not reach; later Felix would write of Sergei and Elisabeth's 'gay and youthful entourage'.[13]

But the gaiety ended with Sergei's assassination. His widow took Marie and Dmitri to Ilinskoe in the summer that followed, and again in 1906, but while they recovered, enjoyed themselves, and grew up, she was embarking on a very different path. In 1905 she established a hospital for the wounded soldiers from the Russo-Japanese war in the park at Ilinskoe, and it absorbed an ever-increasing amount of her time and care. A year later she bought another house outside Moscow for disabled ex-soldiers and by 1910 she had withdrawn from the world completely. She established her own foundation of nursing sisters in a convent on the south side of the river, in the city of Moscow. Ilinskoe passed to Dmitri and in time the estate was sold. It is said that the house itself was pulled down but Lubov Millar, who wrote a biography of Elisabeth, visited Ilinskoe in 1990 and found a high stone wall enclosing the estate and the church. A local priest told her that Lenin used the house for a time, and that later it was completely destroyed by fire. The estate, it was said, had been given to some Americans, and the writer was not allowed to pass the gate. The Russian author and dramatist Edvard Radzinsky did enter Ilinskoe and he describes the avenue of trees that once led to the front door, and the old church. The house he does not mention. He walked the pathway leading down to the river, where once Alexandra Georgievna ran, minutes before her fatal collapse, and he saw the remains of the old landing-stage where she would have climbed into the boat. At Ilinskoe it seems, as at Peterhof, Gatchina and Tsarskoe Selo, there are many mute reminders of a world that is lost for ever.

16

Fast Women and Slow Ships

GRAND PRINCE ALEXEI ALEXANDROVICH

'His was a case of fast women and slow ships.'[1] In a few telling words Grand Prince Alexander Mikhailovich appears to have captured the character of his cousin, Sergei's older brother Alexei Alexandrovich, for ever. It often happens this way: the wittiest, the most articulate commentator is allowed to define our view of events and people, simply because his or her words are so quotable and so memorable. We rarely stop to ask was he right? Was he biased? Was he even honest? Alexander Mikhailovich was writing at a time when all that most people could remember of Grand Prince Alexei was an Admiral-General who lost his command after a series of catastrophic defeats at the hands of the Japanese; who whiled away his few remaining years in Paris and on the Riviera, a rejected, sad man. A few might have looked back further, to one of the juiciest scandals of the 1890s. The living arrangements of Alexei, his cousin Evgeni of Leuchtenberg, and Evgeni's wife Zenaida amused the gossips of Europe for years. 'Fast women and slow ships' seems to say it all. Alexander Spiridovich, chief of security to the last Tsar, recalled that Alexei's death was received with indifference in St Petersburg because naval losses in the Far East had made him so unpopular. But there was much, much more to the story. Alexei Alexandrovich was one of the kindest and least judgemental members of the Romanov dynasty. In October 1905 he dashed across Germany with his luggage strapped to the roof of a car, braving cold and blizzard in response to a cry for help from his nephew Kyrill Vladimirovich without even knowing what the problem was. He was taken aback, at first, to find that he had been selected as principal witness to an illegal wedding, but accepted the situation with good humour. He gave generously to all and, as the fuller picture begins to emerge, it becomes apparent that Alexander Mikhailovich was almost alone in his dislike of his cousin.

Alexei was born in St Petersburg on 2/14 January 1850, exactly four weeks before his cousin Nikolai Konstantinovich. The coincidence was important because, from the moment of birth, Alexei was destined for the navy and he was to be brought up with his cousin, under the eye of Nikolai's father Konstantin Nikolaievich, Admiral-General of the Russian Fleet. On his birthday in January 1857, Alexei was given his first officer's dress uniform. Nikolai was staying with the Tsar's family at the time and the Tsar reported to Konstantin, 'The officer's dress uniform given to Alexei on his seventh birthday, excited not a little envy, but he comforts himself with the thought that soon he too will be favoured. It will be nice to see both our little sailors in identical dress uniforms.'[2] A few weeks later the two boys made their first confession together and by 1859 their parents were discussing a joint education. T he following summer, at the age of ten, they took part in their first naval manoeuvres in the Baltic. They were at sea a little over two weeks and their families were overjoyed to see them safe on dry land. In 1861 they were sent to sea again on the naval yacht *Zabavu*.

Alexei was an attractive, enthusiastic little boy. His cousin Marie of Battenberg met him for the first time at Brückenau in Germany and remembered 'a boy in a white suit, who was very lively, and who used to tease me. I envied him frightfully because he was seven years old, and did not have to be brought in, but was allowed to sit at table with his elders. He was the Grand Duke Alexis.'[3] Seven years would pass before their next meeting and in those years Alexei matured considerably, becoming 'very tall, strong and handsome' in his cousin's eyes. In photographs he often looks rather podgy, but for his contemporaries it was his physical presence that caught the eye and stayed in the memory. He was handsome and always impeccably dressed. At full growth he reached six foot four, and though his brothers were just as tall, or taller, in Alexei the giant stature was combined with an open, friendly personality.

One new member of the imperial family gravitated to him from the start. His sister-in-law Maria Feodorovna did not have an easy time in her first years in Russia, coping with her own lingering grief for the Tsesarevich Nikolai and with her husband's reluctance to adapt to his new role. As Tsesarevich, Alexander was expected to perform an increasing range of the public duties which he hated and his wife handled to perfection. Faced with his own inadequacy he became temperamental. He raged. He sulked. Maria's diary, which has never been published, is said to show that Alexei was a good friend to her at these times, easing the tension by chatting, teasing and listening. In the summer of 1869 the nineteen-year-old Alexei joined the couple on a tour of the Caucasus. There were moments when the strain might have been unbearable if he had not been on hand, to share his sister-in-law's reminiscences about Nikolai and all that her life might have been.

That summer Alexei had problems of his own. He was in love with one of his mother's ladies. In the mid-1860s two of the Tsaritsa's young maids-of-honour drew all eyes at Court and their impact was unforgettable. One was Marie Mescherskaya, Alexander Alexandrovich's old love, the other was her friend Sacha, Alexandra Vassilievna Zhukovskaya, 'who was fair, with large blue eyes and a dazzling complexion. . . . If one was passionate, the other was sentimental, but both were the vogue.'[4] Alexei had fallen for Sacha, whose father had been his own father's tutor. She was almost twenty-seven, he was nineteen, and even as he nursed his feelings he must have known that his brother's love for Marie had ended in an angry row with their father.

It was not an encouraging precedent, but Alexei was not put off. Three years earlier the Tsar had embarked on his affair with Ekaterina Dolgorukaya: at about the same time, his uncle Konstantin started to pursue Anna Kousnetsova. By the 1870s both men had started second families. The gulf between the way Romanov princes were supposed to behave and the way they did behave was hard to ignore, and Alexei responded to the inconsistencies that surrounded him by displaying a marked streak of independence. He made his own rules. Alexander's experience showed that speaking to their father about marriage to a maid-of-honour, even offering to renounce his rights, would achieve nothing, so Alexei decided to settle matters for himself.

There is no documentary evidence of a secret marriage but the tradition is strong. It is said that in 1869 or '70, in Italy, or perhaps at Ilinskoe, Alexei and Alexandra Zhukovskaya contracted an illegal marriage that was later annulled by the Tsar. It could have happened. The Tsaritsa and her younger children spent several weeks at Ilinskoe in the early summer of 1869, though it is hard to believe that any priest would have performed the ceremony under her very roof. Italy seems more likely: the one fact which no one disputes is that Alexandra Zhukovskaya had a son, born in Salzburg on 14 November 1871 and named Alexei after his father.

By this time, though, the relationship was officially over. The Tsar had found out that his son was married or intending to marry, and had taken steps to end the affair. He was holding an official invitation from President Grant to send a member of his family on state visit, as a 'thank you' for Russian support in the American Civil War. Who better to send than Alexei, who was serving as a lieutenant on board the naval frigate *Svetlana*? The United States was comfortably far from Alexandra. So, like his brother, Alexei was sent miles away from the woman he loved. The *Svetlana* sailed west in a three-frigate squadron, and on 19 November, five days after the birth of baby Alexei, they entered New York harbour. The American steamer *Mary Powell* sailed out to meet them, carrying the first of an apparently endless series of welcoming committees, and Alexei was received on board with his dog and members of his suite. The squadron sailed on to New Orleans to meet him at the end of the visit.

Before him lay two packed and exciting months. The tour included a number of American and Canadian cities, from Montreal to St Louis, and everywhere people vied for their share of the glory. Alexei was only twenty-one and would celebrate his twenty-second birthday in America: not unnaturally, press and public curiosity was intense, particularly when their visitor turned out to be so attractive – and so tall. Before long there was predictable talk about his success with the ladies and ambitious mothers across the country pushed their daughters forward to catch the royal eye. In the enthusiastic press coverage of the visit the myth of Alexei the lady-killer was born. But he was less involved than the reporters would have had their readers believe. Writing home in January 1872 he commented, 'Concerning my success among American women, of which the newspapers have written so much, I can honestly say that this is complete nonsense. They look at me as people look at a caged crocodile or a monkey of unusual size, but then, having looked me over, become completely indifferent' – a very realistic assessment of the situation.[5]

In other ways he was fascinated by what he saw and observed considerable differences between America and home. He told his family that American men were intelligent and full of energy but rude; the only ones with any conception of manners were naval personnel. In Europe at this time it was quite normal to think of American women as 'fast' and under-educated but Alexei saw that this was not the case. He found the women 'extremely well brought up', and very beautiful, only differing from Russian women in their free attitude to religion.[6] Everywhere he went Alexei was fêted and treated to speeches, balls and receptions. The warmth of the welcome was almost overwhelming, particularly in the South, where it surprised him that people showed no resentment of the support that Russia had given to the Union cause. He found the Southern landowners much more like European nobility in their attitudes and manners.

As a climax to the visit the Americans had planned a buffalo hunt. Over 1,300 people were involved, including Lieutenant Colonel George Custer, 'Buffalo' Bill Cody and a whole Dakota tribe. Alexei's party arrived in Omaha on 12 January 1872 and were joined by Custer, who took them on by train to North Platte, Nebraska, where Buffalo Bill was waiting. He was to be their guide – and to liaise with the Dakota people who had offered to participate in the hunt. The party travelled to their base, 'Camp Alexis' on Red Willow Creek, by army ambulance, the only vehicle available. The Dakota village was already established on the far side of the creek, and hospital tents had been set up to accommodate the visitors, but Alexei provided his own bed. Bedsteads for men of his height were not easily come by.

On the first morning, Dakota hunters rode out at dawn to round up the buffalo. Custer and Cody led the hunting party out, with Alexei riding the guide's own horse, 'Buckskin Joe'. He wore a green belted riding costume with the imperial arms on every button.

Fifteen miles separated them from the herd, and as they rode Custer showed him the special techniques he would need to shoot moving buffalo. He learned quickly. One of the first animals they encountered surprised the more experienced hunters by charging straight for Alexei's horse but the Grand Prince kept his nerve, rode well and shot cleanly, and the Americans were genuinely impressed. Boyish in his excitement, Alexei cabled his father with the news as soon as he returned to camp.

It must have been a tremendous adventure. On the second night in camp, despite bitter cold, the Dakota performed some of their traditional dances around the camp fire. When the camp broke up Alexei gave generously to everyone involved, and he seized eagerly on Buffalo Bill's offer to drive the party to the station as if they were being chased by hostile natives. The ride left his suite looking very shaken and dishevelled but Alexei was happy. He cabled his father; 'Warm thanks to You and Mother for heartfelt congratulations; returned from the hunt with an escort of Indians! Killed three Bison. Departing for Denver.'[7]

A Union Pacific train took them on for the last leg of the journey, a voyage by river boat down the Mississippi to New Orleans. By Alexei's special request Custer accompanied them all the way and Mrs Custer also joined the party. Telegrams had been sent in advance to towns along the route asking for respectable girls to be brought forward, and Mrs Custer had the job of chaperoning a select group on board. There were no other passengers, and with no worries about security the older members of Alexei's suite relaxed and allowed the young a free rein. Alexei's fellow officers turned the whole thing into a hilarious game, teasing the girls with stories about him, and about the customs of their home, and arranging hectic dances that left everyone breathless. Mrs Custer was amazed by the energy the Russian men brought to their dancing; she had seen nothing like it before. Once again, Alexei's legendary way with women did not seem to be much in evidence. One girl's low-cut dress worried him so much that he bought a woolly scarf in one of the river towns to keep her neck warm. It had been noticed more than once that he found it hard to sit through the interminable speeches of welcome that met him at every stop. Once, one of the girls dressed up in a top hat and cloak to fool him into thinking that another mayor had come on board, and everyone saw his face fall before the joke was revealed.

It was a light-hearted, mad interlude. Watching Alexei, Mrs Custer was struck by the contrast between his stature and his youth – she believed that the downy, fair side whiskers he sported were his first attempt at growing a beard. She also picked up an interesting piece of gossip. Members of the suite were trying to boost his romantic aura by telling the girls of his doomed love, and of his 'wife and son in Switzerland'. It was obvious that someone, probably Alexei himself, was still in contact with Alexandra Zhukovskaya: her baby had not even been born until the squadron was at sea, yet the account Mrs Custer was given was accurate in all but place.[8]

The party ended in New Orleans, where Alexei enjoyed the opera and the theatre. He watched the carnival too, but said that he found the atmosphere forced, 'as if someone had ordered them to dress up like monsters, and pretend they were having fun'.[9] New Orleans appealed to him, reminding him very much of a European city, and overall the tour had been a resounding success. He returned to Russia, complaining light-heartedly to his sister-in-law that there had been too many balls, and that American women danced far too much, though he could not help but admire their beauty.

But had the tour distracted him from Alexandra? Time passed and he fulfilled his naval duties and gave no cause for complaint. All who met him were warm in their praise. Lady Augusta Stanley, meeting him during his sister's wedding celebrations in 1874, commented, 'Alexis is a pickle but intelligent, good looking and sensible. He talked like a book about schools, the training of girls, the drawbacks of institutes – also about National plays, and the theatre in general and the influence of good plays.'[10] 'Pickle' was an odd word to choose for a man in his mid-twenties but it suggests something of Alexei's charm. In Greece, where his cousin Olga Konstantinovna was Queen, Alexei's visits were enjoyed by the whole royal family. The children adored him. 'He was a striking personality and full of fun. Tall, handsome, well-groomed, and with perfect manners, he had an irresistible charm', Prince Nicholas of Greece remembered. Alexei welcomed the family on board the *Svetlana*, and let the children bounce on his bed, and on land he found it easy to persuade the King into anything he wanted. He bathed in the monarch's outsize marble bath, while the King ground out tunes on a musical box. 'My father loved him for his absurdities and wit,' Prince Nicholas wrote, 'and was always delighted to please him.'[11]

True to form, Alexei was the only member of the family, apart from his uncle Konstantin, to accept his father's relationship with Ekaterina Dolgorukaya without a murmur of disapproval. He went out of his way to be kind to her and her children. To his own love life in the '70s there are few clues. Alexandra Zhukovskaya was married in Munich in 1875. Alexei is said to have had a liaison with a St Petersburg cabaret dancer that produced a daughter but, if true, this was a short-lived affair. It is said that in 1880 the Tsar approached the Grand Duke of Hesse on Alexei's behalf to arrange a marriage with Ella, who was then only fifteen. The Grand Duke refused and there is no further evidence in print of Alexei proposing, or even considering marriage, though he was attractive, wealthy and emphatically heterosexual. Writing after his death Mrs Custer suggested that Alexandra Zhukovskaya was the reason he never married; she may have been right, but there was no outward sign of the attachment. Alexei went his own way and apparently enjoyed single life. He visited his sister in England on at least two occasions, once in the summer of 1875, and again in 1881, when the news of his father's murder cut short an anticipated stay with Prince Leopold at Claremont.

The murder changed his life for ever. When the new Tsar, his brother Alexander, dismissed Grand Prince Konstantin from the naval command he had held for almost thirty years, he thrust Alexei into his uncle's shoes. Alexei was not happy. He had respected his uncle from childhood, and was unwilling to take on such heavy responsibility, but he had no choice, and, reluctantly, he settled down and bought his first home in the maritime district of St Petersburg. In 1884, thanks to his brother, his twelve-year-old son

Alexei Alexeievich was recognized and given the title Count Belevsky-Zhukovsky by imperial ukaze.

If Alexander Mikhailovich is to be believed, Alexei's years in office were an unmitigated disaster, but this was not how it was always seen. In the spring of 1884 Prince Wilhelm of Prussia visited St Petersburg, and in a lengthy report to his grandfather the Kaiser he gave a frank assessment of Alexei's competence, observing that he 'has changed remarkably for the better. Since he has taken over the naval administration with its heavy responsibility – although at first with great reluctance – he has become much more serious and grave. In my voyage to Kronstadt I had the opportunity to converse at some length with him, and in the course of our talk he touched lightly on the frightful conditions which he found when he took over; in the walk round Kronstadt also he proved to be well acquainted with the different localities, and gave me any information I wanted with the greatest friendliness and frankness.'[12]

Alexei was taking his new position seriously but it would be naïve to suggest that he could have reformed the navy on his own. In the 1850s his uncle had taken over the Naval Department determined to bring about a complete modernization, and he was as energetic and abrasive as his nephew was easy-going. Even so, he found his intentions frustrated at every turn. If a man of Konstantin's temper had failed to the extent that Wilhelm's report suggests, leaving 'frightful conditions' in the navy, Alexei would have stood no chance at all. There is evidence, at least, that he took a responsible attitude. In the early 1890s his stepmother appealed to him to help her spoilt and feckless son, his half-brother Georgi, Prince Yurievsky. With some misgivings, Alexei allowed the Prince to enter the navy without the usual preliminary examination. He tried to be tolerant, but in the end was forced to take action in the interests of the navy and the other junior officers. The Prince was dismissed and Alexei explained to his mother, 'I must again repeat that I am extremely dissatisfied with his services. Both when on duty and on board during cruises he simply does not want to do anything at all; neither advice, nor the example of others have any effect whatever on him. Laziness, untidiness, and total lack of self esteem make him the laughing stock of his comrades and draw upon him the dissatisfaction of his superiors, who do not know what to do with him. . . . It is very unpleasant for me to have to write you all this, but what can I do?'[13]

Away from his desk, Alexei devoted his time to the good things of life. He entertained generously and collected fine silver and other works of art to adorn his palace. Sometimes he designed his own clothes; his nephew Kyrill remembered a bizarre tennis outfit of red striped flannel: 'He was pleased with it and liked to be seen about in this fantastic get-up. "I am better dressed than any of you fellows," he would say to us.'[14] This description suggests that Alexei did not always take himself too seriously. However, he did take other people very seriously indeed. For Maria Feodorovna he would always be a favourite brother-in-law, who supported her in the long sadness of widowhood as he had in the early days of her marriage. He walked by her side throughout the ordeal of her son's coronation. When her second son Georgi died of tuberculosis, it was Alexei who took the news to the rest of the family, and Alexei who accompanied her on the long journey to Batum in the Caucasus to bring the dead prince's body home. His own son had done well meanwhile, and been chosen as aide-de-camp to his uncle, Grand Prince Sergei. In the summer of 1894 Count Belevsky-Zhukovsky married his aunt's lady-in-waiting, Princess Troubetzkoy, at Ilinskoe. They went on to have four children, Elizaveta, Alexandra, Maria and Sergei, and it would be fascinating to know how much contact Alexei had with them, his only true family.

The celebrated affair with the Duchess of Leuchtenberg must have started some time in the late 1880s. Born Zenaida Skobelyeva, 'Zina' was a strikingly beautiful woman who married Evgeni Leuchtenberg as his second wife in 1870. Alexander II made her Countess de Beauharnais and Alexander III raised her to Serene Highness and Duchess of Leuchtenberg. Alexander Mikhailovich commented that 'women of her maddening pagan appeal should really not be permitted to roam at large', and he was not alone in believing that Alexei was so hopelessly besotted with her that he conducted an affair openly, under her husband's roof and in his full knowledge.[15]

Without documentary evidence it is almost impossible to assess the truth. Evgeni Leuchtenberg was an unwise man who drank away most of his fortune, and for years he and his wife lived off his cousin's generosity. Even after his wife's death the Duke continued to live under Alexei's roof, so it seems reasonable to ask who really was taking advantage of whom in the relationship, around which so many titillating stories were woven.

Decades of comfort and good living eventually took their toll on the high-spirited young man who rode the plains with Custer, but the Grand Prince's suitability for naval command and his record in office are not so clear-cut as they might appear. Alexei was not the architect of war with Japan. Once the fighting started, his squadrons suffered as much from bad luck as bad judgement. A surprise attack by the Japanese on the Russian naval base at Port Arthur, made without declaration of war, took out two of the Far East Squadron's most modern ships. The arrival of the able Admiral Makarov, who did much to boost Russian morale, was followed too soon by his loss at sea, when his ship the *Petropavlovsk* struck a mine. Even the extraordinary decision to send the Baltic Fleet to avenge Russian losses, which involved an epic voyage around the world in full view of the world's press, and ended in disaster at Tsushima, was not of Alexei's devising. He was not in favour of the plan. Unlike his critical cousin Alexander, he did have experience of war, having been given his first naval command on the Danube in the Turkish war of 1877–8, and he could see how dangerous the venture was. It was the press and public who demanded the move in retaliation for Russia's losses: after putting up some resistance, the naval authorities gave way and the fleet sailed. Tsushima left Russia with no navy left to command except the Black Sea Fleet, bound by international treaty not to pass the Bosphorus. For this, Alexei rightly took overall responsibility, though the disaster was not of his making.

The strain he bore through these months is shown most clearly in his reaction to the assassination of Grand Prince Sergei. Security chiefs advised against any member of the imperial family travelling to Moscow for the funeral and the Tsar obeyed but, fearful of breaking the news to his uncle Alexei, he gave his uncle Pavel the task of telling him. Alexei was devastated. According to Grand Prince Konstantin Konstantinovich, he 'sobbed like a child, crying: "What a disgrace!"'[16] In the Russia of his youth Romanov princes had performed their duties in public in defiance of terrorist threats. After this, and the shame of Tsushima, Alexei would spend most of his remaining years in the Paris house which had seemed a terrible extravagance to the family when he bought it in 1897. He was still quick to help anyone who asked him, and there were many who thought of him with kindness. General Mossolov remembered his 'fine athletic figure' and 'infinite charm'.[17] Sergei Witte saw him as a prince of the old school 'incapable of intrigue or murky deeds', and Nicholas II had paid him the highest compliment of all by making him godfather to his only son, the Tsesarevich Alexei. When the Grand Prince died of pneumonia in Paris in November 1908, the Tsar noted in his diary, 'My favourite uncle is dead, a noble, honourable, courageous soul! May the kingdom of Heaven be his!'[18]

Autumn in the South

The revolution of 1905, which came in the wake of the Japanese war and claimed the life of Grand Prince Sergei, made the whole imperial family feel threatened and isolated. Their lives would never be quite the same again. But after a time the upheaval subsided and in 1909, after four years confined to the north of the country on the advice of his security chiefs, Nicholas II decided to take his family back to the Crimea. It was a happy visit but one that was affected nonetheless by the increasing isolation of the Tsaritsa Alexandra Feodorovna, even from members of the Court, and by the illness of her son.

Before the dominance of the car and the aeroplane most holidays began with a train ride. In the last days of August 1909, Nicholas II and his wife and children set off from St Petersburg on their way south. With them was Nicholas's young cousin, Dmitri Pavlovich, who would celebrate his eighteenth birthday during the holiday. It was the first time the family had travelled through Russia for some years; in the aftermath of the 1905 revolution they were confined to the safety of the Baltic coast and the journey would give the country at large a first chance to see the five-year-old Tsesarevich Alexei. Excitement was high. The route was lined with soldiers, facing outwards to watch for trouble, but none was seen, and for six days and nights the family lived in the train. Its luxurious furnishings offered no protection from the heat and dust of late summer, and it was impossible to sleep. The strain told particularly on the Tsaritsa, whose health was causing her family increasing concern. It was for her sake that Dr Evgeni Sergeievich Botkin had advised a trip to the Crimea, placing his faith in the restorative powers of the southern climate as firmly as his father had done.

The imperial train drew into the station at Sevastopol on a fine morning in early September; a light breeze rippled the water where the yacht *Shtandart* lay at anchor, waiting to take the Tsar and his family on the last stage of their journey around the coast to Yalta. The weather was so good and the atmosphere so welcoming that instead they decided to stay in Sevastopol for a week. The Tsar could not have been more surprised; the 1905 revolution had affected the Crimea and the Black Sea Fleet particularly badly and he came prepared to show his disapproval. Now he was completely won over. The town was in holiday mood and enthusiastic crowds lined the hills around the station. There were flags and bunting everywhere and a red carpet marked the path down to the quay, where the guard of honour stood and a small pavilion had been erected for the Tsaritsa and her children. It was hard not to be affected by the general gaiety; when people pushed against the police cordon that surrounded the family, Alexandra, who was known for her timidity in the face of a crowd, sent one of her maids-of-honour to ask the police to stand back and allow them to come nearer. All the family waved to the onlookers, none more energetically than the little Tsesarevich, as they made their way to the launch that would take them to the *Shtandart*.

This reception set the pattern for the days that followed and there was continual traffic to and from the imperial yacht. The Tsar took the opportunity to review the Black Sea Fleet and to attend manoeuvres at sea, and he visited the Admiral's flagship *Pamiat Mercuria* with his son by his side. He made a point of showing the Tsesarevich the Admiral's spartan plank bed, which the little boy prodded in disbelief. 'I was touched,' Nicholas told his mother, 'by the cheering of the crew of every ship each time we left the yacht and especially when they saw Alexei . . . Alexei's pinnace always passed in front of the whole crew and he greeted every ship more loudly than the one before.'[1]

While the Tsaritsa rested on board *Shtandart* her children spent most of their days on land, at the Villa Hollande which belonged to Admiral Boström. To amuse the Tsesarevich, the Boströms created an artificial beach with specially imported sand, and a pond stocked with live fish. While his sisters made a pet of three-year-old Vania, the youngest of the Boström children, Alexei pottered happily by himself, collecting shells and seaweed, but he refused the offer of a fishing line; he said he wanted the fish to stay alive. As the *Shtandart* finally set sail for Yalta signal flags were raised announcing the promotion of the Admiral, and two carrier pigeons were released from the yacht's bridge with letters from the imperial children to the Villa Hollande.

At three that afternoon Yalta came into view. The little town owed its existence as a fashionable resort to the imperial family and its people were happy and relieved to welcome them home. The houses were heavy with flags and flower garlands and a specially selected orchestra was playing in the park, while official delegations and parties of schoolchildren formed up along the pier. As the dignitaries' wives waited in their pavilion on the quay, the honour guard, drawn from the 16th Regiment of Archers, went through its paces for one last time, and all eyes were drawn to the *Shtandart*, now so near that the family could be seen on the bridge. The Tsesarevich was running from side to side in excitement. When they came down the gangplank, preceded by the Tsar, the cheers of the guard and the crowds rose and echoed in the surrounding mountains. There were hands to shake, bouquets to be given and accepted, and a march-past of the guard, then everyone piled into the waiting cars and carriages for the short drive to Livadia, through streets thronged with people. According to tradition Hassan, an elderly Tatar guide, who had taken Nicholas's grandfather Alexander II on excursions into the mountains half a century before, had come out of retirement to ride at the head of the procession. 'Good old Hassan is well and strong', Nicholas told his mother, 'and tears along in front of the carriage on his own horse.'[2]

There were more receptions at Livadia before the imperial family was finally able to settle in at the palace and the suite could disperse to their own houses and hotels, some on the estate and some in the town. As a special favour, they had been allowed to bring their families to the Crimea. Count Fredericks, Minister of the Court, settled into the 'Rossia', Yalta's most fashionable hotel, with his wife and daughter and with General Mossolov; in another hotel were Captain Drenteln, one of the Tsar's aides-de camp, the lady-in-waiting Olga Butzova, and Dr Botkin and his wife. The streets were crowded until late into the night and there were illuminations and firework displays. It gave people an extra thrill to be so close to members of the Court and every girl in Yalta hoped to catch the eye of Grand Prince Dmitri, whose presence added a romantic glow to the whole occasion.

Life at Livadia was easy and relaxing. While Alexandra rested indoors, Nicholas and Dmitri took long walks through the surrounding countryside. On the first morning they reviewed all the guard posts surrounding the estate and relieved any men whose presence seemed unnecessary; by the time they returned to the palace they had collected almost a full detachment of soldiers. This did not please the Tsar's security chiefs, but he was irritated by excessive protection. His daily walks took him through Oreanda, where the ruined palace of his great-uncle Konstantin Nicholaievich stood in a setting of exceptional beauty, and on to his cousins' estates at Harax and Ai-Todor. A hint of mystery surrounded Oreanda, with rumours that Konstantin had been conspiring to take the throne and that the palace had been burnt to destroy the evidence. It was also said that the very path Nicholas used had first been trodden by his grandfather, on secret visits to Princess Dolgorukaya.

The two men would return hot and tired, and swim in the sea with the children. After lunch they would walk again, or ride, or join the archaeological digs being made by Grand Prince Alexander Mikhailovich at Ai-Todor – though Nicholas complained that all the exciting finds were made when he was not there. The four Grand Princesses rode, under the watchful eye of their riding instructor, Karjavine, an officer from the imperial stables. Little Alexei was encouraged to play apart from his sisters, with the ship's boys from the *Shtandart*. His chosen walks took him to Massandra, to the west of Yalta, where he had put up his own tent and had a stove to bake potatoes. The sailor Derevenko was his constant companion and his favourite bodyguard, Kolesnitchenko, acted as a sort of nanny, collecting up his toys and putting them ready for the next day. Spoilt though the little boy undoubtedly was, he had a charm that won and held the affection of all those who came close to him. 'Just now,' the Tsar wrote to his mother, one evening in late September, 'Alexei has come in after his bath and insists that I write to you that he kisses "granny" tenderly. He is very sunburnt, so are his sisters and I.'[3]

As Alexandra's health improved she began to drive out and to take walks with her daughters and her ladies. She preferred to go into the hills, to the waterfall Outchan-Sou or to Eriklik, the wooden house built in the pinewoods for Maria Alexandrovna, which had its own model dairy. Sometimes she went to Oreanda; in the little Byzantine church that still stands on the estate she had once heard the mystic Father John of Kronstadt, and the place held a certain magic for her. She liked to attend vespers and to sing with an impromptu choir made up of her two elder daughters, their lady-in-waiting Mlle Tiutcheva, her friend Anna Virubova and Captain Drenteln. It is said that the Tsaritsa had a very fine contralto voice but her husband was not so sure; he did not like her singing, so she was careful to perform out of earshot. Shopping in Yalta was another pleasure, and a novelty for Alexandra and her daughters. One wet day an assistant in Zembinski's Gallery asked an unknown lady customer to take her umbrella outside before it damaged the parquet floor: with a twinkle in her eye, the Tsaritsa did as she was told.

In a visit that lasted for several months, it was impossible to escape more serious duties. Alexandra was always conscious of the hospitals for tubercular patients in and around Yalta and had financed several of them herself. Now she sent Anna Virubova out to make detailed reports on every aspect of their work and to seek out potential patients who were too poor to pay for treatment. Nicholas received regular reports from St Petersburg by courier, and sometimes a minister would come in person with news of the outside world. There were regimental fêtes to attend and deputations to be received. Once again, the officials surrounding the Tsar made far more fuss about security than he wanted them to. One delegation of local zemstvos included several socialists who had been active in the disturbances of 1905: General Dombadze, the

Commander-in-Chief of the Yalta garrison, was outraged, but the Tsar chatted happily to the men concerned, about their vineyards and about local needs, and both sides came away pleased with the encounter. A Turkish mission visited Yalta and the Emir of Bokhara stayed for several days and, as September gave way to October, Nicholas made plans for a visit to Italy, which could no longer be postponed.

Ostensibly a friendly meeting between sovereigns, the visit would allow secret discussion of the situation in the Balkans following Austria's annexation of Bosnia-Herzogovina in the previous year. The Tsar had hoped that his whole family could go by sea on the *Shtandart* but the Tsaritsa was ill once again so he made plans to travel overland, taking a very long route to avoid Austrian territory. On 6 October he left Livadia and sailed to Odessa. From there the train took him through Poland and on to Frankfurt, where his wife's sisters Victoria and Irene, the Grand Duke and Duchess of Hesse, and Prince Heinrich of Prussia, joined him for tea. His train crossed France overnight and arrived in Italy the next morning. King Vittorio Emanuele and Queen Elena were waiting to greet him at Racconigi, near Turin. He was charmed by the warmth of their welcome and amused to see that they had even more soldiers guarding their trains than he did.

At Livadia the Tsaritsa was miserable without her husband. Custom demanded that their parting had to take place in public, in full view of their suite, which she found especially painful. She spent the first day alone in her room and would not even see the children, but as the days passed her spirits revived. It was fifteen years since she had first set foot in the Crimea; 10 October was the anniversary, and to mark the occasion she was to lay the foundation stone of a new mosque for the Tatars of the Crimean Regiment. This gesture was enormously popular with local people and Nicholas, mindful of his wife's feelings, sent a telegram from Italy on the day naming her head of the regiment. The imam who intoned the ritual prayers at the ceremony announced this to the Tatar soldiers, referring to Alexandra as 'Validé' (mother), and the name stuck, so the mosque was afterwards known as 'Validé-chérif'.

Nicholas returned and life at Livadia settled back into its familiar pattern. That autumn new infantry uniforms were being considered, and he decided to test them for himself before giving his approval. One morning he put on the campaign uniform and equipment of a private in the 16th Regiment of Archers and walked along the coast to Harax. He stopped for breakfast with his cousins before walking back, and was amused to pass the sentry posts unrecognized. A few weeks later he repeated the walk as a private of the Imperial Guard. Some approved of his thoroughness while others found the whole idea beneath the dignity of a Tsar, but Nicholas was unrepentant; after the first walk he filled in an ordinary soldier's identity card as a souvenir. In the space where special privileges were listed he wrote 'not possessing a single privilege until his death'.

Despite the cheering crowds and the bunting, and all the pleasures of a family holiday, an undercurrent of discontent had threatened to sour the atmosphere at Livadia from the start. It was the Court, not the ordinary people, who were quick to find fault and at times assumed a patronizing manner towards their sovereigns. Nicholas had been very young when he came to the throne: Alexandra was younger still and foreign, and had stepped straight into the position of Tsaritsa on her marriage with no time to accustom herself to the country and its ways. Fifteen years had passed, but many senior figures at Court still treated the couple as children in need of guidance. In the autumn of 1909 the Court's disapproval centred on Alexandra's maid-of-honour Anna Virubova. Alexandra favoured Anna because she was young and uncritical and offered total loyalty: she knew that Anna had herself been bullied by some of the older Court ladies. Anna was easy to talk to, but the closer she grew to the Tsaritsa, the more the others disliked her. When Alexandra became ill, the story spread that a St Petersburg specialist had attributed the illness to Anna's influence and advised her dismissal. Instead of attracting sympathy from the Court, Alexandra's very real symptoms only fuelled more gossip, and increased her isolation.

The person who suffered most from this, apart from Alexandra herself, was Dr Botkin. Despite his family's long history of service he had come to be disliked at Court, where he was seen as Anna's protégé. People said that he did not know his job, that he told the Tsaritsa only what she wanted to hear, and that she was using him to hide from her official duties. His personal life also suffered, because he served the imperial family with such wholehearted devotion that his own family, particularly his wife, felt excluded. This autumn, at last, he had been allowed to take her with him, but he had so little free time that she returned to St Petersburg after three weeks, disillusioned and unaware of the problems he was facing. Towards the end of November he wrote to his brother complaining of the backbiting, mischief-making and dishonesty that surrounded him: 'you would need to have a mind as perverted as theirs and a disordered soul to defeat all of their unbelievable plots. I have decided that I am old enough to dare to be myself. I will do the things which I believe to be right, and I am ready to stand up and defend my actions because they are really my own, and have not been forced upon me.'[4] The doctor was too preoccupied to notice his wife's unhappiness and their relationship never recovered; they were divorced a year later.

As the sunshine gave way to grey skies and rain, and snow covered the mountains, the Tsesarevich suddenly became ill. There could be no question of leaving. Secretly, Count Fredericks summoned a French tuberculosis specialist to Yalta and took him to the palace under cover of darkness, but haemophilia was not his province and he could do nothing. Seasonal visitors drifted away from the coast and life became quiet and monotonous. There was little to do except pray for the sick child and play endless games of dominoes, or watch film shows given by Alexander Yagelsky, known as Hahn, the Court photographer. While Alexei was recovering, Nicholas and Alexandra toyed with a project that had been on their minds thoughout the holiday – the building of a new palace. Monigetti's Livadia palace, built in the 1860s, was a simple wooden building. Unused for years, it had become damp and uncomfortable inside, and the heavy balconies shut out the daylight. Ignoring their suite's disapproval, Nicholas and Alexandra commissioned Nikolai Krasnov to draw up new plans. From the old palace they decided to preserve only the dining room's marble fireplace and the chapel, where Alexandra had been received into the Orthodox Church; their new palace would be bright and airy and equipped with every modern convenience.

The sea was rough and forbidding when the family was finally able to set sail from Yalta, in mid-December. As Livadia came into view they stood on the *Shtandart*'s deck and watched Turkish workers begin to demolish the old palace. They would not return for another two years.

18

A House Divided

The wall of misunderstanding that divided Alexandra Feodorovna from
society, from many people at Court, even from members of the imperial
family, seemed to deepen with every year that passed. She was a good woman,
deeply devoted to her husband and his country and painfully aware of her
duty but, like her great-aunt Maria Alexandrovna before her, she could not
communicate her best intentions to the wider world. She was the first Tsaritsa
whom circumstance had forced to step straight from girlhood into the role of
consort and the confidence to manage the transition was simply not in her.
For a century and more, the Tsars of Russia had come to the throne as married
men, with wives who had had years to grow into their new country
and its language and customs in private, to adjust to marriage and raise their
children – Alexandra had no choice but to do all of these things at once, with
the eyes of the world upon her. There was no opportunity for an older woman
to guide her first steps in society – she had scarcely set foot on Russian soil
before she was expected to lead society herself.
Old rivalries ruled out the chance of effective guidance from her husband's
family. His mother Maria Feodorovna had been a successful and popular
consort, and was greatly loved. She was shattered by her husband's early death:
it was not easy for her to see her son step into his shoes. Temperamentally, she
and Alexandra were poles apart and, like all the princesses of her family, she
was a possessive mother. Moreover, by Russian law, the Tsar's mother took
precedence over the Tsar's wife, and this was bound to create tension between
the two women. Grand Princess Elisabeth, who might have been her sister's
main ally, was out of reach in Moscow with her husband. Alexandra could
have turned to her mother-in-law's old rival Marie Pavlovna, Grand Princess
Vladimir, for guidance: the Grand Princess certainly intended that she would,
but Alexandra was intelligent enough to sense the tensions around her and
draw back, trying to rely on herself alone. The imperial family, once so united,
was breaking into rival camps.

203

At Court and in society people watched the tension grow between Marie Pavlovna and the young Tsaritsa. Countess Kleinmichel later described how Marie approached Alix as 'a governess eager to guide all her movements', and took offence when this failed; afterwards she used her considerable influence in society to work against her new rival.[1] General Mossolov, Head of the Court Chancellery, watched her at work. 'When she found herself cold-shouldered,' he remembered, 'Marie Pavlovna, overbearing and irascible by nature, gave full vent to her spleen in acid comment on everything that her niece did or did not do. The Court – her Court – followed the example set to it. It was from the immediate entourage of Marie Pavlovna that the most wounding stories about the Tsaritsa emanated.'[2]

In the memories of the exiles this rivalry was magnified by hindsight. The imperial family was one family still, coming together on official occasions and in the private meetings common to all families. But the undercurrent of tension was real and it was not confined to the women. The need to obey an inexperienced nephew just because he was the Tsar had never entered Grand Prince Vladimir's head. As the new reign began, he and his wife made it clear that they expected to have their own way. In January 1897 Marie Pavlovna was seen entertaining some of her friends in the imperial box at the Mariinsky theatre. She should not have been there without permission and Nicholas wrote a stiff letter to his uncle, telling him that it was never to happen again. 'It is also unfair', he wrote, 'to take advantage of the fact that I am young, and your nephew. Please bear in mind that I have become Head of the Family and I have no right to turn a blind eye to the actions of any member of the Family that I find wrong or inappropriate. More than ever our family needs to remain united and firm. . . . And you ought to be the first to help me in this.'[3]

Independently of his mother and his wife, Nicholas had his own reasons for resenting his uncle's attitude. At the same time, both his mother and his wife had their problems with Marie and, to a lesser extent, with one another. But as Marie and Vladimir watched the younger couple struggle to exercise their new authority, and reacted impatiently when that authority cut across their plans, they must have sensed that fate was moving in their direction. The Heir, Nicholas's brother Grand Prince Georgi Alexandrovich, was consumptive, and in 1891 had to leave St Petersburg for a gentler climate. He died unmarried in 1899, leaving Mikhail Alexandrovich as the only male heir in Alexander III's line. With the young Tsaritsa producing one baby daughter after another, the prospects for the Vladimirovich princes took on a new air of expectation.

Marie Pavlovna was ambitious for her children. In 1898 her daughter Elena became engaged to Prince Max of Baden, but then he changed his mind. The little girl who attacked Thaddeus Jones with a knife had grown into a beauty; her parents were furious with Max, and Marie's subsequent search for a son-in-law excited much gossip. A rumour went round Europe in the spring of 1900 linking Elena with the recently widowed King Ferdinand of Bulgaria. Kaiserin Friedrich heard the news and wrote to her brother, the Prince of Wales. He spoke to his sister-in-law, Maria Feodorovna, and reported back on 16 April: 'she said she knew nothing about it & hoped that there was no foundation. But the Mother of the young lady has become so strange that she would not be surprised at anything – especially as she wants to marry the girl 'a tout prix' as she is in her way! Of course all this is private – & I only mention it – as you wrote to me on the subject.'[4]

It was a spiteful comment from Maria Feodorovna, which says more about the way she and Marie Pavlovna felt towards one another than it does of Elena. The Dowager Tsaritsa was enjoying the situation: a few weeks later she told Grand Prince Konstantin Konstantinovich that Marie had appealed to the Tsar, and Elena to the young Tsaritsa, to help them secure a match with Prince Albert, the eldest surviving son of the heir to the Belgian throne. Later in the year, Konstantin observed that Elena was fond of his nephew, Prince Nicholas of Greece: 'Nicky went for a long ride with Elena, whom he likes, as she does him, but Marie Pavlovna rebuked her daughter for this, and told Georgy that Nicky could not expect to marry Elena, being neither a future King, nor having any fortune.' Konstantin had heard that Marie 'dreams of marrying her daughter to the Heir, Elena's first cousin, imagining that this would be permitted'.[5]

For Konstantin and many other devoutly Orthodox Russians, including the Tsar, marriage between first cousins was almost as repellent as marriage between a brother and sister, and it was forbidden by church law. Marie came from a world where first cousin marriages were common, and she had never tried to understand Orthodox ways. She may well have thought of marrying Elena to Mikhail; it was easy for others to laugh at her ambitions for her daughter but she was simply trying to protect Elena from the frustrations of being a junior princess, which she knew all too well. For the time being Prince Nicholas, a third son like her own husband, stood no chance at all.

At least Marie could take a hand in her daughter's future. She must have been bitterly disappointed in her sons. If only one of them had chosen an acceptable, royal bride. . . . But Kyrill, the eldest, admired Victoria Melita, Grand Duchess of Hesse, the bride at the 1894 Coburg wedding and his own first cousin, a sister-in-law of the young Tsaritsa. Victoria Melita was unhappy in her marriage and in November 1901 it ended in divorce: according to Kyrill, she took this step to be free to marry him. For Russia, the combination of close relationship and scandal was too much, and the Vladimirs did all they could over the next four years to end the relationship.

Boris, their second surviving son, was spoilt by a life in which the good things came too easily. He had affairs but no interest in settling down, and a cousin remembered his lazy charm. 'Gay or sulky by turns, he had an attractive rather husky voice, kind eyes and a humorous smile which crinkled his forehead into unexpected lines . . . a slight lisp added a certain quaintness to his speech.'[6] In the summer of 1901 the youngest son, Andrei, fell in love with the dancer Mathilde Kschessinskaya, who had loved Nicholas II in the days before his accession and marriage. Andrei's affair would have been no problem as a phase he would outgrow, but he was serious. In June 1902 Mathilde gave birth in secret to his son, Vladimir, a fact his mother would never willingly acknowledge. June 1902 must have been a bad month for Marie, as she was also forced then to abandon her hopes for Elena and accept Prince Nicholas of Greece as a son-in-law. But in this she would not be disappointed; the marriage was a success, and in time Elena's three daughters gave her enormous pleasure. The eldest, Olga, was born in June 1903, and Marie went all the way to Greece for the birth, stopping in Paris to buy an expensive layette.

In society the Grand Princess was still a commanding figure. More than ever her Court was the place to be and all manner of interesting visitors found a ready welcome there. The novelists Jerome K. Jerome and Eleanor Glyn knew the Vladimir Palace. Mrs Glyn claimed that Marie invited her to write a book about the Russian Court. She created a fantastic legend about her own kidnap from St Petersburg, arranged, she said, because the central character in her latest bodice-ripping novel was too close for comfort to the Tsaritsa, and someone at Court wanted to do away with her. It was absurd, but one thing in Eleanor Glyn's story does ring true: her original invitation from Marie. 'Everyone always writes books about our peasants. Come and write one about how the real people live.'[7] No one else would have said something so outrageous, and so self-assured.

More dubious visitors could also be found at the Vladimir Palace. One contemporary account credits Marie with introducing the faith healer and religious guru Philippe to Russia, after meeting him on one of her many trips to the Riviera. Philippe would go on to charm his way into the young Tsaritsa's circle, causing untold harm. Rasputin was also invited to the Vladimir Palace when he was a fashionable novelty in the capital; later this was something Marie preferred to forget.

This quest for novelty may have been a sign of boredom; Marie had so few opportunities for real work. But in 1904 Russia's war with Japan gave her a rare opening. Alexandra Feodorovna was pregnant and Marie sprang into action, pulling together the resources necessary to create a successful ambulance train across the vastness of Siberia and the East. The actual nursing she entrusted to her cousin Eleonore Reuss Köstritz; she would no more have dreamed of wearing a nurse's uniform herself than she would of changing places with the scullery maid. But her organization was superb. Her heart must have stopped in April, when Admiral Makarov's ship *Petropavlovsk* was blown up outside Port Arthur with Kyrill on board, but Kyrill survived, and was hailed as a hero.

This brush with death gave Kyrill the courage to act on his feelings. In October 1905 he left Russia and married Victoria Melita in secret, knowing full well that the Tsar had forbidden the wedding. His parents were resigned: they had done their best to prevent the marriage, but it was done, and they expected the Tsar to give Kyrill a ticking-off and then forget all about it. They were stunned, and livid, to hear that their son had been stripped of his rank and titles and banished for his blatant breach of the family laws. Vladimir went to remonstrate with his nephew and Marie had no doubt of who was really to blame. She wrote to her uncle, Heinrich VII Reuss Köstritz: 'the blind vindictiveness and rage of the young Tsarina has, for sheer malice, exceeded everything the wildest imagination could conceive. She stormed and raged like a lunatic, dragging her weak husband along with her until he lent her his power and so made it possible to revenge herself on her ex-sister-in-law for marrying the man of her choice.'[8]

She really believed this and for ninety years her version of events has gone unchallenged. It is only now, as documents are released from the archives in Russia, that we can see how wrong she was. Alexandra did not hate Victoria Melita for the painful end of her brother's marriage. She pitied them both, pleading with her sister-in-law Ksenia not to judge them harshly or listen to gossip about them. It was Nicholas, not Alexandra, who felt obliged to punish his cousin, following a precedent set by his father, and many other members of the family supported the action he took.

But Marie had no patience with Alexandra, and if anyone had tried to explain the truth she would probably not have believed them. Their attitudes to the business of being royal were completely at odds. Marie relished the glamour and believed that princesses should be leaders of fashion and society. She saw the luxurious lifestyle she enjoyed as a vital indicator of the power and wealth of the country, and therefore a duty as well as a pleasure. Consuelo Vanderbilt visited the Vladimir Palace in the winter of 1902, and

Marie showed off some of her treasures 'set out in glass cases in her dressing-room. There were endless parures of diamonds, emeralds, rubies and pearls, to say nothing of semi-precious stones such as turquoises, tourmalines, cat's eyes and aquamarines.'[9]

The Tsaritsa had jewels too, but took after Queen Victoria in her dislike of the wealthy, the aristocratic and the powerful. She believed that the monarchy should devote itself to the poorest people in the country – the 'real' people. Images of the Russia she had encountered at Ilinskoe in the distant summer of 1890 were never far from her mind. Her cherished virtues – honesty, simplicity, and a profound religious faith – did not sit comfortably in Marie's sophisticated circle, and her failings made her an easy target. Taking second place to someone who looked so inept, by her standards, had embittered Marie Pavlovna and brought out the worst in her character.

Kyrill's banishment deepened the divide between the Vladimirs and the imperial couple, but the Grand Prince continued to accept official duties. The Vladimirs represented the Tsar at the wedding of King Alfonso of Spain in 1906, and in September 1907 they arrived in Bulgaria for the unveiling of a monument to Alexander II. This occasion showed Marie at her triumphant best. According to one eyewitness 'she greatly impressed the Bulgarians by her manner and by her kindliness shown . . . to the innumerable men and women who were strangers to her. Her elegant attire and the richness of her jewels contributed to invest her with all the attributes of an Ambassadress of the all-powerful Czar.'[10] But she let her dislike of the Tsaritsa show too clearly when General Mossolov complimented her on her performance and she replied 'One ought to know one's job. You may pass that on to the Grand Court.'[11] She should have known better than to say this to a Court official: her remark indicates the declining respect for the Tsar at the very heart of his family.

In November the Vladimirs were at Windsor, where Edward VII and Queen Alexandra hosted a lunch party for the Kaiser and Kaiserin, the Kings and Queens of Spain and Norway, the Queen of Portugal and a number of lesser royalties. In the official photographs Marie occupies centre stage with absolute poise and self-confidence, while the Kaiserin leans apologetically on the back of her chair. It must have been galling for Marie to know that she was making such a faultless impression as the representative of a Tsaritsa for whom she had so little respect.

The tantalizing possibility that one of her own sons might become Tsar drew closer with the years. The Tsesarevich was a frail child and his uncle Mikhail still single. Kyrill, Boris and Andrei did little to help themselves but their mother would do her utmost. In 1908 she amazed St Petersburg by her conversion to Orthodoxy. It was an extraordinary reversal, but Marie's assertive Protestantism, which had once seemed to spearhead a new freedom, had become an obstacle to her sons' right of succession. She wanted no obstacles. She was pleased when the Tsar, in a conciliatory gesture to mark the funeral of his uncle Alexei, allowed Kyrill to return to Russia and restored his naval rank.

For Kyrill's father the move came just in time. Grand Prince Vladimir forced himself through the New Year celebrations of 1909 by will power alone, but in February he suffered a cerebral haemorrhage at his desk and died within minutes. It was a terrible blow to Marie, who had shared his life for over thirty years in a relationship as strong and as loving as Nicholas and Alexandra's own. She wore mourning for the rest of her life. The Tsar gave Kyrill a full pardon and placed Marie at the head of one of the dragoon regiments of the Imperial Guard. At her own request, he gave her Vladimir's cherished appointment as President of the Imperial Academy of Arts, but a year went by before she felt able to take up her duties.

In her mourning, as in everything else, Marie went her own way with complete confidence. One spring day in 1912 the imperial family was gathered in the Cathedral of St Peter and St Paul for the funeral of the Duke of Leuchtenberg. As they waited in solemn silence, Marie entered holding a vase in the shape of a cockerel, filled with flowers, and placed it on her husband's tomb. Eyebrows were raised. One of the younger princesses was so amazed by the incongruity of it that she laughed out loud, but the vase came from Vladimir's desk, and to Marie it was meaningful, and wholly appropriate.

Widowhood had not made her withdraw from society; she needed company more than ever and dreaded solitude. Her time was filled with receptions and parties and she took particular pleasure in matchmaking. Thanks to her, her cousin Eleonore Reuss Köstritz had married King Ferdinand of Bulgaria, and now she turned her mind to Ferdinand's cousin, the duc de Montpensier. She chose Princess Marina Petrovna, the daughter of Grand Prince Piotr Nikolaievich, as a likely bride, but this caused great amusement in Marina's family. They teased her endlessly about Montpensier's long nose and languid manner, and Marie's plans came to nothing.

Kyrill returned to Russia in 1910, with Victoria Melita and their two small daughters, and once again there were children's parties at the Vladimir Palace. Marie took to her daughter-in-law, and she had always been good with children. At a grand reception in the Nobility Club in St Petersburg in 1912, the little girl who was to make a presentation to her slipped while attempting to curtsey and kiss the royal hand. She would have fallen down several steps if Marie had not changed the gracious gesture into a firm grip, smiling still as if nothing was happening and daring those around her to laugh. It was a kindness the child never forgot.

This incident illustrates the Grand Princess's mastery of her public role. Proud and imperious though she was, she never failed to take notice of the people around her. They went away liking her and feeling that she liked them. If she was perceived as a rival to Alexandra Feodorovna it was because she saw herself that way, particularly in latter years as concern grew about the Tsaritsa's isolation and reliance on Rasputin. Marie never saw how the gossip of her own circle had contributed to that isolation. She never showed any sympathy for Alexandra's failing health. The two women had hardly spoken to one another in private for twenty years, but the First World War was to throw them together, calling for their combined resources. Unfortunately for Russia, the rapprochement came too late, and lasted for too short a time.

At first, the summer of 1914 was deceptively like any other summer. Marie was at Tsarskoe Selo with her family, and just weeks before the declarations of war started flying across Europe she enjoyed a visit from her half-brother Prince Hendrik, consort to the Queen of the Netherlands. One day she took him for lunch with the Tsar at Peterhof. Everything seemed so normal. The war was only a few days old when the French Ambassador Maurice Paléologue dined with Marie in her garden, where 'the table was set . . . in a tent three sides of which were open. The air was pure and soft. From the rose beds a balmy odour filled the air. The sun, which was high in the sky notwithstanding the late hour, shed a soft light and scattered diaphanous shadows around us. Conversation was general, frank and warm. Of course the only subject was the war. . . .'

For Marie, as for so many, war brought a painful personal dilemma. Forty years had passed since she arrived in Russia as a bride, but by birth and upbringing she was German, and many of her relatives lived in Germany still. It had been possible to be both Russian and German before, but now. . . . Drawing the Ambassador aside, Marie told him 'Many a time in the last few days I have turned the searchlight on my conscience. I have seen into the very depths of my soul. But neither in my heart nor in my mind have I found anything which is not utterly devoted to my Russian fatherland. . . . I am only a Mecklenburger on one point: in my hatred for the Emperor William. He represents what I have been taught from my childhood to detest the most – the tyranny of the Hohenzollerns. Yes, it is the Hohenzollerns who have perverted, demoralised, degraded and humiliated Germany.'[12]

The Ambassador was impressed and never saw how disingenuous his hostess was being. Marie's own grandmother, who played a major role in her upbringing, was a Hohenzollern and proud of it. Far from being opposed to Prussian influence, the Mecklenburg of her childhood had embraced Prussia gladly when other German states turned away. Marie had a habit of disavowing any fact when it became inconvenient. In 1914 her sympathies *were* entirely Russian but if she had been more honest about herself, she might have been able to play a more constructive role later, when Alexandra Feodorovna came under attack for her German origins.

As the first Russian troops left for the front, Marie revived the network of ambulance trains and flying hospitals she had created for the Japanese war. She was a gifted administrator and enjoyed the work, controlling ten separate concerns in the front line; the difference in style between her and the Tsaritsa was more apparent now than it had ever been. Marie made an effective figurehead, handling unfamiliar situations with ease; people were impressed with her and drew encouragement from her visits. Alexandra Feodorovna was equally committed to hospital work but she chose to set aside her own physical weakness and train as a nurse. In the wards and operating theatres, where Marie would never have dreamed of going, she dressed wounds, assisted at amputations, and performed countless mundane and unpleasant tasks. She came to know many of the men she nursed as individuals, and befriended their families. She sat with the dying and prayed for them. Her ambulance trains and other services were managed effectively from behind, but the figurehead role never came easily to her.

The two women looked dubiously on each other's efforts at first, but events pushed them together. Both were receiving news from Germany via relatives in the neutral countries. They shared a concern for the fair treatment of prisoners. In September 1915 Alexandra and her elder daughters went to tea at Marie's house in Tsarskoe Selo; it was the first meeting they had ever had there without the Tsar. Marie and her sons were amazed to hear Alexandra speak openly of her difficulties, and of her mistrust of some members of the imperial family. 'It gave us the possibility of understanding Alix', Andrei confessed to his diary. '. . . Nobody really knew her, in fact, or understood her, and the guesses and suppositions that were made, became in time an array of the most varied legends. . . . We saw her in a new light, and realised that many of the legends are false, and that she is on the right path.'[13] The Tsaritsa had no idea how much of a revelation this meeting was. She mentioned it in passing in a letter to her husband, 'we spoke much & they looked at things as one ought to. . . .'[14]

At first the meeting made a difference. When Marie heard from her niece Alexandrine, Queen of Denmark, about a German officer who had been in Kiev when the war began and was still held there as a spy, in terrible conditions, she turned to the Tsaritsa for help.

Alexandra interceded with the authorities and he was transferred to an officers' prison: this delighted Marie, who went to the Alexander Palace for a 'nice and cosy' tea party. In October Alexandra was careful to invite her to the opening of a new church, so as not to offend. Sending details of another of Marie's prisoners to the Tsar at the end of the year, Alexandra added, approvingly: 'she is very careful whom she asks about but also wants us to help set right things if one can, & if an injustice has been committed. . . .'[15]

That November Marie travelled with her ambulance train to Dvinsk, with the Tsaritsa's blessing, taking the British Foreign Office courier Albert Stopford. The railhead was three miles from the front line, and by the light of many torches he and Marie watched the wounded brought in on peasant carts. 'It must have been like that in Napoleon's time,' he wrote, 'the same place and time of year.' But Marie's train was comfortable – luxurious, according to Stopford – and its orderlies came from the St Petersburg ballet. Once the wounded were settled, Marie spoke to each one of them, and on arrival in the city she would not leave the train until every man had been transferred to hospital, though she was quite exhausted. 'It was the most divine time being with her,' Stopford wrote. '. . . We talked of everybody and everything in the world. She is a marvellous woman, and always at her best when there is much to do – sparing herself no trouble.'[16]

Stopford's was just one of a number of friendships Marie enjoyed within the diplomatic community. She had taken him under her wing when he first arrived in the city and shown him the sights, and he was a regular visitor to her palace. Paléologue was given a similar privileged view. In her own mind, Marie was fulfilling a duty the imperial couple neglected: these men represented friendly governments and she believed it was important for the imperial family to be on good terms with them. But she was totally indiscreet, passing on real news, rumour, opinion and gossip without any distinction. While she was in harmony with the Tsaritsa this hardly mattered, but one conversation could not obliterate twenty years of mistrust.

After lunch on 8 February 1916, Grand Prince Boris went to see the Tsar. Two days later Marie had lunch with the imperial couple and discussed Boris's wish to marry their eldest daughter. She went away happy, so they must have managed to hide their shock, but Alexandra was still agonizing over the suggestion weeks later. Grand Princess Olga was an innocent twenty-year-old. Boris was thirty-eight, with a bad reputation and a string of mistresses to his name. Even war had not changed him; he held a few nominal appointments that protected him from danger and did nothing to disrupt his social life. The proposal left both mothers offended on behalf of their children and soured the atmosphere between them even further.

There were other reasons why 1916 saw their new harmony crumble. The Tsar's absence at headquarters had forced Alexandra to take a more active role in government. Behind the scenes was Rasputin, to whom gossip attached vast importance. Insulted for her son, Marie fell back into believing and encouraging the gossip. In February 1916 she summoned Ambassador Paléologue and told him the Tsaritsa was mad and the Tsar too weak to resist her. She gave him a very negative view of the Tsar's relationship with his mother. Others were saying similar things, but it is hard to believe that Marie would have acted in this way if her son had been about to marry the Tsar's daughter. As it was, by talking so unguardedly to foreign representatives, she was actually helping to undermine the imperial government in the eyes of its allies.

The downhill slide gained speed. Marie wanted new statutes to improve the work of the hospitals. In June she approached Alexandra, who was annoyed, though she tried to be generous: 'she can drive one wild . . . only one does not wish needlessly to offend her, as she means well, only spoils all by her jealous ambition.' Correctly, she predicted that Marie's next move would be an approach to the Tsar. A few days later he received an actual draft for the statutes, which he passed on to the relevant authorities. They were both annoyed that their aunt was trying to make decisions that were not hers to make, but she would not give in, and the affair rumbled on for weeks. The Tsar found Marie 'simply insufferable', and the Tsaritsa exploded: 'Hang Miechen on 60 apple trees!'[17]

There were still occasional tea parties. Sometimes Alexandra found Marie 'amiable', but they clashed again in September, when Marie decided to inspect the hospitals in the Crimea, which came under Alexandra's personal management. Marie gave instructions for rooms to be prepared for her at Livadia, Alexandra's property; she had approached the Tsar for permission to do this, without notifying his wife. When Alexandra sent her an angry telegram she took revenge by showing it to General Mossolov, describing the Tsaritsa as 'a woman, and a princess at that, who had to come to me to learn how to behave in society'.[18] As before in Bulgaria, a remark like this made to a Court official, in the hope that it would be reported back, was unforgivable.

Marie returned via Kiev, where she met the Tsar with coldness. The Dowager Tsaritsa went out of her way to avoid her. The family was fragmenting, and as autumn passed into winter Marie sought Paléologue out on several occasions to repeat her complaints about the imperial couple. The idea that the Tsaritsa and Rasputin were single-handedly dragging the country down had become an obsession, and Marie's circle even whispered that Alexandra Feodorovna corresponded with Germany. From Marie, knowing the full circumstances as she did, this was spiteful – particularly as she herself had once been in trouble for a genuine correspondence with the German chancellor. But as yet she only talked – the young men in the family were becoming stirred up enough to act. On the morning of 17/30 December the capital awoke to the news that Rasputin had disappeared in the night.

Society was awash with rumours. It was said that the Guards regiments were about to rise against the Tsar and set his son on the throne, under the regency of Grand Prince Nikolai Nikolaievich. Paléologue reported this in his diary on 5 January, the day Grand Prince Dmitri Pavlovich was sent to Persia for his part in Rasputin's murder. According to Paléologue, Marie's three sons headed the conspiracy, but Stopford, always calmer than Paléologue, describes how Marie sat up through the night of Dmitri's deportation with Kyrill and Andrei and prevented them from taking action; she never contacted Boris at all, for fear of his temper.

Stopford was told this by Marie herself, but others were certain that she wanted action. The Duma chairman Mikhail Rodzianko claimed that after a lunch at the Vladimir Palace in January, Marie expressed the view that the Tsaritsa 'must be annihilated'.[19] On 11 January, Paléologue had lunch at the palace. He describes the tension in the room, as members of the family arrived to talk with Marie in private, and her lady-in-waiting gazed across the Neva to the fortress and talked darkly of imprisonment. Marie told him the family had agreed on joint action:

'"Will it be confined to platonic action?"'

'We looked at each other in silence. She guessed that in my mind was the tragedy of Paul I, as she replied with a horrified stare: "Oh God! Whatever will happen?"'

The French Ambassador spins a good yarn but somebody was overdoing the drama here: the joint action planned by the family – '"And now pray to God to protect us!" She held out her hand; it was trembling violently' – was not an armed rising, or another murder, but just a letter to the Tsar, asking him to have pity on Dmitri. Marie told Stopford she had had it drawn up and signed by the whole family, but many members of the family were not involved at all.[20]

The 'rising of the Grand Dukes' has become part of the mythology of the dynasty's fall. In later years most of the exiles believed that something was afoot at the start of 1917, with Marie and her sons at its centre. Marie is unlikely to have taken interest in Paléologue's scenario, the plot to give Nikolai Nikolaievich the regency. She was as wary of the Nikolaievich branch of the family as the Tsaritsa was, and the move would have done nothing for her sons. On the other hand, Anna Virubova and Grand Prince Alexander Mikhailovich both made later claims that the British Ambassador was conspiring to put Kyrill on the throne: this certainly would have appealed to Marie and she was close to Sir George Buchanan and his staff. Alexander did not think to mention in his memoirs that he himself had written to his brother Nikolai Mikhailovich on 14/27 February arguing the need for 'heroic measures' to remove the Tsaritsa, measures he had discussed with Kyrill.[21] It may have suited him, after the event, to throw the blame for any plotting on the British.

The Tsar, at least, seems to have given credence to rumours of a plot within the family. In January 1917 he began sending his male cousins away from the city. General Mossolov said that he also made one last attempt to reconcile his wife and Marie, for the sake of the country. Alexandra agreed to a meeting on condition that Marie would make the first move and acknowledge that there was fault on both sides. Marie flatly refused. At the end of February she decided to leave for the Caucasus with Andrei, giving depression at the turn of events as her reason for going. Stopford saw her off from the station on 4 March. Ten days later Kyrill broke his oath to the Tsar and declared his allegiance to the Provisional Government.

As the tragedy of Nicholas and Alexandra unfolded behind her, Marie went to Kislovodsk with Andrei. At the end of the month she was placed under house arrest on the orders of the Provisional Government for an indiscreet letter sent to Boris. She was released in June but chose to remain in the Caucasus, where Boris joined her. Both he and Andrei were accompanied by their mistresses but a separate house had to be found for them: revolution or no revolution, there was no way Marie would acknowledge the existence of such women. Life in the Caucasus was not unpleasant. Marie persuaded a Cossack family to guard her and funds were supplied by Stopford, who made the long journey from the capital several times in person: unlike the mistresses, he was allowed to stay in the villa.

By autumn the situation was becoming dangerous. The villa was raided and searched on several occasions; once the revolutionaries came at night and Marie was forced to escape into the hills in her dressing gown. The Bolsheviks took the town in 1918 and tension reigned; one August night Andrei and Boris were arrested. Members of the local Soviet wanted to see them shot, but a friendly local official secured their escape and advised them to get away into the mountains.

The Grand Princess was not capable of the life on the run that now faced her sons, and friends found sanctuary for her in a Cossack village. For months the area was in turmoil, then in October, taking advantage of several Bolshevik defeats, the local White general brought Marie and her sons together and advised them to travel to Anapa in the south, at least for the winter. He arranged a train and an escort of his own men and they left on 19 October, with their own companions and other local refugees. At Touapse a trawler was waiting. It was tiny and squalid, and many of the refugees held back, but Marie took the situation in hand. '"What a wonderfully picturesque setting!"', she announced, 'and, graciously acknowledging the Captain's welcome, she embarked without turning a hair! Sitting imperturbably in a deck-chair on the bridge, she began to look at the crestfallen refugees, who now hastened to follow her example.' Marie had some reason to feel superior, as she was allotted all three cabins while the other ninety-six passengers had to huddle together on the bridge.[22]

The trawler docked at Anapa on 22 October and a house was found for Marie and her sons, while the mistresses were placed in a local hotel. Just before Christmas a British general arrived with his government's invitation to Marie to be taken to safety in Europe. She refused. On 29 March 1919 a British cruiser dropped anchor just outside Anapa and sent two officers ashore by armed motor launch. Once again, they had come for Marie, but she told them it was her duty to remain in Russia. She was alarmed, and angry, when Boris decided to leave for safety with his mistress.

In May, Marie and Andrei decided to return to Kislovodsk. The White armies had retaken the Caucasus and complete victory seemed at hand. But by the year's end it was obvious that the game was over. General Pokrovsky, who had arranged Marie's journey to Anapa, provided a train and an escort, and she and her party set off for Novorossisk. Grand Princess Olga, Nicholas II's sister, was in the port when they arrived, and she could not help admiring the tattered grandeur that still clung to her aunt: 'I felt proud of her. Disregarding peril and hardship, she stubbornly kept to all the trimmings of bygone splendour and glory. And somehow she carried it off. . . . For the first time in my life I found it was a pleasure to kiss her.'[23]

On 13 February 1920 Marie and her party embarked on the long journey into exile, carried by an Italian liner of the Lloyd-Triestino line. A train was waiting in Venice to take her to the south of

France; first to the Grand Hotel in Cannes, and then on to her own villa at Contrexéville. There was one piece of good news waiting: Albert Stopford had risked his life to rescue many of Marie's priceless jewels from the Vladimir Palace and had smuggled them across the border for her, wrapped in newspaper and packed into two Gladstone bags. In early summer Marie visited her daughter in Switzerland and, although she seemed tired and ill, she was still planning for the future. She called on a fellow exile, her husband's sister, the former Duchess of Edinburgh, now Dowager Duchess of Saxe-Coburg. It must have been a strange meeting; war had forced the two women to take opposing sides, abandoning the countries of their birth, and its aftermath had made exiles of them both.

In June Marie Pavlovna was taken ill at Contrexéville and she died on 6 September with her family around her. She had never been an easy woman: she was too forceful and uncompromising, but she fought doggedly for her own and they owed her everything. She would never acknowledge, perhaps never see, the part her own actions had played in the dynasty's fall, but in defeat she was magnificent. 'Her strength of mind rose to the occasion unbeaten by exile or illness. Great characters pass the test of adversity with full honours.'[24]

The story has one final twist. Marie never lived to see her son Kyrill claim the non-existent Russian throne and revive the divisions in the family. In recent years his descendants have emphasized the importance of the Vladimirovich line by taking his body and the bodies of his wife and son to St Petersburg for reburial, alongside the tomb of Grand Prince Vladimir Alexandrovich. But Marie, who worked so hard for her sons, is still buried at Contrexéville. They have not even left a space for her monument among the new graves of her family.

19

The Harsh Light of Day

GRAND PRINCE DMITRI PAVLOVICH

*The murder of Rasputin in December 1916 marked the beginning of the end.
While crowds celebrated in the streets of St Petersburg and Moscow and even
members of the imperial family hailed the event, despite its brutality, in the
countryside the murder only confirmed many ordinary people in their hatred of
the nobility. One of their own kind had come too close to the Tsar, they said, and
the nobility had murdered him. Grand Prince Dmitri's involvement in the murder
was known to all, though the precise details of what happened in the basement of
the Yusupov Palace that December night must always remain open to question.
Some of the conspirators dined out on their involvement for years while others
never spoke at all, but Dmitri had certainly played some part in the cold-blooded
murder of an unarmed man. Many members of the imperial family thought his
punishment harsh, but in the circumstances the Tsar's judgement was remarkably
generous. It also saved Dmitri's life.*

Before he was fourteen, Grand Prince Dmitri Pavlovich had his
own palace in St Petersburg and nominal command of the
2nd Battalion of the Tirailleurs de la Garde. One of his
cousins remarked that he looked so perfect he might have been
made by Fabergé. When he came of age at the 'Blessing of the
Waters' in 1912 and took his Oath of Allegiance, all Russia lay at
his feet. He represented the country in the equestrian team at the
Stockholm Olympics that year and this won him further popularity.
The Tsar and Tsaritsa treated him as one of their own children,
replacing the mother who had died giving him birth and the father
who abandoned him in childhood. His teasing could make even the
Tsaritsa laugh and her daughters adored him; it was widely believed

that one day he would marry the eldest of the four, Grand Princess Olga. Some even wondered if he was being groomed for the position of heir, in case anything should happen to the Tsesarevich. Dmitri began the First World War with a daring rescue under fire of a wounded corporal in the battle of Kaushin, which earned him the Cross of St George and a position at headquarters, yet, before his twenty-sixth birthday he was a penniless exile, pleading for a commission in a foreign army. It was an extraordinary reverse and one entirely due to the Grand Prince's own actions. He would spend the rest of his life coming to terms with what he had done.

When Dmitri turned up in Teheran in the spring of 1917, with nothing but the luggage in his pack and an orderly for company, he was at a low ebb physically and mentally. Nothing had turned out the way he planned. Felix Yusupov was later to say that despite his obvious charm, and the vitality and imagination that drew people to him, Dmitri was a very weak character. Felix was not the only one to feel this way about his former friend. Grand Prince Pavel, Dmitri's father, had worried terribly about the effect that life at headquarters, and the favouritism shown by the Tsar, were having on his son. The Tsaritsa wrote despairingly of Dmitri's activities in town: 'the boy behaves according to the person he for the moment cares for'.[1] His nerves were unreliable and he suffered from palpitations and occasional breathlessness: like many other members of the imperial family he had tuberculosis and was sometimes seen to cough up blood. Even so, he begged for a useful role, in the Caucasus perhaps, or anywhere far away. He complained that his friends had all been killed and he did not like his commanding officer or the other officers of his regiment, who did nothing but drink. On one occasion the Tsar kept Dmitri by his side because 'the boy has got it into his head that he will be killed'.[2] Albert Stopford was Dmitri's friend but still wrote that 'the . . . boy is always helpless and desolate'.[3] Whenever people referred to Dmitri at this time it was always as 'the boy', though he was well into his twenties.

His emotional life was chaotic. According to Felix Yusupov, at one time Dmitri was in love with Princess Irina Alexandrovna, and hoped to marry her until she chose Felix. In December 1914 he saw Grand

Prince Mikhail Alexandrovich's morganatic wife Natalia Brasova at the station, and snatched the earliest opportunity to meet. Soon he was hopelessly in love, and Natalia was flattered by his attention and went out of her way to encourage him, without any serious intent beyond stirring up the feelings of her husband who was away at the front with his regiment. She wrote to Mikhail of their meetings, and of Dmitri's feelings for her, comparing him in his innocence to a 'lily of the valley', and this became the couple's nickname for him. In March 1915 she invited Dmitri to stay with her in Gatchina town and they attended church together. Their relationship may not have been sexual, but Dmitri felt guilty enough to put the telephone down abruptly when Mikhail came home on leave and called to invite him on another visit. Several weeks passed before he contacted Natalia again; then he did and there were further meetings. Her letters suggest that he had tried and failed to put her out of his mind. Again she wrote to her husband about him and again her letters caused Mikhail pain, as she must have intended. Dmitri was being used, and drawn deeper and deeper into a relationship which could lead to nothing but disappointment.[4]

In this state, restless, confused, and intelligent enough to see that outside his own private muddles Russia itself was sliding into chaos, Dmitri was easily drawn by the lure of direct action. Rasputin's reputation was harming the throne, Rasputin must go; but while it was one thing to plan the murder with a group of headstrong young men, each reinforcing the other's boldness, the brutal fact of killing an unarmed man was quite another. There was nothing brave or self-sacrificing about the conspiracy because the murderers never intended to take responsibility for what they had done. If all had gone according to plan, their victim would simply have disappeared, until spring forced the Neva to give up its secrets. Just hours after pushing the dead man's body under the ice, Dmitri was on the telephone to the Tsaritsa asking if he could call for tea that afternoon. He went to the theatre in the evening, and then reality began to dawn. The audience gave him a standing ovation, and he withdrew in embarrassment.

Most of the public attention in the first few days after the murder focused on Dmitri. People cheered him as their hero and lit candles before the icon of St Dmitri in the Kazan Cathedral. He was terrified of this new popularity. He swore to his aunt, Grand Princess Vladimir, that he had left the Yusupov Palace long before the murder; he took a sacred oath before his father that there was no blood on his hands. The people whose good opinion he valued most, his father and the Tsar, were both appalled by the murder. It was obvious, too, that the situation in Russia was not going to improve. Disillusioned and unhappy, Dmitri accepted the Tsar's decision to banish him to a regiment on the Persian front, refusing the chance to escape, and the more melodramatic offers to lead a coup in his name. He left the Nicholas Station in Petrograd at 2 a.m. on 6 January under guard, though his former tutor General Laiming was allowed to accompany him. There was no food on the train and Stopford later heard that 'he had "*une crise de nerfs*", and completely broke down in the train next day in his famished condition'.[5]

Dmitri was welcomed by his new battalion, and he had been with them for barely ten weeks when news came of the Tsar's abdication. The Provisional Government sent a pardon and invited Dmitri to return to Petrograd, but he did not want to go back. His first loyalty had always been to the Tsar and he was still afraid of being praised for an act which now filled him with revulsion. He felt that there was no place for him in Russia and, accompanied by his orderly, he slipped across the frontier into Persia and made his way to Teheran where, according to his sister, 'he lived through a series of painful experiences'.[6] The Russian community ignored him and he turned to the British Legation for help. This was a good move. The British Minister, Sir Charles Marling, and his wife took the exiled Grand Prince into their own home for nearly two years and provided the emotional support he so badly needed.

It is always said that in helping Dmitri Sir Charles acted against the wishes of the British government, putting his own career at risk, but this is very unlikely. In the spring of 1917 Sir Charles Marling was in his mid-fifties, with almost thirty years in the diplomatic service behind him. When the Tsar's cousin turned up on his doorstep asking for a commission in the British army, his first action would have been to inform London, and he was probably told to keep an eye on Dmitri. His career did not suffer at all, on the contrary, from Teheran he went on to become British Minister in Copenhagen and in The Hague, and in 1926, the year of his retirement, he was invested with the highest class, Knight Grand Cross, of the Order of St Michael and St George. The Foreign Office had good reason to take an interest in Dmitri. He was well known to the British Ambassador in Petrograd and his staff and they had watched his treatment after the murder of Rasputin with great concern. Dmitri stood high in the order of succession, he was popular and presentable and, with events in Russia so uncertain, he could become a very important young man indeed. In 1918, during his stay with the Marlings, the Foreign Office received reports that a monarchist group in Russia had recognized Dmitri as heir to the throne. They were not the only ones to take an interest; the German Ambassador in Moscow, Wilhelm von Mirbach, considered Dmitri as a possible regent in the event of a German-led restoration of the throne.

Through 1917 and most of 1918, Dmitri lived with the Marlings and, with little else to do, he made good use of the legation library, acquainting himself with subjects not included in the training of a Russian cavalry officer. Just before the Armistice in November 1918 his commission came through; at the same time, Sir Charles was recalled to London for a new appointment and Dmitri, now a captain in the British army, accompanied the Marlings on their long journey overland to India. At Bombay they boarded a troopship; unfortunately typhoid was rife in the city and affected many of the men on the ship, and Dmitri was one of the first to succumb. Lady Marling and the faithful Russian orderly, who had never left Dmitri's side, took turns in nursing him but he grew weaker by the day. Finally he slipped into unconsciousness and, aware that he was losing the battle, the hard-pressed ship's doctor grabbed Dmitri by the shoulders and shook him roughly, shouting 'Come back, come back!'

It was a desperate measure but it worked. The Grand Prince clung to life and, when the troopship docked at Port Said, he was carried off on a stretcher to complete his recovery in Cairo under the protective eye of the Marlings. Only when he was fully recovered did the little party set out again, crossing the Mediterranean to Marseilles and continuing overland to Paris. Paris held many memories for Dmitri. In the last few years before the war he had kept an apartment at the Hotel Georges V; his father owned a house at Boulogne-sur-Seine and it was there that Dmitri hurried to find news of his family. What he was told sent him reeling. His father was in prison. His sister and step-brother had both disappeared, the Tsar was believed to be dead and nothing certain was known of the Tsaritsa and her children. The Marlings took him to London, where they were able to hand him over to his mother's sister Grand Princess Marie Georgievna. 'He looked desperately ill and weak,' she remembered, '. . . it was only owing to Lady Marling's untiring care that he was saved.'[7]

At least the Grand Princess had some money in hand for Dmitri, the proceeds from the sale of his St Petersburg palace, which had gone through before the Bolsheviks seized power. Dmitri took rooms at the Ritz and spent most of his time with his aunt. They were able to console each other in the weeks of anxiety that followed: the Grand Princess's husband was in prison with Dmitri's father, and together they did all they could to secure a release, or at least to gain reliable news. On 4 February the Grand Princess received a telegram from Finland, which confirmed earlier rumours that all the prisoners had been shot, and she broke the news to Dmitri. His only consolation in this difficult time was the thought that his sister was safe in Bucharest and, as the weeks passed, his old good spirits began to return. Life in England offered many distractions. Dmitri enjoyed company and made friends easily. He was closely related to the King, who is said to have liked him very much. Soon there were house parties and other amusements to look forward to, and a trail of ambitious mothers who saw a handsome Grand Prince as a very good catch. There was also an old flame, newly escaped from Russia. Dmitri had kept in touch with Natalia Brasova from the Persian front and Teheran, and when he heard that she was in England and had taken a house at Wadhurst in Sussex he hurried to see her. For a while he was a regular visitor, but Natalia's thoughts were entirely taken up with the fate of her missing husband, and Dmitri gradually drifted back to his own life.

That summer his sister Marie arrived in London; they had been apart for over two years, and so much had happened to them both. After an emotional meeting at Victoria Station they found that there were many things they were unable to discuss. Marie had remarried during the Revolution; her new husband, Prince Putiatin, knew Dmitri a little and at first the two men got on well. The Putiatins found that the Ritz was too expensive for them and moved out, and shortly afterwards Dmitri followed, taking a house with his sister and brother-in-law in South Kensington. It was an odd household. Dmitri had his English friends and embarked on a study of political economy and social science, but Putiatin still needed to learn the language, and Marie tried to earn money for them both with needlework and knitting – her attempt to produce a pair of pyjamas for her brother reduced them all to hysterics. Dmitri and Marie were at the station to welcome the Dowager Tsaritsa on her arrival in England, and both became regular visitors to Marlborough House in the months that followed.

But beneath the surface all was not well. Dmitri and Putiatin had nothing in common except their war service and that bond could not hold for ever. The Yusupovs had escaped with the Dowager Tsaritsa, and they too settled in London. Felix tried to renew his friendship with Dmitri but the Grand Prince avoided all contact. The conspirators had been sworn to silence about the murder of Rasputin and Dmitri never broke his oath. He was repelled by the pleasure Felix took in recounting the murder because for him it was a living nightmare; his cousin Gavril Konstantinovich remembered that it was many years before Dmitri dared to take communion again, because of the guilt that preyed on his mind. While he stayed away from Yusupov, Marie and Putiatin were drawn more and more closely into the parties and entertainments of the Yusupov set, and tensions mounted in the South Kensington house. In the summer of 1920 the Putiatins moved to Paris. Dmitri followed a few months later, but this time he chose to take rooms at a hotel until he found his own modest two-roomed apartment. He was beginning to have money problems. The proceeds from the sale of his palace had enabled him to live well, but they were not bottomless. He had given generously to other émigrés in need and to Russian charities, and was easy prey for the unscrupulous. An American journalist later quoted him as saying that he 'arrived in Paris with less than a hundred francs . . . and only one extra shirt', and lived on loans. If this was true, he was in more serious trouble than anyone realized, though he still put on an impressive show.[8] He saw relatively little of his sister, but moved in quickly to support her when he knew she had a difficult meeting to face.

Long before war or revolution had entered their lives, Marie had been married to Prince Vilhelm of Sweden and they had a son, Lennart, whom Marie had abandoned when he was little more than a baby. Now she longed to see him again. The King of Sweden understood and was willing to allow a meeting on neutral ground, in Denmark. Dmitri agreed to go with his sister. She needed his support, and for him the visit offered a chance to see the Marlings again; it was arranged that Dmitri and Marie would stay at the British Legation. They set off for Denmark early in the summer of 1921, arriving shortly before the Swedish party. It must have been a strange experience for the twelve-year-old Prince Lennart, but he got on well with his uncle and the holiday was a happy time for them all. The Dowager Tsaritsa was close by in her villa Hvidore, and Dmitri and Marie were able to make several visits to the old lady, whose presence still recalled something of their lost world.

Superficially Dmitri's life was full, but he felt rootless and lonely. He could never escape attention. In 1922 he was still being hailed as 'the hope of Russian imperialism' and a possible future Tsar; his rather brooding good looks were always a talking point. 'He has a figure like Rudolph Valentino's and a face and head like Charles Dana Gibson's,' a journalist wrote, 'he would "go big" in Hollywood.'[9] Dmitri, however, preferred Paris. In the last year before the war he had met an aspiring fashion designer, Gabrielle Chanel. Her lover then had been an Englishman, but he had died, and despite the success of her business – 'Coco' Chanel was becoming the talk of Paris – she needed a new companion. Chanel was older than Dmitri and there may have been a maternal element in their affair, but affair it was, and it is often said that Chanel was the great love of Dmitri's life. He escorted her around Europe and gave her expensive presents, and she understood his needs. 'Princes have always filled me with immense pity', she remarked to a friend. Later, Chanel became close to Dmitri's sister and helped her in her new business venture. Marie had started a company called 'Kitmir', producing fashion embroidery, into which Dmitri sank a substantial investment.

The business did well for some years. Marie's marriage, on the other hand, was crumbling. Dmitri had held himself apart from Putiatin for a long time, but when the couple separated he moved back in with his sister. Circumstances had made the two extremely close as children and Marie was sure that their relationship had never changed, but it is evident from her writings that Dmitri found something claustrophobic in his sister's love. He cared about her and wanted to be on hand to help, but shut her out of important areas of his life. They shared a flat, and later Marie bought a small house at Boulogne-sur-Seine, near to the property their father had once owned, which their stepmother Princess Paley had been forced to sell. Dmitri moved in to the top floor. He had found work for a champagne company at Reims and was out most of the day, but spent his evenings with his sister. They had been together for more than a year when Marie noticed that her brother was becoming increasingly depressed and losing interest in the world around him. His health troubled him more and more, though the doctors could not detect any particular illness. Dmitri needed stability. After years on the move, years of living in rooms and flats and mixing with a shifting set of people, he needed something permanent. He had even lost the undivided attention of Chanel. In 1925 he accompanied her to Monte Carlo where she met and fell for the Duke of Westminster, who became the new man in her life.

The Grand Prince was near to breaking-point when friends invited him and Marie to a tea party at Versailles where he met Audrey Emery, a sophisticated and attractive American heiress in her early twenties. Her prospects had been the talk of Biarritz for some years. Audrey's father was a self-made millionaire. After his death her mother had married the Hon. Alfred Anson, a younger son of the 2nd Earl of Lichfield and, like many an ambitious mother before her, she saw Dmitri as a good catch. He was immediately taken with Audrey; so much so, that he abandoned Marie to find her own way home from the tea party. Romance lifted his spirits, though there were times when his depression returned. He confided in his sister that he felt unworthy to propose marriage because he had so little to offer, but he did propose and Audrey was pleased to accept. She even decided to convert to Orthodoxy, and Grand Prince Kyrill, whose claim to the throne Dmitri never recognized, gave her the title 'Princess Romanovsky-Ilyinsky'. The throne of Russia was still a live issue and Dmitri had many supporters, but he made no attempt to encourage them. In 1928 the Foreign Office notified British Embassies that Kyrill was not to be recognized as Tsar because Dmitri was the true heir to the throne.

The international press took a great deal of interest in Dmitri's wedding at Biarritz, on 21 November 1926. For a few hours it seemed as if the imperial Court had been reborn. Audrey wore the magnificent lace veil once worn by Dmitri's mother and by his sister for their weddings in the chapels of the Winter Palace and the Catherine Palace at Tsarskoe Selo. No one was superstitious enough to remember how short-lived both of these marriages had been. Dmitri was attended by former officers of his regiment (presumably not the ones whose drinking had offended him), and the only spectre at the feast was Marie, who dreaded the parting from her brother and felt that everyone was watching her to see her reaction. Dmitri had been half afraid to tell her about his plans, and she only consoled herself with the idea that Audrey had been her own choice for her brother. After the service and reception, the couple set off for a honeymoon in England where they established their first home.

At last Dmitri really was happy. He had a home of his own and a wife he loved, and the crowning moment came at the beginning of 1928, when Audrey gave birth to a son. They named him Paul, and on the day of the christening the proud father was beside himself with joy. 'I could see how happy Dmitri was,' his sister wrote, 'by the pleasure he took in the minutest details of the arrangements for the occasion. Even the flower decorations he supervised himself. At times he would run up to Audrey's room, where I was keeping her company, and demand that I go down and admire his work . . . bubbling over with enthusiasm as he showed me the rooms filled with flowers.'[10] Between them, the couple could afford a very opulent lifestyle, with homes in London, Biarritz, Neuilly-sur-Seine and Beaumesnil Château, near Caen, and visits to America. Audrey's friends joked that she had produced young Paul in the back of a Rolls-Royce. She certainly had a taste for expensive cars and she and Dmitri owned two Lincolns; one for Paul, his nannies and four or five dogs, to travel in front, and one for themselves, to follow, in style, behind.

But all dreams end, and this one too was bound for a fall. Audrey was much younger than Dmitri and did not want the things that he wanted. After ten years the marriage ended in divorce, and Audrey found another prince, Dmitri Djordjadze, whom she married in 1939. The Grand Prince was devastated. He went back to rooms in the Hotel Georges V and the Ritz, and spent long periods at a sanatorium at Davos in Switzerland. The tuberculosis which had troubled him during the First World War was taking its toll. His son was at school in England, but they were able to spend the school holidays together until war broke out, when it was decided to send young Paul to America for safety. Dmitri saw him off at Genoa; whether Audrey was there or not is unclear, as she plays no part in her son's recorded memories. The Grand Prince may have sensed that this would be the last time he would see his son. He took the boy into a toy shop and bought a huge collection of lead soldiers as a parting gift. Paul boarded the Italian liner *Rex* with his nanny and an ex-Guards officer named Terence Philips, and set sail for America. Two days out from Gibraltar the ship was stopped by a German submarine and boarded, and the Captain was asked for his complete passenger list. The Germans took six Jewish passengers before they would allow the ship to sail; it was a scene young Paul would never forget.

Alone now, Dmitri returned to the sanatorium in Davos. On 4 March 1942 the staff and patients enjoyed a Russian festival he had organized to entertain himself and his friends. The celebrations continued until late into the night, and the next morning Dmitri suffered a sudden attack of uraemia and died. He was only fifty. His nephew Lennart provided his last home, in the chapel crypt of Schloss Mainau, on Lake Constance. For the former 'hope of Russian imperialism', it was a sad end.

20

Surviving

PRINCESS CATHERINE YOURIEVSKY

Dmitri Pavlovich and Grand Princess Vladimir were among the lucky members of the imperial family who escaped the chaos of revolution and found their way to safety. The largest party of survivors were those who accompanied the Dowager Tsaritsa and her family out of Yalta on HMS Marlborough, and they came perilously close to death before rescue arrived. But one of the most remarkable stories of escape and survival belongs to someone who was not, properly speaking, a member of the imperial family at all – though she was a Tsar's daughter.

I t was worthy of a footnote in *The Times*. On Christmas Eve, 1959, an old lady died on Hayling Island, after many years alone and penniless. Her funeral at St Peter's Church, North Hayling, was a small affair; even her two sons stayed away. The paper noted eight mourners including a nephew, her ex-husband, the doctor and the vicar's wife, but if the circumstances sound unremarkable, the lady herself was not. A professional singer who had struggled for years against ill-health, Princess Catherine Yourievsky was the daughter of a Tsar of Russia, and her death was a quiet postscript to one of the most compelling of royal stories.

The Princess was the youngest child of Alexander II and Ekaterina Dolgorukaya, born in the Crimea in September 1878. During her father's lifetime, she and her brother and sister were far too young to realize the scandal attached to their name.[1] Georgi was six when Catherine was born, Olga was almost five, and a second boy, Boris, had died soon after his birth. Their father gave them the name Yurievsky, which their mother took after her marriage, and the rank of prince. He made no secret of the fact that he adored them. His nephew Alexander Mikhailovich described their entry at a tense family meal:

At the end of the dinner the governess brought in the three children.

'Ah, there is my Gogo,' exclaimed the Emperor proudly, lifting the vivacious boy in the air and placing him on his shoulder. 'Tell us, Gogo, what is your full name?'

'I am Prince George Alexandrovitch Yourievsky,' replied Gogo, and started to arrange the side-whiskers of the Emperor, brushing them with his two little hands.[2]

Catherine was not quite two when her father and mother were married in secret. Before she was three, he died; she was too young to be touched by the horror and confusion and in the aftermath of the murder her mother clung to her. She was the only person who could still make the bereaved Princess smile. Her own memories of Russia were entirely cheerful, or so she claimed; once she and her brother and sister played with the new Tsar's children, and she never forgot their excitement as their giant half-brother Alexander III tossed them in a balancing net. 'I well remember the huge enjoyment and shrieks of laughter that accompanied this game, and the amusement of the Emperor, who seemed a playful and kind Goliath amongst all the romping children.'[3]

But beyond her comprehension, an unpleasant atmosphere surrounded the Yurievskys. Even at her husband's funeral the Princess had no place; the Court would never accept her or her children. The Tsar had left his second family a substantial income in his will and made his heir responsible for them: Alexander III respected his father's wishes but he could not change the past, or forget his own resentment, as his comments on their unexpected meeting at Livadia showed. He gave the Princess a palace of her own, the Palais Rose at No. 3 Gagarinsky Street, but she was haunted by her loss. She turned one room into a replica of the study where her husband died, and after a year she left St Petersburg for France, in search of earlier and happier memories.

The little family set out in the spring of 1882, accompanied by nurses, governesses and tutors, a doctor, cooks, maids and footmen, a coachman, and the Princess's beloved dogs. Alexander III provided them with a military escort and they occupied two hotels in Paris before taking a house at No. 52 Avenue Kléber, which the Princess turned into a shrine to the murdered Tsar. Her sister joined her, and her brothers found her useful as a source of funds. An interesting circle of friends gathered around her: Dumas and Ferdinand de Lesseps were frequent visitors to the Avenue Kléber. In time the Princess bought a house at Neuilly-sur-Seine, and this was the first home her younger daughter would really remember.

Catherine was a delicate child with a congenital heart defect which caused fainting and attacks of breathlessness. Georgi and Olga teased her about her size; until she reached the age of twelve she was tiny and they told her she would never grow. Even so, time would prove her the most attractive and gifted of the Yurievsky children, with her mother's looks and temperament. She shared Ekaterina's love of animals. All her life she was devoted to her dogs, and as a child she even had a baby donkey. It was supposed to live in the stables, but she often smuggled it into her nursery. She longed to ride, but was considered too weak and had to be content with a pony cart.

In summer Princess Yurievskaya took the children to Nice or Biarritz, where they were welcomed by the Russian colony, and in 1888 she decided to settle permanently in Nice. She bought a three-storey marble villa and called it the 'Villa Georges'; in time it was furnished with all the treasured reminders of her husband. She brought the children up to know that they were the children of a Tsar and to take a fierce pride in the love that produced them. She behaved like an empress, the rank she might have held if her husband had lived only weeks longer. There was a defiant edge to the attitude she instilled in her children; the world, knowing their story, would always be curious and often spiteful. In compensation she gave them everything a Tsar's children would have had. She tried to be strict with them but wealth without responsibility is a hard mixture to control.

Georgi was the first to show its effects. He was charming, amusing and utterly spoilt, eager to sample all the temptations open to a young man with money. His tutors faced a hopeless task. In 1893 his half-brother Grand Prince Alexei secured him a commission in the Russian navy but he resented the discipline, borrowed money from his fellow officers, ignored orders and finally faced a court martial. After Alexei had been forced to dismiss him a place was found for him in the army. Shaken by his experience, Georgi at last tried to reform.

Olga caused her mother no problems, and the Princess's only immediate anxiety for Catherine was her health. The little girl showed great aptitude for music. She played the piano well, though it bored her, and one evening when her mother was out the maid took her to hear Nellie Melba sing. The atmosphere fired her imagination, and she decided there and then that she too must be a concert singer. At first her mother would not allow her to take lessons because of her heart, but she persisted, and by the end of her teens was training seriously in Milan under the celebrated Polish tenor Jean de Reszke.

Catherine's memories of these years are confused. Her autobiography states that she married while still in her teens and only then was able to follow her two great dreams, singing and riding. In fact, she was twenty-three when she married, and had been studying music and riding for some time. A young Russian visitor to Biarritz in 1900 remembered her clearly. At ten years old, Prince Serge Obolensky was very taken with the tall, beautiful young woman with her polished manners and mezzo-soprano voice. 'She rode to hounds', he wrote, many years later, 'and was a fine horsewoman. Naturally she was very conscious of her position as a daughter of the Emperor.'[4]

The young Yurievskys were children no longer. Marriage was first suggested to Catherine when she was fifteen, but she was not impressed with her would-be husband; she liked his father better. In 1895 Olga married Count Georg Merenberg, a grandson of the poet Pushkin, and settled with him at Wiesbaden. Before the wedding her mother contacted Nicholas II, who should have been her daughter's sponsor, but the old resentments had been handed on to a new generation and the Tsar refused. 'Mama was in despair at the idea,' he told his brother, 'so I politely but firmly declined.'[5] On St Valentine's Day 1900 a magnificent ceremony marked the wedding of Georgi and Countess Alexandra Zarnekau. They moved into the Palais Rose in St Petersburg, while Princess Yurievskaya left Nice with her younger daughter for the Villa Sofia in Biarritz.

It was in Biarritz that Catherine was married, in October 1901. Her husband was Prince Alexander Bariatinsky, the heir to one of Russia's wealthiest families. Like her brother he was spoilt and attractive, and could charm without effort; for some years he had enjoyed a very public affair with the opera singer Lina Cavalieri. Surprisingly, perhaps, the marriage was a success. Catherine was shrewd enough to realize the hold that Cavalieri still had over her husband, and instead of fighting it she made a friend of the singer. She copied Cavalieri's hairstyle – on her it looked stunning – and the three were seen everywhere together. Once, innocently or by design, she admired a collaret of emeralds that the Prince had given to Lina. Quietly, the singer took them off and placed them around Catherine's neck.

Now Catherine was free of her mother's control her life was one long party, with the opera, theatre and balls of Paris, hunting, racing and bridge parties at Biarritz and the outdoor life at Lidenau, Alexander's estate on the Starnbergsee in Bavaria. She had two sons, André, born in 1902, and Alexander, always known as 'Buddie', in 1904, and a pet milk cow was added to the family's travelling caravan. Reality only intruded when the debts became too much, and the couple ran to their parents for help. The Bariatinskys often despaired of their son, and Princess Yurievskaya became used to finding Catherine on the doorstep, wearing all her furs and diamonds to save them from creditors. After a few weeks the couple would return to an emptied house, refurnish and start again. Sometimes Catherine was briefly overwhelmed by remorse. Once she tried to kill herself by cutting the ends off a box of matches and consuming the poison, but the attempt failed and she soon bounced back. It seemed that nothing could hold her down for long.

The game ended in March 1910, when Alexander died. He was recovering from a slight stroke when he collapsed at an afternoon bridge party in Florence and died soon after, despite desperate attempts to revive him. 'He was known all over the Continent,' his sister-in-law wrote, 'and had led an eventful, if perhaps somewhat thoughtless life. But he was a charming man, liked by everyone, and had a winning personality.'[6]

Catherine retired to Lidenau. She had loved Alexander and it was hard to make sense of life without him; her only relief was found in solitude, walking or riding in the hills. But in time she began to sing again and joined in with local society and, as her spirits returned, she became absorbed in an ambitious new project. She decided to take her sons to their ancestral home, Ivanovskoe, near Kiev, and teach them about the management of a great estate.

So far her only experience of money had been spending, which she did with enthusiasm. According to her own account she now took over the running of Ivanovskoe on her elder son's behalf and revolutionized it, saving a fortune in the first year and earning the admiration and gratitude of all concerned. She makes no mention of the fact that her father-in-law was still living on the estate and still very much in control. The Bariatinskys would have welcomed her, for their son's sake. They may have given her some responsibility, and indulged her, as she had always been indulged, allowing her to think that her contribution was vital: if so, they certainly succeeded.

Catherine inspired a protective concern in those closest to her. Her early widowhood was one reason, her health was another. She had spells of breathlessness and would often faint while riding and be found unconscious, miles from the house. When the Bariatinskys decided that the climate at Ivanovskoe was too harsh and sent her to the Crimea, she disappeared on the way and was found unconscious on the floor of the car. Once, in Bavaria, she became so engrossed in a jigsaw that she and her half-sister, the Duchess of Saxe-Coburg, were working on that she passed out and it took some time to revive her. There was no warning before these attacks and they must have been alarming.

In the last years before the outbreak of war, Catherine divided her time between Ivanovskoe, Lidenau and whichever home her mother was using. Princess Yurievskaya returned to Russia in 1912 to visit her husband's grave, and Nicholas II made her welcome. Her existence was even reported in the newspapers for the first time, thirty-two years after her marriage to Alexander II. Nicholas's sister Olga visited her at the Palais Rose, where 'she lived entirely in the past. Time stopped for her on the day my grandfather was assassinated. She always talked about him. She kept all his uniforms and clothes, even his dressing-gown, in glass cases in her private chapel.'[7]

In the spring of 1913 Princess Yurievskaya was staying with Catherine and her grandsons at Lidenau when Georgi joined them, in need of sympathy. His marriage had ended in divorce five years earlier, and he was suffering from an incurable kidney disease. Georgi was the unseen casualty of the bomb that killed his father. He had never really come to grips with life, and at the age of forty-one his life was ending. He still tried to be amusing, but in moments of depression and pain he found comfort in his sister's singing. He stayed for several months, and died at Marburg in September 1913.

The outbreak of war in 1914 found the family scattered. Olga was in Germany with her husband and children and could not communicate with her mother until the fighting ended. Her husband was attached to a Red Cross unit in recognition of his Russian ancestry, but their son fought on the western front and was taken prisoner near Verdun. Catherine was at Munich with her children at the start of the war and they had great difficulty getting back to Russia. They settled at Ivanovskoe, where she ran a makeshift hospital in one wing of the house. She arranged concerts to raise funds, and the soldiers themselves were a captive audience for her singing. Cut off from both daughters, Princess Yurievskaya was glad to be reunited with Georgi's ex-wife and his son Alexander. She sent the boy to school at her own expense, and with his mother became involved in the work of a military hospital in Paris.

In the autumn of 1916 news came that Catherine was to remarry. At a charity bazaar in Yalta that spring, she had met a sick officer of the Chevalier Guard. He was Serge Obolensky, the little boy who once admired her in Biarritz, and both remembered the meeting. She invited him to one of her concerts and her singing moved him.

On the run from a failed love affair, Serge was feeling vulnerable, and Catherine had been alone for six years; by the end of his leave he had proposed. Catherine would give no answer at first, but they exchanged letters, and within weeks she accepted. They were married in Yalta in October 1916. Nicholas II sent a necklace of aquamarines and was represented at the wedding by Count Fredericks. Fourteen-year-old André Bariatinsky was one of the ushers, and Grand Prince Alexander Mikhailovich provided the car that took the couple to Simferopol on their way to a St Petersburg honeymoon. Serge's duties kept them in the north until the February revolution, but after that his regiment effectively ceased to exist, and he and Catherine made their way back to Yalta and the boys.

In the lull between the two revolutions the Crimea was relatively peaceful, and the family enjoyed a brief, idyllic period in Catherine's Mordvinov Palace in the hills above Yalta. Then the Bolsheviks seized power in the north. Catherine was disturbed when Serge told her that he planned to join a rebel force of Tatars and former Guards officers, but he was adamant and they quarrelled for the first time. Just hours after he left, Yalta was bombarded from the sea.

The Princess sent her sons to the cellar and sat by the piano, always her refuge in times of stress. She was singing when a mob of soldiers burst in. The palace was taken, and she sat up all night dreading that Serge might return to his death. In the morning the boys were allowed to leave with their English governess but Catherine, as the daughter of a Tsar, might have faced a firing squad if a friend of Serge's had not bribed one of the guards. She was hurried away from the palace with Bobby, her dog, in her arms; under heavy shell fire she and her protector ran to safety in a friend's house.

Briefly the Tatar force recaptured Yalta. Serge was dismayed to find the Mordvinov Palace ransacked, but friends told him where Catherine was and he made his way there, caked with mud and in fear of his life. He wanted her to join him: she followed him into the dark streets, carrying Bobby, but there was shooting all round, and she had to go back; bullets had even penetrated her coat before she reached the house. As soon as possible she escaped again, and took shelter in another house where she stayed for several days, until the family realized the danger they faced by harbouring her. She agreed to leave, if they would only take care of her dog.

Now she was completely alone. Her husband's former gardener and his wife took her to a farm in the country and she posed as one of the family, caring for the baby, scrubbing floors and doing manual work. Serge was now a resistance fighter with a price on his head; there were persistent rumours that he had been killed. She lived in dread of discovery. Many months passed before she learned that friends had smuggled her husband away to Moscow, drugged to simulate illness. Once there he tried to trace her and the boys and discovered that André and Buddie were safe, but that Catherine badly needed his help.

The same friends who arranged Serge's escape were able to provide Catherine with a new refuge and a new identity. After a twenty-mile walk that left her feet torn and bleeding, she found herself at a boarding house where she became Mlle Hélène, a governess stranded in Yalta by war and revolution. There were Bolshevik soldiers among the guests, and one was keen to learn French; it was a strange situation but she kept her nerve, and after some weeks of teaching, cooking and cleaning, word came that it was time to leave. With a nurse's uniform for protection and a bribed soldier as an escort, Catherine made the nightmare journey to Moscow, where Serge was being sheltered by friends. She travelled by train, perching on the luggage rack of a carriage packed with soldiers. It was dangerous, unpleasant and very frightening but at least she was alive. Far away in France Princess Yurievskaya heard that both Catherine and Serge were dead, and grieved for them. More than a year would pass before she learned the truth.

As the First World War drew to an end, the old Princess's problems were only beginning. For nearly forty years, ever since the terrorist's bomb tore her husband from her, she had lived in the past, but she had also lived in luxury. After the Revolution that security ended; there was no Tsar to pay her allowance now. It was hard for her to accept the change, harder still to believe that the Russia she had known was gone for ever. But at least the return of peace allowed a reunion with her elder daughter, and the last months of 1918 brought exciting news: Catherine and Serge were not dead after all and had reached safety in Switzerland.

They were incredibly lucky to be alive. Reunited in Moscow in the home of an employee of Serge's family, they had to pretend to be strangers. After some months their host was able to find them places with a trade delegation en route for the German-held Ukraine. They travelled by train to Petrograd, then on to the German border at Pskov, passing through some frightening police checkpoints before reaching ironic but real safety in territory controlled by their former enemies. In Kiev they were able to resume their true identities and they moved in with Prince Anatole Bariatinsky, the brother of Catherine's first husband.

Next they had to rescue André and Alexander, who were still in Yalta. Hearing that the Crimea had fallen to the Germans, Serge applied to the German authorities to let him bring the boys to Kiev, with money raised from the sale of some Bariatinsky property in the Ukraine. Permission was given, and the boys arrived safely with Bobby, their mother's beloved dog, but their governess, Miss Picken, and Albert Stannard, who had been the Yurievskys' coachman when Catherine was a child, were turned back. They had protected the young Princes from every danger and Miss Picken was more of a mother to the boys than their own mother but they were English, and the Germans would not allow them to enter Kiev. They had to be smuggled back to Odessa, which was in French hands, and returned to England by sea.

While Serge's greatest concern was the state of Kiev, which might fall to the Red Army at any moment, Catherine was simply overjoyed to be reunited with the dog she had last seen during the fighting in Yalta. Bobby meant everything to her and his disappearance one day caused a major panic. The house was in uproar. Catherine made everyone go out to search the streets: the suggestion that Bobby might have been taken to the pound sent her on a heedless dash, determined to save him. Actually he had been found by a German soldier and was being cared for in the barracks. A friend saw him some days later and reunited him with his distraught mistress, who could then turn her mind to more serious things.

Serge was right about the danger. He applied for permission to go to Vienna, and the family left Kiev just before the Ukraine fell. Most of the funds they had salvaged were lost in the confusion, but they reached Vienna in safety and had settled into a hotel when they realized that here too things were going wrong. When Serge saw mobs forming in the streets he remembered St Petersburg and knew that it was time to leave. They took a train for Switzerland, and after some difficulty at the border they entered the country as the Austrian revolution broke out behind them. After so much turmoil it seemed unreal to be in a country at peace.

The Obolenskys stayed in Berne for a short time before going on to Lausanne, where they were delighted to meet old friends. Prince and Princess Nicholas of Greece were there with their children, and so was the Dowager Duchess of Mecklenburg Schwerin, Grand Princess Anastasia Mikhailovna, who had refused to stay in Germany while the country was at war with her Russian homeland. It was time to consider the future of Catherine's sons; André was sixteen and Alexander fourteen, and their lives had been too unsettled to allow for much education. Serge discussed them with his old tutor and they were placed at a school in Lausanne, which consumed most of the money their parents still had. Alone now, Catherine and Serge were able to relax. They spent Christmas skiing at Gstaad and applied for permits to enter France, for the long-awaited reunion with Catherine's mother.

Princess Yurievskaya had not seen her daughter for five years and Serge had been a child of ten when they last met. The three were reunited in Nice, and Serge was overwhelmed by this encounter with the past. The Princess was seventy now, but in his eyes she looked little more than forty. 'She always wore the same type of mauve dress. She kept fine horses, and drove daily, no matter how she felt, to a small villa in the hills where all her pet dogs were buried. . . . She couldn't sleep, so I used to come into her room in the evenings and talk with her until late at night. It was a fascinating time.'[8]

In Nice Serge had one evening of extraordinary luck at the Casino. He bought a new Peugeot, and he and Catherine spent a lazy month driving around the south of France; for her it must have seemed like a return to her former life, but Serge was not Alexander Bariatinsky, and the world around them had changed. Soon a feeling of unreality and the sense that they were cut off from old friends worried them both. Serge's winnings would not last for ever. They returned to Nice, where Catherine remembered her dream of becoming a professional singer. She began to train seriously with Mme Litvin, the most famous Russian concert singer of her day. She gave small concerts, helped by Dame Nellie Melba, whose singing had inspired her when she was just a child.

Serge became increasingly restless; Catherine's music did not involve him and he needed real work. He sold the car and travelled to Paris, and when life there became too expensive he went on to London. He had studied at Oxford before the war and felt at ease in England; he still had many friends, and with their help he found a job with a subsidiary of the Vickers company, selling agricultural machinery. After some weeks of sleeping on Prince Yusupov's sitting-room couch, he leased a house for himself and Catherine, and then went to Nice to collect her. Together they moved into their first London home in Hill Street, near Hyde Park.

Catherine's determination to sing in public soon became known. She held informal gatherings at Hill Street with the exiled King Manoel of Portugal as her accompanist, and Nancy Leeds asked her to sing at a large dinner party given in her honour. She gave her first professional concert in England on 3 December 1919 at the home of Mrs William Corey in Connaught Place, and won the approval of the music critic of *The Times*. Still there was a certain artificiality about her new career. While some of Serge's friends were supportive and really wanted to help her, others were simply playing. It might be amusing for them to have a real Russian princess to sing at their 'At Homes' but they could not understand Catherine's serious devotion to music, or her need to earn a living, and in time the novelty would wear off.

Catherine found it hard to adjust to life in England. She and

Serge had moved to a house in Connaught Street and the daily round of housekeeping and shopping was something she had never known; on her first visit to Selfridges she was overcome by nerves and rushed away in confusion. It was ironic: in the Crimea she had coped heroically for months in the role of a peasant girl on a farm, but then she knew that she was a princess in disguise and had the adrenaline of fear to spur her on. Now she was just another exile. Serge understood. 'Catherine had a temperament that was magnificent in adversity', he wrote, many years later, 'but it was the petty annoyance of everyday life that she could never cope with.'9 She began to crave solitude and complained that Serge 'made' her meet his friends; the very word she used shows how her resentment was building. Their marriage had survived war, revolution and the threat of death, but ordinary life would prove too great a strain.

Early in 1920, the couple left Connaught Street and moved into a house in Sussex Place, which they shared with Serge's old friend Prince Paul of Yugoslavia. In June Catherine gave an important concert at the Queen's Hall under Melba's patronage, and she chose a mixture of songs, most unlike the conventional concert repertoire. Her programme and her inexperience were criticized, otherwise the evening was very well received, and her career seemed to be on course. She sang at another large concert at the London Coliseum and began to make records. Serge, on the other hand, had decided that there would be more opportunities for him on the other side of the world. He persuaded his company to move him to Australia and left before the year's end. He and Catherine wrote to one another regularly, but for him, the marriage was over – for her, it was not.

In Nice Princess Yurievskaya was becoming very frail, and Catherine began to spend as much time as possible with her. The Princess was saddened by her daughter's need to earn a living and by the unhappiness in her personal life. She liked Serge and hoped that there might be a reconciliation; Catherine too was still hopeful. Serge spent a year in Australia but things did not work out as he had planned. He was staying in Rome with his mother when a letter arrived from Catherine to say that Princess Yurievskaya had died peacefully in Nice on 4 February 1922, severing another link with the past.

The Princess had been obliged to sell much of her property in order to survive, and her estate at death was not large. Anything that would have gone to Catherine was claimed by the French courts, because under French law she was still liable for her first husband's debts. Then she learned that a former secretary of her mother's was about to publish private papers belonging to her father, and she and her sister Olga fought unsuccessfully through the courts to stop him. It was a difficult, painful time, at the end of which Catherine returned to London and set up a home of her own in Kensington, with Miss Picken as her companion, and her beloved dog.

Criticism of her inexperience on the concert stage had stung Catherine into action. She hired a professional teacher and worked hard, practising for three or four hours a day until she had developed a repertoire of two hundred songs in five languages. She began to give concerts in provincial towns, though her range was limited by the need to return to London each night to avoid the cost of hotels. She knew quite well that many managements only engaged her because of her name; sometimes their posters and handbills did not even mention that she was a singer, but the audiences were appreciative and she cherished the comments they made. She came to feel that only the middle and lower classes ever offered true friendship, and blamed her husband's society friends for everything that had gone wrong between them.

Serge was back in London, staying at the Yusupovs, but there would be no reconciliation. He had wanted a divorce for some time: 'Our marriage had been one of wartime delusion,' he wrote, 'of a short, sharp, romantic attachment sought by both of us in a tiny moment of desperate calm.'[10] But for Catherine the marriage meant a great deal more than this and she was unwilling to let it go. She blamed his friends for his change of feelings, claiming that they had made fun of his faithfulness, and that he, 'poor boy', could not handle their laughter. She was twelve years older than Serge; once it had not mattered but now it widened the gulf between them. To her he had become a 'poor boy', unable to form his own judgement, and he started to believe that the age gap was bigger than it really was.

In 1917, hiding from Bolshevik shell fire in a cellar in Yalta, someone had given Catherine a copy of the *Imitation of Christ*. Now, confused, angry, and very much alone, her mind turned again to the comfort she found in the book, and she decided to seek conversion to the Catholic Church. It was her confessor who finally persuaded her, at the end of 1923, to agree to a divorce, and the decree was issued in June the following year.

Catherine's autobiography, published in 1924, shows how deeply she resented Serge at this time: 'my late husband (I ought to put 'ex', but put 'late', for to me he is now dead)'. She believed that friends abandoned her after the divorce, 'finding it more useful to have a bachelor companion again, who, besides being ornamental, is very useful to dance with and amuse them in various ways'.[11] She felt that they made fun of her singing and hated them as deeply as she thought she was hated: it is unfortunate that her attitudes at this moment should have been preserved, because this depth of bitterness was unlike her, and it would have eased. Writing about her over thirty years later, Serge was full of admiration for her courage, honesty and beauty, and was certain that they had remained friends.

Alone now, save for Miss Picken and Bobby, Catherine continued to sing, and built up a social life of her own. She had a few close friends, some of them still 'society' people, despite all her anger against them. She became a keen golfer, though she continually raised eyebrows by ignoring the golf club's treasured rules, and Bobby would keep chasing the ball. In August 1925 her sister Olga died at Wiesbaden, leaving Catherine as the only living reminder of the love story that had once been the sensation of Europe.

There are two surprising omissions from Catherine's account of her life; her sons, André and Alexander. After Lausanne, they disappear from the story altogether, and the reader could forget that she had children. Serge described how 'Catherine's boys, André and Buddy, dropped out of sight for long periods at a time. The only person who managed to keep track of them was their old nurse, Miss Lily Pickens, and she did so when everyone else gave up. From her I learned that Buddy had gone to the United States.'[12] In the 1940s Serge had a chance meeting with Alexander, who was serving in the

American forces. He later became a US citizen, with the surname 'Barry'. His brother stayed in Europe, married and had a daughter.

Catherine kept up her singing career for as long as she could, but the strain on her heart was too much and she had to retire. This left her with no income but help came from a surprising source. Sir Henry 'Chips' Channon provided her with £300 a year, which paid for her basic needs. Why he should have done this is unclear, but he was Serge's closest friend and, despite all that had passed between them, Serge still cared for his former wife. In 1942 Channon paid a surprise visit to Catherine in her house on Hayling Island and his diary records the impression of an irrepressible old lady living in poverty, but still proud of her imperial heritage:

> Her little house is horrible. . . . She is lonely and over 60. But somehow she exudes a certain atmosphere of grandeur, and still has her pearl ear-rings, the only tangible touch of the past. She chatted of her royal relatives, her various nephews and nieces, reigning still or in exile. . . . It was a depressing visit, but she was so cheerful that she has obviously achieved a certain philosophy of life . . . she is one of those people to whom every misfortune falls. She even found her last servant dead in bed a few weeks ago; and her three beloved Pekinese all have died recently.[13]

Catherine had seventeen years more to live. At her funeral on 29 December 1959 the only family mourners were Serge and her brother's son, Prince Alexander Yurievsky. And her voice? Serge called it 'wonderful' and paid tribute to its emotional power. She never achieved the success of Melba, her life-long idol, but her health and perhaps even her title were against her. Next time you pass a box of old 78 r.p.m. records in a junk shop or car boot fair, look very carefully – you may be lucky enough to find the recorded voice of a daughter of a Tsar of Russia.

Cathedral Square in the Fortress

21

The Beloved Grand Prince

GRAND PRINCE PAVEL ALEXANDROVICH

Princess Catherine Yourievsky ended her life poor and alone but at least she died quietly, in a world at peace. Others were not so lucky. Her half-brother, Grand Prince Pavel Alexandrovich, was one of four senior men of the imperial family murdered one January morning in the Peter and Paul Fortress, close to the Cathedral where their ancestors were buried in state. In the last troubled months before the Revolution, as the imperial family became more deeply divided and lost the power to act effectively, Grand Prince Pavel, the last Tsar's last uncle, emerged as the elder statesman of the family. He alone showed the wisdom and understanding to stand between the rival camps and try to mediate, and he retained the trust and affection of all. He is always praised for his attempts to save the dynasty, yet if he had died only a few years earlier he would have been dismissed as an unimportant figure – the architect of a scandal which united the family against him. It was quite a transformation.

Grand Prince Pavel was born at Tsarskoe Selo in the autumn of 1860, the youngest child of Alexander II and Maria Alexandrovna, and from the start he was a family pet. Countess Marie von Keller, who belonged to the household of Pavel's aunt Grand Princess Konstantin, recalled her first meeting with him in 1865: 'the little Grand Duke Paul came in after dinner. He looked so sweet in his Russian smock of white silk, and his little boots with red revers, that I longed to kiss him, but dare not. The Tsarina seemed to guess my thoughts, for she said: "See how my little Puss-in-boots stares at you. You must kiss him." I reddened with pleasure at the permission.'[1]

Pavel's first and closest companion was his brother Sergei. Only three years lay between them and they were friends as well as brothers, clinging firmly together as the shadows of grief, illness, unfaithfulness and terrorism closed around their previously happy family. Like Sergei, Pavel grew up to be a profoundly religious man but he was livelier, more cheerful, more accessible to people he did not know. In later years it would be said that much of Sergei's energy had been expended in protecting his younger brother from the more painful and disturbing realities of their world.

By the mid-1870s study absorbed most of the young Grand Princes' time. Their tutor, Admiral Arseniev, ensured that they were very well versed in artistic as well as military subjects, though, like all the men of the imperial family, Pavel was enrolled in several regiments on the day he was born. At the age of thirteen he was made a sub-lieutenant and he became a full lieutenant before his sixteenth birthday, but he was the only one of the Tsar's sons too young to participate in the Russo-Turkish war of 1877. When Sergei went away it was probably the first time the brothers had been separated. While the Russian army prepared to cross the Danube, Pavel was sent to Darmstadt to represent the family at the funeral of his uncle, Grand Duke Ludwig III of Hesse. A younger cousin, Grand Prince Piotr Nikolaievich, was moved into the Winter Palace for a time and the two became firm friends, racing their bicycles along the gleaming corridors. Eighteen months after the war ended Pavel turned nineteen, and took his Oath of Allegiance before representatives of government, the church and the army.

The deaths of the Tsar and Tsaritsa within a year of each other left their youngest son isolated and unhappy. It is said that Pavel knew nothing of his father's affair with Princess Dolgorukaya until after his mother's death, when the shock of discovery made him ill. He and Sergei were not in Russia when Alexander II was murdered: for years Pavel was haunted by an imaginary picture of his dying father's terrible injuries. He clung to his brother; when Sergei went to England to be vetted by his future wife's grandmother, Pavel went too. Queen Victoria liked Sergei but found Pavel more agreeable. Pavel even shared his brother's honeymoon: when their sister Maria visited Ilinskoe she found them all very happy, and Pavel seemed to her to be the ideal companion, 'he is very discrete and never in the way: his great pleasure is riding about the country for hours'.[2]

As the months passed Pavel continued to live with his brother and sister-in-law, and Elisabeth missed him when he was away. He and Sergei enjoyed reading aloud in the evenings, and acted together in productions at the Hermitage Theatre: Pavel's performance as Prince Christian in *Boris Godunov* was remembered for decades, and the Italian actor Salvini was heard to say that the young Grand Prince was a terrible loss to the stage. Pavel was also an accomplished dancer; it was not long before the gossips of St Petersburg began to count the times he danced with his sister-in-law, and eyebrows were raised at their unusual living arrangements. The three regarded the rumours with the composure of those who have nothing to hide. In the autumn of 1887 they visited Turkey together and Pavel went on to spend the winter in Greece. The next year he accompanied Sergei and Elisabeth again when Alexander III sent them to attend the consecration of the church on the Mount of Olives, dedicated to their mother. They made a pilgrimage around the Holy Land before beginning the homeward journey, travelling via Athens where their cousin Queen Olga and King George of Greece were celebrating their silver wedding. Pavel and Sergei had often visited their cousins in Athens, but this time Pavel had something special on his mind. He proposed to the King and Queen's elder daughter Alexandra, and was accepted. They were married in St Petersburg in June 1889, and the three became four.

A married man, with a wife he loved and a palace of his own, the former Stieglitz Mansion on the English Quay in St Petersburg, Pavel was supremely happy, and Elisabeth and Sergei were as pleased with Alexandra as he was. Elisabeth said that her new sister-in-law had a cheering effect on the brothers, encouraging them to talk about their childhood, which kept them amused for hours on end. None of the others seemed to realize that Alexandra found the adjustment to married life draining, and at times unhappy. She was ten years younger than Pavel and his regimental duties often took him away from home. In November 1889, five months after the wedding, one of the Tsaritsa's ladies found her pale, exhausted by a difficult first pregnancy, and homesick for Greece. Her baby, Marie, was born in the spring and Sergei was chosen as godfather, proudly carrying the baby to the font.

In the autumn of 1890 Pavel took Alexandra home to Greece for a holiday, and on his return he became commander of the Imperial Horse Guards, based at Krasnoe Selo. He was given a suite of rooms in the Catherine Palace at Tsarskoe Selo but was only able to join Alexandra there at weekends. She felt his absence badly, especially when Sergei and Elisabeth left the city for Moscow. Elisabeth told her father that Sergei was particularly troubled by 'the thought of leaving Paul – you know how Serge has always lived for this brother, treating him more like a son'.[3]

As the following summer drew to an end, the two couples were reunited at Ilinskoe, never suspecting the tragedy that was to follow. Alexandra's death left Pavel stunned and bewildered and his brother took charge, both of him, and of the frail baby Dmitri. Marie of Romania described Pavel's grief at his wife's funeral: 'Uncle Sergei, his favourite brother, took him in his arms when he made a desperate gesture of protest when at last they laid the coffin lid over the sweet face he had loved.'[4] Dmitri was christened on 29 October/10 November 1891, the third anniversary of his parents' engagement, and after the ceremony Pavel went to stay with his sister in Coburg before going on to visit Alexandra's family in Greece. The children remained with Elisabeth and Sergei.

Alexandra's death sent a shock wave through the European Courts. She was so young, and the tragedy so unexpected and so cruel. From Balmoral, Queen Victoria petitioned her granddaughter for the full details, and when no satisfactory answer came she turned to Elisabeth's elder sister: 'What brought on the fits? As a usual thing – a wrong state of the kidneys produces these convulsions if not attended to; & the labour must then be brought on (wh is quite easily done) but the danger is very great.'[5] Her heart went out to Pavel's children; Marie was only seventeen months old and Dmitri needed constant nursing for the first few months simply to keep him alive. The Queen hoped that Elisabeth and Sergei would be able to assume responsibility for them both.

As the months passed, Elisabeth kept her grandmother in touch with the progress of her widowed brother-in-law and his family. They were all finding it hard to come to terms with what had happened: Pavel needed emotional support from his brother and sister-in-law but their own grief was still strong. Almost a year after the tragedy Elisabeth and Sergei travelled to St Petersburg to share Pavel's name-day, and she told the Queen, 'it is heart-rending to see him so resigned but so utterly broken down, his little boy was with us until now as we had heavenly weather at Moscow & Ilinskoie. . . . he is a sweet little fat healthy Baby with a merry character but the real beauty is his sister – I have rarely seen a lovelier child. Poor motherless Darlings, it is too sad. . . . how happy all were a year ago. . . . What a year it has been for us all, wherever one looks – sorrow.'[6] Time brought no relief. Another year passed, and Elisabeth wrote, 'Paul comes from time to time to see us – he & the Babies are quite well but his poor aching heart cannot heal although he is in better spirits, yet he never for a moment forgets his sorrow poor poor fellow.'[7] The Queen invited them all to Balmoral and in September 1893 they left Russia with Elisabeth's lady-in-waiting Princess Troubetskoy and the Grand Prince's gentlemen, Count Steinbock and Baron Schilling. The children remained in Russia with their nurses.

The visit to Balmoral was a happy interlude that gave the brothers a rare chance to see their cousin Prince Henry of Battenberg, the Queen's son-in-law, who shared their memories of the childhood autumns at Heiligenberg. Pavel had the same birthday as Henry's youngest son Maurice, which was celebrated at Balmoral, and the Queen was careful to see that her Russian guest was not forgotten. While the two-year-old enjoyed his new toys, Pavel was given a posy of flowers, a wrapper (probably in good Scottish tartan) and a cigarette case. With his brother and cousin he went hunting and visiting in the neighbourhood, while the Queen took every opportunity to speak to Elisabeth and, separately, to her lady-in-waiting: she was a shrewd, inquisitive and caring grandmother who liked to know every detail of the young people's lives, even the things they might not have felt able to tell her themselves. The Russian party left Balmoral very early on the morning of 11 October loaded with gifts and good advice, and more gifts reached them on their arrival in London. They stayed for a few days, then began the long return journey, which was broken by a stay in Darmstadt where the Queen sent more presents, this time for Marie and Dmitri.

The visit to Darmstadt was cut short by a summons from St Petersburg, and, sooner than they had intended, the party left for home. On 20 November Elisabeth wrote to her grandmother: 'Paul's children put on your frocks looking so sweet, they are flourishing thank God – He has just been photographed with them, if a success would you like to have some of their portraits – they are such sweet pretty little things.'[8] A photograph duly followed, with a letter from Pavel, which is still preserved in one of the Queen's albums. 'You had the kindness during my stay in Scotland to ask me for a photograph of my children. I hasten to carry out your request by sending the most recent photograph . . . taken at my home shortly after my return to St. Petersburg. It is with profound gratitude that I often think of my charming stay at Balmoral and of the extreme kindness which Your Majesty showed to me. On returning I found my children, thank God, grown and in good health. The little girl was enchanted with the doll which Your Majesty had the extreme kindness to send her, and knows perfectly well from whom she came. The little white dress she wears every Sunday.'[9]

Pavel could be an enchanting father, with a slight air of distance about him which only increased his attractiveness. 'His love for us was deep and fond, and we knew it,' his daughter recalled, 'but he never displayed towards us a spontaneous tenderness, embracing us only when bidding us good-morning or good-night.'[10] The children lived apart in the second floor nurseries of the palace, which he visited twice a day. His imagination could be a delight: once, at Easter, he slipped a hen's egg under their pet hare and convinced them that the hare had laid it. 'At Christmas he was particularly joyous,' Marie wrote, 'and Christmas was the peak of our year.'[11] But once Christmas Eve was over, with the decorated tree, the presents, and the dangerous thrill of letting off indoor fireworks, Pavel would leave the children in the palace and go away to spend the rest of the holiday with his brother and sister-in-law in Moscow – and this too was typical of him as a father. His attention to the children was erratic. He was absent for much of the time, and every summer sent them to their uncle and aunt at Ilinskoe.

Some time in 1895 or the early months of 1896, the Grand Prince had an encounter that would change all their lives, and seriously damage relationships within the family. He fell in love with Olga von Pistolkors, the wife of a captain in his regiment who was also aide-de-camp to his brother Grand Prince Vladimir. The couple had three young children: nonetheless, Pavel began an affair with Olga. It was a serious abuse of his position, both as Eric von Pistolkors' commanding officer and as a member of the reigning family. In the summer of 1896 he was moved to a different regimental command, but if this had anything to do with the affair it came too late. In January 1896 Olga gave birth to a son, who was not her husband's child.

Pavel had no intention of ending the affair and he must have known that sooner or later it would precipitate a crisis. He began to take more interest in Marie and Dmitri and there were no visits to Ilinskoe in 1897 and 1898; instead he took the children to Europe. He let go of the memory of Alexandra; her clothes, untouched since her death, were sorted out and disposed of, while Marie was moved into her mother's rooms. Pavel was resolved to marry Olga, whose own marriage had effectively ended with the birth of their son, but he knew there would be problems. His cousin Mikhail Mikhailovich had been banished for contracting an unsuitable marriage without permission, and Mikhail's wife was not even a divorcee. In 1900 Pavel began to sound his brothers out on the idea of a morganatic marriage, but he also bought a house in Paris from the Yusupov family. Then he discussed his plans with his nephew, the young Tsar.

Much as Nicholas II liked his uncle he felt bound to refuse him permission to marry. Such a marriage was an open breach of family laws, and the Tsar made it clear that if Pavel were to marry without permission he must lose his position, his income, his right to live in Russia and the guardianship of his children. At the same time, Grand Prince Vladimir was pressing the Tsar to grant Captain von

Pistolkors a divorce. Vladimir was upset and angry because his brother's action had put him in a very difficult position. He was obliged to support his unhappy aide-de-camp, though both he and the Tsar knew that if the divorce became final the way would be open for Pavel to marry outside the law. Vladimir forced his younger brother to swear a solemn oath that he would not marry Olga and finally, with this assurance, in 1902 the divorce was granted.

That August Pavel's brother-in-law Prince Nicholas of Greece was to marry Vladimir's daughter in St Petersburg. As the guests gathered, the tension grew. The King of Greece avoided Pavel, who seemed sad and preoccupied. Pavel argued with Sergei. The day after the wedding he left the country, having arranged for a Court official to meet him at the station with three million roubles. He fled to Italy. Sergei and Elisabeth followed, in a desperate attempt to make him change his mind for the sake of the children. The whole family felt compromised by the scandal and worried about Marie and Dmitri, but Pavel was adamant. He married Olga in the Greek church at Leghorn and wrote to the children to explain what he had done. He settled in his Paris house with his new wife and their son Vladimir, accepting every consequence of his action but one. It must have been in his mind that Marie and Dmitri would be able to leave Russia and join him in Paris, despite what he had been told, and the Tsar's decision to transfer legal guardianship to Sergei, without any consultation, left Pavel angry and very bitter and drove a deep wedge between him and the brother he had always loved.

Pavel had abused his rank. He was wrong, and others paid a high price for what he had done, but as the months passed he gained a new strength of character. Life had always been mapped out for him before and his brother had been on hand to support him when things went wrong: now he had to build a life for himself. He and Olga had given up a great deal to be together and their marriage grew strong. They had two more children, Irina and Natalia, and the awkwardness of their position (neither Olga nor the children had a legal title, or even a surname) was resolved by the Prince Regent of Bavaria. In 1904 he made Olga 'Countess of Hohenfelsen', with the right to pass the title on to her children.

She was able to see the von Pistolkors children for holidays but, far away in Russia, Marie refused to accept that Pavel had abandoned her and her brother and persisted in seeing him as a wounded hero, mistreated by the family. Her anger turned towards her aunt and uncle.

In 1905 Pavel's new happiness was shaken by the news that Sergei had been assassinated in Moscow. The Tsar gave him permission to attend the funeral, alone, restoring to him the rank of lieutenant general, and he travelled to Russia with a package Sergei had given him thirteen years earlier, to be opened in the event of his death. It was found to contain the uniform of the Preobrajensky Guard in which Sergei wanted to be buried, but the terrorist's bomb had done so much damage to the body that it was impossible to do as he asked. Pavel's return to Russia could not help but be uncomfortable and distressing for all concerned. Dmitri was afraid that his father would take him away, and clung to Elisabeth.[12] She could not forgive Pavel for all that had happened, and for him, the death of a favourite brother at a time when they were estranged was a thought too painful to recall. There could be no reconciliation and no hope of renewed friendship. The past was gone, and for the rest of his life Pavel would never speak willingly of his childhood.

His only happiness now lay in Paris. He and Olga enjoyed a simple family life and their house at Boulogne-sur-Seine became a magnet for artists, writers and holidaying Russians. At times it seemed like an outpost of the Russian Embassy. The names of Grand Prince Pavel and Countess Hohenfelsen headed the guest list at social functions, evenings at the opera and ballet, and services at the Russian church. Pavel became familiar with a wider range of people and ideas than he would ever have encountered in Russia. He built up an impressive collection of antiques and works of art too, and extended his house to make room for them. He was able to make brief visits to Russia but Olga was banned until 1907, when she was allowed to attend the birth of her first grandchild.

Meanwhile Marie and Dmitri grew up without their father. In 1907 Marie became engaged to Prince Vilhelm of Sweden: she would say later that the engagement was arranged by her aunt against her will but there is no sense of this in letters written at the time. Her memory may have been coloured by the subsequent failure of the marriage. But at the same time, any pleasure she might have felt in the engagement was severely shaken by her father's reaction: Pavel refused to attend the ceremony unless he could bring his wife. He set two conditions. First, he wanted to see Olga accepted at Court. 'Could you really think that I would leave my wife alone,' he asked the Tsar, 'she whom everyone here loves and respects. . . . I did not make the break and sacrifice everything to let her then be humiliated and insulted without reason.' Second, he wanted the wardship of his children ended, and he refused to be seen on the sidelines of an engagement over which he had had no say.[13] From his own standpoint his arguments must have appeared quite reasonable but the family did not see it that way. 'What incredible heartlessness!', the Tsar's sister Ksenia wrote in her diary. 'I feel so sorry for poor Maria – he's spoilt everything for her!'[14] That October, the Tsar had a slight change of heart, and allowed Pavel and Olga to visit St Petersburg together to see Marie and Dmitri.

Marie was married in 1908 and things went wrong very quickly. The circumstances of her upbringing had made her both selfish and difficult, and her behaviour in her new country earned a bad reputation which worried her father. In 1911 Olga's younger daughter was divorced after only three years of marriage; when Marie also announced her plan to leave her husband and child Pavel must have wondered if the next generation was not following his example rather too keenly. But Dmitri seemed more promising, and stood high in the favour of the Tsar and Tsaritsa. On 6 January 1912, after the traditional 'Blessing of the Waters' in St Petersburg, he took his Oath of Allegiance, and Nicholas II marked the occasion by announcing that Pavel and his family could return to Russia for good. Pavel still owned his palace in the city but he wanted to build a house at Tsarskoe Selo based on his Paris home, for his family and his art collection. His son Vladimir also returned to attend the Corps des Pages. For the others, however, the move took longer, and their house was not finished until May 1914. Within months the First World War began.

Pavel had been away from the army for a long time and he had no experience of active service, but seeing his cousins, nephews and sons in uniform he craved a useful role. He discussed this with the Tsaritsa and as the months passed he became a regular visitor to the Alexander Palace. Over tea they talked about events at the front and at home; other members of the family were closing ranks against Alexandra Feodorovna but Pavel was sympathetic and supportive. He had always been quick to defend victims of injustice, and besides, she was Elisabeth's younger sister and he had known her since she was a baby. He reported to her his conversations with the French Ambassador and confided growing anxiety about Dmitri. Then there was Olga: Pavel passed on her worry that she and the children had only German titles. In the tense atmosphere of wartime this plea was readily understood, and in August 1915 Nicholas II created the title Prince/Princess Paley for her and the children, a few days before Vladimir Paley left for the front. Pavel had eight more months to wait for a front line commission, then he was placed in command of the 1st Corps of the Imperial Guard. After a difficult spell in the trenches, which earned a well-deserved award for gallantry and almost cost him his life, Vladimir became his father's orderly officer.

Pavel spent a brief period at the front under heavy enemy bombardment, then he was moved to a new appointment at headquarters. He took a three-week holiday in the Crimea with his wife and children in the autumn of 1916, and on the journey north was invited to lunch with the Dowager Tsaritsa at Kiev. She wanted to enlist his help, though this did not emerge until the next day when he lunched with his cousin Alexander Mikhailovich, who spoke forcibly and at length about the developing crisis in the country. Pavel was the family's chosen intermediary to speak to the Tsar and Tsaritsa and persuade them of the need for change, in particular, to discuss the influence of Rasputin, which was seen to be so damaging. It was a sensitive subject and when the time came Pavel handled it with great tact, but little success. His friendship with the Tsaritsa was not shaken, however, until his son took part in Rasputin's murder; then several very tense weeks were to pass before he was received at the Alexander Palace again.

The Grand Prince made one last attempt to propose constitutional change. On 28 February 1917, with the assistance of Prince Mikhail Putiatin and the lawyer Nikolai Ivanov, he drafted a constitutional manifesto, underwritten with his own signature and those of Grand Princes Mikhail Alexandrovich and Kyrill Vladimirovich. This was meant to be presented for the Tsar's signature on 1 March, when he returned from headquarters, but his train was held up, and on 2 March, the day of the abdication, Pavel wrote to the chairman of the State Duma, 'As the only living son of the Tsar-Liberator, I entreat you to do all that is in your power to preserve the constitutional throne for the tsar.'15 It was too late. But Pavel's kindness to the Tsaritsa would last until the end. In the chaos of the February revolution, it was Pavel who gave her the shattering news of her husband's abdication and Pavel who supported her through her first meeting with members of the new government. He even offered her the use of his Paris house if she was forced into exile.

Few members of the family were as sympathetic to Alexandra Feodorovna by this time. Most of the younger Romanovs, including his own son Vladimir, were content to blame her for everything. Vladimir Paley was a very gifted young man whose poetry was highly praised. The Tsaritsa had been kind to him despite her reservations about his birth: his first volume of poems was sold to raise money for her charities, but his cartoon drawings of her were vicious. Soon after the February revolution he turned his wit on the Provisional Government, and the result was almost a disaster. His satirical verses and cartoons caused such outrage that Pavel's whole family was placed under house arrest for eighteen days.

This was only the beginning. The danger for all members of the imperial family increased when the Bolsheviks took over the country in October 1917. In the early days of November, Pavel's Tsarskoe Selo house was raided in a search for arms, and he himself was arrested, taken to the Smolny Institute in the city for questioning, then released. Always prone to chest trouble, his health declined rapidly under the new conditions, with fresh food and other essentials in short supply. During the difficult winter of 1917/18 his family ran out of heating fuel altogether and decided to close the house and move into a smaller cottage belonging to Grand Prince Boris Vladimirovich, who had gone to the Caucasus. They had barely moved when their own house was requisitioned and opened as a museum: future residence was forbidden but Olga liked to go in and act as guide, just to keep an eye on her husband's collections.

In March 1918 a decree was issued compelling all members of the imperial family and those related or connected to them to report to the Cheka headquarters in the city for registration. Pavel was ill and Olga went alone, only to be told that a doctor would be sent to Tsarskoe to confirm her story, and that her son must also present himself. Vladimir was to be offered a straight choice; to repudiate his father and go free, or to refuse and be sent into internal exile in Siberia with the other young men of the family. He chose the second option. But the Bolshevik doctor who was sent to Tsarskoe agreed that Pavel was too ill to travel: the Grand Prince remained at liberty, though under close observation. The weeks passed and conditions steadily worsened. In August the Tsar and his family were taken away from the Alexander Palace where they had been imprisoned since the first revolution. This ended the sad spectacle of their walks in the park, which often drew an openly hostile crowd – Pavel had found the idea too painful to contemplate and stayed away, though his wife sometimes went in a vain attempt to show silent support for the Tsar. Their one joy in a time of otherwise unrelieved sorrow was Marie's marriage to Prince Putiatin. On 18 July 1918 – the day following the murder of the Tsar and his family, though none of them knew it at the time – Pavel had the pleasure of holding a new grandchild, Marie's son, at the font.

The Grand Prince must have guessed that the end could only be a matter of time. One day he walked in the garden with his younger daughters: 'He spoke to us at length about all that he owed to our mother, all that she had brought to him which he had never known in his life before, and about all that she had been to him,' Princess Irina Paley remembered. 'He spoke while he walked, and this allowed him to overcome his reserve and his intense shyness. Did he sense then that he had not long to live? I am tempted to believe it and to think that he was asking us to take care of our mother when he could no longer be with her. For me, it was one of the most moving moments I experienced in my life with him.'[16] Some three weeks after the christening of Marie's child, one of Pavel's stepdaughters came to offer him a chance to escape from Russia. He was to wear Austrian uniform, she said, and be moved under the protection of the Danish minister Scavenius who was tireless in his efforts to help members of the imperial family. Pavel flatly refused to hide behind an enemy uniform. He was arrested three days later and taken to Grand Princess Vladimir's Tsarskoe Selo house, which the Bolsheviks were using as their headquarters. Then he was moved to the city, and Olga chose to accompany him. Both were aware that the net was closing, as other male members of the imperial family who had been spared the first exile were being rounded up. In the days before Pavel's arrest his cousins Nikolai and Georgi Mikhailovich and Dmitri Konstantinovich were taken to the Schpalernaia prison in the city. Pavel was held first at the old Cheka headquarters on Gorohovaia Street, then moved to the prison three weeks later. For some time the cousins were held on the same corridor, on the fifth floor of the prison.

The months passed and Olga was allowed occasional visits, alone or with her daughters. She saw Pavel for the last time on Christmas Day 1918 in the prison hospital, for his health had declined sharply in captivity. Concern for him and for his cousins mounted. Olga did her utmost to gain access to prominent Bolshevik officials and appeal for clemency, and from England, where Georgi Mikhailovich's wife and daughters had spent the war, from Denmark and from Spain, there were intense diplomatic efforts to secure the men's release. Friends began to devise an escape plan for Pavel but he refused to cooperate, knowing that if the plan succeeded it would mean the end for his cousins. On Tuesday 28 January 1919, soldiers came and took him away from the Schpalernaia to Gorohovaia Street. The next day he was moved to the Peter and Paul Fortress: his cousins had already made this journey and were locked in the cells of the Troubetskoy Bastion, where Pavel joined them. In the early hours of the next morning, 30 January 1919, the four Grand

Princes, naked to the waist, were led out to an open grave on the square in front of the Cathedral and shot. It is said that Gorky had just obtained an order for their release. It is also said that Nikolai Mikhailovich kept his favourite Persian cat with him until the very last moment, and all accounts agree that one of the victims, either Pavel or Dmitri, died praying for his murderers.

Strelna

Ostashevo

To Belong to the Family

THE KONSTANTINOVICHI

Grand Prince Pavel was an attractive character who fought hard in the last months to overcome the disunity in the imperial family, but his own behaviour in earlier years had been part of the general falling-off of standards. From the beginning of the nineteenth century, law and custom had defined the ways in which members of the ruling family were expected to live, laying down their faith, their marriage partners and their duties. Visible obedience to the Tsar was demanded, even from those who questioned his actions in private. Until the 1870s at least, adult members of the dynasty played an admirable and conspicuous role in the patronage of the arts and sciences and in bringing educational reform, social improvements and up-to-date medical services to the country; their positive contribution outweighed any lapses and contradictions in their lives. There were scandals but these were not acknowledged openly, and if this or that Grand Prince was an unpleasant person in private life, outside the palace no one ever knew. Their sense of duty was strong and they understood why duty mattered.

In part, the change was inevitable. By the end of the century the extended family was enormous: in the place of brothers or cousins brought up together there were so many individual family groups of widely differing ages, who met only on rare occasions. This left room for differences in upbringing, with all the attendant risks of arguments, jealousies and rivalries. Alexander III's reforms to the family law, however understandable, accentuated the distance between the branches of the family and the centre. More and more, as the nineteenth century drew to an end, the Grand Princes of Russia were perceived as living for themselves alone, enjoying a luxurious lifestyle without paying the compensatory balance of duty. They showed little respect even for their own family laws, and people began to resent the high offices that were granted them by virtue of their rank, for which they showed no apparent aptitude or interest.

But the argument is not as straightforward as it sounds. Times were changing –

expectations too. There were many sympathetic, likeable and interesting
characters in the family at the turn of the century – like Pavel. Seen from an
individual standpoint, it is all too easy to understand why they behaved as they
did, particularly on the question of marriage. There were no easy answers, then
or now: the bald fact remains that because individual members of the imperial
family were not seen to respect the standards expected of them, the country lost
respect for the family as a whole and that loss, once set in motion, could not be
halted. In the final crash the best were to suffer with the worst.
In the last generation, one branch of the family stood out as faithful to the old
ways. Grand Prince Konstantin Konstantinovich, the second son of the old
Admiral-General, Konstantin Nikolaievich, was a sensitive, conscientious and
good man, entirely Orthodox and entirely Russian. He had no mistresses, adored
his nine children, and served creditably in his regiment; he gave imaginative
leadership to the Academy of Science and his contribution to the arts in Russia,
both as a patron and as a gifted writer, is respected to this day. As an example of
the very best that a Grand Prince could be, Konstantin Konstantinovich is all the
more remarkable because we know now what his contemporaries did not – that he
carried a tension within his personality which could have unleashed both scandal
and disgrace. By any standards, Konstantin was a fascinating man, but the
respect and love he had certainly earned were to count for nothing in the years of
war and revolution. His children were made to suffer terribly, simply because
their name was Romanov.

The sons of the old Admiral-General were brought up in a tradition which raised adherence to duty above every other imperative, and the disgrace of Nikolai, the adored eldest son, brought that tradition to bear all the more severely on his younger brothers. Konstantin was sixteen when his brother was caught stealing, Dmitri fourteen and Viacheslav twelve; their parents, and particularly their mother, impressed upon them all the stages of Nikolai's fall and they had to promise before her that they would never drink, never give themselves to a life of self-indulgence, never forget that all the privileges of their wealth and rank were meant for use and not enjoyment. In January 1874, four months before the realization of Nikolai's conduct broke on the family, Lady Augusta Stanley visited Russia, representing Queen Victoria at the wedding of her son Prince Alfred and the Tsar's daughter. At the banquet that followed the ceremony she found herself sitting next to young Konstantin Konstantinovich, and took to him instantly. He was 'an enchanting companion,' she said; 'a very young sailor very clever and quite "un homme du monde". I suppose about fifteen or less and very good looking and most conversible.'[1] It is an attractive sketch of Konstantin on the threshold of adult life, which captures his intelligence and something of his charm.

Like their father, the Admiral-General's sons were intended for the sea from the start, though they were given army ranks at birth by family tradition. After early naval training, Nikolai was the first to opt for an army career. Young Konstantin began his naval training at twelve years old, and when Lady Augusta met him he was serving under his cousin Alexei Alexandrovich on board the *Svetlana*. He travelled widely before he too chose a life on land, entering the lists of the Ismailovsky regiment. Viacheslav died in 1879 and Grand Prince Konstantin, adamant that one of his sons must serve in the navy, sent Dmitri to the naval college in St Petersburg, ignoring the boy's love of horses and his wish to join the cavalry. Alone among his brothers Dmitri found that he enjoyed the sea, but he suffered terribly from seasickness, and was forced to face his father with a request to leave the navy. This was no easy decision. Dmitri spent days in prayer to build up his courage and the confrontation was terrible. Konstantin Nikolaievich refused to listen, bellowing that even Nelson was seasick, and it was left to the Grand Princess to intercede for her son.

Brought up under these conditions, it is not surprising that the younger Konstantinovich princes grew into thoughtful, introspective men who took their position seriously. Both were devoutly Orthodox, and this would come to be seen as the defining characteristic of their branch of the family. Like their father, they were also musical, and expressed particular love for Russian church music. In later years Konstantin trained the choir in the private chapel at Pavlovsk, while Dmitri often sang in the chapel choirs at Strelna and the Marble Palace, and the Pokrovsky Convent in Kiev. Dmitri suffered from intense, almost painful shyness. In adult life duty stood at the core of his being and he was fiercely critical of a system which pushed members of the imperial family forward simply because of who they were. He believed that their promotions should be earned, that their official income was meant to be used for the good of the country and the reputation of the dynasty, not for their own amusement. He never married: some said that he hated women or even feared them, but women within the family valued his friendship. Dmitri preferred to avoid society, but on summer evenings at Peterhof he often rode from Strelna to Znamenka, his cousin Grand Prince Piotr Nikolaievich's house, where he was a welcome guest. Piotr's son Roman remembered how his mother would have the tea table brought out onto the terrace for her visitor and would send for raspberries and cream, always his favourite. Then there would be music: Dmitri liked to hear the Grand Princess play the piano and he could usually be persuaded to join in, accompanying his own singing of the Russian folk songs he loved.

In April 1884 Konstantin Konstantinovich married Princess Elisabeth of Saxe-Altenburg, whose father, Prince Moritz, was his mother's cousin, a degree of distance that made marriage acceptable to even the most devoutly Orthodox. She chose to remain a Lutheran: it argues much for Konstantin's broadmindedness that he was able to accept this when his own religious convictions were so strong. The difference would last for the rest of their lives. The new Grand Princess Konstantin, who became Elizaveta Mavrikievna, or 'Mavra', was a gentle, motherly young woman and in all other things she slipped perfectly into Konstantin's world. They were happy. In later years her own children and their cousins would remember her kindness and good humour and her quiet devotion to her husband. She never made a show of her Lutheranism as Marie Pavlovna had done, but loyally attended the services that meant so much to her husband and heard her children sing grace each day before meals, without ever sharing the feelings their observances inspired.

The marriage was happy and the first child, Ioann, was born at Pavlovsk in the summer of 1886. He was the first Romanov to be only the great-grandchild of a Tsar, and his birth prompted Alexander III to control the size of the family by limiting the title

'Grand Prince' (*Velikii Kniaz*) to the Tsar's children and grandchildren. Ioann and any future brothers and sisters, as the great-grandchildren of Nicholas I, would be the first Romanovs to bear the lesser title 'Prince' (*Kniaz*). There were to be brothers, and sisters; Gavril was born a week after Ioann's first birthday, Tatiana less than two years later, then Konstantin, Oleg, Igor and Georgi. In 1905 an eighth child, Natalia, was born, and her death after just two months came as a body blow to the whole family. From Livadia, where he had been sent to escape the northern winter, Prince Oleg wrote to his father to offer what comfort he could and to appeal for photographs of the sister whose birth had caused excited celebrations only weeks before. The eleven-year-old wrote in his diary, 'So we never saw Natusya at all. She died on 10th May. She had peritonitis and inflammation of the brain and had convulsions almost every minute. She suffered and screamed terribly and she died in Mama's arms. Mama was the first to know that our dear little sister had passed away. She was born on the 10th of March, she was christened on the 10th of April and she died on the 10th of May: always the 10th. . . .'[2] A younger sister, Vera, was born the following year.

The Konstantinovich children all seemed pale and prone to illness. Oleg was small for his age and suffered with his chest, while Igor was born blue and had to be swung by the ankle to force air into his lungs. Sophie Buxhoeveden, who was Grand Prince Konstantin's god-daughter, played with them in the well-equipped playground at Pavlovsk and would later remember, 'Alas! I knocked them down, and maltreated them sadly, for they were puny, weedy little fellows, still treated as babies in the nursery, while I was a lusty damsel of nearly six, and tall and strong for my age. Their mother often came with them, a kindly, fair-haired woman, with a perpetual, cheerful laugh that set me at my ease.'[3] But weedy or not, they survived, and had the advantage of growing up in one of the most remarkable households in Russia. Konstantin Konstantinovich was the last Grand Prince to make his house a centre of intellectual excellence. The best writers and musicians were invited to Pavlovsk and the Marble Palace, the latest inventions were examined and the newest theories discussed. The Grand Prince devised a programme of lectures for his children and the children of his Court, inviting guest experts to tell them of archaeological excavations, expeditions into the country's remoter regions and new developments in architecture. Sometimes peasant choirs would perform regional music, or the children would be treated to performances of the early church music which delighted their father, and his interest in education did not stop with his own family.

Konstantin funded free summer courses for elementary school teachers and Sunday classes for slum children. He became patron of a university college for women and of a grammar school for girls. He was still in his twenties when he made his first attempt to raise the intellectual level of army life by founding a literary society within the Ismailovsky regiment, giving evening readings of new Russian novels and poetry. Under his dedicated leadership the society flourished and his own literary aspirations grew. His first collection of poems was published in 1886 under the initials 'K.R.' and won great praise; there would be two further collections of poems and various essays and plays that are admired to this day, though their author was profoundly unsure of his own talent. Others had no doubt. Some of the foremost composers of the time, including Tchaikovsky and Glazunov, vied to write settings for Konstanin's poems. Alexander III suggested that he should translate *Hamlet* into Russian and the work, which took seven years to complete, was performed in the magnificent setting of the Hermitage Theatre in 1896 with Konstantin taking the leading role. Acting was part of his family's life. In the 1909/10 season he staged a series of tableaux at Pavlovsk depicting the history of the Russian theatre, with his children and Court taking part and Nicholas II and his family in the audience.

As a rule, Alexander III preferred to promote his brothers to high office but he made an exception for Konstantin. Through the 1880s and '90s appointment followed appointment for the cousin whose talents were too obvious to be ignored. Konstantin commanded the 15th Tiflis Grenadiers. In 1889 he became President of the Academy of Science. Two years later, in 1891, he succeeded his closest friend in the imperial family, his cousin Grand Prince Sergei Alexandrovich, as commander of the Preobrajensky Guard, Russia's premier regiment. The honours continued into the new reign. In 1899 Konstantin was chosen to head a committee to plan the celebrations for Pushkin's jubilee, and that same year his commitment to education was recognized in the appointment to head Russia's military training schools. He was fully aware of the responsibility and keen to undertake the work; sad only that this would force him to relinquish his regimental command.

Viewed from the outside, Konstantin's story would seem to be an unqualified success. He was loved and respected in his family and in the regiments he served with, his literary work had earned popularity with a wider audience, but within himself he was never at rest. His diary is the painfully honest record of a man with a terrible sense of inadequacy. He did not believe in his own worthiness and needed continual preferment simply for the reassurance it gave. In the early years of Nicholas II's reign there were no new appointments and this preyed on Konstantin's mind: they had enjoyed an easy relationship when Nicholas was the Heir and he the commanding officer, and he feared that others had spoken against him, or that he was too liberal for the new Tsar's tastes. He watched people around him and noticed the tiny signs that betrayed their true thoughts and, though sensitive to real or even imagined slights on his own behalf, he was also acutely aware of the feelings of others and easily moved by their pain. He was a nice man, but far too self critical, and as the 1890s passed and a new century began, one fear obsessed him more than any other.

In 1902 Konstantin confided to his diary, 'How appalled all those people, who love and respect me, would be if they knew of my depravity! I am deeply dissatisfied with myself.'[4] The 'depravity', which had possessed his mind for almost ten years and would continue to do so, was a recurring desire for sex with other men. There was nothing emotional in this; it was a physical urge, quickly satisfied, which left only a profound sense of disgust. Konstantin's understanding of the world offered him no way to justify his needs. A less introspective man, or a less religious one, might simply have accepted the situation, but he struggled against himself – harder at some times than at others – and found the struggle impossible to win. 'My sin is known to no-one,' he wrote, early in 1904, 'I am loved, praised and promoted beyond what I deserve, my life is happy, I have a beautiful wife, who is appreciated and respected by all; delightful children. . . . How is it I can't deal with it?'[5]

The contradiction was made all the sharper by the fact that he deplored the moral slide he observed in the rest of the family. As the Grand Princes one after another entered relationships which the family laws would not allow, and sought to have those relationships made official, he looked on in horror. Pavel was the first in the new century: Konstantin was in no doubt that the Tsar was right to banish the Grand Prince for marrying without permission. He agreed that neither Mikhail Alexandrovich nor Kyrill Vladimirovich should be allowed to marry a first cousin, and he was appalled when the Tsar, whose earlier firmness he had applauded, bent the rules for Nikolai Nikolaievich simply because he was a particular friend, allowing him to marry a cousin's divorced wife. But this was only the beginning. 'What harm our family does to itself and how it undermines the Emperor and the ruling house!' Konstantin wrote in 1907, 'The further we go, the worse it gets.'[6]

At the back of his mind must have been the career of his own elder brother Nikolai, officially non-existent but still very much alive in internal exile in Tashkent. No disgrace could overcome the ties of a close family and Konstantin kept in contact with his brother and visited when he could. He kept him supplied with money, much of which Nikolai used to finance irrigation schemes, churches and village schools, which made him very popular with local people. There was good in him but in his personal life he owned no restraint, and though he was still married to his policeman's daughter and had two sons, officially acknowledged with the title 'Prince Iskander', in 1895 he bought a sixteen-year-old Cossack girl and built a palace round her. They went on to have three children. In 1901 Nikolai became obsessed with a schoolgirl and installed her in another house bought for the purpose, then contracted a bigamous marriage. This was declared illegal and the girl and her family were moved to safety in Odessa. Nikolai became increasingly odd as the years passed. 'His habit of dress was most eccentric', Princess Bariatinsky wrote, after a visit to Tashkent in 1910. 'His head and face were clean-shaven, and he wore an eyeglass. His costume consisted of a red shirt, something in the style of the peasants' garment, a black velvet suit, and, winter and summer alike, a sealskin cap.'[7] He drank and brawled; once he buried his wife up to the neck in one of his irrigation trenches, and her behaviour was as bizarre as his. It was all a very long way from the polite salons of St Petersburg.

In July 1911 their mother Alexandra Iosifovna, the old Grand Princess Konstantin, died in her room at the Marble Palace. Her stern insistence on duty had dominated her family for over fifty years. She never forgot her rank and demanded flawless manners from even the smallest child. When her son Dmitri discovered that his promise not to drink, exacted in the shocked aftermath of his brother's disgrace, made participation in the life of his regiment impossible, he still felt bound to go to his mother to be released from the promise, adult though he was. But even in old age Alexandra was magnificent. At the 1896 coronation 'All eyes were upon her, as she stood in the front row of the princesses in her Court dress of solid cloth of silver, with a magnificent diamond tiara and a parure of sapphires three inches in diameter.'[8] Towards the end a stroke left her unable to walk and she spent the final years of her life at home, confined to a wheelchair and carefully protected from sad or disturbing news, but she was still quite a character. It is said that she had green baize aprons made for the naked statues in the Marble Palace, to protect the modesty of visiting clergymen. She was the last of her generation: Alexander II and Maria Alexandrovna, her own husband Konstantin, the old Admiral-General, Nikolai Nikolaievich and Mikhail Nikolaievich, Viceroy of the Caucasus, she had outlived them all, and her passing was felt by the whole family. Her body was placed in state on a raised dais in the Cathedral of St Peter and St Paul, but the solemnity of the eve-of-funeral service was broken when her son Dmitri bent to kiss the body as custom demanded, misjudged the distance (he was very short-sighted), and tumbled right over the open coffin and down the steps on the other side of the dais.

As one generation passed, another stepped into the public eye. Just weeks after the funeral, Prince Ioann became engaged to Princess Elena of Serbia. Ioann had grown into a tall young man with a long solemn face, very quiet and deeply religious. He became a sub-deacon in the Orthodox Church and considered entering a monastery, so the news that he was to marry amazed the family. 'By the way,' the Tsar wrote to his mother, 'how did you like Yoanchik's engagement to the daughter of the King of Serbia? It happened like a flash of lightning. . . . I should think it must be a risky thing to marry Yoanchik, he ought to become a monk, which he himself talked of doing.'[9] The idea of kissing Ioann sent his girl cousins into fits of giggles; fortunately for him, Elena saw him in a different light and the wedding took place on 3 September. Three days later his sister Tatiana married Konstantin Bagration-Mukhransky, a prince of the old ruling house of Georgia.

Konstantin Konstantinovich loved all his children, but one had a special place in his heart. From the nursery his fourth son, Oleg, had stood out as being quicker, more imaginative and more gifted than the others. The best games were always of his devising and even the older children followed his lead: his nurse remembered one particularly complex role play, 'the journeys of Nansen', which required the involvement of adults and children and a full set of tin soldiers and dogs. As Oleg grew, it became apparent that his talents mirrored his father's, and might even surpass them. He enjoyed studying and needed no encouragement to work hard. He was a gifted artist. Literature fascinated him, and his father decided that for this son a conventional education based on the curriculum of Russia's military academies would not be enough. He sent Oleg to the Alexander Lyceum in St Petersburg. Soon the boy was writing his own poetry and winning high awards but most of the men in the family disapproved heartily: alone among the male members of the family, Oleg had no military uniform. In time he came to feel this lack himself and in 1913, the Tercentenary year, the Tsar noticed his discomfort and gave him a junior commission in the Hussars.

These were the last peaceful years of imperial Russia. In the summer of 1912 Stravinsky and Prokoviev gave concerts at Pavlovsk and Teymuraz Bagration, Konstantin Konstantinovich's first grandchild, was born. His youngest son, Georgi, became the first Romanov boy scout. Konstantin's last verse drama, The King of the Jews, was performed to great acclaim at the Hermitage Theatre in the autumn of 1913 with the author in the role of Joseph of Arimathea and his elder sons in the cast. The Tsar had sanctioned the performance after reading the play at home to his wife. 'It made the deepest impression on me,' he told Konstantin, 'more than once my eyes filled with tears and I had a lump in my throat. I am certain that to see your play on stage and to hear the beautiful paraphrasing of what each of us knows from the Gospels, all this could but produce the most profound effect on the spectator.'[10] In the summer of 1914 Konstantin recited the 'Nunc Dimittis' from his play again, at a reception at Pavlovsk attended by Baroness Buxhoeveden and Nicholas II's two elder daughters. Something about the evening, in that last summer before the storm broke, made his words seem almost prophetic. 'It was a moving and admirable piece of poetry', the Baroness remembered, 'and its author, then already a sick man, with his fine features bearing the stamp of the many emotions of a sensitive spirit, his hair and beard streaked with grey, looked like an inspired patriarch taking leave of the world. My two young Grand Duchesses, the embodiment of happy, buoyant youth, sat still, the smiles gradually fading from their faces. "It is like a farewell", Tatiana Nicolaievna whispered to me. I felt this too. It was the farewell to his work – the last legacy of a true poet.'[11]

Konstantin was in Germany with his wife, taking a cure, when the war began. The Germans detained and would have interned him but Elisaveta used her connections as a German princess to obtain his release. Their homeward train stopped abruptly before reaching the frontier and, despite Konstantin's poor health, they were obliged to walk miles across open country to the first Russian station. Back in St Petersburg they found their sons alight with excitement and ready to throw everything into the struggle. Ioann, the would-be monk, now happily married and the father of a baby son; Gavril, a tall young man, as shy as his brother, whose heart was privately committed to a dancer, Antonina Nesterovskaya; Konstantin, whose world was his regiment; Oleg the poet, already with work in print – for some time Oleg had been in love with Princess Nadejda Petrovna and in 1914 they became engaged unofficially, but war overwhelmed all other hopes and plans; and finally Igor, the most outgoing, lively and argumentative member of the family. Nadejda's brother Roman remembered Igor as one of those people whose voice was always too loud for his surroundings. All five were preparing to leave for the front with the first Guards regiments, and only Georgi was too young to go. In 1914 the departure to war of five brothers seemed splendid and patriotic and the crowds outside the Marble Palace cheered them to the echo. Their parents played their own part by financing the 'Marble Palace Hospital Train', to be run by Elena and Konstantin's niece, the younger Grand Princess Marie Pavlovna. Her grandmother Queen Olga of Greece, Konstantin's sister, had returned to Russia after her husband's murder in 1913, and she opened a hospital of her own at Pavlovsk.

Prince Oleg's war service would be all too brief. On 27 September/10 October, after only two months at the front, he was wounded in an attack on a German position in East Prussia. At first his wound seemed slight and it received no attention. The next day doctors realised that there was serious internal damage and Oleg was moved by ambulance train to Vilno for an emergency operation. His brothers Igor and Gavril were with him and his parents hurried to the hospital, but he could not be saved. Oleg died at 8.20 p.m. on 29 September, happy still because he believed that the death of a member of the imperial family would draw them closer to the country, and thrilled with the medal of St George received from the Tsar in his final hours. He was just twenty-one. His father decided to bury him at Ostashevo, the estate to the west of Moscow which had always been special to them both. It was a simple funeral: the Prince's body, covered in flowers, was carried through the villages on an ordinary gun carriage. Behind were his father, mother and youngest brother, followed by princes, soldiers and peasants, the highest and lowest walking side by side without distinction.

For Konstantin this was a loss that could not easily be overcome, but it was only the beginning. On 1 June 1915 Prince Bagration-Mukhransky was killed in action at Yaroslavl in Galicia, leaving Tatiana Konstantinovna a widow, with two small children. Her father already knew that he himself was dying, and this news was a final blow. Grand Prince Konstantin Konstantinovich died at Pavlovsk two weeks after his son-in-law, and was the last member of the imperial family to be given a state funeral. The Tsar followed his coffin on foot through the streets of St Petersburg, despite increasing unrest in the city. Afterwards four widows dined together at the Marble Palace; Elizaveta Mavrikievna, Grand Princess Konstantin, her daughter Tatiana, Queen Olga and Elisabeth, Grand Princess Sergei, who had always been close to Konstantin and his family. Both she and they felt increasing concern about Rasputin's influence on her sister, the Tsaritsa, but while the older generation only talked, Princes Gavril, Konstantin and Igor were drawn into the excited discussions that led to the murder of Rasputin, carried away by the idea that one man's death could make a real difference to the desperate state of the country.

The murder only accelerated the tumble into chaos, and the Tsar's abdication in the spring of 1917 began a time of frightening uncertainty. There were no more rules: in April 1917 Prince Gavril married the dancer Nestorovskaya. The family spent their last summer at Pavlovsk; Ioann, now at their head, and his wife and two children, his widowed mother, fourteen-year-old Georgi and eleven-year-old Vera. Queen Olga was with them; when her granddaughter Marie Pavlovna was married at Pavlovsk that September Ioann took the father's part because her own father Grand Prince Pavel was under house arrest. Seeing the way that things were moving, and realizing that resistance was not an option, Ioann invited the new government to take an inventory of the treasures at Pavlovsk. His family had always loved the palace but their life there could not go on, and within weeks they accepted advice to leave for the city.

In March 1918 came the call for registration of all members of the imperial family. The younger men were given a few hours to prepare for exile in Siberia: none of those who were sent east would ever return. Only two of Konstantin Konstantinovich's surviving sons escaped death in the Revolution – Georgi, who was still a boy, and Gavril, who was too ill to be sent into exile. In August he and his uncle Dmitri were arrested and taken to the Schpalernaia prison in the city. Gavril was a lucky man. He would almost certainly have shared the fate of his uncle, the brothers Nikolai and Georgi Mikhailovich, and Grand Prince Pavel, if it had not been for his wife. Nesterovskaya was friendly with Gorki and persuaded him to secure Gavril's release and to take them both into safety under his own roof. It has always been said that even Nikolai Konstantinovich, exiled in distant Tashkent, was shot by the revolutionaries in February 1918, but the latest research from Russia suggests that this was not the case. Nikolai welcomed the Revolution – after all, he had little cause to love the Tsars – but he was in his sixties at the time and had suffered from arteriosclerosis and chronic bronchitis for some years. Apparently, on 14 April 1918, he died peacefully in the arms of his illegitimate daughter Daria. Two of his sons were less fortunate: his son Sviatoslav, Daria's brother, was shot by the revolutionaries in Tashkent and later in the year Prince Artemi Iskander died fighting with the White army, but for Nikolai Konstantinovich, the imperial family's most intractable rebel, the Bolsheviks are said to have provided a splendid funeral and a tomb in the Orthodox Cathedral in Tashkent.[12]

No other members of the family could expect such treatment, and for those who survived the massacres in Siberia and in the Fortress, escape to the West was the only hope. Stranded in St Petersburg in the Marble Palace, which had been requisitioned with all its contents, Grand Princess Konstantin and Queen Olga managed a precarious living by secretly selling their own belongings to buy food. The Danish government obtained permission for Queen Olga to leave the country in a train full of repatriating German prisoners but she was almost taken when Bolshevik soldiers attempted to uncouple her carriage. The Grand Princess fled Russia with her four surviving children and attempted to build a new life, though there would always be memories. In 1921 Tatiana was remarried in Geneva to Alexander Korotchenzov, who had once worked for her uncle Dmitri, but he died only three months later. She became a nun, eventually taking charge of the Russian convent on the Mount of Olives in Jerusalem. Her brother Gavril settled in Paris and had the extraordinary experience of finding his own baptismal icon, lost in the Revolution, for sale in an antique shop. In 1950 Gavril's wife died and he married a fellow exile, Princess Irina Kurakine. His nephew Teymuraz grew up to resemble him so closely in speech and mannerisms that even she sometimes confused them.

The younger children never married. Prince Georgi died in New York in 1938 after a chequered career in the States. At one time he worked in a shop selling lamps: for him, as for many of the exiles, the adjustment to a new life, after such upheaval and suffering, was almost impossible to achieve. His sister Vera fared better and in time became the longest surviving member of the imperial family, with memories which could still reach back to their life in Russia before the Revolution.

23

Escape from Ekaterinburg

One of the most remarkable stories to have come out of the Revolution is that of Elena Petrovna, Princess Ioann Konstantinovich, who accompanied her husband to Siberia by choice. She was the only member of the imperial family to fall into the hands of the Ural Bolsheviks and survive, and in the 1950s, when Anna Anderson's claim to be Grand Princess Anastasia was attracting wide publicity, Elena put her story on record. Her motive was simple: after all that she had seen and suffered, she was convinced that Anastasia had died at Ekaterinburg and that it was her duty to say so. Her account was published in a French magazine but it received little attention, and now it is all but forgotten.

For Princess Elena the path to Ekaterinburg was a turbulent one. She was born at Fiume, near the border of Italy and Croatia, in November 1884. Her father, Peter Karadjordjevic, the eldest surviving son of the former Prince of Serbia, had been exiled at the age of fourteen and made his living as a mercenary. In the late 1870s he went to Montenegro to help reorganize the army of his friend Prince Nicolas, but his burning ambition was to return to Serbia and depose the Obrenovic family who had taken his father's title. To re-establish his dynasty he needed a son, and in August 1883 he married the Montenegrin Prince's eldest daughter, Zorka. He was thirty-nine, she was eighteen, and Elena was their first child. A second girl followed but she died before she was two, and in September 1887 Zorka produced the all-important son, Djordje. Peter built a small house in Cetinjé, the Montenegrin capital, and it was there that his second son, Alexander, was born. In Cetinjé Elena had an English governess, Miss Everard, and two young aunts for playmates, but her mother's life was not easy. Peter was a hard, ruthless man. He had spent all his time fighting and there was no gentleness in him. In March 1890 their fifth child, a son, was born but only lived a few hours. Three weeks later Zorka too was dead.

This tragedy seems to have cast a shadow over the friendship between Peter and his wife's parents: he left Montenegro soon after with the children and settled in a rented house in Geneva. Far from the places and people she knew, at six years old Elena had become the only woman in the family. Peter took in clerical work to earn a living and the children went to Swiss elementary schools, but his ambition was not forgotten and he filled their minds with the language and history of Serbia. Despite his harshness, Elena adored him. He called her his 'little firebrand' because she had inherited his fierce temper and would never give way when she thought that she was right.

As the years passed, Zorka's sisters took responsibility for Elena's education. Her life was divided between Italy and Russia, where her aunt Militsa, Grand Princess Piotr Nikolaievich, employed a Russian governess for her. The Montenegrin princesses had all been educated at the Smolny Institute under the patronage of Tsaritsa Maria Alexandrovna, and when Militsa and her younger sister Anastasia graduated in 1889, good marriages were arranged for them. Militsa was a cultured and intelligent woman who taught Elena well and brought her into contact with the imperial family. Elena followed her aunts to the Smolny, and when Nicholas II heard of her family's problems he brought her brothers to St Petersburg too, to study at the Corps des Pages.

It made sense for Russia to cultivate Peter and his sons; the Obrenovic princes, who gained the title of king in 1882, had become something of a disappointment, to Serbia as well as to Russia. In 1903 King Alexander of Serbia and his wife were murdered and Peter was called home to take the throne he had brooded over for so long. He had taken no part in the murders and officially deplored them, but he had conspired to bring down King Alexander's father, and there were people in his household who openly boasted of their involvement in the crime – one of his son's closest friends had opened the palace door to admit the murderers.

Nonetheless Peter was crowned in Belgrade, and after years as a poor relation Elena was transformed into a King's daughter.

It was almost inevitable that she, like her aunts, would marry into the imperial family, and in 1911 her choice was made. Her aunt Elena, Queen of Italy, took on the delicate task of overseeing the arrangements. Elena went to Italy and the Queen wrote to invite Prince Ioann Konstantinovich to stay for a few days. His parents approved, and he stunned everyone by proposing to Elena the minute he arrived. After that, events moved with extraordinary speed. Elena joined her father in Belgrade and arrived in Russia with him a few weeks after the engagement was announced. She sat by the Tsar at a gala dinner at Peterhof on the eve of the wedding, and could not believe her ears when he said that now she was to be a member of his family, she must call him 'Niki'. She told him she could never do it: her father would kill her for showing so little respect. From the other side of the table, King Peter winked in agreement.

In Ioann, Elena had found a partner who supplied the qualities she lacked, and their marriage was a blend of her headstrong nature and fierce sense of duty – sometimes too fierce for her own good – with his gentleness and piety. While he returned to his duties with the Guards à Cheval, she studied medicine at the University of St Petersburg, giving up reluctantly after three years when her son Vsevelod was born. As the great-great-grandson of a Tsar the baby was only a minor member of the imperial family, but he was also the first grandson of the King of Serbia, and his christening was in keeping with his status. 'The baptism of the first grandson of the King of Serbia was extremely solemn', one witness noted. 'The Emperor, who was godfather, attended the service with the two Empresses and the whole imperial family.'[1] It was 1914. When little Vsevelod was barely seven months old the First World War began, with Serbia at the heart of the fighting. Elena took over the management of the Marble Palace Hospital Train and went straight to the East Prussian front as head of the unit, leaving Vsevelod with his grandparents and Miss Irwin, his English nanny. He was in good hands and Russia sorely needed effective medical services.

The first months of war were a tense and sad time for the Konstantinovich family and Elena bore added anxiety for her own family; her father threatened to kill himself rather than leave Serbia. In 1915 it became obvious that the country would fall, but the King retreated over the Albanian mountains with his army. When Grand Prince Konstantin died that summer, worn down by a series of tragedies, he just missed seeing the year's one truly happy event. On 25 July Elena gave birth to a second child, Ekaterina, at Pavlovsk. Even in the darkness of war, Ioann found time to enjoy his children. The writer E.M. Almedingen remembered how his face lit up when he told her class, on one of his regular visits to the school, that little Vsevelod had cut his first tooth.

Elena was soon active again. She involved herself in a hospital in the city to complement her work at the front, and when the Tsar's daughter Tatiana asked for her help with Serb refugees she was quick to respond, travelling all the way to Odessa to review a detachment of Serbian soldiers. Elena was fond of the Tsar and his family and felt particularly close to Olga, the eldest daughter. She had seen signs of affection between Olga and her brother Alexander and hoped that in time something more serious would develop. Sadly for them all, the time was running out.

In February 1917 Elena visited the Alexander Palace to report on her refugee work, and she noticed how exhausted and ill the Tsar looked. He left soon after for army headquarters and, as revolution broke out around them, Elena returned to the palace to offer her help to the Tsaritsa, wearing an ordinary nurse's uniform so that the guards on the gate would allow her to pass unhindered. She was shocked to see that the Tsaritsa's hair had gone grey in just two weeks, and she realized that although Alexandra Feodorovna was outwardly calm, inside she was angry and afraid. Not one man from the imperial family was there to support her. Her children were ill, she had no idea where the Tsar was and she was not allowed to contact him. It was a fear Elena understood all too well – Ioann had not been heard of for some weeks. She offered her own help, and the Tsaritsa's grateful refusal fell on deaf ears.

That evening Elena set off for the city on a troop train,

accompanied by Mme Baltazzi, the lady-in-waiting to Queen Olga of Greece. The Queen knew that when Elena had made up her mind nothing would change it, but had insisted that she must not go alone. The two women found it impossible to call a cab at the station, and had no choice but to walk four miles through the frozen night, taking side roads for safety. The city lay under an unnerving silence, broken at intervals by rifle and machine-gun fire, and the streets were littered with corpses. At the Serb Legation the Minister, Spalaikovich, was outraged by the risk his Princess had taken, but he telephoned the Duma and discovered that the Tsar would be arriving at Tsarskoe Selo within hours. Then he escorted the women back to the station, and the next morning Elena was able to telephone the Tsaritsa with the news. A few hours later she learned of the Tsar's abdication; soon the telephone lines were cut and there could be no more communication with the Alexander Palace.

At Pavlovsk life became harder as the weeks passed. Elena resisted the demands of a revolutionary committee who wanted to dismiss Smirnov, Ioann's steward, and fly the red flag over the palace, but their triumph could only be a matter of time. She was desperate for news of her husband; Spalaikovich had promised to help and one day the Prince arrived unannounced on the doorstep. The epaulettes had been torn from his tunic but he had escaped a general massacre of officers because his men said that he treated them fairly. Feeling dishonoured now in his own uniform, Ioann changed into the dress of a Serb cavalry captain that King Peter had given him on his wedding day. He would wear it for the rest of his life. When Easter came, he and Elena decided to take eggs to the imperial children at the Alexander Palace. They were turned away by the guards, though their gifts were taken in. Denied contact with the Tsar, and realizing that their own peaceful life at Pavlovsk would not be allowed to go on for long, Ioann and Elena reluctantly accepted advice to move to the city. From the windows of the Marble Palace they watched the cruiser *Aurora* fire the opening shots of the Bolshevik Revolution.

In February 1918 Spalaikovich brought them news that all the foreign legations were leaving Russia. He offered to take Elena,

Ioann and the children to Finland under his protection but they refused, believing that it was their duty to stay in Russia. They were throwing away their last chance to escape as a family. A few weeks later all male Romanovs who were fit to travel were ordered to prepare for internal exile. This sealed Ioann's fate, but he was dismayed that Elena wanted to leave the children with his mother and go with him. He could not dissuade her; all he could do was to secure a safe conduct signed by Trotsky that would allow her to return home if the children needed her. Shortly before seven on the evening of 4 April, a sad little party assembled at Petrograd's Nicholas Station; Elena and Ioann, his brothers Konstantin and Igor, Grand Prince Sergei Mikhailovich and his secretary Feodor Romez, and Prince Vladimir Paley, whose distraught mother entrusted him to Elena's care. At seven the whistle blew and the exiles began their long journey.

It took two days and nights to reach Viatka in the Urals, where they were allowed to find their own lodging, though every movement was watched. They spent some days in an inn, then moved into a small house. Revolution had hardly touched the little town and people were sympathetic, bringing gifts and helping the Princes to settle. Nuns from a nearby convent prepared their meals. It was a situation the Bolsheviks could not tolerate. After eleven days two soldiers came while the men were at church and announced that the exiles were to be moved to Ekaterinburg. Prince Paley was deeply depressed by the news and the others teased him for his pessimism, but really all were aware that things could only get worse. The nuns brought food for their long journey and, in thanks for their help, Elena gave the convent her only remaining fur coat. They were loaded into a battered railway carriage by an escort of Red Guards and for three days their train rattled through endless dark forests, sometimes passing high waterfalls that were coloured blood-red by the local soil. The immensity of the landscape and its timelessness were oddly consoling to Elena and her companions; here was a world that would last, whatever lay ahead for them.

On their arrival in Ekaterinburg the Princes asked to go to mass in the Cathedral and the guards took them, leaving Elena alone with the luggage. While she waited a young man came and introduced himself as the manager's secretary from the local bank. He had been sent to help and, finding someone with a cart to carry the luggage, he took her to a hotel run by a Cossack couple named Atamanov. As they walked, he told her that the Tsar and Tsaritsa and one of their daughters had arrived in Ekaterinburg two days earlier. As soon as he was gone, Elena hurried off to find the others and give them the news.

The men were excited to think that the Tsar was nearby and determined to make contact, though it had to be done through Elena because she alone was able to move freely. Mrs Atamanov was afraid and would tell them little: according to Elena's own account of events she would only tell them that Dr Derevenko, one of the Tsar's physicians, was making daily visits to the imperial family in the Ipatiev House and otherwise practising medicine in the town. Elena described how she visited the doctor and appealed for his help but she must have been confusing this with her second stay in Ekaterinburg. There are few precise dates in her account but if she and her companions had arrived two days after the Tsar and Tsaritsa, they reached Ekaterinburg on 2 May when Dr Derevenko was still in Tobolsk, looking after the Tsesarevich. He would remain there until 20 May when his patient was fit to travel. The imperial children arrived in Ekaterinburg on 23 May, and even then it must have taken the doctor some days to set up in business.

Whatever happened on this first occasion, contact with the Tsar was impossible. Elena and her companions had hardly come to terms with this disappointment when another member of the imperial family appeared unexpectedly at the door of their hotel. Elisabeth, Grand Princess Sergei, had been brought to Ekaterinburg under guard with one of her nuns. She had tried to see her sister, the Tsaritsa, and had been refused; now she settled with the others at the Atamanovs'. Within days the Bolsheviks decided that it was dangerous to have this concentration of Romanovs so near to the Tsar and armed guards came to move the whole party to Alapaevsk. They spent twelve hours in a train, passing a post which marked the boundary of Europe and Asia just before the journey's end. This struck Elena as a chilling omen; they had crossed the border of two continents, for them, perhaps, it was also the border between life and death. At the station rough carts were waiting to take them to their destination, a wooden house enclosed by a fence and a high hedge. Once it had been the school house, now it would be their prison.

The seven guards claimed the largest classroom while the others had to settle in as best they could. Elena and Ioann claimed one room, Grand Princess Elisabeth and Sister Varvara another, Ioann's brothers shared a room and so did Sergei Mikhailovich, Romez and Prince Paley. The building was dirty and almost unfurnished, but it did have a kitchen garden which provided them with exercise and food. In the stifling heat of early summer, working in the garden also gave them a precious chance to breathe fresh air, for they were never allowed to open a window. The weeks that followed were a curious, almost peaceful interlude, cut off as they were from the outside world. Occasionally news came in, or they were able to send out a smuggled letter, but for most of the time the prisoners were dependent on one another. Denied prayer books, they improvised church services from memory. Alapaevsk was a small settlement which had grown up around the mines and smelting works. Many of its people had once been convicts, but even here there was sympathy for the imperial family. Unseen hands threw flowers over the hedge and one day an old copy of an illustrated magazine appeared, with photos of Elena and Ioann's engagement. It was a poignant reminder of all that they had lost.

As May turned to June and the days went by with no news, Ioann and Elena became increasingly worried about their children. A smuggled newspaper told them that the palaces had been appropriated and their inhabitants turned away; the city was said to be ravaged by famine and cholera. Ioann decided that it was time for Elena to go back. The prisoners held a family council and decided that as she still had a safe conduct signed by Trotsky she must go, find the children and bring them to Alapaevsk. There was no safety in Petrograd now, and whatever fate lay ahead it was better for the family to be together. Reluctantly, Elena spoke to the local Commissar but Trotsky's signature meant nothing to him; he could only send her to Ekaterinburg to appeal to Beloborodov, the head of the Ural Soviet. To Elena this seemed too uncertain, but the family still insisted that she must go. A cart arrived to take her to the station; it was a terrible moment for her but the guards, seeing her fear, allowed the other prisoners to leave the compound to wave her off. 'I saw all those I loved standing between the guards', she wrote. 'For a moment terror took over, and it seemed to me that they were lined up for an execution. "I don't want to go any more", I shouted to the driver, "stop now!" Without doubt my dear ones realised how I felt. After making encouraging signals to me, they all turned back to the house. The door closed behind them. I was alone. I had left them.'[2]

Ahead lay a terrifying journey through unknown country torn by civil war, with a nurse's uniform as her only protection. In the train from Alapaevsk two soldiers sat opposite her and put their feet on the seat, penning her in with their boots. It took enormous courage to face them as she did, saying that as she was obviously in their way she would stand for the rest of the journey. The boots came down but the soldiers amused themselves with obscene songs until sleep finally claimed them. When the train pulled into Ekaterinburg at five in the morning, Elena hurried to the safety of the Atamanovs' hotel. She was carrying smuggled letters from the prisoners but this horrified Mrs Atamanov, who assured her that if they were found it would mean her death. Sadly, Elena consigned them to the boiler. Beloborodov received her the next day but it seemed that her journey had been wasted: he refused to let her leave the Urals and would not send her back to her husband. She must remain in Ekaterinburg, he said, until a decision was made about her future. Protestations about the children did no good; he just said that a good mother would never have left them in the first place.

Elena returned to the hotel in despair, and at this low point her mind was drawn irresistibly to the only relatives who were still within reach. Beloborodov had refused her request to see the Tsar, but she felt that there was little to lose, and it must have been at this time that she went to see Dr Derevenko. She described how she bought some iodine and bandages and simulated a wound on her arm, then went in search of the doctor. His door was opened by a hard-featured woman who told her that he was attending the Tsar, and allowed her to wait. When he returned, Elena saw recognition in the doctor's eyes, but he said nothing that could give her away. He dismissed the woman and, as he dressed the 'wound', he and Elena conversed in whispers; in this way she learnt that security around the prisoners was fierce. Even the doctor never saw them without a guard and he stood no chance of passing on a message. He advised Elena that any attempt to see the family would put her life at risk; the Bolsheviks were edgy and saw conspiracy all around them.

Even now, Elena was not prepared to give up. Mrs Atamanov was too frightened at first to give directions to the Ipatiev House but finally she gave way, muttering 'if the Serbs are all as headstrong as you, there's no chance of them losing the war!'[3] Elena found the house and calmly, but with a pounding heart, walked towards it, until a sentry stopped her. She asked for his commander, hoping that it might be the officer who had guarded the family at the Alexander Palace; he had been a fair-minded man. While the rest of the guard trained their rifles on her, the sentry went inside – and returned with Commandant Avdeyev – a total stranger. Elena decided to risk everything on the truth: 'I am the wife of a Romanov interned at Alapaevsk, but I am also the daughter of the King of Serbia. . . . As a relative of the Tsar, I have come to hear news of him and, if you allow it, to see him.'[4] Avdeyev must have been stunned. He would not allow her in, but he agreed to tell the Tsar that she had been and to pass on her offer to obtain anything the family needed. He asked where she was living and the interview ended.

She returned to the hotel physically and mentally exhausted. Mrs Atamanov was horrified by what she had done and certain that they would all be shot, and her fears seemed justified when a soldier came to the hotel that evening and asked for 'the Serb': it might have been Elena's last moment but he had only come to say that the Tsar and Tsaritsa thanked her for her message, and assured her that they needed nothing. When he left Elena cried with relief. She slept peacefully that night for the first time since leaving her husband, but her apparent safety was a cruel illusion. At the first light of dawn, two soldiers burst into her room with a warrant for her arrest. She was taken to the headquarters of the Cheka in the Hotel d'Amerique to face a military tribunal.

The Bolsheviks were probably aware of a new development. From the safety of Murmansk, Minister Spalaikovich had sent a four-man mission in search of his Princess. The Serbian Military Attaché's adjutant Jarko Michich and Smirnov, Ioann's former steward from Pavlovsk, now travelling on Serbian papers, had spent months on the road accompanied by two soldiers and were approaching Ekaterinburg. Elena was amazed when the tribunal gave her a pass for Petrograd and released her. She was even more amazed when the Serb mission appeared at the door of the hotel, but it was their turn for amazement when she calmly refused their help. Michich had orders to find her, reunite her with her children, and take them all to Murmansk, but she was determined to take the children back to their father. She would accept the mission's help only as far as Petrograd and would not even think about leaving Russia without Ioann. After coming so far, the Serb mission must have felt like taking her prisoner themselves.

The next evening the little party found seats on a west-bound train, unaware that the Bolsheviks had other plans. While they waited, their carriage was silently uncoupled and surrounded and, as the rest of the train pulled out of the station, they found themselves under arrest. The station Commissar told them that he was following Beloborodov's orders. Michich refused to surrender his sword, or to take the epaulettes from his uniform, and the soldiers took them all to Cheka headquarters, where they were separated. Elena was taken before Yurovsky, soon to be the Tsar's murderer, who had her stripped and searched, and then locked up. The nightmare seemed endless.

Two weeks passed, then the woman who brought food told Elena that the prisoners at Alapaevsk had been set free by the Whites, and that White armies were now approaching Ekaterinburg. The part about Alapaevsk was a cruel trick: Ioann and his fellow prisoners had been murdered, so had the Tsar and his family, but the White armies really were coming. Before daylight the next morning Yurovsky burst into the cell and ordered Elena to dress: she thought that she was about to be shot in reprisal for her husband's 'escape', and found armed guards waiting for her in the street. They told her she was being taken to Moscow, but drove past the station and out into the forest. Elena silently prepared for the worst, but her journey ended in a clearing where a crowd of people huddled miserably together beside a train. The Bolsheviks were evacuating Ekaterinburg with hostages to ensure their safety. There were about forty of them, mostly men, including Mr Atamanov and the Serb mission. Elena noticed Michich, still proudly wearing his epaulettes, but she was pushed towards the only two women in the group. She could hardly believe her eyes. They were the Tsaritsa's lady-in-waiting Countess Hendrikova and her reader Mlle Schneider, both so emaciated and pale that she hardly recognized them; they told her that they had been in prison ever since their arrival in Ekaterinburg.

Soon the hostages were herded into a barred carriage once used for transporting convicts, and as the train steamed to the north-west, the Countess told Elena all that had happened during the imperial family's imprisonment. After three days they reached Perm. The hostages were forced to walk several miles to the prison, where the three women were placed in one cell, and here they learned the true fate of the imperial family. A few days after their arrival a female warder brought news of the massacre in the Ipatiev House: she had heard it from a guard who came with the hostages. He was on duty at the door of the murder room and described the scene in all its horror, and the warder repeated his story to the shocked prisoners. It seemed too awful to be true. For five weeks the women could think of nothing else and expected their own deaths at any moment, then one night two soldiers came for Countess Hendrikova and Mlle Schneider. The young Countess, quite calm, pressed a last message addressed to her sister into Elena's hand, the door closed behind them and they were gone. Left alone in the dark, Elena paced to and fro until dawn, when the warder told her her companions had been shot.

Later an official came and told Elena that her own fate had not yet been decided. Until it was, she was to be moved to a cell with twelve criminals, 'to allow her to meet the real people'. Elena prided herself on the Serbian royal family's closeness to their subjects but she had never seen anything like this. Her new cellmates were women who knew only deprivation and violence. Most were prostitutes, all had killed lovers or husbands, or murdered for money. For the first few days they ignored her, then curiosity overcame them. One girl asked for her story and another attacked her, but Elena was well able to look after herself, and, as the weeks passed, a genuine sympathy grew between her and her companions. Their stories opened her eyes to a world of misery and she made them promise that, if the Revolution ever ended, they would look for her, and she would help them to rebuild their lives.

She spent five months in the cell. In the outside world, the diplomatic community was trying to find out what had become of her.[5] The bodies of Ioann and the other victims of Alapaevsk were found at the end of September. In October the British Consul at Vladivostok received a report that Elena had been taken from Ekaterinburg as a hostage; this was confirmed by the Consul at Ekaterinburg a few days later. He believed that she was being held in Perm and wrote to London at the end of November to 'suggest that some neutral power might make guarantees for [her] safety'.[6] Then refugees from Perm brought news that Elena had been killed by the Bolsheviks on 17 November. In Bucharest her father went into mourning, but Spalaikovich did not give up hope. He obtained Lenin's permission to continue the search, and the Norwegian Minister in Moscow sent out one of his own envoys with rather confused orders – he thought he was looking for the Queen of Serbia. He reached Perm at the beginning of December and Elena was brought from her cell to meet him. No explanation was given, and once again she believed that she was going to her death, but the governor assured her that soon she would be taken to the Norwegian Consulate in Moscow, where a diplomatic passport was waiting. Two days later the prison door opened on an icy morning, twenty degrees below zero. Elena shivered in her thin summer dress and worn-out shoes, as an escort of thirty Red Guards hurried her to the station. After two days and nights they reached Moscow, but their destination was not the Norwegian Consulate.

This was the strangest twist in the story. The soldiers took Elena to the Loubianka prison, to the office of a Lithuanian named Peters whose reputation gave nightmares to little children. Once again Elena expected to die, but the reputation belied the man. Peters was respectful, almost kind. He denied any knowledge of Ioann – this must have been a lie – but he confirmed the story she had been told of the execution of the imperial family. He promised to telephone Petrograd and find out about her children, and was soon able to report that they were safe in Sweden with their grandmother. He told Elena that he was obliged to keep her under guard and, not wanting to put her in the prison, he had prepared rooms for her in the Great Palace in the Kremlin. He said that he would visit her himself as much as possible and went out of his way to make her comfortable. Her first meal was an excellent roast dinner, but after months of prison food she was unable to eat it. One of the guards told her that he had once served Grand Prince Konstantin Konstantinovich, and she gave him the dinner – in return he offered to heat her bath water.

Peters seemed determined to make Elena comfortable. He sent the palace librarian to her with books and offered her the chance to walk outdoors. On learning that she had no coat, he would have given her a free choice of clothes from the Tsaritsa's wardrobe but she felt unable to accept. That same day a box was delivered to her room containing a grey astrakhan coat, still bearing the shop's labels to reassure her of its origin, and she accepted it gladly. It was very emotional for her to be escorted by armed guards through the halls of the palace, now so empty and so full of memories. Her new prison was near to St Catherine's Hall; she had her own hallway, sitting room, bedroom and bathroom, but spent many sleepless nights haunted by thoughts of the past. On her walks, always accompanied by a guard with a fixed bayonet, she watched the removal of icons from the Kremlin churches and grieved to hear that the buildings themselves were to be closed.

Peters asked if Elena knew anyone in Moscow who could visit her. She was extremely reluctant to trust him with names but, reassured by the Norwegian Consul, Mr Kristianson, she gave the address of her former governess, and the woman was allowed to see her each day and share her walks. On their return one day they found Peters waiting with important news. Elena would be free to leave at six the next evening and must be out of Russian territory within forty-eight hours. She wondered how she would achieve this with no money, but Kristianson had sent word that she was to go directly to the Consulate and she did as he said, shivering all the way. Despite Peters' courtesy she was unwilling to be in debt to a Bolshevik and had left the astrakhan coat in her room. She was welcomed by the Consul's wife and given the Norwegian papers which would allow her to leave the country. The Kristiansons were leaving too, and they would travel together to Petrograd, then on to Finland. A few hours remained for Elena to say goodbye to her old governess, and they went together to the nearest church to give thanks for her release.

As the party settled into their reserved compartments on the Petrograd train there was one last surprise. Peters' assistant arrived with a bouquet of flowers for Elena and the Commissar's apology, he had hoped to wave her off in person. The train reached Petrograd the next day and they set off for Finland. At the frontier station of Belo Ostrov the bridge had been destroyed and the passengers were obliged to walk to a waiting train on the Finnish side. They were almost on the border when a Red Guard stopped them and said that he could not allow the Princess to leave Russia. She panicked – death would be better than returning to prison – but Mr Kristianson quickly whispered to her not to be silly. A hefty bribe was all it took to close the soldier's eyes and Elena was free. She turned back for one last glimpse of the skyline of Petrograd, veiled in a winter mist.

In all this time no one had told Elena what had happened to her husband, and she learned the truth in a terrible way. She was met in Stockholm by Prince Schakovskoi, her brother-in-law's former aide-de-camp, who was to take her to the little spa town where her mother-in-law and the children were living. As their train drew near to the station and the long-awaited reunion, he suddenly asked, 'Did you know that your husband was killed with his brothers last July? The Grand Princess was unwilling to believe it and telephoned King George V of Great Britain herself for confirmation, but the King could only give her the answer she feared.'[7] The shock left Elena reeling and she greeted the children in a daze. They hardly knew who she was. It was not the reunion she had longed for, but she hugged her son and daughter and found in them the strength to go on: 'they were there, they were alive and we were together. Life could still have meaning despite the atrocious death of their father.'[8]

His death *was* atrocious. Princes Ioann, Konstantin and Igor Konstantinovich and Vladimir Paley, Grand Prince Sergei Alexandrovich, Grand Princess Elisabeth, Sister Varvara and Feodor Romez had been taken from the schoolhouse at Alapaevsk on the night of 17/18 July 1918 and driven in carts to an abandoned mineshaft. The Bolsheviks pushed them down, threw grenades after them, and covered the mouth of the shaft. Their bodies were found by investigators from the White army and, after post-mortem, given a funeral service and placed in the crypt of the Cathedral at Perm. When it became clear that the area would fall to the Reds, General Dieterichs, who had been made responsible for the investigation, had the eight coffins sent to Chita on the East-Siberian railway line. They were accompanied by Father Seraphim, the Superior of the Monastery of St Seraphim of Sarov who had once been Elisabeth's confessor, and escorted by soldiers. For six months they remained in a monastic cell at the Protection Convent at Chita until the danger once again became too great. On 26 February 1920 Father Seraphim set off with the coffins for China. Within sight of the border a group of communists attacked the train and seized Ioann's coffin but the Chinese border guards rushed to Father Seraphim's aid and retrieved it.

The eight coffins were taken to Peking and placed in a small Russian chapel just outside the north gate of the city, tended carefully by Father Seraphim and the priest who ran the Russian Mission. In July 1920 *The Sphere* published photos of the coffins in the chapel.

This alerted members of the Hesse family and a few months later they arranged for the bodies of Grand Princess Elisabeth and Sister Varvara to be taken to Jerusalem for burial. When Sydney Gibbes, Tsesarevich Alexei's former tutor, visited Peking in the winter of 1928 he found that all was not well. The men's coffins were in the crypt of the cemetery church, tended with respect, but the head of the Russian Mission was elderly and had no funds; his church was crumbling round him and there was no one to say the offices for the dead. Gibbes appealed to the Serbian Minister in London for help. The Minister replied that the families themselves were in severe financial difficulty but he would do what he could. It is said that the coffins were later taken to Jerusalem and buried.

From Sweden Elena went on to Paris with her children. Her brother, Crown Prince Alexander, met them there and took them home to Belgrade, where Elena was reunited with her father. She tried to settle in Serbia, but the country reminded her of Russia and the memories were still too painful. Alexander bought her a villa at Cap Ferrat where she lived for a while until the children were ready for school, then they moved to England. Vsevelod was educated at Eton and Oxford and Ekaterina at Heathfield. Princess Elena died in Nice in 1962, a few weeks short of her seventy-eighth birthday.

24

The Lost Tsar

The exiles settled to their new lives with varying degrees of difficulty. Most, like Elena, had royal relatives somewhere in Europe, to cushion them against financial problems and soften the transition, but it could never be easy. Each had suffered some bereavement – a brother, a cousin, a husband. Each had also to come to terms with that other bereavement, that while they had escaped, or even been allowed to leave, the Tsar and his wife and children were dead, abandoned at the last by all but a few faithful servants. This left a painful emptiness at the heart of the family: it had lost its head, its reason for existing and, in the young Tsesarevich, it had also lost its future. More and more, that loss is coming to symbolize the whole tragedy.

He was tall, and would probably have reached the commanding stature of his Romanov and Hesse ancestors. He was attractive, resembling, it was said, his great-grandfather Alexander II, one of the best of Russian Tsars. He was intelligent and forceful, with a mind of his own, but his potential was never realized because he died in a cellar at the hands of his parents' enemies, a few weeks before his fourteenth birthday. Nicholas II had no legal right to abdicate on behalf of his son: some would take the argument a step further and say that in law the Tsesarevich Alexei became Tsar on his father's abdication, even though his accession was never recognized. It has also been argued that in the accession of Alexei under a regent, which the Duma representatives wanted when they forced the end of his father's reign, lay the final hope for the Russian monarchy. Who knows? The remains of the Tsesarevich, and all that he might have been, lie somewhere in a Siberian forest. In the autumn of 1998 there were reports that his body had finally been discovered, months after the reburial of his parents, but DNA tests will be needed before these findings can be confirmed. Alexei reached such maturity as fate allowed him during the war and the long months of imprisonment. Exposure to sights few children see and a tension at times unbearable made him analyse his family's plight for himself, and he was developing a sharp eye. He was a child still, but at Tobolsk in the autumn of 1917, that child noted in his diary, 'In this place I am beginning to understand the word truth. At Tsarskoe Selo everybody lied. If I become Tsar one day, no-one will dare to lie to me. I will sort things out in country.'[1] It suggests something of what might have been.

His story began in another world. The birth of a Tsesarevich had been anticipated, longed-for, even despaired of; it was no wonder that the proud parents were overwhelmed with joy and gratitude – no wonder that the country was relieved and ready to celebrate. It is all too easy now to underestimate the joy with which the news was received. Knowing the end, knowing too that Alexei's birth came in the middle of the disastrous war with Japan, which tipped the country into the 1905 revolution, we assume that these events must have been prefigured in the public mood at the time. There is no evidence that they were. Across the Tsar's vast empire church bells rang and people clamoured to hear the news. The scenes Baroness Buxhoeveden remembered in her own small village near Kazan would have been repeated across the country. On Sunday the church was packed,

> every man, woman and child had squeezed in to listen to the imperial message. The deacon . . . wore the holiday cloth of silver vestments, much too large for him. . . . He cleared his throat, spat discreetly behind his hand . . . and slowly boomed out: 'We, Nicholas II, by the Grace of God Emperor of Russia, Tsar of Muscovy.' All the imperial titles were rolled out in a crescendo. The men, mostly old soldiers, stood rigidly at attention . . . The women crossed themselves, and bowed low as every title of the Emperor was mentioned. . . . After the crowd had poured out of church, the peasants stood about in groups discussing the event.

'The Tsar now has his own rabotnik (worker),' I heard a man say. 'He will help him with his work as he grows up.'[2]

The war would have been remote from these people but the birth of a Tsesarevich was something all could understand. It promised amnesties and other solid benefits, and gave a reassuring sense of continuity.

The christening at Peterhof on 11 August 1904 was a fairy-tale event, stolen completely by the children. Alexei's sisters took part, and the elder ones wore Court dress for the first time and walked hand-in-hand in the procession. For many of their cousins too this was a first formal appearance, and the little ones looked on in wonder. Eleven-year-old Oleg Konstantinovich and his brothers and sister were summoned from their father's Moscow estate for the ceremony, and he captured the excitement in his diary:

We arrived on the 10th, Papa's birthday. After spending the night at Strelna and putting on full dress uniforms sewn together overnight, we set out for Peterhof. Ioann, Ganya and Tanya took part in the procession. A.M., Kostya, Igor and I walked through the rooms of the palace to the church. We had to pass through large halls, filled with people. There were many Counts, Countesses etc. We passed by the guards, who saluted us, and at last entered the church. Here I saw General Sakharov for the first time. Suddenly all was silent. The procession came in. First the Tsar with Empress Maria Feodorovna. We formed a line: Kostya, myself, Igor – A.M. at the back. The Tsar smiled and made his greetings. It was all very interesting. At last there came Princess Golitsina with a cushion tied to her neck, and on the cushion – Alexei. The service began. It was conducted by Metropolitan Anthony, Father Yanyshev and Father Ioann of Kronstadt; there were 2 archimandrites, 2 deacons and 2 psalm-readers, all in golden chasubles. The Tsar was wearing an Ataman uniform. The others had parade uniforms on. Tatiana was wearing a Russian dress of pink brocade with a pair of pink slippers. Tatiana, G.P. Marie Pavlovna, G.P. Elizaveta Feodorovna and myself all felt our heads spinning, and I stood behind the grille.

Then I went out. When I was behind the grille I was sitting with the Heir Alexei Nikolaievich. He's very sweet: the whole time he played with his fingers.[3]

Awe and interest surrounded Alexei from the start, and his parents delighted in showing him off. On her first visit to the Alexander Palace, Sophie Buxhoeveden was plunged straight into a game of blind-man's-buff with the four little princesses, her eyes covered as she plunged after the squeaking, giggling figures to peals of laughter from their mother. But the mood changed in an instant, as Alexei was brought into the room: "'Stop, all of you . . . Baby's coming." I unbound my eyes and saw the nurse come in, carrying the three-months-old Cesarevich. He was a splendid baby, and no one would have believed that he had in him the germ of any inborn weakness. . . . I shall never forget the look on the Empress's face as she took him from the nurse. She was radiant. . . . "He is so good," she said. "He hardly ever cries, and feel how heavy he is. Just take him in your arms."'[4]

The wider family adored Alexei too and wanted to feel part of his life. Oleg's father described the imperial children's entrance at a family tea party in 1906: 'Their four daughters came into the dining room and also – to the great joy of our children – the two-year-old Tsarevich. After going round the tea table and greeting everyone, he climbed onto his mother's knee; Igor was sitting next to her, and the little Heir willingly moved over onto his lap, calling him, as someone unknown "the new one". Then our boys and the imperial girls had a wonderful time romping with him on the floor.'[5] Before he could walk, Alexei had been carried in his father's arms in front of massed ranks of soldiers. As a toddler he stood behind the Tsar to sample meals served to sailors on the imperial yacht, and solemnly shook hands with officials and dignitaries. He attended troop reviews, and the inhabitants of Tsarskoe Selo became accustomed to seeing him out in a carriage, or at play in the park. Russians whose lives were remote from the capital were made aware of the Heir's existence through photographs, formal and informal, which reinforced the message: the Tsar and his wife were blessed with a robust, beautiful son, and in him lay the dynasty's future. Nicholas II felt handicapped by his own shyness and unpreparedness for public life: he was determined to let his son grow into the role of Heir and feel comfortable with it. In the Tsar's study in the Alexander Palace there was even a small child's table set aside to enable the little Tsesarevich to attend meetings and audiences.

This was a departure from the past. Nicholas I had refused to allow his young Heir to be seen in a formal setting, or to be addressed by his titles, and successive generations had zealously guarded their children's privacy. Modern accounts lay so much stress on the safe, loving domesticity of the last Tsar's family that we tend not to notice how Alexei was being systematically prepared for his public role. Suspicions about the health of royal children are commonplace, but even when there were unmistakable signs of Alexei's illness, no question mark was allowed to touch his future. As late as 1911, an American journalist could still write 'he is a sturdy, whole-some boy in every respect and takes the keenest interest not only in all the wonderful toys that are sent him by kings, emperors and eastern potentates but also in childish sports and games.'[6]

So much attention might turn any child into a monster. Nicholas I protected his son from formality because he feared the effect on his character but in Alexei's case, the risks were overtaken by the benefits. There are many anecdotes of him behaving badly, but it was a tendency he soon outgrew. By the time he was ten, it was obvious that his parents had chosen well. One day in the summer of 1914, for example, he jumped at the chance to go walking with a friend, to relieve the boredom of a long hot day. They were at Ai-Todor in the Crimea and wandered outside the gates to explore the nearby village. Almost immediately Alexei was recognized and surrounded by a crowd, friendly enough, but overwhelming in number and in their determination to touch him. Alarmed as he was, the little boy kept his composure, and worked his way steadily back to the gates, smiling, saluting and shaking hands. He knew how to behave in public.

Another important decision was the choice of companions for him. Alexei needed other boys, but while his father and grandfather had brothers close to them in age, he had only sisters. Alexander II was in a similar position as a child, but when he was eight two boys were chosen to be his constant friends, room mates and classmates. No similar arrangements were made for Alexei, and his haemophilia must have been a factor in this: boys' games were very dangerous for him. He played occasionally with his cousins, the sons of his aunt Ksenia, and with Oleg's younger brothers. Georgi Konstantinovich was a great favourite; when he announced his decision to become a chauffeur in adult life, Alexei readily offered to be his assistant. Ships' boys and army cadets were brought in too. This was a Romanov tradition, known and accepted, but many people were far less happy to see Alexei playing with the sons of his sailor attendant Derevenko; they were thought much too common. The same criticism was laid against his closest friend of later years, the doctor's son Nikolai Vladimirovich Derevenko (no relation), always known as 'Kolia'. Alexei was allowed to visit Kolia at home and to associate freely with his family, and in this too, Nicholas and Alexandra served their son well. In having friendships with ordinary children, Alexei learned not to make false distinctions between people. He approached everyone with the same openness and genuine interest, and this was a good quality in a future ruler. In the early months of the First World War the tutor Gilliard took him on a series of outings, and he remembered how his pupil would talk with peasants in the fields. 'Alexis Nicolaievitch liked questioning them, and they always answered him with the frank, kindly simplicity of the Russian moujik, not having the slightest idea whom they were speaking to.'[7]

War provided Alexei with a very different glimpse of the world outside. Boy-like, he was thrilled with the idea of war, and the first glimpses we have of him speaking with his own voice show this clearly. A few months after hostilities began, he wrote to his father, 'Yesterday we played at war. I took the enemy trench in one moment but was immediately thrown back and taken prisoner. But at that very second I broke away and scrammed!' 'They have made me a soldier's coat, and I stood guard in it today. Today P.V.P.

brought me from Petrograd three entrenching spades in leather cases.'[8] It was quite in line with their general attitude to Alexei that his parents decided to send him to headquarters with his father, and while this too was exciting for him, it very quickly deepened his understanding. In October 1915, wearing an ordinary private's uniform, he stood beside the Tsar at a parade of men fresh from the battlefield. Gilliard saw him 'listening intently to the stories of these men, who had so often stared death in the face. His features, which were always so expressive, became quite strained in the effort not to lose a single word of what the men were saying.'[9] The simple request made at a parade a few weeks later, for all men who had served from the beginning of the campaign to raise their hands, was a stark reminder to the boy of the horror of war. Thousands stood in line that day but the number of hands raised was pathetically few.

Father and son toured the Ukraine and Galicia together, pushing as close to the front line as they could – closer, often, than their advisers would have liked. Once they walked to within five kilometres of the fighting, and at the end of the tour of inspection the Tsar wrote home, 'Alexey climbed everywhere and crept into every possible hole – I even overheard him talking freely to a lieutenant, asking him questions about various matters!'[10] Nor were their visits confined to the trenches. At a front line aid-post protected by dense forest Alexei had his first sight of the sufferings of the wounded, straight from the line. On this, and on visits to military hospitals, he never shrank from what he saw. He knew all there was to know about unbearable pain, and his sympathy was real. His demeanour on these visits made a deep impression and the Council of the Order of St George voted to give both father and son the Medal of St George, one of Russia's highest military awards.

Daily life at headquarters settled into a routine of lessons, walks or drives, and games with two cadets of his own age. Alexei slept with his father, and while the need to watch over a chronically ill child was not the most helpful burden to add to the load of a man already responsible for the running of an empire, and for the command of an army in wartime, the boy's presence did boost morale. Ordinary soldiers were curious to see him and thoroughly approved of his bearing and appearance, and they responded to his obvious interest in them. Senior officers and foreign liaison officers became very fond of Alexei – by all accounts he was extremely likeable. He could be too mischievous, and Gilliard was probably right to worry that long periods at headquarters made him over-excited and unable to concentrate, but he still gained from living in a masculine environment and he was maturing quickly. A severe nosebleed cut short his first spell at headquarters, but by May 1916 he was well enough to return, after a family visit to the Black Sea Fleet and the western Crimea.

In August 1916 Alexei was joined at the Stavka at Mogilev by his English tutor Sydney Gibbes. He was in his element, bombarding his mother with demands for pocket money – 'My salary! I beg you!!!!!. . . . I shall soon start selling my clothes books and will finally die of hunger.'[11] He told Gibbes that he was much happier at Mogilev than at home. The remark may have no great significance, but it is possible that at home he was beginning to sense the growing political tension that centred on his mother. At headquarters all this would seem far away and unimportant; war was the only priority there. Sir John Hanbury-Williams, who was attached to the Stavka, lost his son on the western front that summer. He was touched to receive a visit from Alexei, who slipped into his room one evening, quietly and unannounced, saying that his father thought it better for the General not to be alone. Sensitivity to others would always be one his most attractive qualities.

Before the spring of 1917 the possibility that the Tsesarevich's haemophilia might make him unfit to rule simply did not arise. While he lived, he was Heir, and even though the public must have known that something was wrong with him, his position was never questioned. A strong sentiment was attached to his name and person: this was why people clustered round to see and touch him, and the feeling ran deep – even after the Revolution. So when the capital sank into dangerous chaos, with various factions setting out their own prescriptions for the future, it was natural that Alexei's name would be brought forward. Even revolutionaries could see that immediate abolition of the monarchy would be dangerous because monarchy was central to the organization of the state – and because most people outside Petrograd still wanted a Tsar. It was Mikhail Rodzianko, the chairman of the Duma, who proposed the accession of Alexei under a regent. The catch was his naming of Grand Prince Mikhail Alexandrovich as regent: most senior members of the imperial family were deeply suspicious, feeling that Mikhail (or more likely his wife) was conspiring in his own interest, undermining their attempts to preserve the Tsar's throne with a reformed constitution.

But the regency itself was not a bad idea. However unfairly, public opinion had turned against Nicholas, but sentiment and sympathy was still attached to his son, and a child as Tsar would have offered a rallying point for all but the most extreme revolutionaries. Alexander Guchkov and Vasili Shulgin, the Duma delegates who went to Pskov to negotiate the abdication, were in no doubt of this: 'a beautiful myth could have been created around this innocent and pure child', Guchkov remembered in later years. 'His charm would have helped to calm the anger of the masses.'[12] When they learned of the Tsar's decision to abdicate in Alexei's name the deputies made no attempt to dissuade him, but they were not happy; in law the Tsar had no right to name his own successor. The order of succession was clearly defined in the 'Fundamental Laws' laid down by Tsar Paul, and further laws protected the rights of minors. Besides, there was the emotional aspect: 'We had counted on the figure of little Aleksei Nikolaievich having a softening effect on the transfer of power.'[13]

The story of the abdication is so familiar that its details slip by without question – and they are puzzling. On 1/14 March, the thirty-sixth anniversary of his grandfather's assassination, Nicholas was advised of the need to abdicate in Alexei's favour, and the next morning he telegraphed his agreement. He even signed the instrument of abdication. But by the time the delegates had arrived at Pskov, he had decided to withdraw the inheritance from his son. Why? Gilliard had an answer, which is not even mentioned in the Tsar's diary. In the intervening period, he said, Nicholas had discussed Alexei's illness with his own doctor and was advised that haemophilia was incurable; that Alexei could possibly live to old age, but would always be at risk from accidents. At this, according to Gilliard, Nicholas 'hung his head and sadly murmured: "That's just what the Czarina told me. Well, if that is the case and Alexis can never serve his country as I should like him to, we have the right to keep him ourselves."'[14]

If this is accurate – and Gilliard was not there – it is extraordinary. After all, had the Tsar and his wife not known, almost from the beginning, the nature and implications of their son's condition? The assumption that they had is universal and most would date the discovery to September 1904, when the baby Alexei began to bleed from the navel. The anxiety of those September days is clear in the Tsar's diary. He had surely discussed his son with doctors in the intervening years, and the decisions he made bear witness to this: first, the appointment of sailor attendants to keep a constant watch on the boy, then the very brave decision to draw them back, allowing Alexei to make mistakes and so, in time, to learn how to manage his condition. In the spring of 1912 the Tsaritsa confirmed long-held suspicions in the family by telling her sister-in-law that Alexei had haemophilia. In 1913 a detailed description of the illness was given to Gilliard when he began to teach Alexei, and that same year the Tsar's instruction that his son must be allowed to take risks, and play all the games of a normal boy, was known across the family. Agnes de Stoeckl remembered how worrying it was to watch him play on the giant stride at Harax that summer. Alexei was as capable of serving his country in 1917 as he had been in 1913; in terms of his health, nothing had changed, and the doctor cannot possibly have been telling the Tsar anything he did not know already.

The official reason for Nicholas's decision – the reason stated on the instrument of abdication – is his reluctance to be parted from his son, but that too is puzzling. At first, the Tsar stipulated that he would abdicate in Alexei's favour on the understanding that the boy would not be taken from his family. It may be that after signing the document Nicholas began to worry about this, and the doctor is said to have advised him that separation was likely, but the decision was made long before he had even seen the delegates or discussed the question with them. Their eventual response, that Alexei's future living arrangements had not even been considered, was almost certainly the truth. This was a point that Nicholas could probably have negotiated, had he chosen to try, and surely there were other members of the family to whom he could have trusted his son in the short term. His own mother? His daughters – two of them were grown women by this time, against whom no one had any complaint. Alexei had already shown himself quite capable of living away from home and enjoying it, and he was growing up all the time.

Of course, on a human level the Tsar's decision is all too easy to understand, and it attracts immediate sympathy. He was tired and depressed, hurt by the defections of those whose loyalty he had trusted, and worried about the safety of his family. He wanted to protect them, particularly the son who meant everything to him. The tragedy is that in doing this in the way that he did, he lost what might have been his only chance to turn the tide of events. But one witness suggested that his decision was prompted by more than simple concern for his son. Anna Virubova, the Tsaritsa's friend, was as close to the imperial couple as anyone, and she believed that in abdicating for Alexei, Nicholas was taking his last revenge on the powerful men who had turned against him and forced him to abdicate – generals, politicians, even members of his own family. In her scenario, these men wanted to take power and rule in their own interests, gaining control of Russia and its resources through Alexei. 'My boy I will not give them', she quotes Nicholas as saying. 'Let them get some one else, Michail, if he thinks he is strong enough.'[15]

While his future was being decided, Alexei was at Tsarskoe Selo recovering from measles. He spent the day of the abdication, when he was, for a few hours at least, Tsar Alexei II, building model houses and reading aloud to Gibbes. Two days later the tutor noted that he was 'better but not in very good spirits. Knows nothing of passing events, but feels them all the same. We cast lead bullets and built model houses, and with many visits from the Empress and family the day passed.'[16] It fell to Gilliard to break the news of the abdication to Alexei, and he was struck by the boy's modesty; not once, then or afterwards, did he comment on the abrupt change to his own position. He was concerned for his father and for Russia, and that was all.

In the months that followed the whole family had to learn a new way of life, as prisoners in their own home. It must have been hard for Alexei to witness the changed attitude to his parents and the hostility shown both by guards and officials, and by the people who gathered at the railings to witness the family's walks. He was neither passive nor insensitive, and there must have been times when his temper boiled. It was painful too to see the falling away of people who had presented themselves as loyal friends. One of the most enigmatic figures, and the most intimately involved with Alexei, was the sailor Derevenko. Anna Virubova claimed to have seen Derevenko bullying Alexei, shouting orders at a boy too bemused to fight back. If this was true it would have been a shattering experience, but its truth is not so clear cut as it may seem. According to Anna, it happened on 20 March, two days before her own arrest. After a display like this the sailor would surely have left or been made to go, but he was still at the palace months later. Shortly before the move to Tobolsk in August he submitted an invoice for new clothes and shoes for Alexei to Colonel Kobilinsky, the commandant of the palace garrison. He was asking a huge amount so payment was withheld: when the sailor complained to the Tsaritsa and she intervened on his behalf, Kobilinsky showed her the invoice. She took the Colonel's part. Derevenko was refused permission to accompany the family to Tobolsk, but months after their departure he was still pleading to be allowed to join them. Failing that, he asked for the return of a trunk, which he said had gone to Tobolsk in error. It was found and opened, and inside were the new clothes and shoes, and an icon given to Alexei by his great-uncle, Grand Prince Sergei Alexandrovich.[17] Was Derevenko stealing? Looking after the boy's interests in his own peculiar way? No one will ever know.

After the first shock of imprisonment, the weeks slipped by. Winter gave way to summer and Alexei's time was divided between the classroom, with his parents and members of the suite taking their turn as teachers, and the park. Two walks a day were allowed and he longed to be outside, where he could run barefoot, swim in the lake and play on the island that had been the province of the children of his family for generations. He had his cat and dog for company and one day discovered a baby hare in the park, which he took back to the palace: Alexei adored all living things. Indoors, he practised his balalaika and gave cinema shows to his family and the suite, issuing written invitations and ushering in his guests. Watching him, Count Benckendorff was moved by his many good qualities – intelligence, strength of character and kindness – and mused on the service he might give his country if only he were spared. One aspect of the boy's response to imprisonment was striking. Far from hating the soldiers who guarded his family and enforced niggling and often spiteful regulations, Alexei made friends of many of them. He liked to question them about their lives. He showed little sign of fretting against the limitations of imprisonment but the frustration was there. 'Oh, if only <u>once</u> I could go out for ten minutes' walk,' he was heard to say, 'just beyond the gates.'[18]

The sense of confinement mounted in Tobolsk. Alexei was glad of the break from Tsarskoe Selo and the adventure of a journey even though familiar things had to be left behind, including his beloved cat. In many ways he settled very happily but his diary shows his boredom, as one day followed another with no sign of an end. 'The whole day was just the same as yesterday', 'Everything's just the same', 'I'm so bored with it all', 'Boring!!!' – the refrain runs from day to day, broken only when he was ill. Illness confined him even more, tying him to his bed and to solitary meals upstairs with his mother, while everyone else ate downstairs. Much as he loved the Tsaritsa, there must still have been a sense of release, and added interest, on the days when he was able to write, 'I had lunch downstairs with everyone', 'I had dinner downstairs with everyone else'. In the first three months of 1918, Alexei had German measles and several minor attacks of haemophilia, in the form of painful joints or reaction to minor accidents, but he was always impatient to be well. He was obviously an old hand at monitoring his temperature and looking out for signs of trouble: 'This morning spots started appearing on my body. I put myself to bed. . . . My temperature is normal, 36.1"'; 'In the evening I felt a bit of pain in my right leg. I put a compress on it'; 'Yesterday I banged my left ankle and I had a compress on it all today'.[19]

At Tobolsk the family experienced their first Siberian winter, when the temperature could fall horribly far below zero, making indoor amusements a necessity. Alexei was fiercely competitive, like most boys, and enjoyed cards, 'Nain jaune', and a game called 'the slower you go, the farther you go', which was his favourite. Occasionally he drew caricatures or did jigsaws, but one pastime that drew the whole household together were the plays the captives performed in Russian, English and French, directed by Gibbes and Gilliard, which called for the creation of makeshift scenery and costumes, for actors and, of course, for an audience. Rehearsals could last for days and some plays were put on more than once: Alexei noted them all in his diary, with programmes, recording seven plays in three months. On 4/17 February, for example: 'At nine we practised the play "A La Porte", and at quarter past nine performed an English play "Packing Up". M., A., and I were in it. Everyone was in fits of laughter.'

One regular member of the audience was Kolia Derevenko. His parents had followed the family to Siberia, and after a few weeks Kolia was given permission to play with Alexei. He came and went very freely, and his company provided a vital spark: together the boys played noisy games indoors and ran wild outside whenever they could. Their games were lively, imaginative and often violent, centring at first on the snow mountain they had made in the garden: 'In the afternoon with Kolia we ran to build up speed and jumped in the snow. We poured water on the snow mountain, fought one another and wrestled.'; 'Kolia came. We spent the afternoon sliding from the top of the mountain and kept falling down.' By February, they were becoming more ambitious. They built two fortresses in the snow, then dug a connecting tunnel large enough to crawl through. It took three days; on the afternoon of the fourth day, assisted by Tatiana, they 'made a second tunnel and a new fortress. No.I and no.II and no.III are joined by two tunnels.

We played a lot and it was great fun.' It must have been frustrating when the soldiers decided to demolish the snow mountain only four days later, almost certainly destroying all of these elaborate fortifications in the process. 'In the morning we cleared the snow away from the path', Alexei wrote the next day. 'The mountain was completely spoiled and churned up.'

But the games continued unchecked. The boys made wooden daggers and fought with them. One day they attacked Gilliard, who 'threw us in the snow and saved himself'. Soon wooden guns became part of their arsenal; one afternoon in early March Alexei 'played at cutting wood with an axe, and I made two guns and a dagger'. By mid-March a steady thaw had set in and the boys had found a new interest – archery. They made a bow and arrow on 22 March/4 April, and were so pleased with the results that soon they were making more, particularly arrows, which kept getting lost. But more exciting possibilities opened up a few weeks later. 'A local businessman sent me a sledge and a boat as a present, modelled on the sledges and small boats they use in this area', Alexei wrote on 25 March. 'Kolia and I played with them for ages and we slid down the staircase in the boat. He left at nine.' Melting snow had created a puddle in the garden thirteen metres long, and as soon as the weather allowed them to, the boys dragged the boat outside. To Alexei it might have been a boating lake, but it was all fantasy. 'My brother has a little boat in which we go rowing', Olga told a friend. 'It is more in imagination as there isn't enough water after all, and we therefore move sticks and hands.'[20] His revenge was sweet: Olga fell out and found enough water to get satisfyingly wet.

At Tobolsk as at Tsarskoe Selo, Alexei sought out the company of the soldiers, especially the men of the 1st and 4th Regiments, who still regarded him as 'the Heir' and did their best to amuse him. He chatted to them and picked up their expressions and language. 'In the evening I played draughts in the guard room with the soldiers', 'We talked with the soldiers. These are the best detachment, from the 4th regiment. In the evening after dinner I went to the guard room and played draughts with Lieutenant Malychev and Private Egorov.' It was a situation that deteriorated steadily as familiar men left and others took their place. One day a new guard refused to let Kolia enter the house. On 10/23 February Alexei noted rather sadly, 'I went for a walk in the afternoon. Talked to the soldiers – these were the best ones. Nearly all of them are going home. At six the sisters brought in Adjutant Tour who had come to say goodbye. Mama gave him a little icon for himself and for the others who are leaving. Papa kissed him and so did I. We wished him a good journey.' It was as close as he ever came to mentioning the darker side of imprisonment. He certainly felt it. During a severe attack of internal bleeding in April he was heard to say '"I would like to die, Mama; I'm not afraid of death, but I'm so afraid of what they may do to us here"', but this tension never touches his diary.[21] He probably coped by trying not to think about it, but he could not stop it happening. In the last entry of all he noted, 'During our morning walk a commissar, Demianov, came to have a look at our garden and courtyard, he is also the head of the Omsk detachment of the Red Guard. With him were the commandant and committee of our detachment. The Red Guards have been here for a week.'

The next day Alexei fell victim to an internal haemorrhage which almost killed him. No one knew why; coughing, they guessed, or the rough games he enjoyed so much. There would be no more diary entries, and the last glimpses we have before the door of the Ekaterinburg house closed behind him come in letters to his parents and sister Maria, who were taken from Tobolsk in April, and to Kolia, who was no longer allowed to visit. It upset Alexei particularly that he could not celebrate Kolia's twelfth birthday with him, and he sent a favourite toy cannon as a present. Gibbes later remembered that Alexei was the last member of the family to think of giving presents. On 1/14 May, shortly before leaving Tobolsk, he wrote to his mother, 'The rooms are empty, little by little everything's being packed away. The walls look bare without the pictures.'[22] The strain and sadness was evident but, as if to emphasize that this was a tough little character who could not be held down for long, at the same time Alexei was writing to Kolia, whom he would never see again, 'I hold you in my arms and thrash you with my feet.'[23]

Without the evidence of his diary and letters, Alexei would be lost for ever in a limbo of sympathetic but stifling interpretations, which see him through the eyes of others. But he was not just a pathetic victim, perpetually suffering and surrounded by ministering adults. Alexei was active and spirited, and his own determination to live and be normal must have been as big a factor in his survival as anything the doctors, or Rasputin, or even his loving parents could have done. He survived even in Tobolsk, when all hope was abandoned. He was clever, and although too active to favour books, in captivity he began to develop a taste for Lermontov and Pushkin. Vasili Pankratov, the Commissar in charge of the family in their first months at Tobolsk, was struck by the boy's insatiable appetite for information and very critical of the education he had so far received. Of the whole family, he said, 'They suffocated in the monotonous court atmosphere. They felt real spiritual hunger, a thirst to meet people from another milieu', and this was true of Alexei to the end.[24] A priest allowed into the Ekaterinburg house only days before the murder would later recall, 'his eyes were alive and bright, looking at me, a new person, with noticeable interest'.[25]

25

In Some Enchanted Castle

They are gone now, the good, the bad, and the indifferent, but their fate, and their life before the flood, exert an increasing fascination. Some of the murdered Romanovs remain where they died, but even their fate is changing at a bewildering rate. In the summer of 1998 the remains of the last Tsar and Tsaritsa, three of their daughters and their servants were taken back to St Petersburg – St Petersburg now, not Petrograd or Leningrad – in an official gesture of atonement. The exiles still lie in places as far afield as Canada, Denmark, England, Switzerland and France, who might once have expected to end with them in the Cathedral of St Peter and St Paul. Living Romanovs are scattered, maintaining the imperial heritage in their own way or trying to put it behind them and earn a living, but the divisions which split the family in the final years persist to this day. Once the exiles seemed to hold the only memory of the past, but after the fall of the Soviet Union locked cupboards were opened and forbidden subjects discussed, and it became apparent that an undreamed-of wealth of physical reminders of imperial Russia still exists, hidden away in Russian museum vaults, store rooms and archive boxes. There is so much still to discover. Popular interest in recent years has centred around the Alexander Palace, the most closed and inaccessible of the buildings that were used regularly by the Romanovs before the Revolution. Its story is a fitting place to end, because it draws together the threads of the last imperial century – one of the first homes of the first Nicholas and Alexandra, and the last home of the last – a family at the height of its power, a family in crisis and a family under siege and now, at last, the beginning of a new understanding.

The Alexander Palace has stood for over two hundred years, its sweeping classical façade reflected on the surface of a reed-edged lake. When the sun catches the yellow and white stucco the building looks bright, from a distance, but at close quarters it is sadly neglected, the once cheerful paintwork peeling and grubby. On a dull day, with rain dripping from the trees, the surrounding park is haunted by the sad finale of imperial Russia, when Nicholas II and his family were imprisoned in the Palace, allowed to walk only as far as the bridges and to dig a vegetable patch in the park. The garden façade of the building cannot even be seen as it was meant to be: a high, dark-green fence punctuated by empty watch towers hides all but the upper levels – not a reminder of the last Tsar's imprisonment, this, but the legacy of the Soviet navy who were given the Palace in the 1950s. Today the Alexander Palace seems inseparable from the tragedy of Nicholas and Alexandra, but the building was standing long before their time and carries other associations too, and other memories.

It was in the closing years of the eighteenth century that Catherine the Great decided to create a palace for her beloved eldest grandson, Grand Prince Alexander Pavlovich. In 1792 she commissioned the Italian architect Giacomo Quarenghi to build close to her own favourite palace, the Great, or Catherine, Palace at Tsarskoe Selo, about fifteen miles to the south-east of St Petersburg. The decision had political overtones. Catherine did not get on well with her son, Grand Prince Paul, and it was widely rumoured that she wished to set him aside in favour of her grandson, which was her right under the old law of succession. The siting of Alexander's new palace so near to her own was seen as a physical expression of her plans.

The new palace was a low building on two storeys, with two symmetrical wings on either side of a central courtyard, joined at one end by a suite of state rooms. At the front, an elegant colonnade connected the entrances to the two wings, which looked out onto the courtyard. At the back, the long garden façade overlooking the park had at its centre a wide semi-circular bay with a domed roof. While building work was still underway, in October 1793, Alexander was married to Princess Louise of Baden, who became Grand Princess Elizaveta Alexeievna. He was fifteen, she was fourteen, and the alliance had been arranged by his grandmother. The Alexander Palace was completed in 1796, and Catherine handed it over to the young couple with a traditional offering of bread and salt. She died before the year's end.

Tsar Paul hated Tsarskoe Selo because his mother had loved it, and he visited the town only rarely. He had all building work in the parks and palaces stopped and removed some of the most valuable works of art: fortunately for Tsarskoe Selo his reign was short. When Alexander came to the throne, after his father's murder, the 'Tsar's village' returned to favour, but instead of moving into the Alexander Palace, the new Tsar preferred his grandmother's palace. His own would wait for sixteen years until his younger brother Nicholas Pavlovich found a bride: only then did the Alexander Palace become a family home.

In the late 1820s the Polish Countess de Choiseul Gouffier visited Tsarskoe Selo at Alexander I's invitation, and was given a room on the upper floor of the Alexander Palace. Grand Prince Nicholas and his wife were away in Germany at the time and their children were staying with the Dowager Tsaritsa, so the building was empty. 'The apartment which they had allotted to me', the Countess remembered, 'was . . . at the end of a long open gallery, which opened on the dining-room and served as choir for the musicians at the grand dinners. From all the windows I had charming views of the park and the imperial château, which is about a hundred yards from the Alexander Palace. A mass of green which partly covered the edifice leaves in view the five gilt cupolas of the chapel surmounted by brilliant crosses, which in calm weather are reflected in a bit of water clearly defined and surrounded by a verdant lawn. . . . I was absolutely alone in this great palace, with the exception of my child and the domestics of the court. . . . With the help of the imagination I could have thought myself in fairyland in some enchanted castle.'[1]

Grand Prince Nicholas and Alexandra returned to Russia, and in June 1825, six months before Nicholas succeeded to the throne, their third daughter was born in the Alexander Palace. Grand Princess Alexandra Nikolaievna, usually called 'Alexandrine' or 'Adine' in the family, was a delicately pretty, dark-haired child. In 1826 the artist Piotr Sokolov painted a miniature of her in a high chair, clutching a wooden rattle. Two years later her father, describing her in a letter to his sister in the Netherlands, was less than enthusiastic about her looks: 'Adine', he wrote, 'is very small and very mischievous, but I do not think she is pretty in spite of others' opinions.' When she was eight, he would say she was 'a little moppet, but sweet'.[2]

Only two of the first Nicholas and Alexandra's children were actually born in the Alexander Palace; Alexandra and her younger brother Nikolai, whose birth in 1831 coincided with a severe epidemic of cholera in Russia. This confirmed the imperial couple's preference for the country, and all their family came to know and love the Palace and its park, particularly in spring. In the 1830s the Alexander Palace was a happy place. The interior was extensively redecorated for the family's comfort and pleasure: in one of the formal halls a slide was installed for the children. The 'Hall with the Hill' was a playroom until the Revolution. Outside, close to the west wing of the Palace where the family had their private apartments, a lake and an island were also set aside for the children's use. The Children's Island, reached by its own pull-along ferry, was their domain, with a cottage where the three Grand Princesses, Maria, Olga and Alexandra, learned to cook, a kitchen garden for all the children and a fort for the boys, anticipating the delights Queen Victoria's children enjoyed at Osborne. There was even a cemetery on the island for their pets.

Like the second Nicholas and Alexandra, Nicholas I and his wife were devoted parents who longed for privacy, but the Alexander Palace in their day was not a place to shut out the world – on the contrary, the Tsar made a point of bringing important guests into the domestic circle. In the autumn of 1836 Lord and Lady Londonderry were invited to dinner at the Alexander Palace, and Lady Londonderry described the visit in her diary. They dined in Quarenghi's Semi-Circular Hall, the centrepiece of his design, 'an immense "salle", the bay windowed middle of which was partitioned off on each side by open columns, orange trees and plants. [There was] a horse-shoe table and about sixty people.' After the meal, the Tsar's younger sons were brought in with their nurses and played about on the floor, while the adults mingled and chatted.

Lady Londonderry did not meet the Tsar on this occasion but she could not have been more impressed by Alexandra Feodorovna and the imperial children. 'There is a peculiar charm about this family', she wrote. 'They are gifted by nature more than the generality: tall, handsome, graceful, well made, clever, agreeable and different from most royal persons. They appear conscientiously good . . . living to fulfil "their being's end and aim", to be useful, to do good and to distribute comfort and improvement on a great scale. The children seem carefully educated, and in the interior appears the domestic comfort, affection and simple privacy of a "ménage" in humble life, and this is singularly set off by the immense power, wealth and great magnificence that surrounds them.'[3] Family life was part of the image of monarchy Nicholas I wanted to project to all classes. Residents of Tsarskoe Selo and the surrounding area were encouraged to gather on the Palace lawns each evening to watch the imperial family relaxing together.

In 1842 Nicholas and Alexandra celebrated their silver wedding anniversary in style, with a medieval tournament under the walls of the Alexander Palace. On 23 May sixteen gentlemen rode out onto the lawns, led by the Tsar himself, wearing a genuine sixteenth-century suit of armour from his own collection. The Tsesarevich Alexander and his brother-in-law the Duke of Leuchtenberg rode behind him, also in full armour, and the Tsaritsa was at his side on a white horse, in a medieval dress of gold silk emblazoned with the imperial eagle on a white shield. Her daughters Olga and Alexandra rode with her, also in costume, and the three younger Grand Princes, Konstantin, Nikolai and Mikhail, were dressed as pages in bright blue velvet doublets. The eldest daughter, Maria Nikolaievna, Duchess of Leuchtenberg, served the guests with ice cream and tea in the colonnade. It must have been an extraordinary scene. Nicholas I commissioned the French painter Horace Vernet to produce a family portrait in costume, and was so thrilled with the result that he rewarded Vernet with the Order of Alexander Nevsky, and his own carriage and horses.

Two years after the festival, tragedy came to the Alexander Palace. Grand Princess Alexandra Nikolaievna, the first of the Palace's children, was married in January 1844 to Prince Friedrich of Hesse-Cassel. She was eighteen. That summer she became ill while staying with her parents: some accounts say she had tuberculosis, others that she caught measles. She died in her bedroom on 10 August 1844, giving birth to a seven-month child, a son, who did not survive. Her parents were devastated. Nicholas had his family's private apartments, on the courtyard side of the west wing, completely redecorated, to protect his wife from reminders of that terrible summer. Where his daughter's bed had stood, a small chapel was installed, with an icon of St Alexandra commissioned by the officers of the Preobrajensky regiment from the artist Karl Bryullov. The saint had the features of the dead Princess. Her father also commissioned a monument to be placed on her favourite spot in the park – a statue of her carrying her baby in her arms. A portrait was painted, which has hung at Gatchina in recent years, showing Alexandra Nikolaievna holding a rose: the Alexander Palace appears in the background.

The tragedy was the prelude to a quieter period in the Palace's story, as the imperial children grew up and moved away. By 1844 the future Alexander II was married with a family of his own, but their Tsarskoe Selo home was in the Zubov wing of the Catherine Palace: Alexander II and Maria Alexandrovna rarely used the Alexander Palace. Nicholas I died in 1855, and artists commissioned to record the appearance of the private rooms of the Palace towards the end of his reign showed the bedrooms and schoolrooms of the younger Grand Princes with dust sheets on the furniture: only the Tsar's rooms and those of his wife appeared still to be in use, including her comfortable Raspberry Drawing Room, which was on the corner where the private wing joined the state rooms and had windows overlooking the park on two sides. Nicholas's study was small, almost cramped, its dark green walls providing a striking background for his collection of military models. These were displayed in glass cases, stacked shelf upon shelf up to the ceiling.

After her husband's death, Alexandra Feodorovna chose to remain at the Palace, which held so many memories, gathering her family around her whenever she could. She kept in touch with their news, attended her daughters-in-law during their confinements, and warned her son against his new reform programme: to her the old ways seemed so much safer. She died in the Alexander Palace on 1 November 1860.

Silence fell. For six years the Palace was used only for guests, but in 1866 new apartments were prepared on the garden side of the west wing for a new Tsesarevich Alexander, Nicholas and Alexandra's grandson, and his young wife Maria Feodorovna. Their first child, the future Nicholas II, was born in their bedroom in the Alexander Palace on 6/18 May 1868 and so, in succeeding years, were his brothers; Alexander, who died of meningitis shortly before his first birthday, and Georgi. Towards the end of 1872, rooms in the east wing were prepared as a honeymoon suite for the children's aunt Maria Alexandrovna, who married Queen Victoria's son at the turn of the year. The newlyweds came and went, but throughout the 1870s the Tsesarevich's family enjoyed the Alexander Palace and its park as their grandfather and his brothers and sisters had done before them.

Childhood memories may have drawn Nicholas II back to the Palace after his own wedding in 1894, when he needed to spend a few days in peace with his bride. The suddenness of his father's death and his own accession had left no time to prepare a honeymoon suite: Nicholas stayed in the rooms he had shared with his brother Georgi, and Alexandra used their mother's rooms. They arrived on an icy evening in early December, and the next morning the Tsar noted in his diary, 'It was strange to spend the night in dear Papa and Mama's bedroom, where I was born. I went from the bedroom in a dressing-gown to my own room to dress, through Nikolai Pavlovich's apartment, as I did yesterday evening.' It was not a perfect arrangement, though everything else about those few days seemed sublime, and the young couple could not have been happier. 'Each day that passes,' Nicholas wrote, 'I am grateful to the Lord and I thank him from the depth of my heart for the happiness which He has granted to me.'[4] The Alexander Palace became a part of that happiness. 'It is so nice here,' Alexandra told her grandmother, 'and my room is full of plants and delicious smelling flowers, quite like at home. In the next room my sweet Nicky was born and Georgy and the little brother who died.'[5]

The young couple needed somewhere of their own, for themselves and the family they anticipated. Rooms in the Winter Palace were being prepared for them, but it was not surprising that they also chose the Alexander Palace, which had such pleasant associations. The architect Roman Meltser was commissioned to redesign the apartments in the east wing. He arranged a suite of rooms for the Tsar on the ground floor, overlooking the courtyard, and set out the Tsaritsa's rooms on the other side of the narrow central corridor, looking out on the garden towards the railings that separated the park from the town. The couple saw Meltser's handiwork for the first time in September 1895 and were enchanted. Nicholas told his mother 'we could hardly recover from a feeling of pleasant surprise when we saw that nothing had been left even to remind us of the dreadful old arrangement. . . . sometimes we simply sit in silence wherever we happen to be and admire the walls, the fireplaces, the furniture. . . . The mauve room is delightful – one wonders when it looks better, in the evening or by daylight? The bedroom is gay and cosy; Alix's first room, the Chippendale drawing-room is also attractive, all in pale green; but as not all the furniture is ready yet, it is too early to form a definite opinion about it.'[6]

These were the Tsaritsa's rooms and the 'mauve room' the Tsar described was to become one of the most famous in Russia, central to the daily life of the family. In the memory of the exiles the mauve room was either light, airy, and beautiful, always full of fresh flowers, or tasteless, unattractive and cluttered – depending entirely on how the writer felt about the Tsaritsa. An essential part of her character seemed to be embodied in that one room. In 1898 a corner balcony was built onto the end of Alexandra's suite of rooms by the St Petersburg Metalworks and this too became a favourite place, for sitting outside, drinking coffee and watching the children at play in the garden. In 1903 Meltser converted the Great Concert Hall at the end of the east wing into two rooms joined by a raised gallery; Alexandra's Maple Drawing Room, with its delicate, Art Nouveau interior, and Nicholas's New Study.

From the New Study to the entrance of the east wing on the courtyard side, Nicholas's rooms were consciously masculine, with the dark wood panelling and green leather upholstery he liked. In 1894–5 he had a large sunken bath, almost a swimming pool, installed in his suite of rooms, and he ensured that his architects and decorators took advantage of all the new technologies. Electricity and the telephone were brought to the Palace and in 1899 a hydraulic lift was installed, connecting the Tsaritsa's rooms with the children's suite on the floor above. A private cinema was built in the Semi-Circular Hall.

The whole east wing was developed for family life, though the Tsar never forgot the historical significance of the Palace and, wherever possible, asked for old interiors to be preserved intact behind the new decorations. Facing his own rooms across the courtyard, in the west wing, the Dowager Tsaritsa commissioned Maples of London to redecorate and furnish the rooms that had once been used by the first Nicholas and Alexandra. This 'English suite' was intended for guests, and a special apartment was prepared for the Tsaritsa's sister, Grand Princess Elisabeth. The rooms on the other side of the west wing corridor, where Nicholas was born, were left untouched, partly in memory of Alexander III, partly as a base for Maria Feodorovna to use on visits to her son's family. In the early days no one predicted how rare those visits would become.

Then there were the nurseries. When Nicholas and Alexandra moved into the Palace they were expecting their first baby, who was born in her parents' bedroom on 3/15 November 1895. Grand Princess Olga was the only one of the five imperial children to be born in the Alexander Palace. The nursery suite, on the first floor above the Tsaritsa's rooms, was modest at the time of her birth; it grew with the family, and classrooms were added. Writing in 1906 Miss Eagar, who nursed the four little Grand Princesses, described the children's rooms as she knew them:

> the nurseries at Tsarskoe Selo are very fine, consisting of about eleven rooms. In the bathroom is a stationary bath of solid silver, used for the bigger children. There is a small silver bath for the use of whichever baby reigns. Each child's name is engraved upon it, so it forms a historical record. It was apparently bought for

Nicholas I, and bears his name and those of his family. We also find the names of Alexander II, and of Marie, afterwards Duchess of Edinburgh. The last name added was that of Alexis, the little baby who was born in August, 1904.

The walls of all the new rooms are painted in oil with beautifully executed friezes of the same flowers as appear in the chintz, interspaced with golden butterflies or birds. The bathroom has sea-gulls painted on the frieze. At the end of this suite is the playroom. It has eight windows overlooking the park and gardens. It is all yellow and green, like a bunch of daffodils, and has a frieze of peacocks strutting about amidst greenery. The carpet is a pale sage green, unpatterned. Over each window is a panel, in painted poker work, each representing some scene in animal or bird life.[7]

By 1906 the Alexander Palace had become the young family's principal home: they had been driven from the Winter Palace by the 1905 revolution. They were happy at Tsarskoe Selo, and people in the town became accustomed to glimpsing the children at play in the park, or seeing them ride out with their mother or their nurses. Court officials, government ministers and delegations were continually arriving at the gates: the Tsar worked an extremely long day in his study but he was a fit and active man who enjoyed walking in the park, cycling or boating on the canals. When there was snow on the ground, ice mountains were built for the amusement of children and adults alike. The Palace was not shut away and the family had chosen to live in the wing closest to the road and the town, nonetheless, outside the protected world of Tsarskoe Selo the Tsar's family came to be seen as an isolated little group living for themselves alone. This was not what they intended, but increasingly it was how they were perceived. In the city particularly, people missed their participation and leadership, and grumbled because they stayed away.

They still planned for the future, though, and as late as 1916 the Tsesarevich's rooms, facing the garden on the first floor, were redecorated and extended in recognition of the fact that he was growing older. When official delegations came, or when soldier's meals were brought for the Tsar to taste, the little boy would be present as often as his health allowed. But the work on his rooms was destined to be the last redecoration undertaken for the imperial family. In February 1917 the Tsaritsa and her children were in the Palace when revolution broke out in the city. Three of the five children were down with measles and the others would soon succumb. The park was under deep snow, the lift failed to work, and the air was alive with rumours: it was the last act in the tragedy. On 7/19 March the Provisional Government ordered the arrest of the abdicated Tsar and his wife in the Alexander Palace: two days later, Nicholas was brought home under guard.

The imprisonment lasted until August. Physically, conditions were not too bad, despite the humiliations of house arrest: as the Tsar commented in his diary, 'the thought that we are all <u>together</u> gladdens and consoles'.[8] As the weather improved, the family began to spend as much time as possible outdoors, ignoring the crowds of onlookers who gathered by the railings. In May they started to dig a vegetable garden, assisted by their retainers and some of the soldiers of the guard, and in June Grand Princess Olga wrote to her old Russian tutor describing their new life: 'We walk every day from 2 to 5. We work in the garden. If it isn't too stifling, Mama also comes out and lies on a couch under a tree by the water. Papa walks . . . to the outer reaches of the garden, where they chop and saw dry trees. Aleksei plays on the "children's island", runs barefoot, and sometimes swims.'[9] During the night of 13/14 August the family gathered with their luggage in the Semi-Circular Hall and, after a delay lasting nearly five hours, they were taken out onto the terrace and driven away through the park before the sun rose.

For the Alexander Palace, this was not the end. As chaos descended, a small but determined group of connoisseurs, museum professionals and art historians struggled to preserve the imperial palaces and their treasures. They took inventories, lobbied tirelessly, and found a few supporters in the new Soviet hierarchy, but the fight to save the palaces was a hard one. In Moscow the Bolshevik government pronounced the palaces national property, but local officials were not always willing to comply. Early in 1918 soldiers broke into the Alexander Palace and soon after, Anatoly Lunacharsky, the 'Commissar for Enlightenment', decided to appropriate the building and turn it into a centre for socialist education, distributing the toys and books of the imperial children to local schools and hospitals. Urgent protests managed to save the books, and the idea was soon abandoned. In June the Palace doors were opened to the public for the first time.

For the next twenty-one years, no matter how brutal the reality of life outside became, nothing could stop the growing crowds who came to shuffle round the palaces in respectful silence. In the '20s the Soviet government began to sell off treasures to raise money and many precious items were lost. But the Alexander Palace stayed open, and for twenty kopecks it was possible to explore the state rooms and the apartments of Alexander III in the west wing, while fifteen kopecks bought admission to the family rooms of the last Tsar. In 1937 the Palace acquired a remarkable new director, who did his utmost to defend it in the difficult years ahead.

Anatoly Mikhailovich Kuchumov was born in the Russian provinces a year before the Romanov Tercentenary. Growing up in the drab years of Revolution and civil war, he was fascinated by relics of the past and studied them closely. In 1932, after falling through the ice on one of the canals in the Alexander Park, he talked himself into a junior position on the staff of the Palace museums: after two years he had become a curator. For Kuchumov the Alexander Palace was a very special place. 'It was the first place', he said, 'where one could sense the aroma of the epoch, the character of the people. . . . In the dressing table of Alexandra Feodorovna there were little boxes of medicine. In the bedroom of Nicholas II and Alexandra Feodorovna, there were various relics, icons, a lampadka with icon oil – rose oil. The scent of rose oil remained until the war. One had the impression that the people who had lived there had just gone into another room.'[10]

Kuchumov tried to restore the old arrangement of the rooms, recording the memories of people who had worked in the Palace as servants. He staged a special exhibition of costume in the state rooms and kept the building open until late into the night, playing the music of Chaliapin on an old gramophone. And he recalled the fateful Sunday afternoon in June 1941 when news of the German invasion broke on the cheerful crowds waiting for admission. 'Everyone stood motionless', he wrote. 'Smiles disappeared. . . . The whole happy new life of summer vanished.'[11]

The weeks that followed brought a struggle to save whatever could be saved from the advancing army. Precious items were packed into crates, then into any containers that could be found. Even the trunks that the imperial family had taken with them that August morning in 1917 were pressed into service, though they were still marked with the double-headed eagle and the imperial crown. Their clothing served as emergency packaging. Working through the night under pressure, unable to show a light for fear of enemy bombing, Kuchumov sensed a presence in the silent corridors and believed that the last Tsaritsa's spirit watched over him and approved. In the early hours of 30 June he left the Alexander Palace, just as the sun rose.

The Nazis broke into the Palace on 17 September, and began the systematic removal of any furniture and other treasures which remained. The building was used as a Gestapo headquarters and prison, while the SS dug up the courtyard as a cemetery for their dead. Russian troops returned in 1944 to find the interiors in a desperate state, though the building had suffered less structural damage than the other palaces. Only the west wing had been hit by shell fire, and as evacuated treasures from all the palaces were returned, the Alexander Palace was chosen as a safe temporary store. Kuchumov began to scour Europe for items which had been stolen.

The determination to restore the palaces was alive even before the war ended, and as soon as it could, the work began. The Alexander Park was opened again in 1946, and the exterior of the Palace repaired and painted by 1949, but the work was dogged by uncertainty about the future use of the building. A museum for Pushkin, in whose honour Tsarskoe Selo had been renamed? A restored palace of the eighteenth century, stripped of all reminders of the later Tsars? At first the chosen plan would have preserved some interiors from each period of the Palace's occupation but this idea was revised while work was in progress and the best of the modern interiors, particularly those relating to the last Tsaritsa, were deliberately destroyed. Her balcony was removed. In the mind of postwar Soviet governments, a growing sensitivity attached to the places that had been most intimately connected with the last Tsar and his family. In 1951 the Alexander Palace was suddenly handed over to the Navy Department, the restoration was halted, and public access became impossible. Tomishko's New Palace on the shore at Peterhof, built for Nicholas II, had been damaged in the war but it was actually destroyed in the 1960s, and the Ipatiev House in Ekaterinburg, where the family died, was razed to the ground in the '70s.

Now, once again, the wheel is turning. In the summer of 1997, after preliminary restoration to the roof and to a few rooms, the ground floor of the east wing of the Alexander Palace was opened to the public for the first time in over fifty years. Alexandra Feodorovna's rooms had lost any semblance of the decorations she knew, and an old photograph was used in each room as a reminder of the past. In 1997 and '98, the rooms in Alexandra's suite were used to trace the history of the Palace through four generations of the imperial family, with portraits, clothing, china and original accessories going back to the time of Catherine the Great. By 1999, the decision to restore the rooms to their pre-Revolutionary condition had been made official. Elements of the previous display were then concentrated into the first room, once partitioned as Alexandra's maid's room, bathroom and dressing room, while each of the other rooms in the suite is laid out according to the old photographs, with as much of the original furniture as can be found. Paintings and ornaments have been brought out of storage and returned to their old positions and, to make up the screen of icons in the imperial bedroom, the Russian government has donated a collection of antique icons impounded at customs.

The Tsar's rooms, which complete the tour, have retained much more of their original decoration. Only the bathroom fittings are gone, and this room has been used to house a display relating to the imperial children. There are toys, clothes, a donkey harness given by the King of Italy – even Alexei's christening robe, displayed on the lace cushion that still bears the broad, white ribbons once tied around the neck of the elderly Princess Golitsina, because it was her duty to carry the baby and she was terrified that she might drop him. More has survived the years of oblivion than anyone could have dared to hope, and this is only the beginning. The restoration continues: given funds, goodwill on the part of the other palace administrations, who hold treasures from the dispersed collection, and a favourable political climate, more and more of the Alexander Palace will emerge from its long sleep, and a whole new chapter of the story will begin.

Family Trees

1: Descendants of Catherine the Great

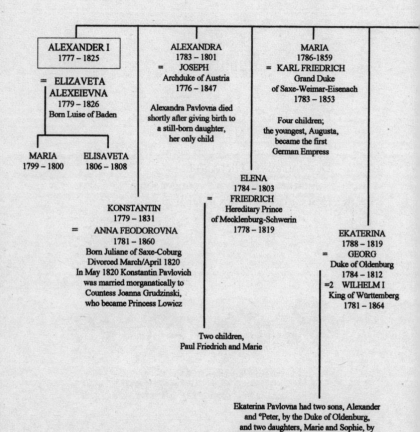

ALEXANDER I
1777 – 1825

= **ELIZAVETA
ALEXEIEVNA**
1779 – 1826
Born Luise of Baden

MARIA
1799 – 1800

ELISAVETA
1806 – 1808

ALEXANDRA
1783 – 1801
= JOSEPH
Archduke of Austria
1776 – 1847

Alexandra Pavlovna died
shortly after giving birth to
a still-born daughter,
her only child

MARIA
1786-1859
= KARL FRIEDRICH
Grand Duke
of Saxe-Weimar-Eisenach
1783 – 1853

Four children;
the youngest, Augusta,
became the first
German Empress

KONSTANTIN
1779 – 1831
= ANNA FEODOROVNA
1781 – 1860
Born Juliane of Saxe-Coburg
Divorced March/April 1820
In May 1820 Konstantin Pavlovich
was married morganatically to
Countess Joanna Grudzinski,
who became Princess Lowicz

ELENA
1784 – 1803
= FRIEDRICH
Hereditary Prince
of Mecklenburg-Schwerin
1778 – 1819

EKATERINA
1788 – 1819
= GEORG
Duke of Oldenburg
1784 – 1812
=2 WILHELM I
King of Württemberg
1781 – 1864

Two children,
Paul Friedrich and Marie

Ekaterina Pavlovna had two sons, Alexander
and °Peter, by the Duke of Oldenburg,
and two daughters, Marie and Sophie, by
King Wilhelm (who was her first cousin).
*Sophie became Queen of the Netherlands

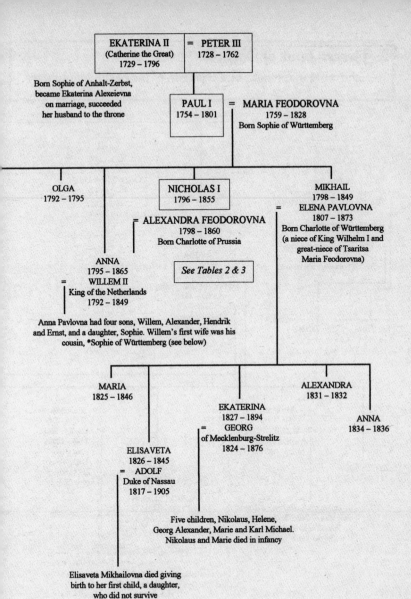

EKATERINA II
(Catherine the Great)
1729 – 1796

= PETER III
1728 – 1762

Born Sophie of Anhalt-Zerbst,
became Ekaterina Alexeievna
on marriage, succeeded
her husband to the throne

PAUL I
1754 – 1801

= MARIA FEODOROVNA
1759 – 1828
Born Sophie of Württemberg

OLGA
1792 – 1795

NICHOLAS I
1796 – 1855

= ALEXANDRA FEODOROVNA
1798 – 1860
Born Charlotte of Prussia

MIKHAIL
1798 – 1849
= ELENA PAVLOVNA
1807 – 1873
Born Charlotte of Württemberg
(a niece of King Wilhelm I and
great-niece of Tsaritsa
Maria Feodorovna)

ANNA
1795 – 1865
=
WILLEM II
King of the Netherlands
1792 – 1849

See Tables 2 & 3

Anna Pavlovna had four sons, Willem, Alexander, Hendrik
and Ernst, and a daughter, Sophie. Willem's first wife was his
cousin, *Sophie of Württemberg (see below)

MARIA
1825 – 1846

ELISAVETA
1826 – 1845
= ADOLF
Duke of Nassau
1817 – 1905

EKATERINA
1827 – 1894
= GEORG
of Mecklenburg-Strelitz
1824 – 1876

ALEXANDRA
1831 – 1832

ANNA
1834 – 1836

Five children, Nikolaus, Helene,
Georg Alexander, Marie and Karl Michael.
Nikolaus and Marie died in infancy

Elisaveta Mikhailovna died giving
birth to her first child, a daughter,
who did not survive

2: Descendants of Nicholas I –
showing marriages and children of the Tsar's daughters

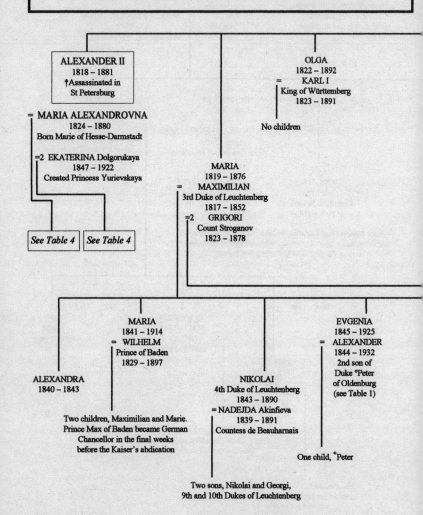

ALEXANDER II
1818 – 1881
†Assassinated in
St Petersburg

= **MARIA ALEXANDROVNA**
1824 – 1880
Born Marie of Hesse-Darmstadt

=2 **EKATERINA Dolgorukaya**
1847 – 1922
Created Princess Yurievskaya

See Table 4   *See Table 4*

OLGA
1822 – 1892
= **KARL I**
King of Württemberg
1823 – 1891

No children

MARIA
1819 – 1876
= **MAXIMILIAN**
3rd Duke of Leuchtenberg
1817 – 1852
=2 **GRIGORI**
Count Stroganov
1823 – 1878

ALEXANDRA
1840 – 1843

MARIA
1841 – 1914
= **WILHELM**
Prince of Baden
1829 – 1897

Two children, Maximilian and Marie.
Prince Max of Baden became German
Chancellor in the final weeks
before the Kaiser's abdication

NIKOLAI
4th Duke of Leuchtenberg
1843 – 1890
= **NADEJDA Akinfieva**
1839 – 1891
Countess de Beauharnais

Two sons, Nikolai and Georgi,
9th and 10th Dukes of Leuchtenberg

EVGENIA
1845 – 1925
= **ALEXANDER**
1844 – 1932
2nd son of
Duke °Peter
of Oldenburg
(see Table 1)

One child, †Peter

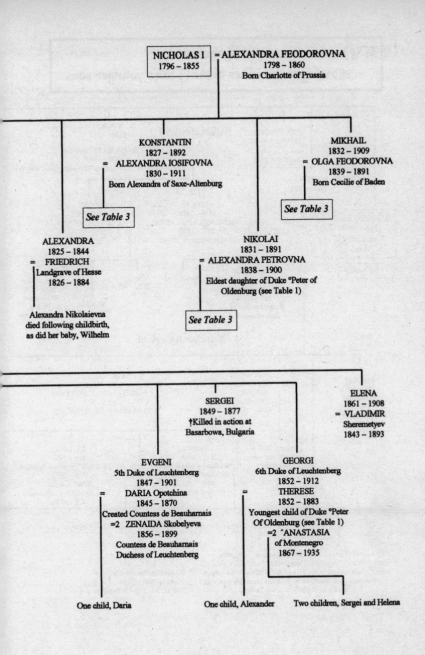

NICHOLAS I
1796 – 1855
= ALEXANDRA FEODOROVNA
1798 – 1860
Born Charlotte of Prussia

KONSTANTIN
1827 – 1892
= ALEXANDRA IOSIFOVNA
1830 – 1911
Born Alexandra of Saxe-Altenburg

See Table 3

MIKHAIL
1832 – 1909
= OLGA FEODOROVNA
1839 – 1891
Born Cecilie of Baden

See Table 3

ALEXANDRA
1825 – 1844
= FRIEDRICH
Landgrave of Hesse
1826 – 1884

NIKOLAI
1831 – 1891
= ALEXANDRA PETROVNA
1838 – 1900
Eldest daughter of Duke °Peter of
Oldenburg (see Table 1)

See Table 3

Alexandra Nikolaievna
died following childbirth,
as did her baby, Wilhelm

SERGEI
1849 – 1877
†Killed in action at
Basarbowa, Bulgaria

ELENA
1861 – 1908
= VLADIMIR
Sheremetyev
1843 – 1893

EVGENI
5th Duke of Leuchtenberg
1847 – 1901
= DARIA Opotchina
1845 – 1870
Created Countess de Beauharnais
=2 ZENAIDA Skobelyeva
1856 – 1899
Countess de Beauharnais
Duchess of Leuchtenberg

GEORGI
6th Duke of Leuchtenberg
1852 – 1912
= THERESE
1852 – 1883
Youngest child of Duke °Peter
Of Oldenburg (see Table 1)
=2 ^ANASTASIA
of Montenegro
1867 – 1935

One child, Daria

One child, Alexander

Two children, Sergei and Helena

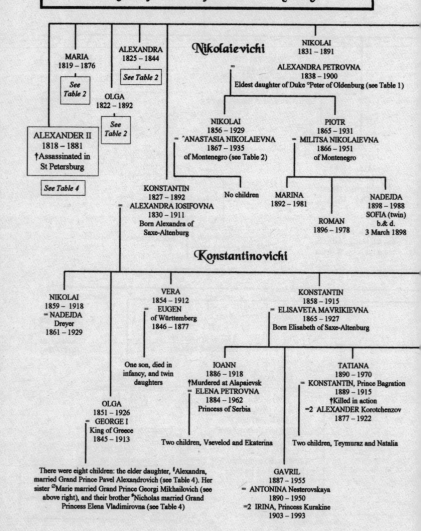

3: Descendants of Nicholas I –
showing the families of the Tsar's younger sons

Nikolaievichi

MARIA
1819 – 1876

See Table 2

ALEXANDRA
1825 – 1844

See Table 2

OLGA
1822 – 1892

See Table 2

ALEXANDER II
1818 – 1881
†Assassinated in
St Petersburg

See Table 4

NIKOLAI
1831 – 1891
=
ALEXANDRA PETROVNA
1838 – 1900
Eldest daughter of Duke °Peter of Oldenburg (see Table 1)

NIKOLAI
1856 – 1929
= ^ANASTASIA NIKOLAIEVNA
1867 – 1935
of Montenegro (see Table 2)

No children

PIOTR
1865 – 1931
= MILITSA NIKOLAIEVNA
1866 – 1951
of Montenegro

MARINA
1892 – 1981

ROMAN
1896 – 1978

NADEJDA
1898 – 1988
SOFIA (twin)
b.& d.
3 March 1898

KONSTANTIN
1827 – 1892
=
ALEXANDRA IOSIFOVNA
1830 – 1911
Born Alexandra of
Saxe-Altenburg

Konstantinovichi

NIKOLAI
1859 – 1918
= NADEJDA
Dreyer
1861 – 1929

VERA
1854 – 1912
=
EUGEN
of Württemberg
1846 – 1877

One son, died in
infancy, and twin
daughters

KONSTANTIN
1858 – 1915
=
ELISAVETA MAVRIKIEVNA
1865 – 1927
Born Elisabeth of Saxe-Altenburg

IOANN
1886 – 1918
†Murdered at Alapaievsk
= ELENA PETROVNA
1884 – 1962
Princess of Serbia

Two children, Vsevelod and Ekaterina

OLGA
1851 – 1926
= GEORGE I
King of Greece
1845 – 1913

TATIANA
1890 – 1970
= KONSTANTIN, Prince Bagration
1889 – 1915
†Killed in action
=2 ALEXANDER Korotchenzov
1877 – 1922

Two children, Teymuraz and Natalia

There were eight children: the elder daughter, ⁸Alexandra,
married Grand Prince Pavel Alexandrovich (see Table 4). Her
sister ⁰Marie married Grand Prince Georgi Mikhailovich (see
above right), and their brother ⁸Nicholas married Grand
Princess Elena Vladimirovna (see Table 4)

GAVRIL
1887 – 1955
= ANTONINA Nesterovskaya
1890 – 1950
=2 IRINA, Princess Kurakine
1903 – 1993

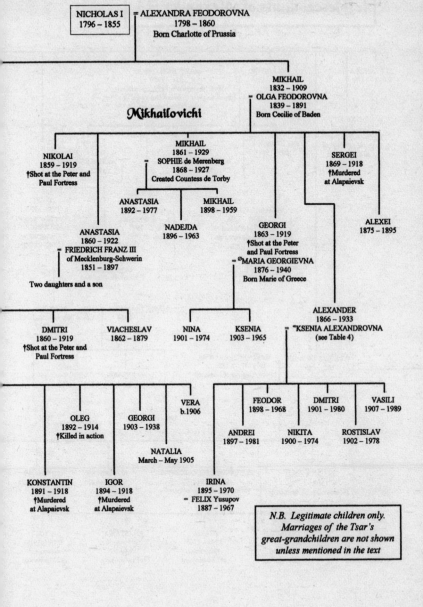

NICHOLAS I
1796 – 1855
= **ALEXANDRA FEODOROVNA**
1798 – 1860
Born Charlotte of Prussia

MIKHAIL
1832 – 1909
= **OLGA FEODOROVNA**
1839 – 1891
Born Cecilie of Baden

Mikhailovichi

NIKOLAI
1859 – 1919
†Shot at the Peter and
Paul Fortress

MIKHAIL
1861 – 1929
= **SOPHIE de Merenberg**
1868 – 1927
Created Countess de Torby

SERGEI
1869 – 1918
†Murdered
at Alapaievsk

ANASTASIA
1892 – 1977

MIKHAIL
1898 – 1959

NADEJDA
1896 – 1963

GEORGI
1863 – 1919
†Shot at the Peter
and Paul Fortress
= ⁂**MARIA GEORGIEVNA**
1876 – 1940
Born Marie of Greece

ALEXEI
1875 – 1895

ANASTASIA
1860 – 1922
= **FRIEDRICH FRANZ III**
of Mecklenburg-Schwerin
1851 – 1897

Two daughters and a son

DMITRI
1860 – 1919
†Shot at the Peter and
Paul Fortress

VIACHESLAV
1862 – 1879

NINA
1901 – 1974

KSENIA
1903 – 1965

ALEXANDER
1866 – 1933
= ⁂**KSENIA ALEXANDROVNA**
(see Table 4)

VERA
b.1906

FEODOR
1898 – 1968

DMITRI
1901 – 1980

VASILI
1907 – 1989

OLEG
1892 – 1914
†Killed in action

GEORGI
1903 – 1938

ANDREI
1897 – 1981

NIKITA
1900 – 1974

ROSTISLAV
1902 – 1978

NATALIA
March – May 1905

KONSTANTIN
1891 – 1918
†Murdered
at Alapaievsk

IGOR
1894 – 1918
†Murdered
at Alapaievsk

IRINA
1895 – 1970
= **FELIX Yusupov**
1887 – 1967

*N.B. Legitimate children only.
Marriages of the Tsar's
great-grandchildren are not shown
unless mentioned in the text*

4: Descendants of Alexander II

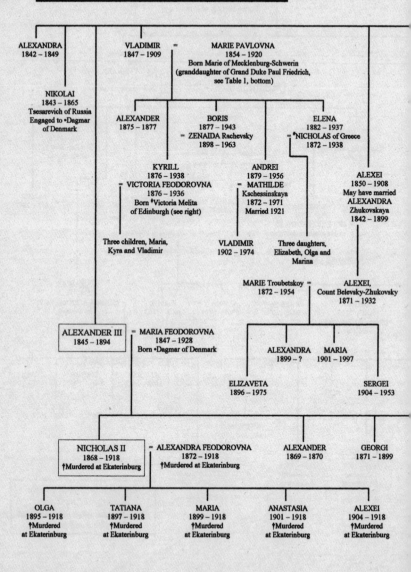

ALEXANDRA
1842 – 1849

NIKOLAI
1843 – 1865
Tsesarevich of Russia
Engaged to •Dagmar
of Denmark

VLADIMIR
1847 – 1909
=
MARIE PAVLOVNA
1854 – 1920
Born Marie of Mecklenburg-Schwerin
(granddaughter of Grand Duke Paul Friedrich,
see Table 1, bottom)

ALEXANDER
1875 – 1877

BORIS
1877 – 1943
= ZENAIDA Rachevsky
1898 – 1963

ELENA
1882 – 1937
= •NICHOLAS of Greece
1872 – 1938

KYRILL
1876 – 1938
= VICTORIA FEODOROVNA
1876 – 1936
Born †Victoria Melita
of Edinburgh (see right)

ANDREI
1879 – 1956
= MATHILDE
Kschessinskaya
1872 – 1971
Married 1921

ALEXEI
1850 – 1908
May have married
ALEXANDRA
Zhukovskaya
1842 – 1899

Three children, Maria,
Kyra and Vladimir

VLADIMIR
1902 – 1974

Three daughters,
Elizabeth, Olga and
Marina

MARIE Troubetskoy =
1872 – 1954

ALEXEI,
Count Belevsky-Zhukovsky
1871 – 1932

ALEXANDER III
1845 – 1894
= MARIA FEODOROVNA
1847 – 1928
Born •Dagmar of Denmark

ALEXANDRA
1899 – ?

MARIA
1901 – 1997

ELIZAVETA
1896 – 1975

SERGEI
1904 – 1953

NICHOLAS II
1868 – 1918
†Murdered at Ekaterinburg
= ALEXANDRA FEODOROVNA
1872 – 1918
†Murdered at Ekaterinburg

ALEXANDER
1869 – 1870

GEORGI
1871 – 1899

OLGA
1895 – 1918
†Murdered
at Ekaterinburg

TATIANA
1897 – 1918
†Murdered
at Ekaterinburg

MARIA
1899 – 1918
†Murdered
at Ekaterinburg

ANASTASIA
1901 – 1918
†Murdered
at Ekaterinburg

ALEXEI
1904 – 1918
†Murdered
at Ekaterinburg

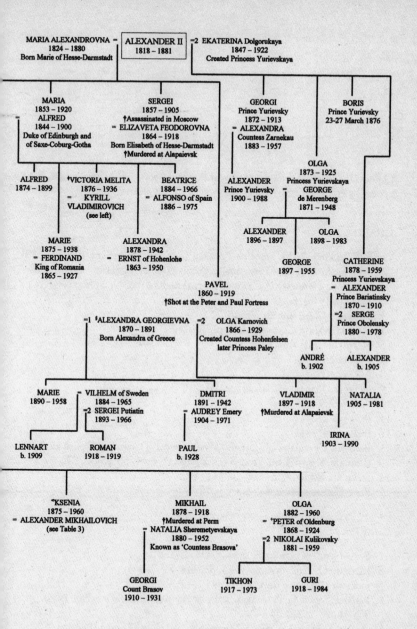

MARIA ALEXANDROVNA =
1824 – 1880
Born Marie of Hesse-Darmstadt

ALEXANDER II
1818 – 1881

=2 EKATERINA Dolgorukaya
1847 – 1922
Created Princess Yurievskaya

MARIA
1853 – 1920
ALFRED
1844 – 1900
Duke of Edinburgh and
of Saxe-Coburg-Gotha

SERGEI
1857 – 1905
†Assassinated in Moscow
= ELIZAVETA FEODOROVNA
1864 – 1918
Born Elisabeth of Hesse-Darmstadt
†Murdered at Alapaievsk

GEORGI
Prince Yurievsky
1872 – 1913
= ALEXANDRA
Countess Zarnekau
1883 – 1957

BORIS
Prince Yurievsky
23-27 March 1876

ALFRED
1874 – 1899

†VICTORIA MELITA
1876 – 1936
=
KYRILL
VLADIMIROVICH
(see left)

BEATRICE
1884 – 1966
= ALFONSO of Spain
1886 – 1975

ALEXANDER
Prince Yurievsky
1900 – 1988

OLGA
1873 – 1925
Princess Yurievskaya
= GEORGE
de Merenberg
1871 – 1948

MARIE
1875 – 1938
= FERDINAND
King of Romania
1865 – 1927

ALEXANDRA
1878 – 1942
= ERNST of Hohenlohe
1863 – 1950

ALEXANDER
1896 – 1897

OLGA
1898 – 1983

GEORGE
1897 – 1955

CATHERINE
1878 – 1959
Princess Yurievskaya
= ALEXANDER
Prince Bariatinsky
1870 – 1910
=2 SERGE
Prince Obolensky
1880 – 1978

PAVEL
1860 – 1919
†Shot at the Peter and Paul Fortress

=1 §ALEXANDRA GEORGIEVNA
1870 – 1891
Born Alexandra of Greece

=2 OLGA Karnovich
1866 – 1929
Created Countess Hohenfelsen
later Princess Paley

ANDRÉ
b. 1902

ALEXANDER
b. 1905

MARIE
1890 – 1958
= VILHELM of Sweden
1884 – 1965
=2 SERGEI Putiatin
1893 – 1966

DMITRI
1891 – 1942
= AUDREY Emery
1904 – 1971

VLADIMIR
1897 – 1918
†Murdered at Alapaievsk

NATALIA
1905 – 1981

LENNART
b. 1909

ROMAN
1918 – 1919

PAUL
b. 1928

IRINA
1903 – 1990

*KSENIA
1875 – 1960
= ALEXANDER MIKHAILOVICH
(see Table 3)

MIKHAIL
1878 – 1918
†Murdered at Perm
= NATALIA Sheremetyevskaya
1880 – 1952
Known as 'Countess Brasova'

OLGA
1882 – 1960
= †PETER of Oldenburg
1868 – 1924
=2 NIKOLAI Kulikovsky
1881 – 1959

GEORGI
Count Brasov
1910 – 1931

TIKHON
1917 – 1973

GURI
1918 – 1984

Notes

Quotations from documents in Royal Archives at Windsor (references RA) appear by gracious permission of Her Majesty The Queen

CHAPTER 1

1 S.W. Jackman (ed.), *Romanov Relations* (London, Macmillan, 1969), p. 313
2 S.W. Jackman (ed.), *Chère Annette* (Gloucester, Alan Sutton, 1990), p. 89
3 Una Pope-Hennessy, *A Czarina's Story* (London, Ivor Nicholson & Watson, 1948), p. 28
4 Jackman, *Chère Annette*, pp. 25, 72
5 Pope-Hennessy, *Czarina's Story*, p. 36
6 Jackman, *Chère Annette*, p. 18
7 *Ibid.*, p. 26
8 *Ibid.*, p. 105
9 Jackman, *Romanov Relations*, p. 190
10 *Ibid.*, p. 252
11 *Ibid.*, pp. 230–1
12 *Ibid.*, pp. 312–13
13 Baroness Georgiana Bloomfield, *Reminiscences of Court and Diplomatic Life* (London, Kegan, Paul, Trench & Co., 1883), vol 1, pp. 254–5, 232
14 Jackman, *Romanov Relations*, p. 314
15 Pope-Hennessy, *Czarina's Story*, p. 27

CHAPTER 2

1 Pope-Hennessy, *Czarina's Story*, p. 29
2 Bloomfield, *Reminiscences*, vol. I, pp. 244–5
3 Jackman, *Romanov Relations*, p. 345
4 Baroness Sophie Buxhoeveden, *Before the Storm* (London, Macmillan, 1938), pp. 315–16
5 Andrei Maylunas, & Sergei Mironenko, *A Lifelong Passion* (London, Weidenfeld & Nicolson, 1996), pp. 10–11
6 *Ibid.*, p. 164

CHAPTER 3

1 Elizabeth Narishkin-Kurakin, *Under Three Tsars* (New York, Dutton, 1931), p. 25
2 Jackman, *Romanov Relations*, p. 95
3 *Ibid.*
4 *Ibid.*, p. 98
5 Jackman, *Chère Annette*, p. 97
6 Jackman, *Romanov Relations*, pp. 153, 159
7 E.M. Almedingen, *Alexander II* (London, Bodley Head, 1962), p. 352
8 Baroness Stackelberg, *The Life of Carmen Sylva* (London, Kegan Paul, 1890), p. 74
9 *Ibid.*, p. 77

CHAPTER 4

1 Pope-Hennessy, *Czarina's Story*, p. 37
2 Jackman, *Chère Annette*, pp. 26, 91, 142
3 Almedingen, *Alexander II*, p. 29
4 *Ibid.*, p. 34
5 E.A. Brayley Hodgetts, *The Court of Russia in the Nineteenth Century*, vol. II (London, Methuen, 1908), p. 12
6 Almedingen, *Alexander II*, p. 36
7 Brayley Hodgetts, p. 21; Almedingen, *Alexander II*, p. 46
8 Almedingen, *Alexander II*, p. 53
9 *Ibid.*, p. 58
10 Jackman, *Romanov Relations*, pp. 283, 284, 285
11 *Ibid.*, p. 288. The letter continues, 'In a few days we are expecting Marie; pray God that everything may succeed according to our wishes and our hopes.' There were several Maries in Nicholas' life, but Jackman takes this to be a reference to Marie of Hesse and if he is right, this would suggest that Marie visited Russia while Alexander was in England, before the engagement negotiations began. A later letter, written by Nicholas in 1840, suggests that he has not yet met the Princess.
12 *Ibid.*, p. 301
13 The Dean of Windsor and Hector Bolitho (eds), *Later Letters of Lady Augusta Stanley 1864–1876* (London, Jonathan Cape, 1929), p. 204
14 Almedingen, *Alexander II*, p. 65
15 M. Iroshnikov, L. Protsai and Y. Shelayev, *The Sunset of the Romanov Dynasty* (Moscow, Terra, 1992), p. 55

CHAPTER 5

In 1951 E. Fricero of Nice, a descendant of Josephine Fricero, whose family still believe that she was Nicholas I's daughter, wrote and published a detailed account in French of the Tsesarevich's last year, based on the memoirs of Feodor Oom and other members of the suite, and on nineteenth-century documents. This account of Nikolai's travels, and of his death, is based on Fricero's pamphlet.

1   E. Fricero, *Nicolas Alexandrovich* (Nice, Meyerbeer, 1951), p. 2 (author's translation)
2   Almedingen, *Alexander II*, p. 206
3   Jackman, *Romanov Relations*, p. 312
4   A.F. Tiutcheva, *Pre Dvore Dvuch Imperatorov* (Moscow, Muisl, 1990), pp. 102–3 (author's translation)
5   Fricero, *Nicolas*, p. 6
6   Quoted in 'Nixa, Minny and Sacha' by Aliya Barkovetz, in *Maria Feodorovna, Empress of Russia*, Exhibition Catalogue, Christiansborg Palace, Copenhagen, 1997, p. 74
7   Fricero, *Nicolas*, p. 2
8   Barkovetz, 'Nixa, Minny and Sacha', pp. 74–6
9   *Ibid.*, p. 76
10 *Ibid.*, p. 80
11 *Ibid.*
12 *Ibid.*, p. 82
13 'Maria Feodorovna through Diaries and Personal Letters' by Preben Ulstrup in *Maria Feodorovna*, p. 112
14 *Ibid.*
15 Fricero, *Nicolas*, p. 10
16 *Ibid.*, p. 7
17 *Ibid.*, p. 15
18 Ulstrup, 'Maria Feodorovna through Diaries and Personal Letters', p. 114
19 Barkovetz, 'Nixa, Minny and Sacha', p. 79
20 *Ibid.*, p. 80
21 *Ibid.*, p. 84
22 Countess Kleinmichel, *Memories of a Shipwrecked World* (London, Brentano's, 1923), p. 49
23 Barkovetz, 'Nixa, Minny and Sacha', p. 82
24 *Ibid.*, p. 84
25 *Ibid.*, p. 84
26 *Ibid.*, pp. 84, 86; Marie left Russia with an elderly aunt, and in Paris she met and married Paul Demidov, Prince of San-Donato. She died in

childbirth in 1868, leaving a son, Elim, who was said to be his mother's double.

27 'The Empress Maria Feodorovna in Memoirs of Russian Political and Public Figures' by Andrey D. Yanovsky, in *Maria Feodorovna*, p. 240

28 *Ibid.*, p. 242

29 Ulstrup, 'Maria Feodorovna through Diaries and Personal Letters', p. 120

30 Barkovetz, 'Nixa, Minny and Sacha', p. 86

CHAPTER 6

1 Anthony Lambton, *The Mountbattens* (London, Constable, 1989), p. 44. The old rumours about Alexander and Marie of Hesse are still repeated, and some still believe them. Much that is said, on both sides of the argument, is demonstrably false, but as Grand Duke Ludwig accepted the children as his own the onus of proof is on the other side; as yet they have produced no convincing evidence, only speculation.

2 Almedingen, *Alexander II*, p. 63

3 Richard Hough, *Louis and Victoria* (London, Hutchinson, 1974), p. 4

4 Princess Alice, *Alice, Princess of Great Britain, Grand Duchess of Hesse, Letters to Her Majesty The Queen* (London, John Murray, 1897), p. 226

5 Irina Bogatskaia, *The Moscow Kremlin in Watercolour* (Paris, Alain de Gourcuff, 1994), pp. 138, 140

6 Alexander II & Grand Prince Konstantin Nikolaievich, *1857–1961; Peesma, Dnevniki* (Moscow, Terra, 1994), p. 53 (author's translation)

7 Marie, Princess of Battenberg, *Reminiscences* (London, Allen & Unwin, 1925), pp. 5–6

8 Marie, Princess of Battenberg, *Reminiscences*, pp. 46, 47–8

9 Princess Alice, *Alice, Grossherzogin von Hessen und bei Rhein; Mittheilungen aus Ihrem Leben und aus Ihren Briefen* (Darmstadt, Arnold Bergsträsser, 1884), p.102 (author's translation)

10 Marie, Princess of Battenberg, *Reminiscences*, pp. 108–9

11 *Ibid.*, p. 110–11

12 *Ibid.*, p. 114

13 Roger Fulford (ed.), *Darling Child* (London, Evans, 1976), p. 163

CHAPTER 7

1 Maurice Paléologue, *The Tragic Romance of Alexander II* (London, Hutchinson, c. 1923), p. 118

2 Almedingen, *Alexander II*, pp. 288–9

3 *Ibid.*, p. 295

4 Fulford (ed.), *Darling Child*, pp. 264–5

5 Almedingen, *Alexander II*, p. 298

6 *Ibid.*, p. 299

7 Paléologue, *Tragic Romance*, p. 107

8 Fulford (ed.), *Darling Child*, p. 268; Narishkin-Kurakin, *Under Three Tsars*, p. 50

9 Alexander Tarsaïdzé, *Katia, Wife Before God* (New York, Macmillan, 1970), p. 211. The account given in chapters six and seven of Alexander's relationship with Ekaterina is largely based on Tarsaïdzé's book, which differs in some interesting respects from the standard view. Tarsaïdzé makes it seem unlikely, for example, that Ekaterina actually moved into the Winter Palace before the Tsaritsa's death – something most accounts accept without question. But the book is based on some very unusual source material, including lengthy quotations from the private correspondence of Alexander and Ekaterina, so its claims have to be taken seriously.

CHAPTER 8

1 Jackman, *Romanov Relations*, p. 141

2 *Ibid.*, p. 145

3 Brayley Hodgetts, *The Court of Russia in the Nineteenth Century*, p. 136

4 Bloomfield, *Reminiscences*, vol. I, pp. 290–1

5 Buxhoeveden, *Before the Storm*, pp. 220–1

6 Alexander II & Grand Prince Konstantin Nikolaievich, *Peesma, Dnevniki*, p. 65 (author's translation)

7 *Ibid.*, p. 209 (author's translation)

8 Almedingen, *Alexander II*, p. 120

9 *Ibid.*, p. 159

10 Kleinmichel, *Memories of a Shipwrecked World*, pp. 25–6

11 Jacques Ferrand,*Il Est Toujours Des Romanovs* (Paris, Jacques Ferrand, 1995), pp. 248–9 (author's translation)

12 Tarsaïdzé, *Katia, Wife Before God*, p. 217

CHAPTER 9

1 Pauline Gray, *The Grand Duke's Woman* (London, Macdonald and Jane's, 1976), p. 39

2 Pope-Hennessy, *Czarina's Story*, pp. 41, 45

3 Tiutcheva, *Pre Dvore Dvuch Imperatorov*, pp. 72–3 (author's translation)

4 Ulstrup, 'Maria Feodorovna through Diaries and Personal Letters', p. 142
5 Ian Vorres, *The Last Grand Duchess* (London, Hutchinson, 1964), p. 39
6 HRH Prince Christopher of Greece, *The Memoirs of HRH Prince Christopher of Greece* (London, Right Book Club, 1938), p. 67
7 Buxhoeveden, *Before the Storm*, pp. 263–6
8 Gray, *The Grand Duke's Woman*, p. 72
9 *Ibid.*, p. 100

CHAPTER 10

1 Quoted in Emmanuel Ducamp (ed.), *The Winter Palace* (Paris, Alain de Gourcuff, 1995), pp. 13–14, 19–20
2 W.A.L. Seaman (ed.), *The Russian Journal of Lady Londonderry* (London, John Murray, 1973), p. 54
3 Quoted in Larissa Yermilova, *The Last Tsar* (London, Parkstone Planeta, 1996), p. 83
4 Stella King, *Princess Marina* (London, Cassell, 1969), pp. 39–40
5 H. Jones Thaddeus, *Recollections of a Court Painter* (London, Bodley Head, 1912), pp. 112–13
6 Grand Duke Kyrill, *My Life in Russia's Service* (London, Selwyn & Blount, 1939), p. 13
7 Grand Duchess Marie of Russia, *Things I Remember* (London, Cassell, 1930), p. 11
8 Edward J. Bing (ed.), *The Letters of Tsar Nicholas and Empress Marie* (London, Nicholson & Watson, 1937), p. 54
9 Vorres, *The Last Grand Duchess*, p. 23
10 *Ibid.*, p. 80. Descendants of Mrs Franklin live in Russia still and they believe that she was buried in Gatchina cemetery, though the grave is now lost. It was Grand Princess Olga who described the burial under a tree in the park.
11 Princess Alice, *Letters*, p. 138
12 Maylunas & Mironenko, *A Lifelong Passion*, p. 133
13 Bing (ed.), *Letters of Tsar Nicholas and Empress Marie*, p. 146
14 Baroness Sophie Buxhoeveden, *The Life & Tragedy of Alexandra Feodorovna* (London, Longmans, 1928), p. 87
15 Nicholas II, *Dnevniki Imperatora Nikolaya II* (Moscow, Orbita, 1991), p. 231 (author's translation)
16 *The Times*, 6 January 1905
17 M. Eagar, *Six Years at the Russian Court* (London, Hurst & Blackett, 1906), pp. 282–3

CHAPTER 11

1   Marie, Queen of Romania, *The Story of My Life* (London, Cassell, 1934), vol. 1, p. 98
2   H.R.H. Princess Wilhelmina of the Netherlands, *Lonely But Not Alone* (London, Hutchinson, 1959), pp. 67–8
3   RA Z25/80
4   RA Add A25/325; 13 January 1872
5   *Alice, Grossherzogin von Hessen und bei Rhein*, p. 313
6   RA Z28/24; Crown Princess Victoria to the Queen, 10 May 1874
7   RA H42/25; 16 September 1874
8   Bülow's anecdote, as quoted in Lambton's *The Mountbattens*, describes Marie pointing out the likeness to the Grancy family in the profile of her sleeping husband. It sounds like the sort of thing she might have said but cannot possibly be true as it stands since he places it in the mid-1860s, when Marie was still a child.
9   Tiutcheva, *Pre Dvore Dvuch Imperatorov*, p. 103 (author's translation). In itself this is only a small anecdote, one of many, but it is interesting that it was set down in writing long before anyone knew that Nikolai really would die young, or had reason to speculate on the relationship between Alexander and Vladimir.
10 Vorres, *The Last Grand Duchess*, p. 58
11 Grand Duchess George, *A Romanov Diary* (New York, Atlantic International Publications, 1988), p. 43
12 Kaiser Wilhelm II, *My Early Life* (London, Methuen, 1926), p. 320
13 Lubov Millar, *Grand Duchess Elizabeth* (Redding, California, Nicodemus Publication Society 1991), p. 59

CHAPTER 12

Factual details and the sequence of events given here are based on the Tsar's diary, as quoted in *A Lifelong Passion*, his letters to his mother (see note 3), *The Times Weekly Edition*, and Queen Victoria's journal, quoted in *The Letters of Queen Victoria*, 3rd Series 1886–1901 (London, John Murray, 1931)
1   Maylunas & Mironenko, *A Lifelong Passion*, p. 45
2   Bing (ed.), *Letters of Tsar Nicholas and Empress Marie*, p. 75
3   Maylunas & Mironenko, *A Lifelong Passion*, p. 47
4   Nicholas's diary, quoted in *ibid.*, p. 47
5   Bing (ed.), *Tsar Nicholas and Empress Marie*, p. 76
6   *The Letters of the Tsaritsa to the Tsar* (London, Duckworth, 1923), *The*

Letters of the Tsar to the Tsaritsa (London, John Lane, The Bodley Head, 1929); various quotations from April 1915 and 1916

7 *The Times Weekly Edition*, 27 April 1894, p. 329
8 Maylunas & Mironenko, *A Lifelong Passion*, p. 50
9 *Ibid.*, p. 52
10 *Ibid.*, p. 51
11 *Ibid.*, p. 50
12 *Ibid.*, p. 54

CHAPTER 13

1 Agnes de Stoekl, *Not All Vanity* (London, John Murray, 1950), p. 115; Anna Viroubova, *Memories of the Russian Court* (London, Macmillan, 1923), p. 37
2 Jackman, *Chère Annette*, p. 99. There has always been a tradition, dismissed by most serious historians, which questions the death of Alexander I. It was said that he staged his own death to escape from the burden of office and walked away from Taganrog under cover of darkness, later settling in Siberia as Feodor Kusmich, a hermit. Nicholas I is said to have made a special trip to meet Kusmich and to have been convinced that it was his brother. Either way, the Crimea played a part in ending the Tsar's reign.
3 Marina Zemlyanichenko & Nikolai Kalinin, *The Romanovs and the Crimea* (Moscow, Kruk, 1993), pp. 37, 158
4 Quoted in Vladimir Poliakoff, *The Empress Marie of Russia and Her Times* (London, Thornton Butterworth, 1926), p. 86
5 According to Zemlyanichenko & Kalinin, *The Romanovs and the Crimea*, Alexander III and Marie were accompanied only by Ksenia and Mikhail. In mid-September the imperial children were all together at Peterhof, without their parents. No precise date is given for the visit to the Crimea: it does seem rather odd that the other children were not present, but the authors of the book had access to original sources, including Alexander III's diary.
6 Quoted in Zemlyanichenko & Kalinin, *The Romanovs and the Crimea*, p. 57 (author's translation)
7 Quoted in Millar, *Grand Duchess Elizabeth*, p. 42
8 Maylunas & Mironenko, *A Lifelong Passion*, p. 101
9 Bing (ed.), *Letters of the Tsar and the Empress Marie*, p. 146
10 Alexander, Grand Duke of Russia, *Once a Grand Duke* (New York, Farrar & Rinehart, 1932), pp. 133, 204

11 de Stoekl, *Not All Vanity*, pp. 119–20
12 Viroubova, *Memories of the Russian Court*, p. 44
13 de Stoekl, *Not All Vanity*, p. 139

CHAPTER 14

1 See Samuel Hoare, *The Fourth Seal* (London, Heinemann, 1930), pp. 314–17
2 Brayley Hodgetts, *The Court of Russia in the Nineteenth Century*, pp. 231–2
3 A.A. Mossolov, *At the Court of the Last Tsar* (London, Methuen, 1935), p. 80
4 It is strange that so thin a man as Sergei should have thought it necessary to wear a corset – if indeed he did. We tend to jump to the most sensational conclusions, but there are possibilities other than effeminacy, or homosexuality, which could explain it. Sergei may simply have suffered from back trouble.
5 Alexander, Grand Duke of Russia, *Once a Grand Duke*, pp. 139–40
6 Tiutcheva, *Pre Dvore Dvuch Imperatorov*, p. 156; by tradition Russian parents did not attend the christening service
7 *Alice, Grossherzogin von Hessen und bei Rhein*, p. 102
8 Princess Alice, *Letters*, p. 77
9 E.M. Almedingen, *An Unbroken Unity* (London, Bodley Head, 1964), p. 30
10 'Dostoevsky and the Imperial Family' by Gennady Belovolov, in *Maria Feodorovna* (Copenhagen, 1997), p. 266
11 Ernst Ludwig, Großherzog von Hessen und bei Rhein, *Erinnertes* (Darmstadt, Eduard Roether, 1983), pp. 76–7
12 *Alice, Grossherzogin von Hessen und bei Rhein*, p. 77
13 Richard Hough (ed.), *Advice to a Granddaughter* (London, Heinemann, 1975), p. 56
14 Alexander Bokhanov, 'Ella & Sergei: a dynastic marriage of love . . . or convenience', in *Royalty*, vol. 12, no. 11, 1994, p. 62
15 Frances Dimond & Roger Taylor, *Crown & Camera* (London, Penguin, 1987), p. 175
16 Roger Fulford (ed.), *Beloved Mama* (London, Evans, 1981), p. 153
17 Bokhanov, 'Ella & Sergei', p. 60
18 *Ibid.*, p. 62. Both parents had of course been dead for some years.
19 David Chavchavadze, *The Grand Dukes* (New York, Atlantic International Publications, 1990), p. 121
20 Bokhanov, 'Ella & Sergei', p. 62
21 Millar, *Grand Duchess Elizabeth*, p. 32

22 Ludwig, *Erinnertes*, p. 76
23 Both quotations from Millar, *Grand Duchess Elizabeth*, pp. 62–3
24 *Ibid.*, pp. 67–8
25 See John Van Der Kiste, *The Romanovs 1818–1959* (Stroud, Sutton Publishing, 1998), p. 137
26 Marie, Queen of Romania, *The Story of My Life*, vol I, p. 94
27 Grand Duke Cyril, *My Life In Russia's Service*, p. 13
28 Grand Duchess George, *A Romanov Diary*, p. 85
29 Meriel Buchanan, *Queen Victoria's Relations* (London, Cassell, 1954), p. 98
30 Princess Radziwill (writing as Count Paul Vassili), *Behind the Veil at the Russian Court* (London, Cassell, 1913), p. 272
31 Grand Duchess Marie of Russia, *Things I Remember*, p. 18
32 Princess Radziwill, *Behind the Veil*, p. 127
33 Ludwig, *Erinnertes*, p. 76
34 Maylunas & Mironenko, *A Lifelong Passion*, p. 149
35 Grand Duchess Marie of Russia, *Things I Remember*, p. 55
36 RA Z90/ 86
37 Grand Duchess Marie of Russia, *Things I Remember*, p. 17
38 Private information
39 Bokhanov, 'Ella & Sergei', p. 64
40 Buxhoeveden, *Before the Storm*, p. 272
41 Maylunas & Mironenko, *A Lifelong Passion*, p. 267

CHAPTER 15

1 Grand Duchess Marie of Russia, *Things I Remember*, pp. 24–5
2 RA Add A20/1625; Marie, Duchess of Edinburgh to Queen Victoria, 17 July 1884
3 *Ibid.*
4 *Ibid.*
5 *Ibid.*
6 *Ibid.*
7 Prince Felix Youssoupoff, *Lost Splendour* (London, Jonathan Cape, 1953), p. 83
8 Grand Duchess Marie of Russia, *Things I Remember*, p. 30
9 Vorres, *The Last Grand Duchess*, p. 89
10 Marie, Queen of Romania, *The Story of My Life*, vol. II, p. 76
11 Grand Duchess Marie of Russia, *Things I Remember*, p. 22
12 Prince Felix Youssoupoff, *Lost Splendour*, p. 84
13 *Ibid.*, p. 98

CHAPTER 16

1 Alexander, Grand Duke of Russia, *Once a Grand Duke*, p. 139
2 Alexander II & Grand Prince Konstantin Nikolaievich, *Peesma, Dnevniki*, p. 17 (author's translation)
3 Marie of Battenberg, *Reminiscences*, pp. 5–6
4 Kleinmichel, *Memories of a Shipwrecked World*, p. 49
5 *Jewels of the Romanovs* (Exhibition catalogue, The American-Russian Cultural Cooperation Foundation, 1997), p. 13
6 *Ibid.*, pp. 12–13
7 *Ibid.*, p. 13
8 John S. Manion, Jr. (collected, transcribed and annotated by), 'Custer, Cody and the Grand Duke Alexis by Elizabeth B. Custer', *Research Review, The Journal of the Little Big Horn Association*, vol. 4#1 (New Series), January 1990
9 *Jewels*, p. 14
10 Dean of Windsor and Hector Bolitho (eds), *Later Letters of Lady Augusta Stanley*, p. 209
11 HRH Prince Nicholas of Greece, *My Fifty Years* (London, Hutchinson, 1926), p. 42
12 Wilhelm II, *My Early Life*, p. 320
13 Tarsaïdzé, *Katia, Wife Before God*, pp. 283–4
14 Grand Duke Cyril, *My Life In Russia's Service*, pp. 42–3
15 Alexander, Grand Duke of Russia, *Once a Grand Duke*, pp. 151–2
16 Maylunas & Mironenko, *A Lifelong Passion*, p. 268
17 Mossolov, *At the Court of the Last Tsar*, p. 79
18 Maylunas & Mironenko, *A Lifelong Passion*, pp. 240, 314

CHAPTER 17

The facts and sequence of events in this chapter are based on the Tsar's letters, Alexandre Spiridovitch, *Les Dernières Années de la Cour de Tzarskoie-Sélo* (Paris, Payot, 1928); Viroubova, *Memories of the Russian Court* and *A Romanov Diary*.
1 *Letters of Tsar Nicholas and Empress Marie*, p. 248
2 *Ibid.*, p. 249
3 *Ibid.*, p. 250
4 Tatiana Botkine, *Au Temps des Tsars* (Paris, Grasset, 1980), p. 52

CHAPTER 18

1 Kleinmichel, *Memories of a Shipwrecked World*, p. 207

2 Mossolov, *At the Court of the Last Tsar*, p. 78

3 Maylunas & Mironenko, *A Lifelong Passion*, p. 161

4 RA Add A4/156

5 Maylunas & Mironenko, *A Lifelong Passion*, p. 199

6 Marie, Queen of Romania, *The Story of My Life*, vol. II, p. 74

7 Anthony Glyn, *Eleanor Glyn* (London, Hutchinson, 1955), p. 178. The idea of Alexandra Feodorovna as a seductive Balkan Queen touring Europe in search of a pure young Englishman to father her son is irresistible, but highly unlikely.

8 John Van Der Kiste, *Princess Victoria Melita* (Stroud, Sutton, 1991), p. 90

9 Consuelo Vanderbilt Balsan, *The Glitter and the Gold* (London, Heinemann, 1953), p. 127

10 Anna Stancioff, *Recollections of a Bulgarian Diplomatist's Wife* (London, Hutchinson, nd), p. 223

11 Mossolov, *At the Court of the Last Tsar*, p. 79

12 Maurice Paléologue, *An Ambassador's Memoirs* (London, Hutchinson, 1923), vol. I, pp. 71–2

13 Maylunas & Mironenko, *A Lifelong Passion*, pp. 438–9

14 *The Letters of the Tsaritsa to the Tsar*, p. 137

15 *Ibid.*, pp. 188, 240

16 *The Russian Diary of an Englishman* (London, Heinemann, 1919), p. 33

17 *Letters of the Tsaritsa to the Tsar*; *The Letters of the Tsar to the Tsaritsa*; various letters, June 1916

18 Mossolov, *At the Court of the Last Tsar*, p. 47

19 Van der Kiste, *Princess Victoria Melita*, p. 117

20 Paléologue, *An Ambassador's Memoirs*, vol. III, p. 162. Princess Paley, Dmitri's stepmother, said that she had written the petition herself, but it is usually attributed to Marie.

21 Maylunas & Mironenko, *A Lifelong Passion*, p. 532

22 Mathilde Kschessinska, *Dancing in Petersburg* (London, Doubleday, 1961), p. 190

23 Vorres, *The Last Grand Duchess*, p. 167

24 Stancioff, *Recollections of a Bulgarian Diplomatist's Wife*, pp. 151–2

CHAPTER 19

1 *Letters of the Tsaritsa to the Tsar*, p. 279

2 *Letters of the Tsar to the Tsaritsa*, p. 243

3   *The Russian Diary of an Englishman*, p. 93
4   See Rosemary and Donald Crawford, *Michael and Natasha* (London, Weidenfeld & Nicolson, 1997)
5   *The Russian Diary of an Englishman*, p. 93
6   Grand Duchess Marie, *A Princess in Exile* (New York, The Viking Press, 1932), p. 20
7   Grand Duchess George, *A Romanov Diary*, p. 239
8   Frederick Collins, *This King Business* (London, T. Werner Laurie, 1923), p. 8
9   *Ibid.*, p. 5
10 Grand Duchess Marie, *A Princess in Exile*, p. 278

CHAPTER 20

In Russia both mother and daughter would have been 'Ekaterina Yurievskaya'. The spelling used here for the younger Catherine is the Anglicized spelling she used herself in later years.
1   The genealogies all cite St Petersburg as Catherine's birthplace, but she herself believed that she was born in the Crimea. This seems likely, given that she was born in September when the Tsar and his family made their autumn visits to Livadia.
2   Grand Duke Serge, *Once a Grand Duke*, pp. 50–1
3   Princess Catherine Yourievsky, *My Book* (London, Eveleigh, Nash & Grayson, 1924), p. 6
4   Serge Obolensky, *One Man in his Time* (London, Hutchinson, 1960), p. 50
5   Maylunas & Mironenko, *A Lifelong Passion*, p. 133
6   Princess A.M. Bariatinsky, *My Russian Life* (London, Hutchinson, 1923), p. 156
7   Vorres, *The Last Grand Duchess*, p. 98
8   Obolensky, *One Man in his Time*, p. 194
9   *Ibid.*, p. 193
10 *Ibid.*, p. 208
11 Princess Catherine Yourievsky, *My Book*, p. 115
12 Obolensky, *One Man in his Time*, p. 238
13 Robert Rhodes James (ed.), *Chips: The Diaries of Sir Henry Channon* (London, Weidenfeld & Nicolson, 1967)

CHAPTER 21

1   Kleinmichel, *Memories of a Shipwrecked World*, p. 151
2   RA Add A20/1625

3 Lubov Millar, *Grand Duchess Elizabeth*, p. 68
4 Marie of Romania, vol. I, pp. 214–15
5 Richard Hough (ed.), *Advice to a Granddaughter* (London, Heinemann, 1975), p. 112
6 RA Z90/27; Grand Princess Elisabeth to Queen Victoria, July 1892
7 RA Z90/46; the same, 9/21 May 1893
8 RA Z90/62; the same, 8/20 November 1893
9 Grand Prince Pavel's letter and the photograph of his children are in a volume entitled 'Photographs and Portraits', vol. 7/65, p. 8, in the Royal Photograph Collection
10 Grand Duchess Marie of Russia, *Things I Remember*, p. 11
11 *Ibid.*, p. 12
12 Hugo Mager, *Elizabeth, Grand Duchess of Russia* (New York, Carroll & Graf, 1998), p. 214
13 Maylunas & Mironenko, *A Lifelong Passion*, p. 302
14 *Ibid.*, p. 303
15 Mark D. Steinberg and Vladimir M. Khrustalëv (eds), *The Fall of the Romanovs* (Yale University Press, 1995), p. 91
16 Princess Irina Paley, 'Souvenirs de mon père', in Jacques Ferrand, *Le Grand-duc Paul Alexandrovitch de Russie* (Paris, Jacques Ferrand, 1993), p. 12

CHAPTER 22

1 The Dean of Windsor & Hector Bolitho (eds), *Later Letters of Lady Augusta Stanley*, p. 217
2 *Kniaz Oleg* (St Petersburg, 1915, reprinted by Kazan, Star, 1995), p. 43
3 Buxhoeveden, *Before the Storm*, p. 146
4 Maylunas & Mironenko, *A Lifelong Passion*, p. 231
5 *Ibid.*, p. 240
6 *Ibid.*, p. 305
7 Bariatinsky, *My Russian Life*, p. 168
8 Buxhoeveden, *Before the Storm*, p. 153
9 *Letters of Tsar Nicholas and Empress Marie*, p. 263
10 Maylunas & Mironenko, *A Lifelong Passion*, p. 353
11 Buxhoeveden, *Before the Storm*, p. 225
12 See R.G. Krassioukov's article, originally published in a Russian journal in 1994, reprinted in French translation in *Il est Toujours des Romanovs*, pp. 248–54

CHAPTER 23

Most of the details in this chapter are based on Princess Elena's own account of her adventures, published in the French magazine *L'Illustré* in the 1950s in six parts, under the title 'J'étais à Iékatérinburg'.

1   Postcard dated 15/28 January 1914; private collection
2   'J'étais à Iékatérinburg', part 3, p. 30
3   *Ibid.*
4   *Ibid.*
5   Jarko Michich and the other members of the Serb Military Mission had also survived their captivity in Perm: Captain Paul Bulygin records their arrival in Harbin in June 1920.
6   Public Record Office FO 371 3330
7   'J'étais à Iékatérinburg', part 6, p. 33
8   *Ibid.*

CHAPTER 24

1   Eugénie de Grèce, *Le Tsarévitch; enfant martyr* (Perrin, Paris, 1990), p. 198
2   Buxhoeveden, *Before the Storm*, p. 237
3   *Kniaz Oleg*, pp. 37–8. Ioann, Ganya (Gavril), Kostya (Konstantin) and Igor were Oleg's brothers, A.M. (Maximov) their tutor, and Tanya (Tatiana) their sister. The mention of Sakharov is an interesting hint of feeling about the war then in progress: he was the War Minister. An English schoolboy in 1914 would have had a very similar reaction to his first glimpse of Kitchener.
4   Buxhoeveden, *Before the Storm*, pp. 246–7
5   Maylunas & Mironenko, *A Lifelong Passion*, p. 296
6   Kellogg Durland, *Royal Romances of To-day* (London, T. Werner Laurie, nd), p. 208; references to ages and events in the text suggest the date was 1911.
7   Pierre Gilliard, *Thirteen Years at the Russian Court* (London, Hutchinson, nd), p. 126
8   Maylunas & Mironenko, *A Lifelong Passion*, pp. 410, 411; P.V.P. was the tutor Piotr Vasilievich Petrov.
9   Gilliard, *Thirteen Years at the Russian Court*, p. 149
10   *Letters of the Tsar to the Tsaritsa*, p. 102
11   Maylunas & Mironenko, *A Lifelong Passion*, p. 481
12   Steinberg & Khrustalëv, *The Fall of the Romanovs*, p. 409, n. 53
13   *Ibid.*, p. 97
14   Gilliard, *Thirteen Years at the Russian Court*, p. 196
15   Viroubova, *Memories of the Russian Court*, p. 215

16 J.C. Trewin, *Tutor to the Tsarevich* (London, Macmillan, 1975), p. 52
17 See *Le Tsarévitch; enfant martyr*. The story that Derevenko became a
    wealthy Commissar, seen by Grand Prince Paul Alexandrovich in prison at
    Christmas 1918, is based on a misreading of an anecdote in Princess Paley's
    Memories of Russia. What she says, both in the English translation and in
    the original French, is that her husband had a chance encounter with 'an
    assistant to the sailor Derevenko', not with the man himself.
18 Baroness Sophie Buxhoeveden, *Left Behind* (London, Longmans, 1929), p. 29
19 Alexei's diary for 3/16 January–30 March/12 April 1918 (the day he fell
    victim to an attack of internal bleeding which almost killed him) is
    published in full in *Le Tsarévitch; enfant martyr*, in French. The original was
    written in Russian. The quotations that follow on p. 247 are all drawn from
    Alexei's diary.
20 Olga Nikolaievna from Tobolsk, 4/17 April 1918, printed in *The Romanovs;
    documents and photographs relating to the Russian Imperial House* (Sotheby's,
    London, 1990), item 35
21 Trewin, *Tutor to the Tsarevich*, p. 95
22 Eugénie de Grèce, *Le Tsarévitch; enfant martyr*, p. 278
23 *Ibid.*, p. 279
24 Steinberg & Khrustalëv, *The Fall of the Romanovs*, p. 273
25 Trewin, *Tutor to the Tsarevich*, p. 111

CHAPTER 25

1 Madame la Comtesse de Choiseul-Gouffier, *Historical Memoirs of the
   Emperor Alexander I and the Court of Russia* (Chicago, A.C. McClurg,
   1900), pp. 271–2.
2 Jackman, *Romanov Relations*, pp. 145, 252
3 *The Russian Journal of Lady Londonderry 1836–7*, p. 54
4 *Dnevniki Imperatora Nikolaya II*, p. 50. The date of their arrival was 22
   November by the old calendar then in use in Russia – 3 December is the
   modern date.
5 Maylunas & Mironenko, *A Lifelong Passion*, p. 115
6 *Letters of Tsar Nicholas and Empress Marie*, p. 103
7 Eagar, *Six Years at the Russian Court*, pp. 21–2
8 Steinberg & Khrustalëv, *The Fall of the Romanovs*, p. 156
9 *Ibid.*, p. 153
10 Suzanne Massie, *Pavlovsk* (London, Hodder & Stoughton, 1990), pp.
   178–9
11 *Ibid.*, p. 183

Bibliography

All books published in London unless stated otherwise.

Alexander II and Grand Prince Konstantin Nikolaievich, *1857–1961; Peesma, Dnevniki*, Moscow, Terra, 1994

Alexandra Feodorovna, Tsaritsa of Russia, *The Letters of the Tsaritsa to the Tsar, 1914–1916*, Duckworth, 1923

——, *The Last Diary of Tsaritsa Alexandra* (with an introduction by Robert Massie), Yale University Press, 1997

Alexander, Grand Duke of Russia, *Once a Grand Duke*, New York, Farrar & Rinehart, 1932

Alice, Princess of Great Britain, Grand Duchess of Hesse, *Letters to Her Majesty The Queen*, John Murray, 1897

Alice, Princess, *Grossherzogin von Hessen und bei Rhein; Mittheilungen aus Ihrem Leben und aus Ihren Briefen*, Darmstadt, Arnold Bergsträsser, 1884

Almedingen, E.M., *Alexander II*, Bodley Head, 1962

——, *An Unbroken Unity*, Bodley Head, 1964

——, *The Empress Alexandra*, Hutchinson, 1961

Anon., *Petrodvorets, The Cottage Palace*, St Petersburg, guide book, 1990

Anon., *Russian Court Memoirs, 1914–16*, Herbert Jenkins, 1917

Anon. (Albert Stopford), *The Russian Diary of an Englishman*, Heinemann, 1919

Bardovskaya, L.W. and G.D. Chodassevich, *Deutsche Prinzessinnen auf Russichem Thron*, Berlin, Felgentreff und Goebel, 1992

Bariatinsky, Princess A.M., *My Russian Life*, Hutchinson, 1923

Barkovets, Alia, Vadim Znamenov and Sergei Mironenko, *Nicholas II, the Imperial Family*, St Petersburg, Abris Publishers, 1998

Belyakova, Zoia, *Grand Duchess Maria Nikolayevna and her Palace in St. Petersburg*, Hazar, 1994

——, *The Romanov Legacy*, Hazar, 1994

Bing, E.J. (ed.), *Letters of Tsar Nicholas and Tsaritsa Marie*, Ivor Nicolson & Watson, 1937

Bloomfield, Baroness Georgiana, *Reminiscences of Court and Diplomatic Life*, Kegan, Paul, Trench & Co., 1883

BIBLIOGRAPHY

Bogatskaia, Irina, *The Moscow Kremlin in Watercolour*, Paris, Alain de Gourcuff, 1994

Bokhanov, Alexander and others, *The Romanovs, Love Power and Tragedy*, Leppi Publications, 1993

——, 'Ella and Sergei: a dynastic marriage of love . . . or convenience', *Royalty* vol. 12, no. 11, 1994

Botkin, Tatiana, *Au Temps des Tsars*, Paris, Grasset, 1980

Botkin, Gleb, *The Real Romanovs*, New York, Putnam, 1932

Brayley Hodgetts, E.A., *The Court of Russia in the Nineteenth Century*, 2 vols, Methuen, 1908

Buchanan, Meriel, *Queen Victoria's Relations*, Cassell, 1954

Bulygin, Captain Paul, *The Murder of the Romanovs*, Hutchinson, 1935

Buxhoeveden, Baroness Sophie, *Before the Storm*, Macmillan, 1938

——, *Left Behind*, Longmans, 1929

——, *The Life and Tragedy of Alexandra Feodorovna, Empress of Russia*, Longmans, 1928

Chavchavadze, D., *The Grand Dukes*, New York, Atlantic International Publications, 1990

Choiseul-Gouffier, Madame la Comtesse de, *Historical Memoirs of the Emperor Alexander I and the Court of Russia*, Chicago, A.C. McClurg, 1900

Christopher, HRH Prince of Greece, *The Memoirs of HRH Prince Christopher of Greece*, Right Book Club, 1938

Clarke, William, *The Lost Fortune of the Tsars*, Weidenfeld & Nicolson, 1994, Orion, 1996

Collins, Frederick, *This King Business*, T. Werner Laurie, 1923

Constant, Stephen, *Foxy Ferdinand, Tsar of Bulgaria*, Sidgwick and Jackson, 1979

Corti, Count Egon, *The Downfall of Three Dynasties*, Methuen, 1934

Cowles, Virginia, *The Romanovs*, Collins, 1971

Crawford, Rosemary and Donald, *Michael and Natasha*, Weidenfeld & Nicolson, 1997

Dehn, Lili, *The Real Tsaritsa*, Thornton Butterworth, 1922

Dimond, Frances and Roger Taylor, *Crown and Camera*, Penguin, 1987

Ducamp, Emmanuel (ed.), *The Winter Palace*, Paris, Alain de Gourcuff, 1995

Duff, David, *Hessian Tapestry*, Muller, 1967

Dupuy, Marie-Bernadette, *Katia Dolgorouky et Alexandre II*, Paris, Éditions Le Soleil de Minuit, 1993

Durland, Kellogg, *Royal Romances of Today*, T. Werner Laurie nd, c. 1910

Eagar, M., *Six Years at the Russian Court*, Hurst & Blackett, 1906

Ernst Ludwig, Großherzog von Hessen und bei Rhein, *Erinnertes*, Darmstadt, Eduard Roether, 1983

Eugénie de Grèce, *Le Tsarévitch; enfant martyr*, Paris, Perrin, 1990

Ferrand, Jacques, *Il Est Toujours Des Romanov*, Paris, Jacques Ferrand, 1995

——, *Le Grand-duc Paul Alexandrovitch de Russie*, Paris, Jacques Ferrand, 1993

Fricero, E., *Nicolas Alexandrovitch*, Nice, Meyerbeer, 1951

Fulford, Roger (ed.), *Darling Child*, Evans, 1976; and later volumes of the same series

Gatchina; Imperatorski Dvorets, St Petersburg, Lenart, 1994

George, H.I. and R.H. Grand Duchess, *A Romanov Diary*, New York, Atlantic International Publications, 1988

Geyrot, A., *Opysanie Peterhofa*, 1868; modern Russian reprint, no details given

Gilliard, Pierre, *Thirteen Years at the Russian Court*, Hutchinson, nd

Gould Lee, Arthur, *The Empress Frederick Writes to Sophie*, Faber & Faber, 1955

de Gourcuff, Alain (ed.), *Imperial Palaces in the Vicinity of St Petersburg*, Paris, Alain de Gourcuff, 1992

Graham, Stephen, *Alexander II*, Ivor Nicholson and Watson, 1935

Granin, Gurevich, Khodasevich, Belanina, *Risen From the Ashes: Petrodvorets, Pushkin, Pavlovsk*, Leningrad, Aurora, 1992

Gray, Pauline, *The Grand Duke's Woman*, Macdonald and Jane's, 1976

Grebelsky, P. and A. Meervees, *Dom Romanovich*, St Petersburg, 1992

Heu, Christopher, 'The Controversial Grand Duchess', *The Monarchist*, January 1981

Hoare, Samuel, *The Fourth Seal*, Heinemann, 1930

Hough, Richard (ed.), *Advice to a Granddaughter*, Heinemann, 1975

——, *Louis and Victoria*, Hutchinson, 1974

Iroshnikov, M., L. Protsai and Y. Shelayev, *The Sunset of the Romanov Dynasty*, Moscow, Terra, 1992

Jackman, S.W. (ed.), *Chère Annette*, Gloucester, Alan Sutton, 1990

——, *Romanov Relations*, Macmillan, 1969

Jewels of the Romanovs, Exhibition Catalogue, The American-Russian Cultural Cooperation Foundation, 1997

King, Stella, *Princess Marina*, Cassell, 1969

Kirichenko, Evgenia and Mikhail Anikst, *The Russian Style*, Lawrence King, 1991

Kleinmichel, Countess, *Memories of a Shipwrecked World*, Brentano's, 1923

Kniaz Oleg, St Petersburg, 1915, reprinted by Kazan, Star, 1995

Knodt, Manfred, *Ernst Ludwig*, Darmstadt, H.L. Schlapp, 1978

Kschessinska, Mathilde, *Dancing in Petersburg*, Doubleday, 1961

Kyrill, HIH Grand Duke, *My Life In Russia's Service*, Selwyn & Blount, 1939

Lambton, Anthony, *The Mountbattens*, Constable, 1989

Lieven, Dominic, *Nicholas II*, John Murray, 1993

Lowe, Charles, *Alexander III*, Heinemann 1895

Majolier, Nathalie, *Stepdaughter of Imperial Russia*, Stanley Paul, 1940

Malafyeva, S.L. (compiler), L.V. Ivanova and U.A. Poliakov, *Tsarskiye i Imperatorskiye Dvortsi, Staraya Moskva*, Moscow, Mosgorarhiv, 1997

Manion, John S., Jr. (collected, transcribed and annotated by), 'Custer, Cody and the Grand Duke Alexis by Elizabeth B. Custer', *Research Review, The Journal of the Little Big Horn Association*, vol. 4#1 (New Series), January 1990

Maria Feodorovna, Empress of Russia, Exhibition Catalogue, Christiansborg Palace, Copenhagen, 1997

Marie, Grand Duchess of Russia, *Things I Remember*, Cassell, 1930

——, *A Princess in Exile*, New York, Viking Press, 1932

Marie, Princess of Battenberg, *Reminiscences*, Allen & Unwin, 1925

Marie, Queen of Romania, *The Story of My Life*, 3 vols, Cassell, 1934–5

Massie, Robert, *Nicholas and Alexandra*, Gollancz, 1968

Massie, Suzanne, *Pavlovsk*, Hodder & Stoughton, 1990

Maylunas, Andrei and Sergei Mironenko, *A Lifelong Passion*, Wiedenfeld & Nicolson, 1996

Michael of Greece, Prince, *Imperial Palaces of Russia*, Tauris Parke, 1992

Millar, Lubov, *Grand Duchess Elizabeth*, Redding, California, Nicodemus Orthodox Publication Society, 1991

Mossolov, A.A., *At the Court of the Last Tsar*, Methuen, 1935

Narishkin-Kurakin, Elizabeth, *Under Three Tsars*, New York, Dutton, 1931

Nicholas II, Tsar of Russia, *Dnevniki Imperatora Nikolaya II*, Moscow, Orbita, 1991

——, *The Letters of the Tsar to the Tsaritsa, 1914–1917*, John Lane, 1929

Nicholas, HRH Prince of Greece, *My Fifty Years*, Hutchinson, 1926

Nikolai i Aleksandra, Exhibition Catalogue, State Hermitage, St Petersburg, 1994

Obolensky, Serge, *One Man in his Time*, Hutchinson, 1960

Paléologue, Maurice, *An Ambassador's Memoirs*, Hutchinson, 1923

——, *The Tragic Romance of Alexander II*, Hutchinson, c. 1923

Paley, Princess, *Memories of Russia, 1916–1919*, Herbert Jenkins, 1924

Pless, Daisy, Princess of, *From My Private Diary*, John Murray, 1931

Poliakoff, Vladimir, *The Empress Marie of Russia and her Times*, Thornton Butterworth, 1926

Pope-Hennessy, Una, *A Czarina's Story*, Ivor Nicholson & Watson

Radzinsky, Edvard, *The Last Tsar*, Hodder and Stoughton, 1992, and as *Gospodi . . . Spasi i usmiri Possiyu*, Moscow, Bagrus, 1995

Radziwill, Princess Catherine (as 'Count Paul Vassili'), *Behind the Veil at the Russian Court*, Cassell, 1913

Ramm, Agatha (ed.), *Beloved and Darling Child*, Stroud, Alan Sutton, 1990

Rhodes James, Robert (ed.), *Chips: The Diaries of Sir Henry Channon*, Weidenfeld & Nicholson, 1967

Romain, Serge, *Joseph Fricero*, Paris, Jacques Ferrand, 1993

Romanow, Prinz Roman, *Am Hof Des Letzten Zaren*, Munich, Piper, 1995

The Romanovs; documents and photographs relating to the Russian Imperial House, London, Sotheby's, 1990

Seaman, W.A.L. (ed.), *The Russian Journal of Lady Londonderry*, John Murray, 1973

Spiridovitch, Alexandre, *Les Dernières Années de la Cour de Tzarskoïé-Sélo*, Paris, Payot, 1928

Stackelberg, Baroness, *The Life of Carmen Sylva*, Kegan Paul, 1890

Stancioff, Anna, *Recollections of a Bulgarian Diplomatist's Wife*, Hutchinson, nd

Steinberg, Mark D. and Vladimir M. Khrustalëv (eds), *The Fall of the Romanovs*, Yale University Press, 1995

de Stoeckl, Agnes, *My Dear Marquis*, John Murray, 1952

——, *Not All Vanity*, John Murray, 1950

Tarsaïdzé, Alexander, *Katia, Wife Before God*, New York, Macmillan, 1970

Tiutcheva, A.F., *Pre Dvore Dvuch Imperatorov*, Moscow, Muisl, 1990

Trewin, J.C., *Tutor to the Tsarevich*, Macmillan, 1975

Van Der Kiste, John, *Princess Victoria Melita*, Stoud, Alan Sutton, 1991

Viroubova, Anna, *Memories of the Russian Court*, Macmillan, 1923

Von der Hoven, Baroness Helena, *Intimate Life Story of HRH the Duchess of Kent*, Cassell, 1937

Vorres, Ian, *The Last Grand Duchess*, Hutchinson, 1964

Warth, Robert D., *Nicholas II, The Life and Reign of Russia's Last Monarch*, Connecticut, Preager, 1997

Windsor, The Dean of, and Hector Bolitho (eds), *Later Letters of Lady Augusta Stanley 1864–1876*, Jonathan Cape, 1929

Yermilova, Larissa, *The Last Tsar*, Parkstone Planeta, 1996

Yourievsky, Princess Catherine, *My Book*, Eveleigh, Nash and Grayson, 1924

Youssoupoff, Prince Felix, *Lost Splendour*, Jonathan Cape, 1953

Zemlyanichenko, Marina and Nikolai Kalinin, *The Romanovs and the Crimea*, Moscow, Kruk, 1993

Index